Irish Divorce/Joyce's *Ulysses*

Irish Divorce/ Joyce's *Ulysses*

Peter Kuch

palgrave
macmillan

Peter Kuch
University of Otago
Dunedin, New Zealand

ISBN 978-1-349-95755-2 ISBN 978-1-137-57186-1 (eBook)
DOI 10.1057/978-1-137-57186-1

Softcover reprint of the hardcover 1st edition 2017

Printed on acid-free paper

This Palgrave Macmillan imprint is published by Springer Nature
The registered company is Nature America Inc.
The registered company address is: 1 New York Plaza, New York, NY 10004, U.S.A.

"Ignorantia juris non excusat."
"Every man is presumed to know the law."

For Declan

Preface

This book offers a revisionist reading of Joyce's *Ulysses* by examining Irish attitudes to marriage and the wide-ranging English, Irish, American, and French debates about divorce that were conducted between 1904, when Joyce's novel of adultery is set, and 1922, when it was published. It draws attention to an Irish practice that, even though it was known at the time, has since disappeared from the critical, historical, and legal literature about *Ulysses* and about Irish divorce.

It is well known that Joyce was an avid reader of newspapers, the most common and popular source of information about divorce.[1]

[1] Garry Leonard, *Advertising and Commodity Culture in Joyce* (Gainesville: University Press of Florida, 1998); Barbara Leckie, *Culture and Adultery: The Novel, the Newspaper and the Law 1857–1914* (Philadelphia: University of Pennsylvania Press, 1999); Declan Kiberd, "*Ulysses*, Newspapers and Modernism," in *Irish Classics* (London: Granta Books, 2000), 463–81; Barbara Leckie, "The Simple Case of Adultery," *James Joyce Quarterly* 40, no. 4 (2003): 729–52; Katherine Mullin, *James Joyce, Sexuality and Social Purity* (Cambridge: Cambridge University Press, 2003); James A. Reppke, "Journalist Joyce: A Portrait," *James Joyce Quarterly* 45, nos. 3–4 (2008): 459–68; R. Brandon Kershner, *The Culture of Joyce's "Ulysses"* (New York: Palgrave Macmillan, 2010); Jennifer Wicke, "Modernity Must Advertise: Aura, Desire, and Decolonization in Joyce," *James Joyce Quarterly* 50, nos. 1–2 (2012–2013): 203–21; Margot Backus, *Scandal Work: James Joyce, the New Journalism, and the Home Rule Newspaper Wars* (Notre Dame, IN: University of Notre Dame Press, 2013).

It is also well known that Joyce was fascinated by accounts of divorce hearings that appeared almost daily in the Irish press from Dilke (1886) to Parnell (1890), to the establishment of the Free State in 1922,[2] and with increasing frequency in the English press between the 1857 Act to Amend the Law Relating to Divorce and Matrimonial Causes in England and the 1926 Judicial Proceedings (Regulation of Reports) Act, which enforced a measure of restraint.[3]

What has not been realized is that the dual time-scheme of *Ulysses*, set in 1904 but written while Ireland was violently renegotiating its relationship to Empire, provided Joyce with a stance from which to interrogate ways in which sometimes rival and sometimes collusive Imperial and Ecclesiastical hegemonies forged the Edwardian Irish social imaginary. What unwittingly resulted from this complex, shifting contestation for control of the Irish mind was the provision of a space that gave Irish litigants, from 1858 to 1922, limited access to the Probate, Divorce and Admiralty Division of the King's Bench, which sat only in London.

Consequently, no one has investigated the extent to which Bloom's "Divorce, not now" and Molly's "suppose I divorced him" are realistic possibilities rather than passing fantasies (17.2202; 18.846), and no one has investigated the extent to which Bloom's and Molly's thoughts about divorce, thoughts that find expression in the early hours of 17 June 1904, arise from and color all eighteen episodes of *Ulysses.*

Irish Divorce / Joyce's "Ulysses" demonstrates that divorce was a realistic option for the Blooms—whether whim, fantasy, wish, or conviction—following Molly's affair with Hugh Boylan. It does so, in an attempt to avoid presentism,[4] by cross-referencing the fifty-fourth edition of *Every Man's Own Lawyer* (1919) Joyce is known to have possessed with contemporary Ecclesiastical and Parliamentary debates, public

[2] Diarmaid Ferriter, *Occasions of Sin: Sex and Society in Modern Ireland* (London: Profile Books, 2009), 105–6; Peter Martin, *Censorship in the Two Irelands, 1922–1939* (Dublin: Irish Academic Press, 2006), 32.

[3] See Gail Savage, "Erotic Stories and Public Decency: Newspaper Reporting of Divorce Proceedings in England," *The Historical Journal* 41, no. 2 (1998): 511–28. The Judicial Proceedings Act can be accessed at http://bailii.austlii.edu.au/uk/legis/num_act/1926/ukpga_19260061_en.html.

[4] Martin Jay, "Historical Explanation and the Event: Reflections on the Limits of Contextualization," *New Literary History* 42 (2011): 557–71.

enquiries, relevant legal texts, and the 1912 Royal Commission on divorce. It also cross-references 1,500 divorce cases reported in various detail in the Irish and English newspapers that Joyce read whenever he could get access to copies with some 850 Divorce Court Minutes deposited in the National Archives in London, particularly those that relate to Irish pleas of the period.

The book further engages with a rich vein of Joyce scholarship revealed by Richard Brown's *James Joyce and Sexuality* (1985), Joseph Valente's *James Joyce and the Problem of Justice: Negotiating Sexual and Colonial Difference* (1988), Vicki Mahaffey's *Reauthorizing Joyce* (1988), Marian Eide's *Ethical Joyce* (2002), Andrew Gibson's *Joyce's Revenge* (2002), Katherine Mullin's *James Joyce, Sexuality and Social Purity* (2003), and Luca Crispi's *Joyce's Creative Process and the Construction of Characters in "Ulysses": Becoming the Blooms* (2015).

It concludes that the Blooms' commitment to one another is more provisional than has previously been realized and that the engorged full stop at the end of "Ithaca" and Molly's final "Yes." represent temporary accommodations rather than forgiveness, qualified commitment, or separation. And it maps several of the paths by which Bloom and Molly become interpellated by the heuristic and legal discourses associated with divorce.

Irish Divorce / Joyce's "Ulysses" is not a book about Joyce's attitude or attitudes to divorce or about divorce in Joyce's corpus, as relevant as some critics believe *Exiles* and *Giacomo Joyce* are to understanding Bloom's situation. Nor is it a book about divorce in *Finnegans Wake*, or what might happen to the Blooms after 16 June 1904.

Instead, it proposes that known Irish access to the Probate, Divorce and Admiralty Division of the King's Bench, the prominence given to divorce in Edwardian print culture, and the extent to which divorce was being expunged from the Irish social imaginary even while *Ulysses* was being written challenged Joyce to reconfigure his domestic odyssey as a novel of adultery by interrogating ways in which competing narratives, multiple voices, and self-reflexivity were played off against one another within a patriarchal legal discourse about divorce that had been and was being widely discussed in England, Ireland, and France (though not Italy[5]) throughout the first two decades of the twentieth century.

[5] Mark Seymour, *Debating Divorce in Italy: Marriage and the Making of Modern Italians* (London: Palgrave Macmillan, 2006).

As he was writing *Ulysses*, Joyce came to realize that Irish recourse to the English jurisdiction for decrees absolute provided him with a space to dramatize one way of subverting the power of "the imperial British state" (utilizing the state's definition of "domicile" against itself) and the "holy Roman catholic and apostolic church" (obtaining a *decree absolute*) even while it drew attention to what was actually happening in Edwardian Ireland (the "Ireland" of "odd jobs") (1.641–44).

Finally, *Irish Divorce / Joyce's "Ulysses"* raises the provocative and timely questions: why was Irish recourse to the English divorce court expunged from Joyce criticism, from Irish history, and from the Irish social imaginary between 1922 and 1986, and what does this tell us about the state and the nation?

Acknowledgments

Much of this book has been written in what Edmund calls "Grandpa's think-house," and much of it has been read of an evening to Liz on the "think-house" porch. I am very grateful for her love and support and for the love and encouragement of my three children, Erin, Anna, and Declan, and my grandson, Edmund. The research, conducted in England, Ireland, Australia, and New Zealand, was facilitated by a sabbatical leave granted by the University of Otago and made possible by the generosity of the Eamon Cleary Trust. I owe a great debt of gratitude to the remarkable generosity of the late Eamon Cleary and to his family and to those associated with the Trust's Otago administration: Warren Cant, Alison Finigan, and Philip Kearney.

Mary McAleese and Paul Doolan have generously commented on legal matters, for which I am most grateful, while Tony Thwaites, Andrew Gibson, and Julie-Ann Robson have offered illuminating advice on substantial portions of the final draft. Vicki Mahaffey has been a great source of encouragement. I am also indebted to Will Martin and Rick Miller for their comments on Chapter 4. Megan Kitching, Lisa Marr, and Vanessa Manhire have saved me from many errors; their friendly guidance is much appreciated, as is that given by the team from Palgrave Macmillan: Allie Bochicchio, Ben Doyle, Ryan Jenkins, the reader, and Brigitte Shull.

I am enormously grateful to the librarians at the University of Otago, particularly Jacinda Boivin, Charlotte Brown, Paula Hasler, and Kate Thompson; to Ka-Neng Au at Rutgers Law Library; and to Gillian Knight and Katy Davies, librarians at the Institute of Chartered Accountants of England and Wales. I am equally grateful to the staff of the National Archives in Kew; the National Library of Australia; the Fisher Library, University of Sydney; the British Library; the Main and the Law Library at the University of New South Wales; and the Robert Stout Law Library at the University of Otago.

My Irish Studies students have been a significant source of inspiration, particularly those in the *Modernism: Joyce* course I taught at the Trieste Joyce Summer School, the University of New South Wales, and the University of Otago. Working with postgraduates on Irish topics—Jennifer Beckett, Mavis Brown, Leila Crawford, Peter Denney, Anthony Finn, Kerri Haggart, Andy Hirt, Justin Lucas, Ruth Macklin, Ailbhe McDaid, Lisa McGonigle, Paul Sheehan, Diane Stubbings, Iain Sutherland, Christopher Thompson, and Andrew Watts—has been intellectually exciting.

Finally, there are those special people whose support is once again gratefully acknowledged: Richard and Mary Ellmann, and John and Chris Kelly for the wonderful Oxford years; Justice John O'Meally for his "bangers and mash" lunches for visiting Irish judges in his Sydney chambers; and the following, for encouragement and enrichment: Terence Brown, Andrew Carpenter and Lucy Collins, Max and Stephanie Charlesworth, Elisabetta d'Erme, Francis Devlin-Glass, Denise Flanagan, Alistair Fox and Hillary Radner, Luke Gibbons, Warwick Gould and Deirdre Toomey, Nicky and Eleanor Grene, Harlene Hayne, Marjorie Howes, Belinda Humfrey, John Ingleson, Michael and Rhona Kenneally, Brendan Kennelly, Dermot and Anne Keogh, Declan and Beth Kiberd, Jeff and Robin Kildea, Margaret MacCurtain, Trevor McClaughlin, John McCourt, Ronan McDonald, Iggy and Eileen McGovern, Liam and Val McIlvanney, Niamh McMahon, John and Helen Milfull, Brian Moloughney, Maureen Murphy, Helen Nader, John Niland, Richard O'Brien, Bernard and Heather O'Donoghue, Shaun Richards, Ann Saddlemyer, Haun Saussy, Christabel Scaife, Peter Scott and Judy Robinson, David Skegg, Anne Stevens, Rodney Walsh, Anne Webster, and Noel White.

Researching and writing this book has proved by turns emotionally taxing and intellectually exciting. Reading hundreds of affidavits and court reports detailing the circumstances and hurt that alienated people from one another has been harrowing. Relationships are what connect, sustain, and define us. We are our wives, husbands, partners, siblings, relatives, circle of friends, and perhaps even acquaintances. But it has been stimulating and exciting to recover a significant aspect of Irish history that has escaped scrutiny for almost a century. And it has made the lonely travel and the long hours in archives worthwhile. That Joyce knew it was possible for the Irish to petition the English court for divorce confirms the breadth of his understanding of Irish society, and his realization that if he was to decolonize the Irish mind he must challenge both priest and king. And he too, I suspect, probably shared my sense that while it was imperative to know that *ignorantia juris non excusat* (ignorance of the law does not excuse), it was also likely that *ignoranti legis non excusat, sed noscere gerras delectatio multis est* (ignorance of the law is not an excuse, but knowing the gossip is a joy to many).

Contents

Abbreviations

AC	Law Reports, Appeal Cases (Third Series)
Add Cas	Addams's Ecclesiastical Reports
All ER Rep	All England Law Reports Reprint
CA	Court of Appeal
CA [****] * KB	Court of Appeal [date] King's Bench
CCR	Court for Crown Cases Reserved
ChD	Law Reports, Chancery Division (2nd Series)
Cir Cas Palles CB	Circuit Cases, Palles Chief Baron (who sat between 1874 and 1916)
Consis. Ct.	Consistory Court
Cox CC [****], CA	Cox's Criminal Cases [date], Court of Appeal
DC	District Court
ER	English Reports
Exch	Exchequer Reports
Hag Con	Haggard's Consistorial Reports
HL	House of Lords
ICLR	Irish Common Law Reports (2nd Series)
ILT	Irish Law Times
ILTR	Irish Law Times Reports
ILTSJ	Irish Law Times and Solicitors' Journal
IR	Irish Reports
IR Eq	Irish Reports, Equity (3rd Series)
Ir Jur	Irish Jurist
JP	Justice of the Peace Reports
Jur NS	Jurist Reports, New Series
KB	King's Bench
L&C	Leigh and Cave's Crown Cases Reserved
LJ	Law Journal Newspaper

LJ Ch	Law Journal Reports, Chancery New Series
LJ CPD or LJCP	Law Journal Reports, Common Pleas New Series
LJEx	Law Journal Reports, Exchequer New Series
LJKB	Law Journal Reports, King's Bench New Series
LJP	Law Journal Reports, Probate, Divorce and Admiralty New Series
LJP&M or LJPM&A	Law Journal Reports, Probate and Matrimonial, New Series
LJQB	Law Journal Reports, Queen's Bench, New Series
LR	Law Reports (1st Series)
LR HL	Law Reports, English and Irish Appeals
LR CP	Law Reports, Common Pleas
LR Ir	Law Reports, Ireland (4th Series)
LR P&D or P&D	Law Reports, Probate and Divorce Cases
LT	Law Times
LTOS	Law Times Reports, Old Series
M&A	Montagu & Ayrton's Bankruptcy Reports
M&W	Meeson & Welsby's Exchequer Reports
Mans	Manson's Bankruptcy and Companies Winding-up Cases
Matr. Ct.	Court for Divorce and Matrimonial Causes
NA J/77/***/****	National Archives (Kew)/numerical case identifier of court minutes
NI	Northern Ireland Law Reports
P	Law Reports, Probate
P&D	Law Reports, Probate, Divorce and Admiralty Division
Peake Add Cas	Peake's Additional Cases at Nisi Prius
QBD	Queen's Bench Division
Sim	Simon's Vice Chancellor's Reports
SJ or Sol Jo	Solicitors' Journal
Sw & Tr	Swabey and Tristram's Probate and Divorce Reports
TLR	Times Law Reports
WR	Weekly Reporter

List of Cases

Key: [] = year as primary method of locating case; () = year for chronological purposes; NA = National Archives, London, followed by collection number and file number for court minutes of divorce cases heard in the Divorce Court in the Probate, Divorce and Admiralty Division of the King's Bench, London.

à Beckett v. De Burgh (1912), *Irish Times*, 29 February 1912, 4.
Abrahams v. Abrahams and Neuberger (1903), NA J77/798/4289.
Adams v. Adams and Colter [1867] LR 1 P&D 333; 36 LJP&M 62; 16 LT 69.
Alexander v. Alexander and Amos (1860) 2 Sw&Tr 95; Sea&Sm 153; 29 LJPM&A 56; 6 Jury NS 56; 8 WR 452; 164 ER 928.
Allen v. Allen and Bell (1893), NA J77/512/15602.
Allen v. Chivers (1900), *Times* (London), 31 March 1900, 17.
Anderson v. Anderson and Rising (1903), NA J77/779/3724.
Astley v. Astley [1828] 162 ER 728.
Bailey v. Bailey (1903), NA J77/778/3688.
Balfour v. Balfour [1919] 2 KB 571 CA.
Bamberger v. Bamberger and Symonds and Leeson and Stephenson and Stein (1920), *Daily Mail*, 11 March 1920, 5.
Bank of Ireland v. Caffin [1971] IR 123.
Barnett v. Barnett and Freakes [dismissed] (1904), NA J77/812/4694.
Bater v. Bater (1906) P 209.
Beck v. Beck and Spittal (1919), *Daily Mail*, 26 February 1919, 3.

Bell v. Bell and Anglesey (Marquis) (1859) 1 Sw&Tr 565; Sea&Sm 110; 29 LJP&A 159; 1 LT 243; 8 WR 178; 164 ER 861.
Bennett v. Bennett (1902), NA J77/753/2920.
Bennett v. Bennett and McKay (1901), NA J77/730/2193; *Times* (London), 1 February 1902, 5.
Boddington v. Boddington and Mossiter [1858] 27 LJP&M 53.
Boyce v. Boyce and Brook (1920), *Daily Mail*, 24 March 1920, 4.
Breen v. Breen [1964] P 144.
Brodrick v. Brodrick (1903), NA J77/783/3846; *Times* (London), 26 January 1904, 4.
Brooke v. Bushe [1886] 49 & 50 Vict., c. 181.
Brown v. Brown [1865] LR 1 P&D 46; 35 LJP&M 13; 13 LT 645; 11 Jur NS 1027; 14 WR 149.
Brown v. Brown and Robey (1869) 21 LT 181.
Bud v. Bud and Green (1894), NA J77/537/16387.
Burdon v. Burdon [1900], NA J77/708/1527; P 52; 69 LJP 118.
Burne v. Burne and Helvoet [1920] P17; 89 LJP 18; 122 LT 224; 64 Sol Jo 132.
Butterworth v. Butterworth [1920] P 126.
Carson v. Kingstown Urban District Council [1906] 40 ILTSJ 287.
Chapman v. Chapman [rescinded] (1918), NA J77/1368/1909; *Times* (London), 15 March 1919, 4.
Chapman v. Chapman and Buist [dismissed] (1910), NA J77/1010/648.
Clarke v. Clarke (1865) 34 LJPM&A 94.
Close v. Close (1904), *Times* (London), 5 February 1904, 13.
Codrington v. Codrington and Anderson (1865) 4 Sw&Tr 63; LJPM&A 60; 11 Jur NS 287; 13 WR 527; 164 ER 1439.
Coleman v. Coleman (1866) 1 P&D 81.
Courtney v. Courtney (1923) 2 IR 31; ILTR 42 CA.
Cox v. Cox and Warde (1906) P 267; 75 LJP 75; 95 LT 546; 22 TLR 557.
Cramp v. Cramp and Freeman (1918), NA J77/1391/2680; P 158; All ER Rep 164.
Crawford v. Crawford and Dilke [1886] 11 PD 150; 55 LT 305; 34 WR 677; 2 TLR 768, CA.
Croghan v. Colter (1909), *Irish Times*, 20 March 1909, 5.
Cunnington v. Cunnington and Noble (1859) 164 ER 820.
Curl v. Curl (1902), NA J77/753/2926.
Curtis v. Curtis (1868) 38 LJP&M 9; 19 LT 610.
Curtis v. Curtis (1905) 21 TLR 676.

D'Arcy v. D'Arcy [1887] 19 LR; Ir 369 (Matr. Ct.).
Davidson v. Davidson (1856) 164 ER 526.
Deck v. Deck (1859), NA J77/13/D3; 28 LJP&M 30n.
Dillon v. Dillon (1842) 163 ER 663; 3 Curt 84; 1 Notes of Cases 415; 6 Jur 422; 163 ER 663.
Dixon v. Dixon (1859), NA J77/13/D8; LJP&M 96.
Doherty v. Mullins (1909), *Irish Times*, 15 May 1909, 3; 43 ILTR 174.
Duplany v. Duplany (1890), NA J77/462/4065; P 53; 61 LJP 49; 66 LT 267; 8 TLR 169.
Durdin v. Durdin (1858), NA J77/13/D4.
Edwards v. Martin (1865) LR 1 Eq 121; 35 LJ Ch 186; 13 LT 236; 14 WR 25.
Egan v. Egan [1928] NI 159.
Evans v. Evans [1844] 163 ER 1000.
Evans v. Evans and Wilson [dismissed] (1902), NA J77/744/2629; *Times* (London), 23 January 1904, 4.
Evans v. Thomas (1903), *Times* (London), 2 December 1903, 10.
Field v. Field (1905), *Irish Times*, 14 September 1905, 3.
Foley v. Faunt (1903), *Irish Times*, 20 November 1903, 4.
Foster v. Foster [1864] 33 LJCP 150.
Fraser v. Fraser (1921), *Irish Times*, 25 April 1921, 2.
Frasier v. Spindelow (1904), *Daily Mail*, 19 March 1904, 3; *Times* (London), 19 March 1904, 4; continued *Times* (London), 21 March 1904, 2.
Friedberg v. Friedberg (1908), NA J77/930/8227.
Gaston v. Gaston (1865) 13 LT 412.
Gillis v. Gillis [1874] 8 IR Eq 597.
Gladney v. Murphy (1891) 26 ILTR 651.
Goodfellow v. Goodfellow and Keys (1902), NA J77/754/2959.
Gordon v. Gordon and Gordon [1904] P 163; [1904–7] P 92; 72 LJP 34; 88 LT 578; All ER Rep 702; 73 LJP 41; 90 LT 597; 52 WR 389; 20 TLR 272; 48 Sol Jo 297, CA.
Haddon v. Haddon [1887] 18 QBD 778; 56 LJMC 69; 56 LT 716; 51 JP 486; 3 TLR 574, DC.
Harraden v. Harraden and Bohan [dismissed] (1902), NA J77/753/2932; *Times* (London), 3 June 1904, 3.
Harriman v. Harriman [dismissed] (1907), NA J77/929/8195.
Harris v. Harris (1906), *Weekly Irish Times*, 17 November 1906, 20.
Harrison v. Harrison (1904), *Daily Mail*, 13 February 1904, 3.

Hart v. Hart (1881) 18 ChD 670; 50 LJ Ch 697; 45 LT 13; 30 WR 8.
Hartford v. Power [1868] 16 WR 822 (IR); 3 IR Eq 602.
Hegarty v. Shine (1878) 4 LR Ir 228.
Hodgson-Roberts v. Hodgson-Roberts and Whitaker (1903), NA J77/798/4300; *Daily Mail*, 9 March 1904, 3.
Huckman v. Fernie (1838) 3 M&W 501; 150 ER 1245.
Hudson v. Hudson [1863] 3 Sw&Tr 314; 33 LJPM&A 5; 9 LT 579; 9 Jur NS 1302; 12 WR 216, 354; 164 ER 1296.
Hunt v. Hunt [1856] 164 ER 522.
Hunter v. Hunter [1905] P 217; 74 LJP 157; 93 LT 451; 53 WR 666; 21 TLR 602.
Hyde v. Hyde and Woodmansee (1864), NA J77/28/H212; [1866] 1 LR P&D 130.
Hyman v. Hyman and Goldman [dismissed] (1903), NA J77/796/4211; P 403.
In re Simon [1909] 1 KB 201; 78 LJKB 392; 100 LT 133; 53 Sol Jo 117; 16 Mans 96, CA.
In the matter of R. F. Young, a bankrupt (1890) 25 LR Ir 372.
Irvine v. Irvine (1920), NA J77/1728/3792; *Irish Times*, 12 May 1921, 3.
Jackson v. Jackson [1910] P 230; 79 LJP 82; 103 LT 79; 26 TLR 476.
Jenkins v. Jenkins (1903), NA J77/791/4064; *Times* (London), 20 January 1904, 4.
Jolly v. Jolly and Fryer (1919) 63 SJ 777.
Jones v. Jones and Saunders and Cook (1902), NA J77/755/2984.
Joseph v. Joseph and Wentzel (sometimes Wenzel) (1865) 34 LJP M&A 96.
Keers v. Kane (1904), *Irish Times*, 22 November 1904, 3A.
Kellner v. Kellner (1939) 3 All ER 957; P 411; 108 LJP 138; 55 TLR 1058; 83 Sol Jo 832.
Kingham v. Kingham (1897) 1 IR 170; 29 ILTR 5.
Kirk v. Kirk (1902), NA J77/768/3378; P 145; 71 LJP 78; 87 LT 148.
Lagan v. Gibson (1878) 10 ILTSJ 6.
Laidler v. Laidler [1920] 36 TLR 510.
Laverton v. Laverton (1921), *Irish Times*, 24 June 1921, 3.
Le Mesurier v. Le Mesurier [1895] AC 517, 540.
Levi v. Levi and Abrahams [rescinded] (1908), NA J77/953/8926.
Light v. Light and Evans and Perry [struck out] (1903), NA J77/798/4297.
Livingstone v. Livingstone (1904), NA J77/819/4884; *Times* (London), 17 May 1905, 3.
Long v. Long and Johnson [1890] 15 PD 218.

Loveden v. Loveden (1810) 2 Hag Con 1; 161 ER 648 (Consis. Ct.).
Maguire v. Maguire (1903), NA J77/778/3700.
Malone's Validation Divorce Bill [1905] AC 315 HL (IR).
Mansford v. Mansford (1904), *Daily Mail*, 18 February 1904, 3.
Mavro v. Craven (1900), *Times* (London), 6 September 1900, 13.
Maxwell v. Maxwell (1901), NA J77/735/2351; *Daily Mail*, 10 August 1904, 3.
Mayo-Perrot v. Mayo-Perrot [1958] IR 336; 93 ITLR 77.
MacBride v. MacBride (1906), *Irish Times*, 18 December 1906, 7.
McCord v. McCord, Ogle and Coxton (1875) 3 LR P&D 237.
McGregor v. McGregor (1888) 21 QBD 424; 57 LJQB 591; 52 JP 772; 37 WR 45; 4 TLR 760, CA.
Mendoza v. Ruben (1901), *Times* (London), 14 December 1901, 15.
Methofer v. Methofer and Bain (1904), NA J77/800/4343; *Daily Mail*, 28 July 1904, 3.
Milne v. Milne (1902), NA J77/754/2958; 40 LJP&M 13.
Mitchell v. Torrington Union [1897] Div. Ct quoted in *Law Journal*, 10 July 1897.
Morgan v. Morgan and Porter (1869) 1 P&D 644.
Moss v. Moss [1897] P 263.
Moutray v. Moutray [1892] 26 ILTSJ 146.
Moyst v. Moyst and Wilcox and Essling (1902), NA J77/765/3284.
Murphy-Grimshaw's (Validation) Bill HL [1907] WN 134; 51 Sol Jo 529 HL (IR).
Nachimson v. Nachimson [1930] P 217.
Narese v. Narese and Jones [rescinded] (1904), NA J77/753/2905.
Neligan v. Neligan (1904), *Times* (London), 5 February 1904, 13.
O'Shea v. O'Shea and Parnell (1890), NA J77/440/3419; [1890] 15 PD 59; 59 LJP 47; 62 LT 713; 38 WR 374; 6 LTR 221; 17 Cox CC 107, CA.
Ogden v. Ogden (1906), NA J77/886/6900; [1908] P 46; [1904–7] All ER Rep 86; 77 LJP 34; 97 LT 827; 24 TLR 94, CA.
Owen v. Moberly (1900), *Times* (London), 2 February 1900, 15; 64 JP 88.
Palgrave v. Palgrave (1904), NA J77/811/4669.
Palgrave v. Palgrave and Lutifer (1904), NA J77/806/4512; *Times* (London), 15 July 1904, 14.
Pollard v. Pollard (1904), *Daily Mail*, 27 April 1904, 3; *Times* (London), 13 June 1904, 11; *Times* (London), 26 October 1904, 9 et seq.
Preston v. Neele (1879) 12 LR CP 760; 12 ChD 760.
Pritchard v. Pritchard and Sims [1967] P 195 at 212–13.

Rayment v. Rayment and Stuart (otherwise Stewart) (1910), NA J77/1008/582.

Read v. Legard [1851] 6 Exch 636; 20 LJEx 309; 17 LTOS 145; 15 Jur 494; 155 ER 698.

Reed v. Royal Exchange Assurance Company (1795) Peake Add cas 70.

Regina. v. Marsden [1868] CCR 131; [1891] 2 QB 149.

Regina. v. Elliot (1861) Le & Ca 103.

Regina v. Hall [1845], *Times* (London), 3 April 1845, 7–8.

Regina v. Mawgridge (1707) 84 ER 1107.

Rex (Ferris) v. Londonderry Justices [1903] 2 IR 747.

Ricketts v. Gaskell (1903), *Times* (London), 31 March 1903, 3.

Rickhard v. Rickhard and Bowles (1902), NA J77/753/2925.

Roberts v. Roberts and Drew (1902), NA J77/754/2937.

Roberts v. Roberts and Foulkes (1901), NA J77/733/2303.

Roberts v. Roberts and Whitaker, Daily Mail, 9 March 1904, 3.

Roberts v. Roberts and Sanlon and Nixon [dismissed] (1903), NA J77/794/4147; *Freeman's Journal,* 11 August 1904, 2, 3.

Roberts v. Scott (1901), *Times* (London), 17 July 1901, 10.

Robinson v. Robinson [1883] 8 PD 94.

Robinson v. Robinson and Dearden (1902), NA J77/763/3213; P 155; 72 LJP 63; 89 LT 74.

Robson v. Robson (1904), *Times* (London), 3 February 1904, 3; 68 JP 416, DC.

Rogerson v. Rogerson and Drummond [dismissed] (1904), NA J77/800/4341; *Daily Mail,* 1 June 1904, 3; *Daily Mail,* 2 June 1904, 3.

Rosenthal v. Rosenthal (1904), *Daily Mail,* 30 June 1904, 3.

Russell and Mulcahy (1897) 31 ILT 215.

Russell v. Russell [1924] AC 687 HL.

Ryan v. Ryan (1903), NA J77/793/4126; *Times* (London), 15 June 1904, 3; *Times* (London), 22 June 1904, 3; *Times* (London), 24 June 1906, 4.

Sadgrove v. Hole [1901] CA 2 KB 1.

Sedden v. Sedden and Doyle [1862] 2 Sw & Tr 640.

Sharpe v. Sharpe and Penny (1921), *Irish Times,* 21 December 1921, 7.

Shaw v. Gould [1868] LR 3 HL 55.

Shaw v. Shaw [1904] 20 TLR 795.

Sheppard v. Sheppard [1905] P 185; 74 LJP 102; 93 LT 433; 53 WR 608; 21 TLR 526.

Simpson v. Simpson and Henshill (1903), NA J77/800/4349; *Freeman's Journal*, 26 April 1904, 4.
Sinclair v. Sinclair (1896) 1 IR 603.
Slater v. Slater (1902), NA J77/753/2912.
Slon v. Slon [1929] 1 All ER 759.
Smith v. Smith and Bothera and Barnes (1903), NA J77/798/4275; *Daily Mail*, 29 April 1904, 3; P 249; 74 LJP 113; 93 LT 457; 54 WR 220.
Smyth v. Smyth (1903), NA J77/785/3881.
St Paul v. St Paul and Farquhar (1869) LR 1 P&D 736; 38 LJP&M 57; 21 LT 108; 17 WR 1111.
St Paul v. St Paul and Farquhar (1870) LR 2 P&D 93; *sub nom St Paul v. St Paul and Farquhar* 39 LJP&M 50; 23 LT 196; 18 WR 1007.
Stace v. Stace (1868) 33 LJP&M 51; 18 LT 740; 16 WR 1176.
Story v. Story and O'Connor (1887) 12 PD 196.
Sutton v. Sutton and Adams and Lloyd and Loveless (1904), NA J77/806/4520.
Symington v. Symington [1875] LR 2 Sc & Div 415.
Symons v. Symons [1897] P 167; TLR 353.
Thelwall v. Yelverton (1862) 14 ICLR 188; 14 Ir Jur (IR); 14 Ir Jur 347.
Thomas v. Young (1901), *Times* (London), 22 July 1901, 12.
Tidswell v. Ankerstein (1792) Peake 151 NS.
Todd v. Todd [dismissed] (1904), NA J77/826/5131.
Tulk v. Tulk (1906) 23 TLR 120.
Usher v. Usher [1912] 2 IR 445.
Watson orse Horsley v. Watson (1902), NA J77/754/2940; 89 LT 78; 19 TLR 567.
Webb v. Webb and Mekin (1903), NA J77/778/3690.
Weightman v. Weightman (1906), *Times* (London), 14 March 1906, 3; 94 LT 620; 70 JP 120; 22 TLR, 362, DC.
White's Divorce Bill (no. 1) HL [1920] 2 IR 343.
Wiedemann v. Walpole [1891] 2 QB 534; 60 LJQB 762; 40 WR 114; 7 TLR 722, CA.
Wild v. Harris [1843–60] All ER Rep 413.
Wilkins v. Wilkins and McCoy [rescinded] (1904), NA J77/822/5005.
Williams v. Thorp (1828) 2 Sim 257; 57 ER 785.
Williams v. Williams (1904), NA J77/801/4378; *Times* (London), 3 February 1904, 3; P 145; 73 LJP 31; 90 LT 174; 68 JP 188; 20 TLR 213, DC.

Wisdon v. Wisdon and St Vincent Parker-Jervis (1920), *Daily Mail*, 23 January 1920, 4.
Woodey v. Woodey (1874) 31 LT 647; 23 WR 386.
Worsley v. Worsley and Worsley (1904) 20 TLR 171.
Wyke v. Wyke (1902), NA J77/768/3361; *Times* (London), 1 December 1903; *Times* (London), 12 December 1903; *Times* (London), 29 January 1904, 13; P 149; 73 LJP 38; 90 LT 172; 20 TLR 193.

CHAPTER 1

Reading Sex, Love, and Divorce in *Ulysses* as Certain Uncertainties

There is an unresolved conflict in much critical writing about the ways sex, love, adultery, and divorce relate to one another in *Ulysses*. Most critics agree that *Ulysses* is a "novel of adultery": as many have pointed out, Joyce deconstructs this form of the novel, specifically the aesthetic, religious, political, and sexual presuppositions from which it traditionally draws its language, structure, and values.[1] As Richard Brown observed some thirty years ago, "Joyce, like so many of the great European novelists of the nineteenth century, relies upon the affective power of adulterous situations for many of his most central scenes and most powerful emotional effects."[2] Most critics also agree that *Ulysses* is about sex and about love; and most persuasively theorize the ways in which sex, love, and adultery

[1] The most memorable dissenting voice is Hugh Kenner, "Molly's Masterstroke," in *"Ulysses": Fifty Years*, ed. Thomas Stayley (Bloomington: Indiana University Press, 1974), 19: "Trysts, assignations, adulteries, these are banal. It seems part of Joyce's art to relegate that order of melodrama to the wings, and focus our attention instead on the perdurable texture of the ordinary." See also Tony Tanner, *Adultery in the Novel: Contract and Transgression* (Baltimore: Johns Hopkins University Press, 1979). For genre, see Jacques Derrida, "The Law of Genre," trans. Avitall Ronell, in *On Narrative*, ed. W. J. T. Mitchell (Chicago: University of Chicago Press, 1981), 51–77.

[2] Richard Brown, *James Joyce and Sexuality* (Cambridge: Cambridge University Press, 1985), 17.

P. Kuch, *Irish Divorce / Joyce's Ulysses*,
DOI 10.1057/978-1-137-57186-1_1

relate to one another. Several have observed that divorce is mentioned in *Ulysses*, but none to my knowledge have investigated whether or not the Blooms could divorce. What *Irish Divorce / Joyce's "Ulysses"* shows is that obtaining a *decree absolute*—rather than a separation order or a separation from bed and board—was not as much of an unlikelihood in Edwardian Ireland as has been thought within and beyond Joycean criticism.

There are perhaps a number of reasons why Bloom's "Divorce, not now" and Molly's "suppose I divorced him" have not been thoroughly investigated. First, it has been accepted as an established fact that divorce in Ireland was too expensive, too complicated, and too socially, culturally, and religiously stigmatized for it to be a realistic option for either of them. The default position is that the Irish do not divorce. And if anybody doubts this, there is a cornucopia of sociological, historical, and statistical evidence to show that Ireland's divorce rate was so low when compared with other Western countries as to be negligible. Second, it can be argued the likelihood of the Blooms petitioning for a divorce does not merit investigation because divorce was inimical to the Irish since it functioned as "other" in their conception of themselves. The following exchange in the House of Commons on 4 May 1906 during a debate about introducing a single divorce law for England, Ireland, Scotland, and Wales (and by extension for the Dominions and Colonies) is particularly instructive in this regard:

> §MR. EUGENE WASON (Clackmannan and Kinross) I beg to ask Mr. Attorney-General whether his attention has been called to the observations of Mr. Justice Gorell Barnes on the question of divorce in England; and whether he will be prepared to consider the propriety of bringing the Divorce Law of England into conformity with that of Scotland and other civilised countries.
>
> §SIR W. ROBSON I believe my Hon. and learned friend the Attorney-General is aware of the observations referred to in the Question. I do not think that either he or I is entitled in the present state of public business to say that the Government are likely to introduce any legislation on the subject.
>
> §MR. WILLIAM REDMOND With regard to the last sentence in the Question will the Hon. and learned Gentleman and the House bear in mind that the most civilised country in the world, Ireland, has no divorce law.
>
> §MR. FLAVIN asked when England ceased to be a civilised country.

> §MR. EUGENE WASON said the words at the end of his Question were not his but those of the learned Judge.[3]

There are at least three aspects of this exchange that merit attention. First, William Redmond (1861–1917), who was the member for East Clare at the time, could risk his provocative remark that "no divorce law" equates to "civilization" because the ecclesiastical condemnation of divorce was so embedded in the Irish social imaginary that it was unquestionably accepted as evidence of a native spirituality and civility that not only distinguished the Irish from their imperial masters but also endorsed their presence in the world.[4] Secondly, Mr. Justice Gorell Barnes, who was President of the Probate, Divorce and Admiralty Division of the King's Bench, had recently argued that a single divorce law for the entire United Kingdom would prevent plaintiffs from manipulating domicile, a practice, as I will show, that is essential for understanding the relationship between sex, love, adultery, and divorce in *Ulysses*. Third, the pitting of the English, Scottish, and Irish jurisdictions against one another in a bid to be deemed the most civilized reveals how much each country, despite their belonging to the United Kingdom, invested in the integrity of their own legal and moral interpretation of matrimonial causes. So perhaps a third reason why Joyceans have not investigated the significance of divorce for the Blooms relates to the untested assumption that the Blooms are only able to petition the Irish jurisdiction, and that Ireland, as Redmond boasted in his exchange at Westminster, "had no divorce law." What *Irish Divorce / Joyce's "Ulysses"* will show is that not only were the three jurisdictions not hermetically sealed with respect to one another but that, despite various judicial and legislative attempts, a number of Irish litigants between 1858 and 1922 were successfully petitioning the English court. In fact, Justice Gorell Barnes's 1905 ruling was just one of several attempts to restrict a provision in English law that

[3] Parl. Deb., H. C., 4th ser., 3 May 1906, vol. 156, col. 729–30, reported as "House of Commons," *Times* (London), 4 May 1906, 6.

[4] Charles Taylor defines "social imaginary" as "the way in which our contemporaries imagine the societies they inhabit and sustain," in *Modern Social Imaginaries* (Durham, NC: Duke University Press, 2004), 6; see also Cornelius Castoriadis, *The Imaginary Institution of Society* (Cambridge, MA: MIT Press, 1987).

it was known in legal, ecclesiastical, and parliamentary circles that the Irish were using for redress.

A fourth reason why the significance of divorce in *Ulysses* has not been thoroughly investigated relates to the characterization of Bloom. As Kerri Haggart has recently observed, critics have tended to characterize Bloom in ways that blur the distinction between the ways other characters see him and the ways critics represent him.[5] In "Cyclops," for example,

> where the patrons of the bar remark that Bloom is "prudent" (12.437), "humane" (12.843), "talkative" (12.895–6), "a dark horse" (12.1557), a "kno-wall" (12.838), and a swindler (12.1575), Joyce scholarship similarly views Bloom as "prudent,"[6] "humane,"[7] "complacent and miserly,"[8] and as an

[5] Kerri Haggart, "Bloom's Situated Mind in James Joyce's *Ulysses*: Decoding Character in a Social Storyworld" (PhD diss., University of Otago, 2015), 123.

[6] David Hayman, *"Ulysses": The Mechanics of Meaning* (New York: Prentice Hall, 1970), 251; Fritz Senn, "Dynamics of Corrective Unrest," in *Joyce's Dislocutions: Essays on Reading as Translation*, ed. John Paul Riquelme (Baltimore: Johns Hopkins University Press, 1984), 284; Hugh Kenner, "Circe," in *James Joyce's "Ulysses": Critical Essays*, ed. Clive Hart and David Hayman (Berkeley: University of California Press, 1977), 359; William Stephenson, "Eroticism and Lightness in 'Wandering Rocks'," in *Joyce's Wandering Rocks*, ed. Andrew Gibson and Steven Morrison (Amsterdam: Rodopi, 2002), 122; Frank Budgen, *James Joyce and the Making of "Ulysses" and Other Writings* (1934; London: Oxford University Press, 1972), 286; Margot Norris, *Virgin and Veteran Readings of "Ulysses"* (New York: Palgrave Macmillan, 2011), 190. For discussions regarding Bloom's "prudent inclination to avoid taking action," see Nicholas A. Fargnoli and Michael Patrick Gillespie, eds., *Critical Companion to James Joyce: A Literary Reference to His Life and Work* (New York: Checkmark, 2006), 138.

[7] A. Walton Litz, "Ithaca," in *James Joyce's "Ulysses": Critical Essays*, ed. Clive Hart and David Hayman (Berkeley: University of California Press, 1977), 401; see also Robert M. Adams, "Hades," in *James Joyce's "Ulysses": Critical Essays*, ed. Clive Hart and David Hayman (Berkeley: University of California Press, 1977), 106.

[8] Adaline Glasheen, "Calypso," in *James Joyce's "Ulysses": Critical Essays*, ed. Clive Hart and David Hayman (Berkeley: University of California Press, 1977), 59.

> "outsider,"[9] a "dark horse,"[10] or, "someone marginalized in Dublin society."[11] Contradictorily, Bloom is also viewed as "sensitive"[12] and generous.[13]

Particular behaviors in crisis situations are not always revelatory of character, for behavior is not always a simple matter of being either "in" or "out" of character. What Alexander Pope observed of the *Odyssey*—that "Homer has taken in *all* the inward Passions and Affections of Mankind to furnish his Characters"—is equally true of Joyce. That *Ulysses* is a book, as Joyce termed it, about adultery and that Joyce's imagination was as much engaged by "Bloom" as text, intertext, and context as it was by Bloom as a character has not always been sufficiently appreciated because it has not been fully understood that Molly's affair, which provides Bloom with grounds for a divorce, has begun of itself to construct both of them as potential litigants.

For example, some critics view Bloom as an early twentieth-century version of Charles Bovary—well meaning, kind, but perhaps a bit limp. They take him to task for not interrogating, or at least questioning, a wife he strongly suspects is about to commit adultery. Some view him as an archetypal "Everyman";[14]

[9] Karen R. Lawrence, *Who's Afraid of James Joyce?* (Gainesville: University Press of Florida, 2010), 144, 146.

[10] Harry Blamires, *The New Bloomsday Book: A Guide through "Ulysses"* (1966; London: Routledge, 1996), 40, 105.

[11] Patrick McCarthy, "*Ulysses*: Book of Many Errors," in *Joycean Unions: Post-Millennial Essays from East to West*, ed. R. Brandon Kershner and Tekla Mecsnóber (Amsterdam: Rodopi, 2013), 207.

[12] Fargnoli and Gillespie, *Critical Companion*, 138.

[13] Budgen, *Making of "Ulysses"*, 286.

[14] It is noteworthy that many of the key descriptions of Bloom are problematized by irony, intertextuality, context, attribution, and speaking position. Quotations from James Joyce, *"Ulysses": The Corrected Text, Student Edition*, ed. Hans Walter Gabler with Wolfhard Steppe and Claus Melchoir (Harmondsworth: Penguin, 1986) appear in the footnotes as *U* plus episode number plus line reference. As "Everyman," "What universal binomial denominations would be his as entity and nonentity? Assumed by any or known to none. Everyman or Noman" (*U*17.2007–8). As kind, "John Wyse Nolan opened wide eyes. —I'll say there is much kindness in the jew, he quoted, elegantly" (*U*10.979–80).

some as an androgynous "outsider";[15] and some as an Edwardian "New Man" sufficiently attuned to his wife's desires to grant her the independence and the personal space to explore her sexuality further and to forgive and forget if it all goes wrong.[16] To do so is to emphasize Bloom as a character at the expense of Bloom as text, intertext, and context.

Some critics err the other way. Both Bloom as a husband and the fact that Molly has committed adultery seem to fade in a blaze of theoretical speculation that, while offering a variety of exciting ways to read *Ulysses*, elides Joyce's engagement with the Irish society of his day—the context—for which his writing is justly praised. Garry Leonard, for example, has argued that Molly is essentially a consumer. Blazes Boylan, he observes, is "not so much a character as a nexus of the latest semiotic signifiers—an erection with an attitude."[17] But to see Bloom solely in these terms is to remove text from intertext and context. To situate Molly's affair within advertising and commodity culture—as influential as they were, particularly within a colonial society—and to theorize it solely in terms of Foucault and Baudrillard is to reduce adultery to sexual consumption and to remove it from two of the most powerful institutional discourses that pervade *Ulysses*—English Law and the Roman Catholic Church.

Some critics, whether or not intentionally, seem to want to overwrite Bloom and 1904 Ireland almost entirely. In *James Joyce and the Politics of Desire* (1990), Suzette Henke proposed, "A female story dialogically emerges from Joyce's master narrative, appropriates its textual authority, and gradually deconstructs the linguistic codes essential to the logocentric and phallocentric discourse not only of 'dear dirty Dublin' but of western patriarchal culture."[18] Such a focus ignores, as Emer Nolan has crisply remarked, "the class or colonial factors which shape gender in Ireland"

[15] "DR DIXON: (Reads a bill of health) Professor Bloom is a finished example of the new womanly man. His moral nature is simple and lovable" (*U*15.1798–99).

[16] Bloom the enlightened forgiver. The problematic passage here is *U*16.1533–42, where Bloom is represented parodying the Victorian "forgiveness scene." For a pictorial representation, see the triptych *Past and Present* (1858) by Augustus Leopold Egg, RA (1816–63), Tate Gallery, London.

[17] Garry Leonard, *Advertising and Commodity Culture in Joyce* (Gainesville: University Press of Florida, 1998), 8.

[18] Suzette Henke, *James Joyce and the Politics of Desire* (London: Routledge, 1990), 212.

and makes it seem that they "were entirely incidental issues."[19] If "the female story" does dialogically emerge, then the other interlocutor in that exchange is the social imaginary that is Edwardian Dublin. Even something as "safe" and traditionally "scholarly" as the Homeric parallel has been used to diminish the significance of adultery in Ireland in 1904. Keri Ames, for example, has argued that "Joyce found a means to forgive Molly's adultery by allowing Penelope's defense of Helen's infidelity (as forgivable sin, the result of divinely inspired blindness) to find nuanced expression in Molly's trivialization of adultery in her soliloquy."[20]

But in 1904 Edwardian Dublin, the Dublin inhabited by Bloom and Molly, adultery was not interpreted mythically or post-structurally or viewed as a trivial matter; and nor was it a trivial matter in 1922 when *Ulysses* was published, despite a significantly increased number of people seeking divorces through what had become a much simplified process. However illuminating theoretical approaches prove to the present-day reader, to ignore the relationships between sex, adultery, and divorce in *Ulysses* is to occlude "the particularity of the Irish historical experience" that arguably generated the book and to ignore the "social dialogue" that distinguished both its conception and reception.[21] Embedded within the historical social imaginary in which Bloom moves, whose conservatism is shown by the fact that *criminal conversation* remained a tort in Ireland until 1976, was the argument advanced by Lord Chief Justice John Holt that a man having sexual relations with another man's wife was "the highest invasion of property" and that "a man cannot receive a higher provocation"[22]—as

[19] Emer Nolan, *James Joyce and Nationalism* (1995; London: Routledge, 2003), 9–10.

[20] Keri Elizabeth Ames, "The Oxymoron of Fidelity in Homer's *Odyssey* and Joyce's *Ulysses*," *Joyce Studies Annual* 14 (2003): 147: "By relegating adultery to a vulgar and trite error inflicted by the gods, Penelope's excuse becomes an intertextual authorization of Molly's trivialization of infidelity." However, what might be true for Molly (respondent) is not necessarily true for Bloom (petitioner).

[21] Nolan, *Joyce and Nationalism*, xii; John Nash, *James Joyce and the Act of Reception: Reading, Ireland, Modernism* (Cambridge: Cambridge University Press, 2006), 98–130.

[22] *Regina v. Mawgridge* (1707) 84 ER 1107 at 1114–15, as discussed in Kate Fitz-Gibbon, *Homicide, Law Reform, Gender and the Provocation Defense: A Comparative Perspective* (London: Palgrave Macmillan, 2014), 23–25.

offensively sexist, phallocentric, materialist, and violent as this seems to the present-day reader. Interpretations that view Molly's adultery as "self-fulfillment," "self-realization," "sexual license," an "indiscretion," a "dalliance," a "misdemeanor," or a "sin," whether or not they employ these terms, ignore the fact that, as far as the laws of the United Kingdom in 1904 were concerned, adultery, although not deemed a felony, could still carry significant financial and social penalties.

As William Cornish has pointed out in his analysis of the Parliamentary debates that took place during the framing of An Act to Amend the Law Relating to Divorce and Matrimonial Causes in England (28 August 1857), "There was even a Lords' amendment seeking to criminalize adultery, but neither House was remotely likely to expose either sex to that minatory prospect. Instead, largely at the behest of the Commons, some vestige of a male lover's liability to pay *crim. con.* damages was kept as part of divorce proceedings."[23] To ignore such complex social, legal, and financial consequences of adultery and not explore its relationship to sex and love is also to ignore the textual evidence that both Bloom and Molly explicitly consider divorce—a realistic and achievable course of action, and, however stigmatized, one that was historically available to them in 1904. It is this textual, legal, and historical evidence that this book explores in detail, specifically as it relates to the various ways sex, love, adultery, and divorce can be read in *Ulysses*.

* * * *

Regardless of how Bloom is viewed, questions about his apparent inaction strike most readers as perplexing. In the main, whether implicit or explicit, such questions go something like this: Why doesn't Bloom continue to question Molly about the letter she receives from Boylan in the morning post, a letter he himself delivers to her while she is still in bed (4.310)? Why doesn't he return to 7 Eccles Street on some pretense or other during the

[23] 1857 Act, ss 33, 59, cited in William Cornish, "Marital Breakdown: Separation and the Coming of Judicial Divorce," in *The Oxford History of the Laws of England: Volume XIII: 1820–1914 Fields of Development*, ed. William Cornish, J. Stuart Anderson, Raymond Cocks, Michael Lobban, Patrick Polden, and Keith Smith (Oxford: Oxford University Press, 2010), 784; see also 734.

morning or the afternoon (8.633 *et seq.*)? Why doesn't he confront Boylan at the entrance to the National Museum or at the Ormond bar (8.1167–72; 11.337–38)—or, if not confront, why doesn't he affirm or assert his status as Molly's husband by simply standing next to the fellow? Why does he stay away from his own home, leaving the field open, as it were, to his rival? It is not that these questions cannot or should not be asked, but such questions, framed in this way, take for granted presuppositions that conflict with the consensus that Joyce deconstructs the conventional novel of adultery.

What such questions assume, in the main, is that Bloom is a stock "wronged husband," a husband who, if he does not raise his voice, blandish his fists, or employ a private detective, will simply evaporate in the intensity of the illicit lovers' passion. They also presuppose that Bloom is a psychologically "unrealistic person" in terms of late nineteenth- and early twentieth-century discourses of masculinity or an ineffectual or flawed "character" in terms of the dynamics of the narrative, and that the only humanly comprehensible course of action realistically available to him is some form of intervention—whether gentle, spirited, or forceful. Such questions also fail to take account of the trajectory of the *Ulysses* narrative as the representational realism of the early episodes, derived as they are from a mimetic narrative technique that elicits a sense of verisimilitude, develops into what Patrick Hogan has recently termed "communicative realism," where the determination is "truth and not some form of simple resemblance."[24] I take "communicative realism" to mean that whatever is read as "truth" to life, to individual experience, to the period and setting, or any other aspect of what is represented, simultaneously calls into question the very presuppositions that have enabled its expression, that have brought it into language.

Facilitating this process are the occurrences of irony, allusion, ambiguous generic and historical contexts, and what Marcus Hartner has termed multiperspectivity[25]—with the result that even though the *Ulysses* narrative becomes increasingly synthetic and meta-fictional and the challenge to

[24] Patrick Hogan, *"Ulysses" and the Poetics of Cognition* (London: Routledge, 2014), 119. I am indebted to Kerri Haggart for drawing my attention to this passage and the passage from Hartner, though my approach differs from hers.

[25] Marcus Hartner, "Multiperspectivity," in *The Living Handbook of Narratology*, ed. Peter Hühn et al. (Hamburg: Hamburg University Press), para. 2, last modified 15 October 2012, http://wikis.sub.uni-hamburg.de/lhn/index.php/Multiperspectivity.

interpret Bloom increasingly complex, it does not unmoor either Bloom or the book from its historically informed fictional story-world or leave it adrift in indeterminacy. The complexities of contemplating divorce in early twentieth-century Ireland and the consequences of those complexities for love and sex within a marriage are as quintessential to Joyce's project of "narrating the nation" as are the complex relationships between modernism and divorce or between modernity and nationalism.[26]

While it is certain, as I will show, that Molly entertains and that Bloom considers divorce in a strategically legal way and while it is certain, as I will also show, that they can actually obtain a *decree absolute*, the fact that *Ulysses* ends as it does means that it remains uncertain that this is what they will do. But this does not mean that they cannot do it.

* * * *

By including the words "certain" and "uncertainties" in Chapter 1 of this book and not including the word "indeterminacy," I wish to draw a distinction between what is printed in the text ("certain," as it relates to the *OED* definition: "determined, fixed; not variable") and the ways in which what appears in the text might defensibly be interpreted ("uncertainty," as it relates to the *OED* definition: "outcomes"). "Uncertainties" implies that "outcomes" may be achieved even though those "outcomes" are not considered definitive or final, whereas "indeterminacy" implies a postponement or destabilizing of "outcomes" because of a potential plurality of "meanings." The distinction between "uncertainties" and "indeterminacy" thus provides a way of distinguishing between readings ("outcomes") that can be defended in terms of their acknowledged presuppositions and readings that are more provisional because they are haunted by a plurality of "meanings."[27] As Alan Roughley admitted in his preface to *Reading Derrida*

[26] See, for example, Richard Brown, "'Perhaps she had not told him all the story': Observations on the Topic of Adultery in Some Modern Literature," in *Joyce, Modernity and Its Mediation*, ed. Christine van Boheemen (Amsterdam: Rodopi, 1989), 99–111.

[27] I am indebted to Declan Kuch for advising me that Wynne's typology draws a similar distinction. See Brian Wynne, "Uncertainty and Environmental Learning: Reconceiving Science and Policy in the Preventive Paradigm," *Global Environmental Change* 2, no. 2 (1992): 112–24.

Reading Joyce (1999), he was tempted to give his book "the title *(Im) possibilities*," to signal the potential "impossibility in ever fully comprehending all the polysemous meanings and complex textual operations."[28]

By concentrating on the text and on reading, I am distinguishing my approach from Phillip Herring's *Joyce's Uncertainty Principle* (1987), where "uncertainty" becomes entangled, despite his protestations to the contrary, with issues of authorial intention.[29] In the same way, I differ in my approach from Joseph Valente's claim that Joyce "formulated" his skeptical epistemology.[30] I am equally reticent about Brian Cosgrove's rigorously pursued analysis of "a persistent indeterminacy" derived from Schlegel and Flaubert that "makes it impossible to adjudicate between not just contradictory but mutually exclusive interpretations." For Cosgrove, Joyce's "proliferation of narrative perspectives" and his "preoccupation with quotidian particularism" mean that readers "lose any sense of a hierarchy of meaning."[31] Despite Hirsch's defense of intentionality,[32] I am skeptical of statements about a writer's "aim," though I thoroughly agree with Joseph Valente that the uncertainties we encounter in *Ulysses* do enrich our "human experience by developing our interpretative capacities."[33] Nevertheless, as Clive Hart has said, "as with some questions of modern physical theory, it is not that we could know but don't; it is rather that the information, the certainty, that we

[28] Alan Roughley, *Reading Derrida Reading Joyce* (Gainesville: University Press of Florida, 1999), xvi.

[29] Phillip Herring, *Joyce's Uncertainty Principle* (Princeton, NJ: Princeton University Press, 1987), xi: "I have tried to avoid the morass of intentionalism. Still, in adding 'principle' to 'uncertainty' in the title I admit that my aim was to suggest a devious authorial strategy the Irish have always associated with Joyce."

[30] Joseph Valente, "Beyond Truth and Freedom: The New Faith of Joyce and Nietzsche," *James Joyce Quarterly* 25, no. 1 (1987): 88.

[31] Brian Cosgrove, *Joyce's Negations: Irony, Indeterminacy and Nihilism in "Ulysses" and Other Writings* (Dublin: University College Dublin Press, 2007).

[32] E. D. Hirsch, *Validity in Interpretation* (New Haven, CT: Yale University Press, 1967). For problems with "intention," see Oscar Wilde's "The Decay of Lying" and Roland Barthes's "The Death of the Author."

[33] Valente, "Beyond Truth and Freedom," 88.

are seeking, does not exist."[34] As Justice Adrian Hardiman has pointed out in a seminal article titled "Law, Crime and Punishment in Bloomsday Dublin," it is evident that "Joyce had a marked partiality for doubtful cases where guilt and innocence seemed difficult to discern."[35]

* * * *

The emphasis placed on "reading" in this book is designed to draw attention to the enticing challenges and rewarding complexities of reading, as they have been explored in works from Wolfgang Iser's *The Implied Reader* (1974) and *The Act of Reading* (1978) to Lubomír Doležel's *Heterocosmica: Fiction and Possible Worlds* (1998). Doležel's claim that "fictional entities may have actual prototypes in the real world" and that this gives them a "transworld identity" immediately struck a chord. It also furnished a theoretical framework for moving freely between textual representations of what Auden called "the strange intimacies of marriage"; the intensely self-referential institutional discourses of parliamentary debate, family law, and the divorce court; the Habermasian public sphere of the newspapers; Edwardian and modern popular culture; and the multiple worlds of *Ulysses*. In this respect, I have been guided by Derek Attridge's advice that writing about *Ulysses* requires "rediscovering the literary work in its original time and place while making it anew for the reader's time and place."[36] What Fritz Senn terms "inductive scrutinies," the teasing out of "small but significant aspects and their implications for the book's language," has proved an invaluable prompt for such

[34] Clive Hart, "*Finnegans Wake* in Perspective," in *James Joyce Today: Essays on the Major Works*, ed. Thomas F. Stayley (Bloomington: Indiana University Press, 1966), 162.

[35] Adrian Hardiman, "Law, Crime and Punishment in Bloomsday Dublin," in *Lawyers, the Law and History: Irish Legal History Society Discourses and Other Papers, 2005–2011*, ed. Felix M. Larkin and N. M. Dawson (Dublin: Four Courts Press in association with the Irish Legal History Society, 2013), 56. Again on p. 68, remarking the references to the Flower and Harvey cases, Hardiman observes, "Both cases deal with a type of uncertainty that fascinated Joyce."

[36] Derek Attridge, *Joyce Effects: On Language, Theory, and History* (Cambridge: Cambridge University Press, 2001), 23.

rediscovery.[37] As the narrator of the "Eumaeus" episode points out, Bloom prefers "Sherlockholmesing" (16.831)—employing probabilistic inductive reasoning—in his search for evidence about what has happened between Molly and Boylan. This should be accepted as more than a nod to the reader that they too should adopt the same reasoning as they read.

I also owe a considerable debt to Margot Norris's inspirational and challenging *Virgin and Veteran Readings of "Ulysses"* (2011), particularly her illuminating idea that productive reading involves dynamically adopting and re-adopting opposing stances—the "virgin," or first-time reader, and the "veteran," or the reader who has read *Ulysses* at least once if not more times. "Virgin" nicely captures notions of initial, first-time, and naïve reading in the sense that the experience is anticipated but not foreclosed,[38] despite an unwelcome association with sexuality that "novice" and other antonyms of "veteran" do not have. "Veteran," however, nicely captures the sense of being experienced and cultivated yet somewhat damaged—the idea that multiple encounters with the complexities of the text, its intertexts and contexts, and its plethora of reading communities can produce responses that might become rigid, because such encounters can prove as exhausting as they are exhilarating. The virgin–veteran binary also enhances the way Joyce considered *Ulysses* should be read. "I don't think the difficulties in reading it are so insurmountable," he is said to have remarked. "Certainly any intelligent reader can read and understand it, if he returns to the text again and again. He

[37] Fritz Senn, *Inductive Scrutinies: Focus on Joyce*, ed. Christine O'Neill (Dublin: Lilliput Press, 1995). I have also benefitted from Joseph Brooker, *Joyce's Critics: Transitions in Reading and Culture* (Madison: University of Wisconsin Press, 2004); Jean Paul Riquelme, "Preparatory to Anything Else: Joyce's Styles as Forms of Memory—The Case of 'Eumaeus'," in *"Ulysses" in Critical Perspective*, ed. Michael Patrick Gillespie and A. Nicholas Fargnoli (Gainesville: University Press of Florida, 2006), 9–34; Margot Norris, "Narratology and *Ulysses*," in *"Ulysses" in Critical Perspective*, ed. Michael Patrick Gillespie and A. Nicholas Fargnoli (Gainesville: University Press of Florida, 2006), 35–50; Nash, *Joyce and the Act of Reception*, 98–130; and David Pierce, *Joyce and Company* (London: Continuum, 2006), 38–54, 57–82.

[38] Margot Norris, in "Narratology and *Ulysses*," 46, explains that a "virgin" reading is "a linear reading from beginning to end limited to the knowledge incrementally unfolded by the narration."

is setting out on an adventure with words."[39] Adopting the stance of "virgin" reader is one way of refreshing these repeated readings.

To all the stances I have just outlined, I would add the electronically assisted reader (EAR). An EAR is a reader who approaches the text of *Ulysses* as hypertext. It is someone who, whether "virgin" or "veteran," is seduced and shaped by immediacy, who engages in the type of glossing and source-hunting that is not as readily available to the reader of the printed text. A subset of the EAR is the aural reader, who comes to either the printed or the electronic text after listening to readings or dramatizations on YouTube, CD, or audio file.

* * * *

The remaining terms in the introduction, "Sex, Love, and Divorce," point to the extent to which certain uncertainties become a way of reading the historical, phenomenological, cultural, and psychological discourses that co-exist within *Ulysses*. To link sex, love, and divorce to one another and to certain uncertainties takes account of the extent to which early twentieth-century divorce hearings were sites of certain uncertainty: predictably certain as to process, but sometimes uncertain as to outcomes. As Cornish has pointed out in his authoritative account of the divorce hearings that took place in the realm of the United Kingdom (that is, in the courts of England, Ireland, Scotland, and Wales[40]) during the period in which *Ulysses* was being written,

> All in all, the case law in this realm developed with "more fluctuation and obscurity than in any other" relating to husband and wife. Its thrusts and feints occurred because individual judges differed in their instincts over how far the Christian view of marriage as an indissoluble union could be qualified by voluntary arrangements where the relationship had broken down. The judges had to deal with the perplexities of policy, while listening to histories of deep personal unhappiness. Often enough each spouse would tell a very

[39] Willard Potts, ed., *Portraits of the Artist in Exile: Recollections of James Joyce by Europeans* (New York: Harcourt, Brace and Jovanovich, 1986), 83.

[40] Unlike Ireland and Scotland, Wales did not have its own court. Welsh cases were heard by the Probate, Divorce and Admiralty Division of the King's Bench, which sat only in London.

different story about why the arrangement to separate had unraveled. Little wonder that so much remained unpredictable.[41]

By offering a reading of *Ulysses* mediated by divorce court reports in newspapers that were familiar to Joyce, this book will show that Bloom possesses a working grasp of English divorce procedure (16.1358–1403; 16.1480–95), sufficient to give credence to his early morning 17 June 1904 consideration, "*Divorce, not now*" (17.2202; emphasis mine). It will closely examine the textual evidence that Joyce revised "*Divorce not yet*" to "*Divorce not now*" when the manuscript of the "Ithaca" episode first came back from the typist,[42] and the fact that Bloom thinks and acts in terms of the English rather than the Irish or Scots jurisdictions. And the two elements of his thought, "*Divorce*" and "*not now*"—a rider that postpones but does not dismiss divorce as an option—will be considered in terms of their legal implications and their significance for the narrative.

* * * *

While Richard Brown has written extensively about the books on marriage and adultery that Joyce had in his library and how they relate to his work,[43] he has overlooked the one that was central to Joyce's knowledge of the law, particularly as it applied to marriage and adultery. This was *Every Man's Own Lawyer: A Handy Book of the Principles of Law and Equity, by A. Barrister; Fifty-fourth Edition*, published by Crosby, Lockwood and Son in 1919.

[41] Cornish, "Marital Breakdown," 773–74.

[42] James Joyce, *"Ulysses": A Critical and Synoptic Edition, Prepared by Hans Walter Gabler with Wolfhard Steppe and Claus Melchior* (New York: Garland, 1984), 3, 1622.

[43] Brown, *Joyce and Sexuality*, 22–49. See also Michael Patrick Gillespie, "A Critique of Ellmann's List of Joyce's Trieste Library," *James Joyce Quarterly* 19, no. 1 (1981): 27–36; Michael Patrick Gillespie, *Inverted Volumes Improperly Arranged: James Joyce and His Trieste Library* (Ann Arbor: UMI Research, 1983); Michael Patrick Gillespie, ed., *James Joyce's Trieste Library: A Catalogue of Materials at the Harry Ransom Humanities Research Center* (Austin: University of Texas, 1986); Thomas E. Connolly, *The Personal Library of James Joyce: University of Buffalo Studies* 22, no. 1 (Buffalo, NY: University of Buffalo Bookstore, 1957).

Running to some eight hundred pages, it contains chapters on marriage and divorce, public health and good order, and insurance, and an extensive *Dictionary of Legal Terms*. Doubtless the short title appealed to Joyce's conception of Bloom as "Everyman or Noman" (17.2008), his protagonist's penchant for miscellaneous erudition, and as a convincing source for Bloom's legal vocabulary. As I have already indicated, Joyce and Bloom were more conversant with the law than has been recognized.

Careful attention will also be paid to the decisions Joyce made regarding divorce and the Blooms as he was writing *Ulysses*, as revealed by Phillip Herring's *Joyce's "Ulysses": Notesheets in the British Museum* (1972) and *Joyce's Notes and Early Drafts for "Ulysses": Selections from the Buffalo Collection* (1977), and articles by Myron Schwartzman and Michael Groden in the Groden 1974–1975 issue of *James Joyce Quarterly*.[44] I owe a considerable debt to Luca Crispi's *Joyce's Creative Process and the Construction of Characters in "Ulysses": Becoming the Blooms* (2015) for evidence from genetic criticism to support my contention that divorce is something that occurs to both Bloom and Molly, not in any deliberate or programmatic way, but rather as a potential course of action, freighted as it is with fantasies, hope, and the preservation and the potential reconstitution of the self.

Nevertheless, this book will argue that despite Bloom's conflicted feelings about his own polymorphous sexuality, his wife's adultery, and his fears about court procedure and divorce reporting, he is more strategic and more forensic than has hitherto been acknowledged. His rejoinder to Molly when she accuses him of philandering—"You have no proof" (18.65–66)—reveals much about his attitude to marital infidelity. And his conversation with Stephen in "Eumaeus" where he refers to the "King's Proctor" and to the "*decree nisi*" with *nisi* subsequently "made absolute" shows that it is the English court he has in mind, the Divorce Court of the Probate, Divorce and Admiralty Division of the King's Bench that sat only in London (16.1490–92). *Irish Divorce / Joyce's "Ulysses"* will also argue that Molly's "*suppose I divorced him*" is not one of those "cracked things that come into [her] head sometimes" (18.846; emphasis mine; 18.1487–88)—though, compared with Bloom's resolution, it is a comparatively late interpolation in

[44] Myron Schwartzman, "The V.A.8 Copybook: An Early Draft of the 'Cyclops' Chapter of *Ulysses* with Notes on Its Development," *James Joyce Quarterly* 12, nos. 1–2 (1974–1975): 64–122; Michael Groden, "'Cyclops' in Progress, 1919," *James Joyce Quarterly* 12, nos. 1–2 (1974–1975): 123–68.

the text[45]—but it is a course of action that is realistic, can be undertaken (she makes no attempt to conceal the evidence), and has the potential to be achieved in and be sanctioned by law.

* * * *

There were seven ways for Irish people to dissolve their marriage at the time that *Ulysses* is set. This is not to claim that all seven ways were available to the Blooms in 1904. But it is to take account of the way in which the movement of people within the Empire, and the variety of traditions and mores they brought with them, meant that each jurisdiction had to judge each case on its own merits. Jurists, politicians, and the religious of all faiths were aware of the complexity of the issues and the growing demand in many countries for rational, humane, and affordable methods for legally dissolving failed marriages, as the numerous enquiries, symposia, and conferences on divorce that were convened in the Empire and in Europe and America attest. As an avid reader of the newspapers, Joyce would have become familiar with Irish ways of dissolving a marriage while he was writing *Ulysses*. Two of the seven ways were comparatively straightforward. One could prove complex. Four were complicated by issues of "domicile" (where the parties legally reside) and "comity of nations" ("the principle that one sovereign nation voluntarily adopts or enforces the laws of another sovereign nation out of deference, mutuality or respect").[46]

I have deliberately retained the somewhat dated term "comity of nations" rather than "conflict of laws" as the former not only reflects the emphasis on "nation" that characterized the politics of the period, but it also signals the uncertainty embedded in the legal term and its practice. In

[45] Joyce, *Ulysses* (1984), 3, 1682. The interpolation occurs as the third of five known revisions to the typescript. See also *James Joyce's "Ulysses": The Manuscript and First Printings Compared*, annotated by Clive Driver (New York: Octagon Books, 1975), 712.

[46] Legal Information Institute, "Comity of Nations," in *Wex Legal Dictionary and Encyclopedia*, Cornell University, http://www.law.cornell.edu/wex/comity_of_nations. For a legal history of "comity," see A. V. Dicey, J. H. C. Morris, and Lawrence Collins, *Dicey, Morris and Collins on the Conflict of Laws*, 15th ed. (London: Sweet and Maxwell, 2012), 1:5–9.

this respect, the *Oxford English Dictionary* entry for "comity" is instructive. Definition a: "The courteous and friendly understanding by which each nation respects the laws and usages of every other, so far as may be without prejudice to its own rights and interests" is elegantly subverted by the next entry, definition b: "*erron*[eous]. The company of nations mutually practicing this." The significance of "domicile" and "comity of nations" for Bloom and for Molly will be investigated in Chapters 6 and 7;[47] but it is important to note for the present that, in simple terms, domicile is a question of fact and intention, and that while legally a person may have only one domicile, they may choose that domicile on the grounds that it is where they wish to reside permanently. Such a choice, however, is open to legal interpretation.[48] As Dicey, Morris, and Collins have pointed out, when "judicial divorce was introduced into English law by the Matrimonial Causes Act 1857," the Act "contained no rules as to jurisdiction of divorce. After a long period of uncertainty, the Privy Council held in *Le Mesurier v. Le Mesurier* (1895) that the only court which had jurisdiction to dissolve a marriage was the court of common domicile of the parties."[49] From 1895, it was the husband's domicile which determined the jurisdiction in which he could petition for separation or divorce. It is also important to note, as an authoritative Irish legal historian has pointed out,

[47] Diane Urquhart, "Irish Divorce and Domestic Violence, 1857–1922," *Women's History Review* 22, no. 5 (2013): 820–37. See "domicile" in Glossary.

[48] John O'Brien, *Conflict of Laws* (London: Routledge, 1999), 66–67. Note also A. V. Dicey and J. H. C. Morris, *Dicey and Morris on the Conflict of Laws*, ed. Lawrence Collins, 13th ed. (London: Sweet and Maxwell, 2000), 1:109–10, §6-008: "After Ireland was divided in 1921 into Northern Ireland and what is now called the Republic of Ireland, it was held in Ireland that a man could be domiciled in Northern Ireland in 1907 or in the Republic in 1898, in each case because he had his home in what subsequently became Northern Ireland and the Republic respectively. In neither of these cases did the court refer to an Order in Council made in pursuance of the Government of Ireland Act 1920, which provides that 'for the purpose of determining the domicile of any person, Northern Ireland shall be deemed always to have been a separate part of the United Kingdom.' 'Separate' in this Order no doubt means 'separate from the Republic.'"

[49] A. V. Dicey, J. H. C. Morris, and Lawrence Collins, *Dicey, Morris and Collins on the Conflict of Laws*, 14th ed. (London: Sweet and Maxwell, 2010), 2:866, §18-002, citing *Le Mesurier v. Le Mesurier* [1895] AC 517, 540.

> The domicile of the husband is communicated to a wife immediately upon solemnization of the marriage and during the subsistence of the marriage she is unable to acquire an independent domicile of her own. This applies even if spouses are living apart, whether or not they are doing so in pursuance of a separation agreement or a decree of divorce *a mensa et thoro*. Thus, if a husband deserts his wife and goes to live in England acquiring an English domicile of choice, even though his wife never sets foot in England, she also acquires under Irish law, an English domicile.[50]

The question of the ways in which "comity of nations" might be applied within the realm of the United Kingdom in 1904 is itself open to legal argument. For a jurisdiction to apply the principle within what is considered to be one sovereign entity—the realm of the United Kingdom—is to imply that the recipient jurisdiction (Ireland or Scotland) might itself be sovereign.[51] What let this particular genie out of the bottle in terms of divorce was the infamous *Thelwall v. Yelverton* (1861–1865) case,[52] which saw the English, Scots, and Irish jurisdictions pitted against one another, provoking considerable debate in both the Commons and the Lords and filling columns of newsprint with legal interpretation about domicile, bigamy, the validity of mixed marriage in Ireland, and what constituted determination. The decades that Westminster and then the English, Scots,

[50] Alan Joseph Shatter, *Family Law in the Republic of Ireland*, 2nd ed. (Dublin: Wolfhound Press, 1981), 117. Note: "*Held*, that the wife's domicile is that of her husband." *Gillis v. Gillis* [1874] 8 IR Eq 597. The case of *Brown v. Brown*, reported as "Hungarian Lady's Divorce," *Daily Mail*, 13 July 1904, 3, is a contemporary illustration of this point of law. The ruling no longer applies. Following the Domicile and Recognition of Foreign Divorces Act, 1986, which came into force from 2 October 1986, Irish courts recognize a divorce granted in a country where either spouse is domiciled at the date of the institution of proceedings. Domicile may take account of "ordinarily resident or ordinary residence." See also *Egan v. Egan* [1928] NI 159 where it was held by Moore, L. C. J. that the plaintiff could elect either to be domiciled in Northern Ireland or in the Free State, and that the petitioner having elected to be domiciled in Northern Ireland, the court could entertain the petition for divorce *a mensa et thoro*.

[51] For some of the complexities involved in the early twentieth-century English definition of domicile, see Dicey, Morris, and Collins, *Conflict of Laws*, 15th ed., 1:109, §6–007.

[52] *Thelwall v. Yelverton* (1862) 14 ICLR 188; 14 Ir Jur (IR); 14 Ir Jur 347.

and Irish judiciary spent trying to negotiate these complexities, as case law accumulated and public attitudes to divorce shifted, particularly during and after the First World War—complexities and shifts that were widely discussed in the newspapers—provide a highly recommended and illuminating context for reading the novel of adultery that is *Ulysses.*

Although there were seven ways Irish people could end their marriage in 1904, this is not to claim that all the ways were equally well known, widely known, or thoroughly known in their intricate legal detail. Some cases, however, such as Madame Maud Gonne MacBride's attempt to obtain a civil dissolution of her marriage to the Irish Boer War hero John MacBride while she was living in France, were reported in detail in the Irish and colonial press.

1. Separation orders: Ireland. Apart from silent cohabitation or informally agreeing to live separately, separation orders provided the most common solution to marriage breakdown in Ireland. In the Irish jurisdiction, prior to disestablishment in 1869, they were determined by the Ecclesiastical Courts and then, consequent on disestablishment, in the civil courts, though the Catholic Church continued not only to grant separation orders after 1869 but also to grant them for reasons other than adultery.[53] Because "Section 13 of the Matrimonial Causes and Marriage Law (Ireland) Amendment Act, 1870 required the civil courts to proceed on principles 'which in the opinion of the ... Court[s], shall be as nearly as may be conformable to the principles and rules on which the Ecclesiastical Courts of Ireland have heretofore acted and given relief,'" judgments made in the civil courts reflected the teachings of the Church.[54] Irish separation orders, unlike their English counterparts, did not make provision for maintenance or custody but, as in *Moutray v. Moutray* (1892), were more lenient with respect to living arrangements.[55] As David

[53] Shatter, *Family Law*, 145–47, 151.

[54] *Report on Nullity of Marriage*, The Law Reform Commission: *An Coimisiún um Athchóiriú an Dlí* (LRC 9–1984), 523, http://www.lawreform.ie.

[55] *Moutray v. Moutray* (1892) ILTSJ 146: "A deed of separation mutually entered into between husband and wife, consequent upon prior differences, does not require the validation of a trustee to render it valid; and mere living in the same house together after its date, without cohabitation, will not avoid it. Under such a deed the wife can sue."

Fitzpatrick has pointed out, "many wives of Irish clerks, artisans and labourers" who did obtain separation orders found it difficult "to compel their husbands to maintain them":

> A deserted wife might insist upon her right of *consortium* by seeking a decree for restitution of conjugal rights, in default of which the wife might be allowed alimony . . . Otherwise she might pledge his credit with shopkeepers, if he had credit, to an amount which the husband deemed appropriate for the subsistence of a wife and children. Her only other remedy was to seek a magistrate's order for maintenance in a case of desertion, under an act of 1886, which was at first thought to be inoperable in Ireland. In 1909, only 80 such orders were issued by Dublin magistrates, and 96 elsewhere in Ireland.[56]

In *Rex (Ferris) v. Londonderry Justices* (1903), however, a Board of Guardians successfully prosecuted a husband at Petty Sessions "for willfully neglecting to maintain his wife, so that she became destitute, and was relieved in their workhouse."[57] Financially independent women did not encounter the same problems. In the opening paragraph of "The Boarding House" in *Dubliners*, Joyce vividly depicts the breakdown of

[56] David Fitzpatrick, "Divorce and Separation in Modern Irish History," *Past & Present* 114, no. 1 (1987): 176. In *Russell and Mulcahy*, 31 ILT 215: "that the wife had no authority to pledge her husband's credit for a debt of that amount for which it was impossible for him to pay out of his earnings; and that there was a duty cast upon a trader of informing the husband of the debt his wife was incurring." In *Sheppard v. Sheppard* (1905), Gorell Barnes ruled that "Sect. 26 of the Matrimonial Causes Act, 1857, absolutely puts an end to the right of a wife who has obtained a decree of judicial separation to pledge her husband's credit or to contract on his behalf during the continuance of the judicial separation except where alimony has been decreed and has not been duly paid."

[57] *Rex (Ferris) v. Londonderry Justices* [1903] 2 IR 747. Note *Every Man's Own Lawyer*, 369, regarding the Married Women's Property Act 1882 (45 & 46 Vict. §20): "Where the husband of any woman having separate property becomes chargeable to the parish, the Justices may make such an order against the wife for the maintenance of her husband out of her separate property as they may make against a husband for the maintenance of his wife." But note also *Every Man's Own Lawyer*, 371, citing *Mitchell v. Torrington Union* (1897): "A husband is not bound to maintain a wife who has committed adultery, and is living apart from him, and who afterwards becomes chargeable to the union."

an Irish marriage, the empowerment of the woman as petitioner, and the apparent ease with which the wife obtains a separation order:

> MRS. MOONEY was a butcher's daughter. She was a woman who was quite able to keep things to herself: a determined woman. She had married her father's foreman and opened a butcher's shop near Spring Gardens. But as soon as his father-in-law was dead Mr. Mooney began to go to the devil. He drank, plundered the till, ran headlong into debt. It was no use making him take the pledge: he was sure to break out again a few days after. By fighting his wife in the presence of customers and by buying bad meat he ruined his business. One night he went for his wife with the cleaver and she had to sleep in a neighbour's house.
>
> After that they lived apart. She went to the priests and got a separation from him with care of the children. She would give him neither money nor food nor house-room; and so he was obliged to enlist himself as a sheriff's man.[58]

There is very little that Mr. Mooney can do because his sole legal redress, a petition to the court for a restitution of his conjugal rights, would almost certainly fail, given *Stace v. Stace* (1868), *Woodey v. Woodey* (1874), and *D'Arcy v. D'Arcy* (1887).[59] As *Every Man's Own Lawyer* advises, "A decree for restitution of conjugal rights obtained by a husband is practically valueless, where the wife chooses to ignore it."[60] And were Mrs. Mooney to allege "habitual drunkenness," Mr. Mooney

[58] James Joyce, *Dubliners*, ed. Hans Walter Gabler with Walter Hettche (New York: Garland, 1993), 219–20. For what was most often the case, however, see Urquhart, "Irish Divorce and Domestic Violence," 825–27. For legal argument over the definition of a "drunkard," see "Drink and Divorce," *Daily Mail*, 3 February 1904, 3; for divorce granted to a Limerick woman by the Dublin courts from a husband who boasted he could drink 21 pints of porter in a day, see "From Far and Near: Limerick," *Daily Mail*, 4 February 1904, 3.

[59] William Latey, ed., *The Law and Practice in Divorce and Matrimonial Causes*, 15th ed. (London: Longman, 1952), 200, §2.359: "In an Irish case (*D'Arcy v. D'Arcy* [1887]) it was held that violent and uncontrolled temper, habitual intemperance, violent conduct in the presence of the husband's guests, assaults on him, acts or threats of violence and offensive language towards his servants, constituted a legal defense to a suit brought by the wife for restitution."

[60] *Every Man's Own Lawyer*, 379.

might well find himself charged under the 1902 Inebriates Act that had been specifically amended to strengthen some of the provisions of the 1895 Summary Jurisdiction (Married Women) Act, though whether or not the latter applied to Ireland remains in doubt.[61] Despite Ireland's much vaunted belief in the sanctity of marriage, the Mooneys are not entirely untypical, for, as David Fitzpatrick has convincingly demonstrated, "if divorce was scarcely known in Ireland separation in its many guises was ubiquitous."[62] Should she wish to remarry, Mrs. Mooney, as a Catholic, would need to petition her Bishop to have her marriage annulled. Since a marriage between Catholics *eo ipso* was indissoluble, she would have to submit to an investigation by "a Catholic Marriage Tribunal, under the direction of a Bishop" to declare "whether or not the essential conditions of a sacramental marriage were present at the time of the marriage."[63] Essentially a pre-Reformation Ecclesiastical Court system, the Irish court remained attentive to Papal encyclicals such as *Dum Multa* (24 December 1902), which affirmed that "as it is evident that every Christian marriage is a sacrament" and that while the contract that governs marriage

> means the civil authority retains in full its right to regulate the so-called civil effects, the marriage itself is subject to the authority of the Church. It follows then that the marriage of Christians when fully accomplished is holy, indivisible, and perfect. It cannot be dissolved for any reason other

[61] See *Robson v. Robson* as reported in *Times* (London), 3 February 1904 for the first prosecution under this Act. For a discussion of the Inebriates Act, 1898, see *Irish Law Times and Solicitors' Journal* 38 (1904): 162. Note however, *Hudson v. Hudson* [1863], "The court will not grant a decree of judicial separation to protect the wife from more unhappiness resulting from an ill-assorted marriage nor from the destruction of domestic comfort caused by drunkenness"; and *Brown v. Brown* [1865], "Habitual drunkenness, and a series of anonymous and extraordinary behaviours on the part of the husband, do not constitute legal cruelty."

[62] Fitzpatrick, "Divorce and Separation," 174.

[63] Simon O'Byrne, *Civil Divorce for Catholics* (Dublin: Frederick Press, 1982), 22. See John T. Noonan, Jr., *Power to Dissolve: Lawyers and Marriages in the Courts of the Roman Curia* (Cambridge, MA: Belknap Press of Harvard University Press, 1972), 159–238.

than the death of either spouse according to the holy words: "What God has joined, let no man divide."[64]

2. Separation orders: English domicile: For the Irish domiciled in England, after the 1895 Act, from the County Courts, where agreements were made orders. These agreements could be reached orally, as with *McGregor v. McGregor* (1888), or in writing and could contain covenants.[65] As in the cases of *Balfour v. Balfour* (1919) and *Courtney v. Courtney* (1923), "mutual oral promises simply not to cohabit, if intended to have legal effect, [were] enforceable."[66] Such an agreement did not end the marriage, but it did allow the spouses to live separately. It also required the husband to give an allowance to his wife if he had been guilty of a matrimonial offense.[67]

[64] "Dum multa: Encyclical of Pope Leo XIII on Marriage Legislation," Papal Encyclicals Online, 24 December 1902, accessed 18 July 2016, http://www.papalencyclicals.net/Leo13/l13multa.htm.

[65] "A deed of separation between husband and wife generally requires the intervention of trustees. But in a recent case, where husband and wife had agreed to live apart on terms that cross-summonses which they had taken out for assault should be withdrawn, and that the wife should receive a weekly allowance from the husband and should indemnify him against claims for debts contracted by her, it was held by the Court of Appeal that the parties had power to make such a contract without the intervention of a trustee, and that such a contract need not be in writing (*McGregor v. McGregor* [1888] 21 QBD 424)." *Every Man's Own Lawyer*, 378.

[66] Shatter, *Family Law*, 121, cites *Balfour v. Balfour* [1919] 2 KB 571 (CA) (on the need for intention to create legal relations) and *Courtney v. Courtney* (1923) 2 IR 31; (1923) ILTR 42 (CA). *The Law Reports of the Incorporated Council of Law Reporting for Ireland: "The Irish Law Times" and the Incorporated Council of Law Reporting for Northern Ireland: Digest of Cases Decided by the Superior and Other Courts in Ireland from the Commencement of Hilary Sittings, 1919, to the End of Michaelmas Term, 1928*, ed. R. H. Ryland. (Dublin: J. Falconer, 1930), col. 175 also notes, "Such a contract need not be in any particular form, provided there is evidence of an agreement made for valuable consideration; nor is it necessary that it should contain an express covenant not to sue to be a bar to subsequent proceedings for divorce, if that can be shown to have been the real character of the agreement entered into by the parties."

[67] "Misbehaviour, such as adultery, desertion, or cruelty, by a party to a marriage . . . provided grounds for divorce and was important in applications in magistrates' courts for financial relief during the marriage." *A Dictionary of Law*, ed. Jonathan Law and Elizabeth A. Martin, 7th ed. (Oxford: Oxford University Press, 2014),

Though the Court of Appeal in 1888 had ruled that a "judicial separation could only be granted where the petitioner came to the court with clean hands, free from all matrimonial misconduct," the effect of this and similar decisions, as Latey points out, "was all but nullified by the discretion given to the court in all cases of judicial separation."[68] A comparatively simple and inexpensive procedure, legal separation became the most popular of matrimonial proceedings in England from 1857 to 1945.[69] However, a petition for divorce could be lodged if either the husband or wife, after having their agreement confirmed as a court order, subsequently discovered that adultery had occurred prior to the agreement being entered into, as in *Weightman v. Weightman* (1906).[70] But, in the case of *Harriman v. Harriman* (1907) as reported in the *Times*,[71] the Court of Appeal upheld a judgment by Mr. Justice Bucknill that "a wife who has been deserted by her husband and who has not obtained a separation order within two years

256, http://www.oxfordreference.com/view/10.1093/acref/9780199551248.001.0001/acref-9780199551248-e-2425.

[68] Latey, *Law and Practice*, §2.345.

[69] Gail Savage, "The Operation of the 1857 Divorce Act, 1860–1910: A Research Note," *Journal of Social History* 16, no. 4 (1983): 105.

[70] This was an appeal by Joseph Weightman from a refusal by Mr. Yates K. C, the Manchester stipendiary, on 24 January 1906, to discharge "on fresh evidence" an order dated 16 March 1904, whereby the said Joseph Weightman was adjudged to have deserted Sara Eliza Weightman, who was granted a separation order. The grounds of the appeal were (1) that it was proved that the wife had committed adultery on 13 March 1904, and that the husband did not become aware of the fact until 21 December 1905, and that the Magistrate was wrong in holding that there was no "fresh evidence" on which he could discharge the order of 16 March 1904. (2) That having "found as a fact that the husband had applied to discharge the order promptly and without delay, the Magistrate was wrong that he had no jurisdiction to discharge the said order because six months had elapsed since the said order was made. Decision: The appeal must therefore be allowed and the order of 16 March 1904, discharged." "Probate, Divorce and Admiralty Division," *Times* (London), 14 March 1906, 3. Court Minutes at NA J77/870/6446, Filed: 13 February 1906; Final Decree: 13 March 1906.

[71] *Harriman v. Harriman*, NA J77/929/8195, Filed: 30 December 1907; Set Down: 14 January 1908; Dismissed: 29 April 1908; Appeal Lodged: 30 April 1908; Appeal Dismissed: 9 February 1909. William Vines Harriman had left Lily Isabel Harriman on 18 July 1902.

from the time when the desertion commenced, thereby loses her right to plead such desertion under the Matrimonial Causes Act, 1857, and, after proof of adultery, to obtain against her husband, who has continued to desert her, a decree of divorce."[72] As has been pointed out, "over this delicate issue, the case law long remained unclear. Only in 1929 would the House of Lords settle that a divorced wife was not bound by the earlier terms, even if they were expressed to continue when there was a subsequent matrimonial wrong."[73]

3. Emigration, which was known colloquially as "the Irish solution," though it was also commonly used by the English[74]—to Australia, New Zealand, India, and some states of America, though not to all provinces of Canada.[75] This was an option taken by those Irish people who were contemplating an exogamous marriage or who were seeking a *divorce a*

[72] *Times* (London), 10 February 1909, 13.

[73] Cornish, "Marital Breakdown," 773.

[74] "Before we proceed; to what extent have you found in your practice that men and women are deserted by a spouse proceeding off to a foreign country or to the colonies?—O, a great many cases. A common thing?—A common thing." Joseph Charles Priestley, K. C., quoted in *Minutes of Evidence Taken before the Royal Commission on Divorce and Matrimonial Causes: Presented to Parliament by Command of His Majesty* (London: His Majesty's Stationery Office, 1912), 1:189, §4526–27.

[75] Diane Urquhart, "Ireland and the Divorce and Matrimonial Causes Act of 1857," *Journal of Family History* 38, no. 3 (2013): 314. Urquhart points out on p. 315 that "Divorce Irish style—which in popular parlance referred to desertion or agreed separation by means of migration—provided a solution of sorts for many more unhappy marriages than divorce." For Canada, which Urquhart includes but does not qualify, see D. Mendes da Costa, ed., *Studies in Canadian Family Law*, 2 vols. (Toronto: Butterworths, 1972), 362: "In Newfoundland and Quebec the courts did not, before the Divorce Act (1968), possess jurisdiction to grant a decree of divorce." "In Ireland, and in Canada in the provinces of Ontario, Quebec, and Manitoba, and in the Northwest Territories absolute divorce can be obtained only by means of a special act of Parliament, although in Ireland and Quebec judicial separations may be obtained through the courts." S. N. D. North, *Marriage and Divorce 1867–1906: Part 1 Summary, Laws, Foreign Statistics*, Department of Commerce and Labor Bureau of the Census (Washington, DC: Government Printing Office, 1909), 331.

vinculo matrimonii (a *decree absolute*). Although alleged desertion might prove a complication, emigration to a Crown Colony gave emigrants access to the Probate, Divorce and Admiralty Division of the King's Bench in London, provided they fulfilled certain conditions. While such a course of action might be complicated by allegations of bigamy and issues of domicile and comity of nations, English divorce law had devised classifications of adultery, one of which made provision for separation consequent on emigration. These classifications were "accidental adultery," where there was no reason to believe that the other spouse was still alive;[76] "unwilling adultery," where, for example, a husband forced his petitioner wife into prostitution; and "condoned adultery," where the respondent had fully forgiven the adultery.[77] If, having been charged with bigamy, either or both parties could prove "accidental adultery" to the satisfaction of the relevant court, they could then be granted leave legally to marry. Ginger S. Frost has pointed out, "According to the *Judicial Statistics of England and Wales*, bigamy trials occurred 5,327 times between 1857 and 1904, an average of 98 per year,"[78] while Gail Savage has found "that in divorce cases using bigamy as a grounds, only one in eight was prosecuted."[79] How many of these 5,327 were Irish who had gone to live in England or in the colonies has yet to be determined. A strategy that was sometimes employed was for the woman to "change her name by deed-poll to correspond with that of the man with whom she is residing, where one or both of them are

[76] Not to be confused with "accidental adultery" as discussed in the debates leading up to the 1857 Act. For a discussion of these debates relevant to *Ulysses*, see *Report of the Royal Commission on Divorce and Matrimonial Causes* (London: His Majesty's Stationery Office, 1912), §214.

[77] Cornish, "Marital Breakdown," 794. The cases cited are *Joseph v. Joseph and Wentzel* (sometimes Wenzel) (1865) 34 LJPM&A 96; *Coleman v. Coleman* (1866) 1 LR P&D 81; *Clarke v. Clarke* (1865) 34 LJPM&A 94; and *McCord v. McCord, Ogle and Coxton* (1875) 3 LR P&D 237.

[78] Ginger S. Frost, *Living in Sin: Cohabiting as Husband and Wife in Nineteenth-Century England* (Manchester: Manchester University Press, 2008), 72.

[79] Gail Savage, "Defining the Boundaries of Marital Sexuality: Bigamy, Incest and Sodomy in the Divorce Court, 1857–1907" (paper presented at the Mid-Atlantic Conference on British Studies Annual Meeting, New Brunswick, NJ, 22 March 2003), cited in Frost, *Living in Sin*, 72.

already married to someone else."[80] Needless to say such a relationship was regarded in law as bigamous.

4. Divorce: Scottish domicile. The Irish domiciled in Scotland could petition for a *decree nisi* and then a *divorce a vinculo matrimonii* from the Scottish jurisdiction in terms of The Marriage (Scotland) Act of 1856 and The Marriage Notice (Scotland) Act of 1878. (Court of Sessions cost could be as low as £12, but parties were required to attend at Edinburgh; the figure of £12 does not include any payment for maintenance that might be granted with the settlement.) Both parties were then able to remarry, although not necessarily in England prior to 1861.[81] Divorce after "Irregular marriages," or marriages that were not conducted by a minister in a church, was permitted under certain circumstances. Domicile for these marriages was defined by the 1856 Act as follows: "no irregular marriage contracted in Scotland by declaration, acknowledgement, or ceremony shall be valid unless one of the parties had at the date thereof his or her usual place of residence there, or had lived in Scotland for twenty-one days next preceding such marriage; any law, custom, or usage to the contrary notwithstanding."[82] In the case of *Watson orse Horsley v. Watson* (1902), the petitioner was able to obtain a *decree absolute* in the English court on the grounds that neither spouse "had her or his usual place of residence in Scotland" or had "lived in Scotland for 21 days preceding such [an irregular] marriage," and the "said Petitioner be pronounced to have been and to be free from all bond of marriage with the said Respondent."[83] As William Cornish in *The Oxford History of the Laws of England* points out,

[80] Shatter, *Family Law*, 151.

[81] "Formerly the law of England did not recognize the jurisdiction of the courts of Scotland when they annulled a marriage on the ground of adultery." Parl. Deb., H. C., 3rd ser., 14 May 1861, vol. 162, col. 2062: Mr. Whiteside. See also Dicey, Morris, and Collins, *Conflict of Laws*, 14th ed., 2:884–85, §18–045, §18–046.

[82] Latey, *Law and Practice*, 217, §2.408. Note that "'irregular marriages' included those in which the parties, before the Sheriff and in the presence of two witnesses, declared themselves married." Commonly known as Gretna Green marriages.

[83] *Watson (orse Horsley) v. Watson*, NA J77/754/2940, Filed: 14 June 1902; Set Down: 13 November 1902; Decree Nisi: 26 January 1903; Final Decree: 3 August 1903.

> The Reformation left Calvinistic Scotland with a provision for divorce by order of a court. Scots law did not belittle wives to the extent of empowering their husbands to divorce them as and when they chose. Nor did it give the pair the power simply to agree upon an end to the relationship. For the court to intervene, one party had to commit an essential breach of the tie—either adultery or desertion for four years. The grant of a divorce did terminate the marriage, freeing the wronged party to marry another, and the wrongdoer also to marry anyone save (so it seems) the adulterer cited in the proceedings. The divorce itself was *a vinculo matrimonii*—from the very bond. By the mid-nineteenth century, the Edinburgh Commissary Court was making some 20 divorce orders a year, nearly half of them in favour of women.[84]

The perceived intransigence of the Scots to any modification of their divorce laws proved to be a significant impediment to the Lords' and Commons' attempts to have the 1857 Act apply equally to England, Ireland, Scotland, and Wales.[85] In the event, the Act applied only to England and Wales. Scotland retained its own system, shaped as it was by Calvinism.

5. Civil dissolution: French domicile, as a provision *de la Loi du 29 juillet 1884* (Naquet Act). This provision was much discussed in French and English newspapers in the year in which *Ulysses* is set, as 1904 marked the centenary of the *Code Napoléon*.[86] Both petitioner and respondent had to be domiciled in France. Recourse to divorce in France (civil divorce was reintroduced in 1894)[87] was much more common than in England, and, as Gail Savage has shown, "prior to the First World War an estranged

[84] Cornish, "Marital Breakdown," 767; see also p. 801 n. 1, which refers to various legal obscurities about the details of Scots law on the subject.

[85] See, for example, Parl. Deb., H. C., 3rd ser., 14 May 1861, vol. 162, col. 2052: Sir Hugh Cairns: "When the House remembered . . . the tenacity with which the people of Scotland had adhered to their own system of law, the House would see that an endeavour to conduct the inquiry with the view of assimilating the marriage law of the three countries would raise a strong hostility in Scotland against any measure founded upon the inquiry, and thus obstruct the wholesome regulations he proposed to introduce with respect to Ireland."

[86] See Nicholas White, *French Divorce Fiction from the Revolution to the First World War* (London: Legenda, 2013).

[87] Brown, *Joyce and Sexuality*, 45.

couple would have simply found it far easier to obtain a divorce in France than in England."[88]

> French courts could grant a divorce upon the demonstration of one of three different types of offenses: adultery, sentencing to severe criminal punishment (*condamnation à une peine afflictive et infamante*), and cruelty or insult (*excès, sévices ou injures graves*).[89] According to statute, a court must grant a divorce upon the proof of one of the first two offenses. The latter category of marital offense, although subject to the discretionary judgement of the court, represented the most common grounds for a successful divorce suit. Of the 48,024 divorces pronounced between 1907 and 1910, the courts granted 21,337 on these grounds. In contrast, divorces involving adultery totaled 7,661 or only sixteen percent of all those granted in that four-year period.[90]

In 1905, while she was living at Colville-sur-Mer, Maud Gonne MacBride petitioned for a civil dissolution of her marriage.[91] To the

[88] "In 1901 . . . the French divorce rate (which stood at 23 per 100,000 population) exceeded the English rate by almost twelve times, even though the English divorce rate had doubled from 1891 to 1901 increasing from 1 divorce per 100,000 population to 2 divorces per 100,000": "French law also recognized several different grounds for divorce and allowed women to invoke the same grounds as men." Gail Savage, "Divorce and the Law in England and France Prior to the First World War," *Journal of Social History* 21, no. 3 (1988): 500, 502.

[89] Leon Barbie, *Guide Pratique du Divorce* (Paris: Librairie Générale de Droit et de Jurisprudence, 1927), 12, cited in Savage, "Divorce and the Law," 505.

[90] Savage, "Divorce and the Law," 505.

[91] See Herbert F. Goodrich, "Jurisdiction to Annul a Marriage," *Harvard Law Review* 32, no. 7 (1919): 818, http://www.jstor.org/stable/1327742, for a detailed discussion of *Ogden v. Ogden* [1908] where the English "Court of Appeals held that a decree of a French court annulling a marriage in England between a Frenchman and an Englishwoman was not entitled to recognition in England, and the woman's second marriage, entered into after the French decree, was rendered bigamous." See *Ogden v. Ogden née Philip*, NA J77/886/6900, Filed: 30 July 1906; Set Down: 28 August 1906; Decree Nisi: 10 December 1906; Stayed: 25 September 1906; Final Decree: 18 January 1908. *Ogden v. Ogden* [1908] P 46; [1904–7] All ER Rep 86; 77 LJP 34; 97 LT 827; 24 TLR 94, CA. See also *Ogden v. Ogden*, http://www.uniset.ca/other/cs5/1908P46.html.

disgust of the *Irish Independent*, because of her husband's intervention in the French hearings, she was only granted a divorce *a mensa et thoro* (a judicial separation from bed and board). John MacBride subsequently sued the *Independent* for libel, and though he was awarded derisory damages of £1, costs were awarded against him. He was sharply reprimanded by Maud Gonne's counsel: "This unhappy woman would have got a divorce from you in the French Court had it not been that your counsel raised the point that you were domiciled in Ireland."[92] That the case attracted considerable attention in Ireland and in the Irish diaspora can be seen from reports published in Australian and New Zealand newspapers as various as the *Kalgoorlie Miner* (Western Australia), the *Brisbane Courier* (Queensland), *Freeman's Journal* (New South Wales), the *Hobart Mercury* (Tasmania), the *Southern Cross* (South Australia), the *Geelong Advertiser* (Victoria), and the *Evening Post* (Wellington).[93]

6. Divorce: English domicile: Seeking a *decree nisi* and then a *divorce a vinculo matrimonii* from the Probate, Divorce and Admiralty Division in the English jurisdiction. Some court costs were as low as £30 to £35 in 1904, though this figure does not include maintenance. For parties domiciled outside London, costs might be greater; both parties were required to attend at London, though many cases were heard undefended. When the caseload increased during the latter part of the First World War, some provincial courts were granted the right to hear divorce cases. Costs might also be substantially increased should the case be challenged by the King's Proctor, who, on further examination, might rescind both *decree nisi* and the divorce *a vinculo matrimonii*. (For Bloom's familiarity with the

[92] *Irish Times*, 18 December 1906, 7.

[93] See "Irish Divorce Suit," *Kalgoorlie Miner*, 10 August 1906, 5; "Cable News in Brief," *Brisbane Courier*, 10 August 1906, 5; "Everyday Notes," *Freeman's Journal*, 18 August 1906, 16; "Divorce Suit," *Mercury*, 1 March 1905, 5; "Items of Interest," *Southern Cross*, 20 October 1905, 15; "Divorce Proceedings," *Geelong Advertiser*, 1 March 1905, 3; all of which can be accessed through http://trove.nla.gov.au; and "Various Cabled Items," *Evening Post*, 10 August 1906, http://paperspast.Natlib.govt.nz.

jurisdiction of the King's Proctor, see Chapter 6.)[94] Petitions were determined by An Act to Amend the Law Relating to Divorce and Matrimonial Causes in England (28 August 1857) and subsequent Acts.[95] English law essentially recognized only adultery as the determining grounds for divorce. Husbands were simply required to establish proof of the wife's adultery, although as we will see and as Bloom discovers, this was not quite so straightforward as it might seem. But wives in the English jurisdiction, between 1857 and 1923, were required to establish that an adulterous spouse had also committed an additional offense—incest, bigamy, cruelty, rape, sodomy, bestiality, or failure to comply with a decree for restitution of conjugal rights. These requirements were not as rigorously enforced during and following the First World War because of the increased demand for divorce. Nor do they appear to have been as much of a deterrent to women seeking divorce or a judicial separation as is sometimes thought. As Allen Horstman has noted, "For the half century after 1857 divorces outnumbered separations four to one, and wives sought separations ten times more than husbands."[96]

Jewish law for those domiciled in the United Kingdom contained significant variations to these provisions. In general, divorce was considered inimical for the Jewish wife, though, as the Chief Rabbi explained to the 1912 Royal Commission on Divorce, "If [her husband] became impoverished and unable, or if he were unwilling, to support her adequately, if he denied her conjugal rights, she could, by rules adopted at various times, claim the right to freedom

[94] Note however, Savage, "Divorce and the Law," 506: "Between 1886 and 1908 the number of interventions fluctuated between a low of 11 (in 1898) and a high of 35 (in 1903). The success rate of these interventions fell below 60 percent only once (in 1899), and in several years (1889, 1900, 1906, 1907) every single intervention resulted in the rescinding of the decree. The average success rate stood at 85.48 percent for those years. Those who wished to patronize the Divorce Court must have regarded such an action by the court as both an unwelcome and a real possibility." See also Latey, *Law and Practice*, "Interventions by the Queen's Proctor," 857–63, §4, 880–95.

[95] For an authoritative summary of the relationship between the 1857 Act and subsequent Acts, see William Rayden, *Rayden's Law and Practice in Divorce and Family Matters*, ed. Joseph Jackson, 14th ed. (London: Butterworths, 1983), 1: 7–8, §10.

[96] Allen Horstman, *Victorian Divorce* (London: Croom Helm, 1985), 101.

(*Kethboth* v. 8–9). Indeed, such treatment on his part was a breach of contract made in the 'marriage deed' in which he had contracted to do all these things."[97] However, she could not, for example, sue for divorce on the grounds of her husband's sexual relationship with an unmarried woman.[98] Bloom and Molly have been married as "Irish" Catholics, but it is possibly this aspect of Jewish law that lies behind Molly's midnight thought that Bloom will not attempt to get a divorce from her by having an affair with Josie Breen because "hed never have the courage with a married woman that's why he wants me and Boylan" (18.1253–54). She is correct, because a Jewish husband was required immediately "to put away his wife" on proof of her adultery, though, following an agreement struck between the Chief Rabbinate of England and The Registrar General in 1866, he could not request the *Beth-Din* for an annulment or a divorce until a *decree absolute* had been granted in the relevant English court.[99] If successful, petitioners were able to marry. The significance of these aspects of Jewish law for the Blooms and the relationship between Jewish custom and English law in 1904 will be examined in Chapter 6. It is worth emphasizing here that divorce reports such as "Divorced by a Rabbi: Strange Method of Getting Rid of a Wife," which appeared on page 3 of the *Daily Mail* on 28 January 1904, and "Solomon's Bad Example," on 30 April 1904 on page 3 in the same newspaper, meant that the public was to some extent kept informed about Jewish divorce procedure.

7. Divorce: Irish domicile: Seeking a *decree nisi* and then a divorce *a mensa et thoro* (from bed and board) in the Irish jurisdiction; as determined by the Matrimonial Causes and Marriage Law (Ireland) Amendment Acts of 1870 and 1871 and the Irish Judicature Act of 1877 as heard before the King's Bench Division of the Irish High Court. Neither party was able to remarry unless a *decree absolute* or an *annulment* was obtained from the

[97] Adler, quoted in *Minutes of Evidence*, 3:232, §38,407.

[98] Molly obviously does not have a high opinion of Josie's husband: "hed never have the courage with a married woman that's why he wants me and Boylan though as for her Denis as she calls him that forlornlooking spectacle you couldn't call him a husband" (*U*18.1253–56).

[99] Adler, quoted in *Minutes of Evidence*, 3:406, §41,384.

House of Lords;[100] costs, except for the wealthy, were generally considered to be prohibitive.[101] Before proceeding to the Lords, male petitioners were routinely instructed to institute a common law suit for *criminal conversation* against the male respondent since *criminal conversation* remained a tort in Ireland until 1976.[102] Again, costs were considered to be prohibitive. In essence, as I have already pointed out, the Irish jurisdiction retained and perpetuated the juridical stance of the pre-1857 Ecclesiastical Courts which "regarded themselves as administering the universal law of Christian marriage in which questions of conflict of laws could not arise."[103]

* * * *

Several critics acknowledge that divorce is a course of action available to Bloom that does not involve some form of confrontation or immediate

[100] "Lord Cranworth reminded the noble Lord (Lord Monteagle) that at present a person in Ireland seeking a divorce was compelled to prosecute for damages in the Irish Courts, and then to come to the Legislature at great expense to get the marriage annulled; whereas the principle Parliament had adopted was to get rid of this cumbrous and discreditable machinery; and the clause now proposed would enable him to come over and obtain a divorce in the Imperial Court." Parl. Deb., H. L., 28 July 1859, 3rd ser., vol. 155, col. 512.

[101] Cornish, "Marital Breakdown," 782.

[102] "In Ireland . . . divorce *a vinculo* of parties there domiciled is obtainable (as in England before 1857), by private Acts of Parliament, after a divorce *a mensa et thoro* has been granted by the King's Bench Division of the Irish High Court (which now exercises the powers of the older Ecclesiastical courts), and (if the suit be by the husband) after judgment has been obtained in an action in the Irish Courts for *crim. con.*, the minimum expense of such proceedings being between £450 and £500." Parl. Deb., H. L., 28 July 1859, vol. 155, col. 512; *Report of the Royal Commission on Divorce and Matrimonial Causes* (1912), 18. See also Cornish, "Marital Breakdown," 777–78, 782.

[103] Rayden, *Rayden's Law and Practice*, 14th ed., 1:35, §2. The most notorious example in *Ulysses* involves Surgeon McArdle, alleged to be "a damned good surgeon but a notorious womanizer. Made buckets of money but lost a lot in *crim con.* actions the husbands brought against him." John Garvin, *James Joyce's Disunited Kingdom and the Irish Dimension* (Dublin: Gill and Macmillan; New York: Barnes and Noble, 1976), 76.

intervention—and some, such as Barbara Leckie, Brandon Kershner, and Patrick Collier,[104] point to the ways divorce in one form or another plays on Bloom's mind throughout the day—yet all, without exception, dismiss this as a compensatory fantasy on the grounds that the only type of divorce available to people living in Ireland post-1857 and pre-1921 was a divorce *a mensa et thoro*, or what was commonly known as a judicial separation from bed and board. They further point out that in order for Bloom to be granted a divorce *a vinculo matrimonii*, a judicial release from the bonds of marriage, or what was known as a *decree absolute*, he would have to petition the House of Lords, an action, it is claimed, that was so costly only the wealthy could afford it.

These "facts" are then generally buttressed by citing statistical evidence,[105] and by aligning them with some reference to the expunging of divorce from the Irish social imaginary, dominated as it was by Roman Catholic faith and practice.[106] The official statistics published in comparative studies of rates of divorce—studies that were periodically undertaken as divorce rates soared between 1900 and 1921—affirm that there were very few officially registered divorces in Ireland. For example, in 1904, the US government commissioned the Department of Commerce and Labor Bureau of the Census to prepare a comprehensive report, *Marriage and Divorce 1867–1906*, about all the countries from which America was drawing migrants. The report noted that

> In Ireland separation and divorce are not frequently resorted to, as indicated by the fact that during the twenty years from 1887 to 1906 only 105 marriages were thus dissolved. Of this number, only 19 were dissolved by absolute divorce and the remainder, 86, by divorce *a mensa et thoro*, or separations granted by the courts.... The tendency towards an increase in the divorce rate in most other countries is not at work in Ireland. The highest number of divorces and separations granted in any one year was

[104] Barbara Leckie, "The Simple Case of Adultery," *James Joyce Quarterly* 40, no. 4 (2003): 729–52; R. Brandon Kershner, *The Culture of Joyce's "Ulysses"* (New York: Palgrave Macmillan, 2010), 79–127; Collier, *Modernism on Fleet Street*, 125–28.

[105] Collier, *Modernism on Fleet Street*, 125–28. The most common source for statistics appears to be Fitzpatrick, "Divorce and Separation."

[106] See Roderick Phillips, *Putting Asunder: A History of Divorce in Western Society* (Cambridge: Cambridge University Press, 1988), 578–81; and Noonan, *Power to Dissolve*.

> 11, reported in 1896 and again in 1898. The smallest number was 1, which was reported in the years 1875, 1882, 1883, and 1889.[107]

This view is also supported by a large number of respected legal authorities. To cite but one:

> It is impossible to obtain a decree of divorce from the bonds of matrimony in the courts of Ireland. The only divorce decree granted is from bed and board (*mensa et thoro*), and amounts in effect to what is termed a judicial separation in England.
>
> The grounds for the limited form of divorce granted by the courts are adultery, cruelty or unnatural practices.
>
> In order to obtain a decree of complete divorce the petitioner must promote a bill in the House of Lords to dissolve the marriage and allow the petitioner to marry again, which bill must be founded upon and follow a divorce from bed and board obtained in the Irish courts.[108]

Historians likewise agree. As David Fitzpatrick has argued,

> The Irish law of judicial separation petrified, while in England procedure with respect to separation as well as divorce was simplified and extended to lower courts ... In Ireland ... in 1853 the cost of an undefended action exceeded £300, while even under civil jurisdiction in 1910 it amounted to £100. Consequently the number of actions was small, being 57 between 1840 and 1843, 203 between 1901 and 1909, and 357 between 1970 and 1979. Few could afford to protect themselves through judicial separation, while those who did so could only hope for alimony if they were "innocent" wives, or for custody of children if they were husbands whether "guilty" or otherwise.... Only thirty-nine Irish divorces were so obtained between 1857 and 1910 (all by Protestants).[109]

Even the newspapers Joyce is known to have read when he was writing *Ulysses* occasionally carried items emphasizing the distinctiveness of the

[107] North, *Marriage and Divorce 1867–1906*, 481.

[108] Hyacinthe Ringrose, *Marriage and Divorce Laws of the World* (London: Musson-Draper, 1911), ch. 4, http://www.gutenberg.org/files/35760/35760-h/35760-h.htm.

[109] Fitzpatrick, "Divorce and Separation," 172–96.

Irish jurisdiction. On 26 July 1904, for example, the *Daily Mail*, under the headline "Dublin" and the sub-heading "Where Divorce is Rare," reported, "There is no congestion of business in the Dublin High Court according to the parliamentary return for 1903 just issued. During last year only two decrees of divorce were granted, and these were *a mensâ et toro* [*sic*], for it requires an Act of Parliament to dissolve a marriage in Ireland."[110]

Quod erat demonstrandum it seems; divorce, whether from bed and board or absolute, is not a practical option or even a potential option for Bloom or for Molly as far as the Joyce critic or the historian of Irish matrimonial causes is concerned.

However, it was possible for Irish people who had been living in Ireland between 1857 and 1921 to obtain *decrees absolute* in the Probate, Divorce and Admiralty Division of the King's Bench. As James Roberts, an Irish lawyer with considerable experience, pointed out in his authoritative *Divorce Bills in the Imperial Parliament* published in Dublin in 1906:

> In the case of *Le Mesurier v. Le Mesurier* it was held by the Privy Council that "according to International Law the domicile for the time being of the married pair affords the only true test of jurisdiction to dissolve the marriage" [[1895] AC 517, 540]. According to that decision persons domiciled in Ireland can resort only to Parliament for a dissolution of marriage.
>
> *But* in many cases persons who were at the time domiciled in Ireland have resorted to the English Court and there have *obtained decrees of absolute divorce, as distinguished from that of judicial separation* [emphasis mine]. The question arises as to whether, when a decree has been obtained without fraud or collusion in the English Court, such can or may be recognised in Ireland.[111]

As Roberts "enjoyed an extensive practice in the House of Lords in Divorce Bills," it is not surprising that, when his book was reviewed in the *Irish Times* on 16 March 1906, he was commended for making the "whole law clear and intelligible," for "propounding it in a clear and

[110] "Dublin," *Daily Mail*, 28 July 1904, 3.

[111] James Roberts, *Divorce Bills in the Imperial Parliament* (Dublin: John Falconer, 1906), 12, https://archive.org/stream/cu31924017814389/cu31924017814389_djvu.txt.

scholarly manner," and for "providing a useful addition to Legal literature" that contained "Abstracts of illustrative cases not elsewhere reported."[112]

Seven years later and in a markedly different context, the Church of Ireland archdeacon, Harry Vere White, also declared, the "common notion that Irish marriages are *absolutely indissoluble is mistaken*" (emphasis mine).[113] In White's case it is important to remember that any statement about divorce from a Protestant cleric in 1913, the year after 100,000 Ulster Protestants took the Solemn Oath and Covenant, needs to be read in terms of Protestant and English unease about the legality of *Ne temere* (1908); the *Report of the Royal Commission on Divorce and Matrimonial Causes*, published in 1912; and the conflicted loyalties bedeviling Irish and English politics at that time.[114] In his evidence to the 1912 Royal Commission, Mr. J. Willock, a lawyer with an extensive divorce practice, politely suggested that the relationship between an Irish accent and English domicile was not always clear. And in response to the Chairman's observation that "domicile" was not always tested in undefended cases, "unless you happen to hear the Irish accent or something of that sort," Willock replied, "Then it does not follow, because they come to England and live here."[115] The practice must have been common enough

[112] "Irish Divorce Procedure," *Irish Times*, 16 March 1906, 9. For information on James Roberts, see *Minutes of Evidence*, 3:463, §42,597. Roberts, who specialized in the application of English law to Irish cases, had been practicing at the Bar since 1887.

[113] Harry Vere White, "Divorce," *Irish Church Quarterly* 6, no. 33 (1913): 94. White was later Dean of Christ Church Cathedral, Dublin (1918–21), and Bishop of Limerick, Adfert and Aghadoe (1921–33). Quoted in Urquhart, "Ireland and the Act of 1857," 301.

[114] See Parl. Deb., H. L., 28 February 1911, 5th ser., vol. 7, col. 165–211 for a speech by the Earl of Donoughmore on the legal complications for divorce law raised by *ne temere*, http://hansard.millbanksystems.com/lords/1911/feb/28/marriage-law-the-ne-temere-decree—particularly the McCann case of 1907. See William Corkey, *The McCann Mixed Marriage Case: An Address by the Rev. Wm. Corkey, with an Authorised Translation of Ne Temere Decree and Translation of Bull of Excommunication* (Edinburgh: The Knox Club, 1912); Jesse Buck, "The Role of *Ne Temere* in the Decline of an Irish Custom Regarding the Religious Affiliation of the Children of Mixed Marriages," *Australasian Journal of Irish Studies* 11 (2011): 28–43.

[115] Mr. J. Willock, quoted in *Minutes of Evidence*, 1:198, §4747–48.

to prompt Justice Gorell Barnes, then President of the Divorce Court, to introduce Divorce Rule 220 on 8 July 1905 that "all divorce petitions filed in court would have to swear to English domicile. Claiming a false domicile would act as a bar to proceedings."[116] Rule 220 stated,

> By direction of the President the following matters as they stand at the time of the institution of the suit must be inserted in the body of the petition:—
>
> 1. The description of the husband.
> 2. The place of residence of each of the parties to the marriage.
> 3. The domicil of the parties of the marriage—but, unless the petitioner is asserting a domicil of the wife different from that of the husband, it will be sufficient if the domicil of the husband is stated.[117]

However, in May 1905, even before the rule was published and well before it came into effect, in the case of *Livingstone v. Livingstone* (1904), Mr. Justice Bargrave Deane sharply reminded counsel who was arguing English domicile on behalf of his Scots client,

> I have received the most specific instructions from the Lord Chancellor to grant no decree in a suit unless the English domicile of the parties is clearly established. In a case which came to this court some years ago it appeared after a decree had been granted that the parties had an Irish domicil and were not within the jurisdiction of this court. They have both married again, and there have been children, and now it has been found necessary to have a special English Act of Parliament passed to put things right.[118]

[116] Urquhart, "Irish Divorce and Domestic Violence," 831.

[117] *The Law Reports: Ten Years' Digest, 1901–10 of All the Cases Reported in the "Law Reports" and in the "Weekly Notes" from the Commencement of 1901 to the End of 1910 together with References to the More Important Statutes, Rules and Orders and Parliamentary Papers*, compiled by Myron White-Winton (London: The Council, 1911), cols. 950–51: §23 reporting *Weekly Notes*, 8 July 1905. Rule 220 became operative on 24 October 1905.

[118] "Probate, Divorce and Admiralty Division. (Before the Hon. Sir Henry Bargrave Deane.)," *Times* (London), 17 May 1905, 3. *Vide* "Malone's (Validation) Divorce Bill," *Times* (London), 11 May 1905. *Livingstone v. Livingstone*, NA J77/819/4884, Filed: 2 June 1904; Set Down: 5 December 1904; Judicial Separation: 1 June 1905.

The special Act, Malone's Validation Bill, established that "where there are doubts as to the operation in Ireland of a decree under the English Divorce Acts, for the dissolution of the marriage of a domiciled Irishman, the proper course is to apply for an Act of Parliament confirming the decree and removing doubts."[119] However, as late as mid-December 1910, James Roberts, in presenting his evidence to the 1912 Royal Commission on Divorce, assured Lord Gorell (formerly Justice Gorell Barnes), President of the Commission, that "since Le Mesurier's case, counsel have been more careful, but at the same time there may be cases, in which I have reason to believe that the same thing has been done (*viz.* taking a house in London and paying rates for 6 months); one quite recently."[120]

As *Irish Divorce / Joyce's "Ulysses"* will show, the Irish and English jurisdictions prior to 1904 and between 1904 and 1921 were not as hermetically sealed with respect to one another as many historians and Joyce scholars have assumed. The book will also show that the issue of Irish domicile and English law continued to prove a problem for English judges and politicians and a source of redress for Irish litigants, particularly during the First World War. It appears that for some time prior to 1904 and at least until 1921, it was possible for Irish people to obtain a *decree absolute* in England, despite opposing views held by the respective jurisdictions about the nature of marriage (whether it was sacramental, symbolic, or contractual); despite legal issues relating to the ways "comity of nations" might function within the United Kingdom and the Empire; and despite the way the petitioners' and respondents' domicile might be interpreted. That both Bloom and Molly think in terms of the English rather than the Irish jurisdiction chimes with recent research into early twentieth-century divorce, which demonstrates convincingly that perceived court procedure and case law that has become common knowledge (often via gossip) generally exert more influence on a decision to proceed with divorce than contemporary social attitudes, financial considerations, or whether or not a person's religion sanctions divorce.

Once Parliament began to debate the merits of a single legal process for divorce within the United Kingdom after passing An Act to Amend the

[119] HL (D) [1905] AC 315. See also Murphy-Grimshaw's (Validation) Bill, HL [1907] WN 134.

[120] Roberts, quoted in *Minutes of Evidence*, 3:465, §42,631.

Law Relating to Divorce and Matrimonial Causes in England in 1857, it was soon recognized that determining domicile might prove extremely problematic. At the committee stage of debating an 1859 Divorce Bill in the Lords that was intended to introduce a single system within the United Kingdom, the Earl of Donoughmore diplomatically outlined the difficulties:

> Although he was firmly persuaded of the general purity of marriage life in Ireland, he thought it was but fair that when persons there were unfortunately under the necessity of seeking for a dissolution of marriage they should have the power of doing so. He had been informed by one of the advocates in the existing Divorce Court that there were at this moment upon the files of that Court three petitions from Ireland. Those were cases in which parties had been married and domiciled in that country, and it was there likewise that the alleged adultery had taken place; but as the law stood it was exceedingly doubtful whether any relief could be afforded to them in the English Divorce Court. In order, however, to bring themselves within its powers they had come over to this country, taken houses, and paid rates, in order to obtain such a domicile as would enable them to take advantage of the English Divorce Court.

The Earl's closing remarks, that "the question was one of considerable difficulty, and he did not pretend to give an opinion with regard to it; but it was certainly one as to which considerable uncertainty existed,"[121] not only predate but are also strikingly similar to James Roberts's 1906 admission that, according to the law, prolonged Irish residency, which in the normal course of events would constitute Irish domicile, should preclude an English divorce—though there were a sufficient number of cases to demonstrate that it didn't. Roberts, however, does not cite any specific cases.

He could have cited *Simpson v. Simpson and Henshill* (1903), which was reported in the *Freeman's Journal* on 26 April 1904, the very newspaper for which Bloom canvasses. Married at the Registry Office in Islington on 9 July 1886, the Simpsons went to live in Giltown, County Kildare. Shortly afterwards, it was alleged, the wife began drinking, neglecting their children, and frequenting the military camp at the Curragh. In

[121] Parl. Deb., H. L., 28 July 1859, 3rd ser., vol. 155, col. 512–13: The Earl of Donoughmore.

January 1903—that is, seventeen years after they were married—the Simpsons moved from Giltown to Number 143 Great Britain Street, Dublin. As the marriage continued to encounter problems, Mr. Simpson, who was employed as a butler, moved to London and petitioned for a divorce. On 25 April 1904, he appeared before Sir Francis Jeune, President of the Divorce Division of the Probate, Divorce and Admiralty Division of the King's Bench in London, and, having had his undefended case corroborated by witnesses, he was granted a *decree nisi*.[122]

A second case contemporary with the Blooms' marital problems is *Roberts v. Roberts and Sanlon and Nixon* (1903). The Roberts were married on 6 July 1891 in the Church of Our Immaculate Lady of Refuge in Rathmines. Canon Fricker officiated; her parents, John and Mary Haverty, were witnesses. They then went to live at Station Hospital, Naas, Kildare, and subsequently at 62 Newport Street, Belfast. They had four children, two boys and two girls. On 6 August 1903 he filed a petition with the Probate, Divorce and Admiralty Division of the King's Bench alleging her adultery. Even though neither was required to provide further particulars, the Registrar signed an order on 22 September 1903 that "the proceedings in this Cause are correct and the pleadings in order." On 20 November 1903 she filed an affidavit alleging that he had treated her with "great unkindness and cruelty" and that he had committed adultery. Some of the paperwork was delayed because the respondent pleaded poverty, so on 12 January 1904 the Registrar granted leave for her to proceed *in formâ pauperis*. The case was eventually heard before Sir John Gorell Barnes on 11, 14, and 20 June 1904 at a sitting of the Divorce Division of the King's Bench. After hearing oral evidence from both petitioner and respondent and witnesses on their behalf and counsel on their behalf, neither co-respondent appearing to defend, the Judge dismissed the case and awarded the respondent costs, as it was evident both petitioner and respondent had

[122] "Butler's Divorce Suit," *Freeman's Journal*, 26 April 1904, 4. In the Court Minutes, *Simpson v. Simpson and Henshill*, NA J77/800/4349, Filed: 6 November 1903; Set Down: 31 December 1903; Decree Nisi: 25 April 1904; Final Decree: 31 October 1904. Edmund Albert Simpson (sometimes misspelt Edward) lists his address as 14 Knowle Road, Brixton, London, but he does not explicitly claim English domicile in his petition or supporting affidavit. No damages.

committed adultery.[123] Neither, in legal parlance, had come to court with "clean hands."[124] Again, the case was reported on 11 August 1904 in the newspaper for which Bloom solicits advertisements, the *Freeman's Journal.*[125]

A third case contemporary with the Blooms' marital difficulties is *Bailey v. Bailey* (1903). On 20 January 1897, Janet Christopher married Benjamin Bailey "at the Register Office in the City of Dublin." She was registered as living at the Royal Hospital, Kilmainham; he at the Richmond Barracks. She was pregnant, their first child, a boy, being born 25 June 1897, as she affirmed, "in wedlock." Shortly after, he deserted her and "on or about the 8th day of January 1899" went through "a form of marriage" with a woman in Battersea. Janet Bailey then moved to Dundee in Scotland, where she filed a petition and affidavit *in formâ pauperis*. At a hearing before Sir John Gorell Barnes on 23 November 1903, she was granted a *decree nisi* on the grounds of "adultery coupled with bigamy and desertion . . . for two years and upwards without reasonable excuse." The decree was made absolute on 23 November 1903.[126]

The case of *Smyth v. Smyth* (1903) provides a fourth example contemporary with the Blooms' marital situation. The Smyths were married on 2 July 1888 at the Roman Catholic Chapel of St. Agatha in the Registrar's District of No. 1 East, in the Union of North Dublin. He was an etcher by trade. After the marriage they "lived and cohabited" at "19 Richmond Cottages in the County of Dublin and at divers other places." They did not have any children. At some time in May or June of 1896, she committed adultery "with a man whose name is unknown," with the result that she gave birth to a male child "on the 8th day of March 1897 at the Rotunda Hospital Dublin Ireland." He filed his petition from 30 Great Percy Street, Percy Circus in the County of London, on 12 May 1903 and listed his trade as Etcher. Neither the petition nor the

[123] *Roberts v. Roberts and Sanlon and Nixon*, NA J77/794/4147, Filed: 10 August 1903; Set Down: 31 December 1903; Decree Nisi: 10 August 1904. Dismissed.

[124] Latey, *Law and Practice*, §2.345.

[125] "The Roberts Divorce Suit Judgment," *Freeman's Journal*, 11 August 1904, 2, 3.

[126] *Bailey v. Bailey*, NA J77/778/3688, Pauper Cause, Filed: 25 February 1903; Set Down: 20 March 1903; Decree Nisi: 11 May 1903; Final Decree: 23 November 1903.

affidavit makes any reference to domicile. The case was heard before the Honorable Sir Thomas Townsend Bucknill on 30 October 1903. It was not defended; the respondent was found guilty of adultery, and the petitioner was granted a *decree nisi*. Costs were not determined. A *decree absolute* was granted on 9 May 1904.[127]

The fifth example, *Todd v. Todd* (1904), was a petition by the wife for dissolution of her marriage. Though the Todds had married and lived "at divers places" in England, they had separated. She had gone to live in Dublin, so she gave "9 Leinster Place, Rathmines in the County of Dublin" as her address on the petition. The case was heard before Sir John Gorell Barnes on 30 January 1905. Because the court was satisfied that she was able to prove cruelty and adultery and because neither he nor his counsel contested the suit, she was granted a *decree nisi*. At that point the King's Proctor filed plea, with the result that the *decree nisi* was rescinded and the petitioner condemned to costs on the grounds that she had been working as a prostitute in Dublin from 1896 to 1904. Though she did not defend the case, she did request her Dublin solicitors to advise the King's Proctor that "there was absolutely no foundation for the general charge" and that her solicitors themselves had found "the general allegations... most unexpected."[128] What is pertinent to my argument is that while her husband's English domicile legally entitled her to approach the court, it was still a course of action that both she and her Dublin solicitors believed she could and should take. What is also pertinent is the amount of detailed information that the King's Proctor was able to include in his plea. Small wonder that Bloom mentions the intervention of the King's Proctor to Stephen when he is talking about divorce in the cabman's shelter prior to bringing him back to 7 Eccles Street for a cup of Epps cocoa (16.1490–91).

Irish recourse to the Probate, Divorce and Admiralty Division of the King's Bench continued until the year Joyce finished writing the final episodes, 1921, as evidenced by the cases of *Sharpe v. Sharpe and Penny* and *Laverton v. Laverton*.[129] Two further cases, *Fraser v. Fraser* (1921)

[127] *Smyth v. Smyth*, NA J77/785/3881, Filed: 12 May 1903; Set Down: 25 June 1903; Decree Nisi: 30 October 1903; Final Decree: 9 May 1904.

[128] *Todd v. Todd*, NA J77/826/5131, Filed: 20 September 1904; Set Down: 27 October 1904; Decree Nisi: 30 January 1905; Petition dismissed.

[129] "Army Officer's Divorce Suit," *Irish Times*, 21 December 1921, 7; "Laverton Divorce Suit," *Irish Times*, 24 June 1921, 3. *Decree nisi* with costs.

and *Irvine v. Irvine* (1920), merit comment.[130] In the former, reported on 25 April 1921 in the *Irish Times*, where both petitioner and respondent gave Merrion Street, Dublin, as their address, the petitioner was granted a *decree nisi* in 1921 from a marriage with the respondent at the Registry Office in Dublin in 1908 on the basis of the respondent's misconduct in Dublin with "a man unknown." In the latter, Elizabeth Irvine, who resided at 139 University Street, Belfast, was able to obtain a *decree absolute*, on the grounds of adultery and cruelty, from her husband, Samuel Irvine, who, at the time of the hearing, resided at 1 Vernon Place, Leyland, in the County of Lancaster.[131] Her petition could be heard by the English divorce court because he claimed English domicile.

To summarize: from 1858 (vide *Durdin v. Durdin*),[132] the year after An Act to Amend the Law Relating to Divorce and Matrimonial Causes in England was passed, until at least 1921 (vide *Irvine v. Irvine*), Irish people who had been living and working in Ireland were able to use and were using the English court to petition for divorce, either because their purported domicile was not challenged in court or because they claimed and were able to affirm English domicile. This did not mean that some or all of these people were fraudulently claiming English domicile in order to "game" the system. What it does mean is that successfully affirming English domicile brought petitioner and respondent within the jurisdiction of the Probate, Divorce and Admiralty Division of the King's Bench, which in 1904 sat only in London.

[130] "Irish Divorce Suit," *Irish Times*, 25 April 1921, 2. *Decree nisi*. "Irish Divorce Suit," *Irish Times*, 12 May 1921, 3. *Decree nisi* with costs.

[131] *Irvine v. Irvine*, NA J77/1728/3792, Filed: 16 November 1920; Set Down: 14 December 1920; Decree Nisi: 11 May 1921; Final Decree: 5 December 1921.

[132] *Durdin v. Durdin* (1858), NA J77/13/D4. This is most likely one of the cases referred to by the Earl of Donoughmore in the House of Lords committee referred to above. James Roberts, in his *Minutes of Evidence*, 3:465, §42,631, cites *Deck v. Deck* as a case where a wife claiming English domicile to secure a divorce *a vinculo* was successful. For *Deck v. Deck* (1859), see NA J77/13/D3. For other cases where the English rule (*vide* Dicey) that in divorce the domicile of the wife must follow the domicile of the husband has not been applied, see H. F. G., "The Domicile of a Wife," *Michigan Law Review* 20, no. 1 (1921): 86–90, http://www.jstor.org/stable/1277099.

Despite the vigilance of the King's Proctor, restorative Acts of Parliament (vide Malone), cases in which domicile was specifically raised (*Le Mesurier v. Le Mesurier*), and warnings from the Bench, some Irish, as my analysis of the newspapers and court records shows, still managed to secure English divorces. None of these divorces, it needs to be pointed out, appear in the official statistics for Irish divorce. None of them are discussed in terms of their implications for pre-1921 Irish divorce in the standard English law texts, such as Latey's *The Law and Practice in Divorce and Matrimonial Causes* (fifteenth ed.), *Rayden's Law and Practice in Divorce and Family Matters* (fourteenth ed.), and Dicey, Morris, and Collins's *Conflict of Laws* (thirteenth, fourteenth, and fifteenth eds.). Furthermore, they did not cease—as evidenced by the case of *Gaffney v. Gaffney* (1973)[133]—with De Valera's insistence that the 1937 Irish Constitution contain a clause that "no law shall be enacted providing for the grant of a dissolution of marriage" and a clause precluding the recognition of foreign divorces.[134] Both of these clauses were enacted at the insistence and with the blessing of Archbishop John Charles McQuaid. Nor were those "Irish" divorces obtained in England between 1857 and 1921 subjected to legal scrutiny in Ireland itself until several key cases were considered in a dissenting opinion following legal argument in *Mayo-Perrot v. Mayo-Perrot* (1958).[135] Judge T. C. Kingsmill

[133] Shatter, *Family Law*, 153. See also *Family Law*, ed. Geoffrey Shannon, 4th ed. (Oxford: Oxford University Press, 2011), 172, 178.

[134] *Bunreacht na hÉireann*, 41.3.2; 41.3.3. "De Valera also refused to accept the advice of Catholic writers who pointed out to him that the clause on marriage (article 41, section 3, subsection 30) denied Catholics rights which the Church permitted—that is remarriage in Ireland, following a lawfully granted civil dissolution abroad, after a civil marriage to a non-Catholic." Tim Pat Coogan, *De Valera: Long Fellow, Long Shadow* (London: Hutchinson, 1993), 497.

[135] *Mayo-Perrot v. Mayo-Perrot* [1958] IR 336; 93 ITLR 77. "The plaintiff had obtained a divorce *a vinculo* in England, where she and her husband were domiciled. Having been awarded the cost of the petition by the English court, she sought to recover the sum remaining unpaid in the Irish courts, her former husband having come to reside within the jurisdiction of the Irish courts." "Held by Murnaghan J., and affirmed by the Supreme Court (Maguire C. J., Lavery, Kingsmill Moore, O'Daly and Maguire J J.) that the order for costs is not severable from the substantive order for divorce, and cannot be enforced by action in Ireland as creating a separate and independent cause of action *in personam*."

Moore, the author of the dissenting opinion, "concluded that prior to 1921 Irish courts would have recognized a divorce decree granted by a foreign court within the jurisdiction of the common domicile of the parties."[136]

Given this depth of silence, historians and Joyceans, without exception, appear to have come to accept as "fact" a circular argument that goes something like this: Ireland resisted divorce reform (demonstrable "fact"); statistics show few divorces in Ireland (demonstrable); therefore, QED, the Irish did not divorce. What this book will show is that, like the Irish recourse to abortion post-1967,[137] an unknown number of Irish who wished to divorce, within the time-frame of *Ulysses*—that is, 1904 to 1921—sought redress in the English jurisdiction.

The assertion that petitioning the House of Lords for a *decree absolute* would prove prohibitively expensive, perhaps involving a cost of £500,[138] is also somewhat mistaken. It assumes that the suit will be contested; and it is not derived from an analysis of the fees and costs of relevant case

Regarding Article 41.3 of *Bunreacht na hÉireann*, Kingsmill Moore observed, "The words do not declare that such a person cannot *anywhere* contract 'a marriage valid within our jurisdiction,' but merely prohibit the contracting *within our jurisdiction* of a valid marriage. It is the contracting of the second marriage within the jurisdiction which is prohibited. There is nothing to make it invalid if contracted elsewhere." *Mayo-Perrot v. Mayo-Perrot* [1958] IR 336; 93 ITLR 77.

[136] Quoted in Shatter, *Family Law*, 153.

[137] Louise Ryan, "'A decent girl well worth helping': Women, Migration and Unwanted Pregnancy," in *Ireland beyond Boundaries: Mapping Irish Studies in the Twenty-First Century*, ed. Liam Harte and Yvonne Whelan (London: Pluto Press, 2007), 135–53. As Ryan points out on pp. 138–39, "In the wider context, however, 'going to England' was and is a time-honoured Irish 'solution' to an Irish problem, one that saw 6,625 Irish women travel to Britain for an abortion in 2001 alone. This number has risen steadily over the last 20 years—in fact, the figures have doubled since 1980—so that abortion rates per 1,000 women aged 15–44 are now 7.5. In all, at least 98,565 Irish women have travelled to British abortion clinics during the 21 year period."

[138] "Thus the petitioner domiciled in Ireland, alone in the British Isles, was still obliged to submit a private bill to parliament. The usual cost of an undefended petition, together with necessary preliminary actions in the Irish courts such as those for judicial separation and for 'criminal conversation' on the part of a wife's lover, exceeded £500 in 1910." Fitzpatrick, "Divorce and Separation," 173–74.

histories. The figure of £500, sometimes cited by historians and Joyceans, apparently originates in a sarcastic comment made by Justice Maule during a famous bigamy trial, *Regina v. Hall*, on 1 April 1845, at the Warwick Assizes, when he advised the petitioner on the intricate procedures he should have followed in order to rid himself of his first wife. His Honour opined that in order to obtain a *decree absolute* from the House of Lords, the petitioner "might perhaps object . . . that he had not the money to pay the expenses, which would amount to about £500 or £600—perhaps he had not so many pence—but this did not exempt him from paying the penalty of committing a felony."[139] In his evidence to the Royal Commission in 1910, James Roberts endorsed the figure of £500, though his admission that it was almost impossible to obtain a comprehensive disclosure of fees and costs renders the figure uncertain.[140] As Cornish has pointed out, the "notion of huge expenditure which confined parliamentary divorce only to the extremely well-off was often exaggerated by reformers, since it related to the comparatively few instances where there was real opposition and expensive counsel were involved."[141] As the *Digest of Cases Decided by the Superior and Other Courts in Ireland* (1919–1928) notes, "In a proper case the House of Lords will allow a petitioner in a divorce bill to prosecute his bill *in formâ pauperis.*"[142] The copy of *Every Man's Own Lawyer* that Joyce had in his library provides a clear explanation of the procedure involved:

> [B]efore either husband or wife will be allowed to proceed *in formâ pauperis*, he or she must lay a case before a Barrister, and obtain his opinion that there is reasonable ground for the proceeding. The case must contain a full and true statement of the facts upon which the applicant seeks the assistance

[139] "*Regina v. Hall, Times* (London), 3 April 1845," repr. in Louis Blom Cooper, ed., *The Law as Literature: An Anthology of Great Literature in and about the Law* (London: Bodley Head, 1961), 285–87; and a letter to the editor from J. E. Latton Pickering, Librarian, Inner Temple Library, EC. 4 published in *The Spectator*, 12 June 1920, 16, alerting readers to the similarities between Maule's remarks and the conversation in *Hard Times* (1854) between Mr. Bounderby and Stephen Blackpool about the cost of divorce.

[140] Roberts, quoted in *Minutes of Evidence*, 3:463, §42,597*ff.*

[141] Cornish, "Marital Breakdown," 782.

[142] White's Divorce Bill (no. 1), HL [1920] 2 IR 343.

> of the Divorce Court, and an affidavit verifying the facts as true. If, in the Barrister's opinion, the applicant has reasonable grounds for proceeding, the case, with opinion thereon and affidavit, should be sent or delivered to the Registrar of the Probate Division of the High Court, at the Royal Courts of Justice, London: it must be also accompanied by an affidavit of the party applying—if by the husband, as to his income and means of living, and that he is not worth £25, beyond wearing apparel, after payment of just debts;—if by the wife, as to her husband's means, and that she has no separate property worth £25.[143]

In examining both costs and accessibility, Gail Savage, Diane Urquhart, Kelly Hager, and others have recently shown that obtaining a *decree absolute* in the English jurisdiction was more common, cost much less, and was achieved by a somewhat broader social range than has been popularly thought.[144] So when, for example, Patrick Collier claims that "practically it would be quite difficult for Bloom to divorce—divorce was legally available under English law, but it was costly enough to be largely a prerogative of the wealthy,"[145] he is reiterating what has become a view among Joyceans: yet such a view is no longer tenable because of recent research in family history, studies of representative case histories, analyses of Parliamentary debates on the subject, and further research into English and Irish divorce law undertaken for this book. Not only, as demonstrated by *Roberts v. Roberts and Sanlon and Nixon* (1904), could provision be made for one of the parties to appear *in formâ pauperis*, but court costs could be as low as £15-14-3 in uncontested cases such as *Pettigrew v. Pettigrew* (1904) or as high as £631-14-2 in contested cases such as *Carstairs v. Carstairs and Francis* (1903). As Joyce's source of legal knowledge, *Every Man's Own Lawyer*, makes clear,

[143] *Every Man's Own Lawyer*, 49. Note that, according to the Bankers Books Evidence Act, 1879, Bloom would be required to disclose his finances in full.

[144] Gail Savage, "They Would if They Could: Class, Gender, and Popular Representation of English Divorce Litigation, 1858–1908," *Journal of Family History* 36, no. 2 (2011): 173–90; Urquhart, "Ireland and the Act of 1857," 301–20; Kelly Hager, "Chipping away at Coverture: The Matrimonial Causes Act of 1857," BRANCH: Britain, Representation and Nineteenth Century History, accessed 6 July 2016, http://www.branchcollective.org/?ps_articles=kelly-hager-chipping-away-at-coverture-the-matrimonial-causes-act-of-1857.

[145] Collier, *Modernism on Fleet Street*, 132.

> As the wife is generally supposed to have no separate income, she is entitled to have her costs taxed from day to day as against her husband, and whether she is petitioner or respondent. When the costs have been taxed, a summons may be taken out, returnable before the Judge Ordinary, who may then order the husband to pay them, and also to pay a further sum to the Court, to give security to meet the wife's costs of the hearing.
>
> If in a matrimonial suit the wife be unable to go to trial in consequence of the non-payment of her costs by the husband, she should either apply at the Judge's Chambers to have the case stand over, or appear in Court on the day of the hearing and state her inability to proceed (*Curtis v. Curtis* 38 LJP&M 9).
>
> Although a wife is in general a privileged suitor with regard to costs, where she has separate property she is liable, like any other unsuccessful suitor, to be condemned in costs (*Milne v. Milne* 40 LJP&M 13).
>
> Upon the principle that the whole property is supposed in law to belong to the husband, he is generally obliged to pay the expenses of litigation on both sides: except in cases where the wife is found guilty of adultery with a Co-respondent; in which case the Court generally orders the Co-respondent to pay the costs of both sides.[146]

In English law, it was possible for Bloom and Molly to divorce one another without necessarily incurring legal costs themselves: Boylan is the one who would be required to pay should judgement go against him.[147] What is more, given the provisions of The Married Women's Property Acts of 1882, 1884, 1893, 1907, and 1908, Molly, as a divorcee—as a *feme sole*—was legally "entitled to retain for her separate use all her property, whether real or personal."[148]

[146] *Every Man's Own Lawyer*, 380–81.

[147] "The exercise of the discretion as to costs vested in the court by Matrimonial Causes Act 1857 (c. 85) section 34 . . . depended upon the conduct of all the parties in each case." *Codrington v. Codrington and Anderson* (1865) 4 Sw&Tr 63; LJPM&A 60; 11 Jur NS 287; 13 WR 527; 164 ER 1439. For wealthy co-respondents, however, see, for example, "Wife's Cash Value: Rich Co-Respondents Must Pay," *Daily Mail*, 11 February 1920, 7.

[148] Sheena Grattan, "Of Pin Money and Paraphernalia, The Widow's Shilling and a Free Ride to Mass," in *One Hundred and Fifty Years of Irish Law*, ed. Norma Dawson, Desmond Greer, and Peter Ingram (Belfast: SLS Legal Publications; Dublin: Round Hall Sweet and Maxwell, 1996), 228. See Cornish, "Marital Breakdown," 761–66.

* * * *

While I will be focusing on Bloom and English and Irish divorce law, it is worth observing that according to Jewish law a wife's adultery not only automatically entitled the husband to a divorce but also empowered him to control her future prospects by whether or not he withheld her "*get*."[149] The understandings of "Jew," "Jewish," and "Jewishness" I am employing here derive in the main from Neil Davison's *James Joyce, "Ulysses", and the Construction of Jewish Identity* (1996) and John McCourt's *The Years of Bloom: James Joyce in Trieste, 1904–1920* (2000), particularly Davison's argument that "Bloom's 'Jewishness' can be measured by his desire to (re) attach himself to an identity that empowers him as an adjusted male, a character who can get on with living."[150] I am also indebted to Marilyn Reizbaum's argument that Bloom is "culturally Jewish even if he remains (mostly) unobservant religiously,"[151] though I have tempered this insight with the observations about the secularization of Jews made by the Chief Rabbi in his submission to *The Royal Commission on Divorce* (1909–1912).[152] The Dubliners in *Ulysses* certainly think of Bloom as a Jew, for the two provisions for divorce most relevant to his Jewish heritage, "*get*" and "*decree nisi*," are both uttered in his presence in the "Cyclops" episode (12.1199; 12.1159). Molly is also somewhat puzzled by Bloom's occasional spontaneous reversion to Jewish custom, such as kissing the doorpost of 7 Eccles Street when they first take possession of the house (18.1406), or sleeping naked on the floor, "the way the jews used when somebody dies"

149 "—Their syphilisation, you mean, says the citizen. To hell with them! The curse of a goodfornothing God light sideways on the bloody thicklugged sons of whores' gets!" (*U*12.1190–1201). See Dicey, Morris, and Collins, *Conflict of Laws*, 14th ed., 2:878, §18–030.

150 Neil Davison, *James Joyce, "Ulysses", and the Construction of Jewish Identity* (Cambridge: Cambridge University Press, 1996), 9–10.

151 Marilyn Reizbaum, *James Joyce's Judaic Other* (Stanford, CA: Stanford University Press, 1999), 3–5. See also Cormac Ó Gráda, *Jewish Ireland in the Age of Joyce: A Socioeconomic History* (Princeton, NJ: Princeton University Press, 2006).

152 In 1910, the Chief Rabbi of England, Rev. Dr. Hermann Adler, tendered a comprehensive explanation of this term, as recorded in *Minutes of Evidence*, 3:407, §41,369.

(18.1246–47), when she initially refuses one of his sexual demands. While Bloom's friendships with the small Jewish community in Dublin appear to belong more to his past than his present and while the extent to which he thinks and instinctively acts as a Jew remains uncertain, he nevertheless retains warm memories of his courtship of Molly when they were socializing with their Jewish friends. These friends' expectation would be that adultery necessitates divorce. Evidence from a number of leading authorities on Jewish attitudes to adultery presented to the 1912 Royal Commission makes it clear that condonation was regarded with intense disfavor, while the idea that "a man should be compelled to retain an adulterous woman as a wife" was unquestionably deemed to be "the height of immorality."[153] As the Chief Rabbi of England affirmed in his evidence, "The husband was required to put away his wife when she committed adultery, this offence not being viewed merely as an injury inflicted on the husband, which might be condoned, but as a crime which saps the foundation of marriage, and makes its continuance impossible."[154] Nevertheless, as *Hyman v. Hyman and Goldman* (1903) shows, this was not always the case. When the King's Proctor revealed that the petitioner had "resumed cohabitation" and that the petitioner and respondent "are still living together . . . as man and wife," the *decree nisi* was rescinded.[155] The significance of condonation for understanding the ways Molly and Bloom react to or plan to react to one another is discussed further in Chapters 2 and 7. What the evidence from the Royal Commission also makes clear is that for a Jewish divorce to be deemed legal, even though it should be initiated prior to civil proceedings, it must follow civil proceedings, as with *Friedberg v. Friedberg*.[156] But even as late as 1910, some foreign Rabbis and Rabbis in England were still granting divorces and condoning

[153] *Minutes of Evidence*, 3:234, §38,422–23.

[154] *Minutes of Evidence*, 3:406, §41,369.

[155] *Hyman v. Hyman and Goldman*, NA J77/796/4211, Filed: 12 September 1903; Set Down: 29 October 1903; Petition Dismissed: 18 July 1904. Hyman had originally claimed damages of £1,500.

[156] *Friedberg v. Friedberg*, NA J77/930/8227, Filed: 9 January 1908; Set Down: 8 April 1908; Decree Nisi: 12 October 1908; Final Decree: 3 May 1909. According to the Court Minutes, the Friedbergs lived for a period of their married life at 25 Greenville Terrace, South Circular, Dublin. See Cormac O'Grada, "Settling In: Dublin's Jewish Immigrants a Century Ago," *Field Day* 1 (2005): 87–99.

remarriage (*Levi v. Levi and Abrahams*),[157] regardless of whether a divorce *a vinculo matrimonii* had been obtained from the English Court.[158] In *Levi v. Levi and Abrahams*, the respondent's re-marriage was declared null and void.

* * * *

It is also worth noting that Molly's thoughts about going on the stage in "Penelope" arguably relate to more than financial independence, a desire for celebrity, and greater personal freedom. As Gail Savage explains, "cases involving the theatrical profession suggest that a wife able to support herself enjoyed greater latitude of action if she wished to shed herself of an unsatisfactory husband."[159] The peripatetic nature of the profession gave such women an advantage because it meant that "domicile" was easier to establish and "geographical distance did not represent any significant impediment to litigation."[160] From 1857, as Cornish points out, "a considerable number of petitioners were wives. They would gain between 38 and 46 per cent of divorces granted in the years to 1914."[161] Molly's passing fancy that she might marry Boylan and perhaps have a child by him implies that thinking of herself as "my being jewess" she might have considered herself already

[157] *Levi v. Levi*, NA J77/953/8926, Filed: 11 September 1908; Set Down: 7 October 1908; Decree Nisi: 7 December 1908; King's Proctor: 29 December 1909; Rescinded: 17 February 1910. The King's Proctor successfully showed "that at all material times the Petitioner was well aware that the alleged dissolution of his marriage with the Respondent was invalid and ineffectual according to the law of England." Costs: £95-1-0.

[158] *Minutes of Evidence*, 3:235, §38,438–39; 3:407, §41,384; and 3:412–15, §41,467–§41,507. There were no fees for obtaining a divorce in the Jewish court, though some foreign Rabbis living in England and Scotland did charge a fee.

[159] Savage, "They Would if They Could," 179–80. Savage's and the present writer's research contradicts Mark Osteen, *The Economy of "Ulysses": Making Both Ends Meet* (Syracuse, NY: Syracuse University Press, 1995), 429: "A real Molly Bloom would not have been allowed to get a separation or retain custody of Milly even if divorce had been possible"; nor would she have "had the right to the money she earned by singing . . . nor could she have invested money or held property in her own name" (Shloss, "Molly's Resistance to the Union," 537).

[160] Savage, "They Would if They Could," 181.

[161] Cornish, "Marital Breakdown," 787.

divorced or that she might have been thinking in terms of the English rather than the Irish jurisdiction (18.1184). For the Irish jurisdiction, controlled as it was by Catholic faith and practice, the theological distinction between a divorce *a mensa et thoro* and a divorce *a vinculo matrimonii* was that the latter, despite the dissolution of the marriage, preserved a commitment to the sacramental rather than the contractual nature of marriage. That this distinction was deeply embedded in the Irish social imaginary is evident in the "Scylla and Charybdis" episode. When Buck Mulligan betters Stephen's account of Shakespeare and the "second-best bed," he immediately interjects, "*Separatio a mensa et a thalamo*" (9.716), since this was, essentially, the only form of divorce available to Shakespeare. In Elizabethan England marital issues were determined by the Ecclesiastical Courts, and marriage was still, for the most part, deemed a sacrament. The sly implication of Mulligan's quip is that Imperial England's bard, despite his literary eminence, was subject to a judicial system that defended marriage as defined by the apostolic Roman Catholic Church.

In summary, what *Irish Divorce / Joyce's "Ulysses"* proposes is that the bricolage that characterizes the *Ulysses* text uncannily echoes much of what is recorded as having taken place in 1904 and subsequently in the sole English court where pleas for a *decree absolute* were heard—the Probate, Divorce and Admiralty Division which sat only in London—and what was reported in considerable detail in the English newspapers in 1904 and which filtered through to Dublin via newspapers ranging from the *Irish Times* to *Tit-bits* and the *Police Gazette*.[162] Here, it is worth noting that even the newspaper for which Bloom canvasses, the pro-Catholic *Freeman's Journal*, despite its shrill endorsement of Catholic teaching, "often reprinted divorce bills from the English press."[163] That Bloom and Molly think of divorce in terms of the

[162] "*Titbits from All the Most Interesting Books, Periodicals and Newspapers in the World*, a sixteen page penny weekly (published on Thursdays, dated Saturday)." Don Gifford with Robert J. Seidman, *"Ulysses" Annotated: Notes for James Joyce's "Ulysses"* (1974; Berkeley: University of California Press, 1988), 80. For information on Joyce's knowledge of *Tit-bits* and the authenticity of "Matcham's Masterstroke," see John Simpson, "Philip Beaufoy and the Philosopher's Tone," James Joyce Online Notes, accessed 23 July 2016, http://www.jjon.org/jioyce-s-people/beaufoy; and Pierce, *Joyce and Company*, 39–43.

[163] Urquhart, "Ireland and the Act of 1857," 301–20.

English rather than the Irish jurisdiction raises significant issues for reading *Ulysses*, issues that will be examined in the course of this book.

* * * *

Though various legal terms and relevant case law will be explained in the following chapters, there are some definitions that need to be established. In English law marriage is defined, following the 1857 Divorce and Matrimonial Causes Act and according to the ruling delivered by Lord Penzance in *Hyde v. Hyde* (1864), as "the voluntary union for life of one man and one woman to the exclusion of all others."[164] Assumed in the Irish jurisdiction and vigorously defended by its ecclesiastical and legal institutions, this foundational definition was complicated shortly after the introduction of the English Divorce and Matrimonial Causes Act by the anomalies, confusions, and disagreements between the English, Irish, and Scottish jurisdictions brought so sensationally to public attention by *Thelwall v. Yelverton* (1861–1865)[165]—anomalies, confusions, and disagreements that I will discuss as they become relevant to the argument.

The definition of marriage recited in *The Book of Common Prayer* (Protestant) and the definition of marriage as stated by the twenty-fourth Session of The Council of Trent (Catholic) are not as relevant in English law post-1857 as the definition established by *Hyde v. Hyde*, which "is understood to involve four conditions: a marriage must be voluntary; the parties must intend it to be for life; it must be monogamous; and it must be between parties of a different sex."[166] Bloom has been baptized as a Protestant and married as a Catholic;[167] and while attending a burial mass, he recalls a phrase from *The*

[164] *Hyde v. Hyde and Woodmansee* (1864), NA J77/28/H212; [1866] 1 LR P&D 130.

[165] See Rebecca Gill, "The Imperial Anxieties of a Nineteenth-Century Bigamy Case," *History Workshop Journal* 57 (2004): 58–78.

[166] Shatter, *Family Law*, 38, citing [1861–73] LR 1 P&D 130; (1866) LR 1 P&D 130 at 133; and *Nachimson v. Nachimson* [1930] P 217.

[167] Note Shatter, *Family Law*, 54: "A marriage of Roman Catholic parties celebrated by a Roman Catholic Priest with no witnesses present is a valid civil marriage *per verba de preaesenti* but is not valid in the eyes of the Church, such ceremony not being in compliance with the decree of the Council of Trent." The case cited is *Usher v. Usher* [1912] 2 IR 445. William Rayden, *Rayden's Law and*

Book of Common Prayer (6.986); but religion is not the determining factor in his thinking. There is, at least in Molly's mind, some doubt that Bloom believes in the existence of the soul. He is shown dismissing the spiritual efficacy of the confessional and whimsically associating trans-substantiation with cannibalism. Consequently, his reactions to what he strongly suspects is Molly's impending affair are largely emotional, quasi-philosophical, and strategic. So when the idea of divorce occurs to him, it is his view of what constitutes marriage that predisposes him to the English rather than the Irish jurisdiction. To understand the essential difference between the two, it is important to remember that, over time, the general effect of the 1857 Act was to shift the public perception of marriage from a metaphysical union symbolizing the relationship between Christ and his Church (Protestant) or a sacrament (Catholic) to a form of civil contract. As stated in the nineteenth edition of *Every Man's Own Lawyer*,

> Marriage is considered in law as a contract, and with but few exceptions the ordinary principles which in law attach to contracts in general apply to the marriage contract.
>
> But "while habitually speaking of marriage as a contract, English lawyers have never been misled by an imperfect analogy into regarding it as a mere contract, or into investing it with all the qualities and conditions of ordinary civil contracts. Thus the parties who contract a marriage cannot at their will dissolve it."[168]

Practice in Divorce and Family Matters in All Courts, 13th ed. (London: Butterworths, 1979), 544: "By virtue of the provisions of the Evidence Act, 1851 (a), sections 10 and 14, certificates of marriages in Ireland are receivable in evidence in the English Courts to the same extent and for the same purpose as they are receivable in any Court of Justice in Ireland."

[168] *Every Man's Own Lawyer*, 356, citing Sir F. Jeune, in *Moss v. Moss otherwise Archer* [1897] P 263. Note: Immanuel Kant, *The Philosophy of Law: An Exposition of the Fundamental Principles of Jurisprudence as the Science of Right*, trans. W. Hastie (Edinburgh: T. & T. Clarke, 1887), 101: "In every Contract there are *four Juridical Acts* of Will involved; *two* of them being *preparatory Acts*, and *two* of them *constitutive Acts*. The two Preparatory Acts, as forms of treating in the Transaction, are Offer (*oblatio*) and Approval (*approbatio*); the two Constitutive Acts, as the forms of *concluding* the transaction, are Promise (*promissum*) and Acceptance (*acceptatio*)."

Nevertheless, given the emphasis on marriage's civil and contractual nature rather than its metaphysical or sacramental nature, the preservation of Bloom's relationship with Molly becomes dramatically imbricated with self-preservation even as he begins to think about divorce. 7 Eccles Street ceases to be a "home" and becomes either an "asset" or a "known address" where the "petitioner" is "domiciled"; in the same way, Molly ceases to be his "wife" and becomes "the respondent," provisionally with the same "domicile."

Hence the emphasis in this book is on Spinoza's proposition VI from "On the Origin and Nature of the Emotions": "Everything, insofar as it is in itself, endeavours to persist in its own being."[169] As many marriage guidance counselors and divorce lawyers will attest, discovering evidence that indicates infidelity generally shocks the innocent party into immediately focusing on how they can protect and secure themselves.[170] Bloom, who possesses a handsome copy of *Thoughts from Spinoza* (17.1372), is no different, as shown by his reaction to the sight of Boylan's torn betting tickets discarded on the apron of the kitchen dresser when he eventually returns to 7 Eccles Street (17.319–21; 18.424). Despite experiencing "perturbations," Bloom immediately opts for avoidance and denial as he attempts to "persist in his own being." He promptly reminisces about the "coincidences" associated with obtaining something by chance and then discarding it (17.323). Though these "reminiscences" lead him to recall his encounter with Bantam Lyons (5.323–41; 8.1023), he avoids, whether from timidity, caution, or self-doubt, associating either Bantam Lyons or the tickets with Boylan. And the avoidance behavior continues. "What qualifying considerations," the arranger then asks, "allayed his perturbations" (17.342). The first part of the answer to this question offers a critique of jumping to conclusions, of arguing *post hoc, ergo propter hoc*, and of formulating hypotheses about or drawing conclusions from data that might or might not be representative, relevant, or statistically meaningful: "The difficulties of interpretation since the significance of any event followed the occurrence as *variably* as the acoustic report followed the electrical discharge and of counterestimating against an actual loss by failure to interpret the total sum of possible losses

[169] Benedictus de Spinoza, *Ethica Ordine Geometrico Demonstrata*, trans. R. H. M. Elwes, Part III, On the Origin and Nature of the Emotions, Proposition VI, http://www.gutenberg.org/cache/epub/3800/pg3800.txt.

[170] Shelley Day Sclater, *Divorce: A Psychosocial Study* (Aldershot: Ashgate, 1999), 133–52.

proceeding originally from a successful interpretation" (17.343–47; emphasis mine). Bloom, we are then told, takes comfort in the belief that "He had not risked, he did not expect, he had not been disappointed, he was satisfied" (17.349–50). Whether or not as readers we would want to accuse him of excessive prudence, self-deception, indifference, docility, or timidity—but it is very late, he is tired, and he has a guest—what marks his reaction as characteristic of an injured party is his preoccupation with self-preservation, with the persistence of his own being. "What satisfies" Bloom and stills his perturbations, the arranger proposes, is that he tells himself that he has "sustained no positive loss" (17.351–52). Whether or not this is true, of course, is another matter.

Thus, central to my reading of *Ulysses* is an image of the "textual Bloom" as the "wily and cunning Odysseus," as a strategist. The word "strategist" is used in Bourdieu's sense of someone attuned to "*le sens du jeu*";[171] and "textual Bloom" in the sense that "Bloom" signifies a site where authorial intention, aesthetic demands, generic expectations, competing discourses, and the author's insights into human behavior, institutions, and history coalesce. "*Jeu*" is interpreted as the marriage game with its divorce subplot. This is not to argue that Bloom, as a "realist character" or as a "possible person," is a strategist, however much his reactions, feelings, and emotions speak to our own experience or achieve a verisimilitude, despite the radical and complex ways in which they are presented. As James Phelan and Peter J. Rabinowitz have persuasively argued, characters can be both "synthetic" and "mimetic"; that is, they "do resemble possible people, they are artificial constructs that perform various functions in the progression [of the storyworld], and they can function to convey the political, philosophical or ethical issues being taken up by the narrative."[172] As the political and ethical issues being considered in this book involve the relationships between sex, love, adultery, and divorce, I would argue that the noun "Bloom" serves as a repository for Joyce's research into and knowledge of the marriage game with its divorce subplot. Joyce acquired this knowledge

[171] Pierre Lamaison and Pierre Bourdieu, "From Rules to Strategies: An Interview with Pierre Bourdieu," *Cultural Anthropology* 1, no. 1 (1986): 110–20.

[172] James Phelan and Peter J. Rabinowitz, "Character," in *Narrative Theory: Core Concepts and Critical Debates*, ed. David Herman, James Phelan, Peter J. Rabinowitz, Brian Richardson, and Robin Warhol (Columbus: Ohio State University Press, 2012), 111.

progressively, even if somewhat randomly, by reading the English and Irish press between the time of his interest in the divorce case of *Harris v. Harris* reported in the *Irish Times*, 17 November 1906,[173] and the eventual publication of *Ulysses* in 1922 with its echoes of *Fraser v. Fraser*, 25 April 1921. It is now possible to search this corpus electronically because most of the major and many of the minor newspapers and journals that Joyce read have been digitized.

Not that discussion about divorce was confined to the newspapers at the time Joyce was writing *Ulysses*. As Barbara Leckie has pointed out, "between 1857 and 1914 adultery was, in fact, everywhere in English print culture: it was discussed in parliamentary debates; it was a front-page 'Divorce Court' story in most of the daily newspapers for at least twice a week for over fifty years; it was a topic of heated discussion in literary and cultural interest reviews; it was represented in popular novels, and it was the central feature of novels that were eventually canonized as great."[174]

This book, however, focuses on those newspapers Joyce is known to have read on a regular basis when his circumstances permitted: the *Daily Mail*, the *Irish Times*, the *Times* (London), and the *Freeman's Journal*. Arthur Power recalled one room of the Joyces' Paris flat being "full of books and old newspapers."[175] Writing to Harriet Shaw Weaver in 1923, Joyce himself mentions "three sacks of newspapers" that would have to be stored when they vacated the flat for the summer.[176] The *Daily Mail* and the *Times* have been included because both regularly reported on divorce court proceedings and because Ireland accounted for approximately one-third of the *Times*'s pre–First World War distribution.[177] Irish newspapers were also a rich source of information. A search of the digital database of the *Irish Times*, for

[173] James Joyce to Stanislaus Joyce, 13 November 1906, in *Letters of James Joyce*, ed. Richard Ellmann (London: Faber, 1966), 2:189, 194.

[174] Barbara Leckie, *Culture and Adultery: The Novel, the Newspaper and the Law 1857–1914* (Philadelphia: University of Pennsylvania Press, 1999), 1.

[175] Arthur Power, *Conversations with James Joyce* (London: Millington, 1974), 42.

[176] James Joyce to Harriet Shaw Weaver, 10 June 1923, in *Letters of James Joyce*, ed. Richard Ellmann (London: Faber, 1966), 3:76.

[177] Brown, *Joyce and Sexuality*, 5. Apparently Nora was also a *Daily Mail* reader. See John McCourt, *The Years of Bloom: Joyce in Trieste, 1904–1920* (Dublin: Lilliput, 2000), 18–19.

example, reveals that there were some 6,445 references to divorce between 1904 and 1921—that is an average rate of one a day for the entire period.

To propose that Joyce's major source of legal information on divorce was a book published in 1919 and that he selectively drew from newspaper accounts of divorce hearings published between 1904 and 1921 is not to argue that his use of legal information is anachronistic, that it violates the contemporaneity of the book, but it is to accept, as several critics have pointed out, that *Ulysses* is informed by a number of time-schemes and that, as Cheryl Herr has shrewdly observed, "the newspaper is put forth as a key cultural institution and primary shaper of consciousness in modern Dublin."[178] Indeed, as Declan Kiberd has convincingly shown, *Ulysses* could be read as a newspaper, though, not surprisingly, given the silence on Irish divorce, he omits one of the most common features of the late nineteenth- and early twentieth-century broadsheet: the divorce report.[179] While the overwhelming majority of "events" recorded in *Ulysses* are events that occurred on 16 June 1904, a number of critics have conclusively demonstrated that whatever Joyce came across in the newspapers from that year and during the time he was writing the book became grist for the mill. As Richard Ellmann claims, one of the many generative events for *Ulysses* was *Harris v. Harris*, heard in Dublin between 5 and 17 November 1906.[180] Nor was Joyce shy when it came to drawing on his own journalism. His recycling parts of his own article on foot-and-mouth disease, published in the *Freeman's Journal* on 10 September 1912, for Mr. Deasy's letter in the "Nestor" episode contravenes the chronology of *Ulysses* on two counts: because a

[178] Cheryl Herr, *Joyce's Anatomy of Culture* (Urbana: University of Illinois Press, 1986), 3. Herr goes on to explain on p. 4, "I have used the term 'institution' to mean any collective creator of discourse that tends to repeat its messages and to shape social behavior through that repetition."

[179] Declan Kiberd, "*Ulysses*, Newspapers and Modernism," in *Irish Classics* (London: Granta Books, 2000), 463–81.

[180] "Harris Matrimonial Suit," *Weekly Irish Times*, 17 November 1906, 20, http://search.proquest.com/docview/850750793/fulltextPDF/103BFD3AA7FB4ADFPQ/1?accountid=14700; Richard Ellmann, *James Joyce* (1959; New York: Oxford University Press, 1982), 230 n., 161–62: "Joyce was punched after speaking to a woman not realizing she was 'accompanied.' A man called Hunter, rumored to be Jewish and to have an unfaithful wife, came to his aid." Recent scholarship has cast considerable doubt on this story.

newspaper item from 1912 is used to inform a letter supposedly written in 1904, and because foot-and-mouth disease was not a significant problem in Ireland in 1904. When it comes to borrowing or parodying language, it is register, tone, lexis, and syntax that appear to be the determining factors, not chronology. As R. Brandon Kershner has pointed out,

> Once we read *Ulysses* with an awareness of the conventions of the periodical publishing industry of the time, we are aware of a double chronological focus (which to some extent characterises every historical novel): some of the most bizarre details regarding newspapers are often startlingly accurate, even while others, which on the surface seem reasonable historical details of 1904, in fact point to the 1920s. It is in part this slippage in *Ulysses* that gives us the impression of an Edwardian life-world being dragged rapidly, if reluctantly, into full-scale modernity.[181]

Nowhere is this doubling more evident than with divorce court reporting. While Joyce did draw from a number of divorce cases that were reported in the press in 1904, it would seem that much of his knowledge about the emotional and psychological effects of infidelity and much of his information about the intricacies of divorce that inform *Ulysses* were gleaned from divorce cases published in the years just preceding and just succeeding the First World War. By then divorce rates had soared, and the newspaper reporting of divorce had become almost formulaic.

Finally, what Joyce acquired fortuitously or as a consequence of careful research needs to be distinguished from what we as readers can be persuaded to accept that Bloom, or for that matter Molly, knew or might reasonably know in Dublin in 1904. In the episodes leading up to and including "Eumaeus," as I will show, Bloom reveals that he has a rough working knowledge of English divorce law: but it is the way he deals with his suspicions and the way he collects and assesses evidence in "Ithaca" that reveal his implicit understanding of English divorce court procedure. Not that verisimilitude is the defining test; and not that anything about divorce that appears in *Ulysses* is to be dismissed as anachronistic if it could not be known by the Blooms in 1904, even though Joyce might have come across it in the newspapers that he was reading sometime between 1906 and 1921. To subject *Ulysses* to these tests is to ignore the valuable work of Adams, Shloss, Brown, Herr, Kershner, Wicke, Leonard, Kiberd,

[181] Kershner, *Culture of Joyce's "Ulysses"*, 96.

Mullin, Leckie, Reppke, Backus, and many others, who have all convincingly demonstrated that Joyce was fascinated by journalism, particularly divorce court journalism, and that divorce, as commodified by popular culture, plays on Bloom's mind throughout 16 June 1904. And yet all of them have either ignored or dismissed Bloom's "Divorce, not now" and Molly's "suppose I divorced him" to become "Mrs Boylan" as temporary thoughts or passing fantasies (17.2202; 18.846), as a course of action not available to people domiciled in Ireland between 1904 and 1921.

While owing a considerable debt of gratitude to this work and to that of other critics, as well as social, cultural, and legal historians, a debt that will be progressively acknowledged in the course of the book, *Irish Divorce / Joyce's "Ulysses"* refutes what has become a truism about divorce in modern Ireland. It invites readers to see *Ulysses* in terms of "communicative realism"; to approach its ironies, allusions, ambiguous generic and historical contexts, and its multiperspectivity with the knowledge that obtaining a divorce *a vinculo matrimonii* (a *decree absolute*) was a possible course of action for Dubliners in 1904.[182] It also invites readers to consider that Bloom's moral dilemma is more challenging and more complex than has so far been realized and that his and Molly's sex lives and love for one another could change in a variety of unpredictable ways, though not inevitably nor necessarily for the worse.[183] Both Bloom and Molly seem to know this and to have begun on 16 and 17 June 1904 to explore its complex consequences, particularly in terms of the respective narratives they have constructed for themselves and about one another. For readers to recall that Molly suspects "slyboots," as she characterizes her husband, is "up to something" should sharpen our attention to detail. For readers to know that for the Blooms a *decree absolute* is possible should encourage a careful re-reading of a great work of literature that repeatedly challenges us to understand it as we come to understand ourselves.

[182] Hartner, "Multiperspectivity." See n. 25 above.

[183] Sclater, *Divorce*, 2: "In psychological terms, divorce is about coming to terms with 'loss', but our findings show that it is about much else besides. It is also a positive process of the reconstruction of identity, and the pursuit of identity as a new and valued goal."

CHAPTER 2

"Not now"—Breakfast at No. 7

The family who eats together stays together.

—Proverbial

As one of the drafts of *Ulysses* reveals, Joyce contemplated using gossip about the way breakfast was taken at 7 Eccles Street to give credence to rumors that Molly was so frustrated sexually that she and Bloom had considered divorce some time before 16 June 1904. The Buffalo manuscript contains the following:

> —I know some talk one time that they were going to be divorced, says Hynes.
> —Restitution of conjugal rights, says Mac Hugh:
> What, Jack?
> —Still, they say he's always dancing attendance on her. Brings up her breakfast in the bed every morning and has his own bit down in the kitchen.
> —*Separatio a mensa et a thoro*, says J. J. & lt;
> —Ay, says Ned, that's right. & gt; Separation from bed and breakfast, says young Dedalus.
> —Breakfast in bed! says Ned, its something else she wants in the bed. What you call a rough and tumble.
> Call it specific performance, says J. J.[1]

[1] Luca Crispi, *Joyce's Creative Process and the Construction of Characters in "Ulysses": Becoming the Blooms* (Oxford: Oxford University Press, 2015), 238 n. 79: Buffalo MS 6, f. [4r]. See also Groden, "'Cyclops' in Progress, 1919," and James Joyce, *Joyce's Notes and Early Drafts for "Ulysses": Selections from the Buffalo Collection*, ed. Phillip F. Herring (Charlottesville: University Press of Virginia, 1977), 181–82.

P. Kuch, *Irish Divorce / Joyce's Ulysses*,
DOI 10.1057/978-1-137-57186-1_2

This passage is from a draft of the "Cyclops" episode in which Bloom's masculinity, sexuality, and nationality are subjected to ribald attack. What Joyce retained of this draft will be discussed shortly and again in the conclusion to this book. But the notion of "restitution of conjugal rights," the legal term "*separatio a mensa et thoro*," and the term "specific performance" all invite analysis, as does the gossip that Bloom dances "attendance on her." "J. J." is Joyce's shorthand for the lawyer J. J. O'Molloy. His advice to Molly, were he to be appointed her counsel—for the draft implies that she is the one who would initiate proceedings—is brutally simple. The way to achieve "restitution of conjugal rights" is not to seek help from the Church and not to petition the English court, but to commence proceedings in the Irish Court of Equity for "specific performance." "Specific performance" is the legal term for

> an extraordinary equitable remedy that compels a party to execute a contract according to the precise terms agreed upon or to execute it substantially so that, under the circumstances, justice will be done between the parties.... Specific performance grants the plaintiff what [was] actually bargained for in the contract rather than damages (pecuniary compensation for loss or injury incurred through the unlawful conduct of another) for not receiving it; thus specific performance is an equitable rather than legal remedy. By compelling the parties to perform exactly what they had agreed to perform, more complete and perfect justice is achieved than by awarding damages for a breach of contract.... An important advantage to this remedy is that, since it is an order of an equity court, it is supported by the enforcement power of that court. If the defendant refuses to obey that order, [they] can be cited for criminal contempt and even imprisoned.[2]

Molly, as readers come to learn, prefers enticement, seduction, and harnessing the envy-politics of rivalry to commencing legal proceedings, as complex as a court action for "specific performance" might prove (it would seem J. J. O'Molloy is referring to *Hart v. Hart* (1881));[3] it is

[2] "Specific Performance," The Free Dictionary, accessed 23 July 2016, http://legal-dictionary.thefreedictionary.com/Specific+Performance. Note that *Every Man's Own Lawyer, Dictionary*, 31, defines specific performance as "The remedy sought by a plaintiff who, instead of damages for a breach of contract, seeks the enforcement of the terms of the contract."

[3] *Hart v. Hart* (1881) 18 ChD 670; 50 LJ Ch 697; 45 LT 13; 30 WR 8.

Bloom who, much later in the day, imagines himself in court charged with failing to meet the conjugal obligations of his marital contract. As we will see in Chapter 5, Bloom fantasizes about J. J. O'Molloy acting on his behalf when he is cross-examined in *Driscoll v. Bloom* in "Circe" about his marriage, his sexual fantasies, and about allegations of sexual misconduct brought by Mary Driscoll, a servant who had once been employed by the Blooms when they lived in Ontario Terrace (15.859–1005).

For the present, however, I wish to concentrate on the significance of this passage from the Buffalo manuscript for reading "Calypso," "Lotus Eaters," and "Hades." What it suggests is that Joyce chose to retain the scenario of the separate breakfasts for Bloom and Molly, his protagonists for his "novel of adultery," as a way of suggesting that they were already divorced Irish style: that Bloom's eating downstairs and Molly's taking breakfast upstairs and their sleeping head to toe implies that prior to 16 June 1904 an actual if ambiguous separation from bed and board has already taken place.

But, to draw the reader into the epic journey of the day, it was a state of affairs that needed to be implied to maintain suspense. In introducing his protagonists, Joyce needed to find ways to suggest that the tensions in the Blooms' marriage, which had led them to consider divorce, still lingered; that Molly was still sexually frustrated; and that, in anticipation of the ways the story-world of *Ulysses* would develop, divorce in Ireland in 1904, despite all its legal complications, social stigma, and ecclesiastical condemnation, was still possible. To have minor characters display a sufficient knowledge of legal terminology to joke about divorce in the episode that introduces the Blooms, or in an episode which interpreted that introduction, would have robbed *Ulysses* of its dramatic tension. To have the nature of that divorce defined—whether *separatio a mensa et thoro* or *a vincula matrimonii*—would have limited the exploration of the emotional complexities of the relationship and denied readers the pleasure of engaging in their own probabilistic inductive reasoning.[4]

[4] Rosa Maria Bollettieri Bosinelli, "The Reader as Detective: Sherlockholmesing Joyce's Texts," in *The Benstock Library as a Mirror of Joyce*, ed. Rosa Maria Bollettieri Bosinelli and Franca Ruggieri, Joyce Studies in Italy 7 (Roma: Bulzoni Editore, 2002), 167–75.

Separate breakfasts also provided a way of enacting an implied divorce free from the need to explain its legal status and free from representing the passive-aggressive combativeness of the infamous Irish "silent marriage."

Bloom has often been read as a caring husband, an atypical Irish male, thoughtfully, perhaps even punctiliously, preparing his wife's breakfast even though theirs is a troubled marriage.[5] But the "Cyclops" draft prompts other readings. This chapter will argue that Bloom is more strategic and more self-protective than is generally thought; that the breakfast is more conventional, more class-conscious, and more gendered than has hitherto been recognized; and that his post-midnight consideration—"divorce, not now"—is prefigured by his several denial-driven decisions during the day not to return to 7 Eccles Street to confront Molly with his suspicions.

* * * *

While some readers have regarded Bloom's dietary preferences as somewhat perverse, his partiality for the "inner organs of beasts and fowls," his fondness for "thick giblet soup, nutty gizzards, a stuffed roast heart, liverslices fried with crustcrumbs, [and] fried hencods' roes" (4.1–3), and his passing consideration of "ham and eggs" is utterly conventional according to the English diet favored by the *petite bourgeoisie* of Edwardian Dublin.[6] As the detailed instructions for their preparation in Mrs. Beeton's *Every-Day Cookery* make clear, they all belong to the

[5] Declan Kiberd, *"Ulysses" and Us: The Art of Everyday Living* (London: Faber, 2009), 83–84, argues that Bloom enjoys being a "housewife," but it is Mrs. Fleming who will come to No. 7 at eleven o'clock to tidy, dust, and clean. Osteen, *Economy*, 72–73: "In bringing Molly breakfast in bed, he is practicing the art of husbanding his wife." But see Glasheen, "Calypso," 51: "Mrs Bloom seems mistress of the house and Bloom stands at the bedside like a detached, respectable upper-servant, calm to the very bowels."

[6] Ariela Freedman, "'Don't eat a beef steak': Joyce and the Pythagoreans," *Texas Studies in Literature and Language* 51, no. 4 (2009): 447–62; Marguerite M. Regan, "'Weggebobbles and Fruit': Bloom's Vegetarian Impulses," *Texas Studies in Literature and Language* 51, no. 4 (2009): 463–75.

conventional Edwardian breakfast.[7] Bloom even follows the conventional method for frying a pork kidney for his own breakfast.[8]

Although it seems he is taking great care preparing a tray for his wife, who is still upstairs in bed, his mind is actually focused on what he himself enjoys—or rather on what it seems he has already digested, at least mentally. The main item for his own breakfast, the anticipated kidney, is said to be already "in" his mind before he has purchased it, assured that grilled mutton kidneys always "gave" to his "palate a fine tang of faintly scented urine" (4.4–5). Well before he has boiled the kettle for his own and his wife's cup of tea, he is shown achieving a form of self-gratification even as he attends to her needs. Although he has taken great care to arrange her tray in exactly the way she likes, he then apparently abandons the bread and butter to the mercy of the cat when he leaves the kitchen to go to the butcher's for the kidney he wants for himself. At least that is what seems to be the case. Though we see him talk to the cat and the cat apparently respond, we are not shown Bloom covering the tray, though we are informed that he glances round and says to himself, "Nothing she can eat? . . . No" (4.48). Even a reader who is very familiar with *Ulysses* might be tempted to accept this assurance at face value, recalling that whether or not the bread and butter is covered is what Kenner has notably called a Joycean "narrative skip" and Hart a "narrative gap."[9] But alert readers would doubtless call into question Bloom's assurance that there is "nothing she can eat" once they realize how little he knows about cats and how much cats like butter. Wondering whether or not trimming cats'

[7] Isabella Beeton, *Mrs Beeton's Everyday Cookery: With about 2,500 Practical Recipes* (London: Ward, Lock, 1923). Instructions for preparing "thick giblet soup" (129); "stuffed roast heart" (78–79, 280, 295; stuffing, 164); "liver slices fried with crustcrumbs" (240, 247); "fried hencods' roes" (180, 524); "ham and eggs" (543–44). For another recipe for "ham and eggs," see Mrs. Isabella Beeton, *The Book of Household Management* (London: Ward, Lock, 1861), §813, http://www.gutenberg.org/cache/epub/10136/pg10136.txt.

[8] Bloom's breakfast is clearly non-Kosher: it is a pork kidney, and it has not had the blood drained from it. For cooking kidneys, see Beeton, *Household Management*, §724.

[9] Hugh Kenner, *"Ulysses"* (1980; Baltimore: Johns Hopkins University Press, 1987), 48; Clive Hart, "Gaps and Cracks in *Ulysses*," *James Joyce Quarterly* 30, no. 3 (1993): 435.

whiskers prevents them from catching mice because their whiskers will no longer shine in the dark or that mice never squeal when attacked are not speculations designed to engender confidence in Bloom's knowledge of cats.

The tray that he prepares for Molly is conventionally appropriate for her image of herself. Food historians have noted that around 1900 the custom was "Early morning. 8 a.m. For the fortunate, a tray with tea and bread and butter brought to them, while still in bed, by a maid."[10] The fortunate, that is, those who could afford servants, also tended to be comparatively late risers. To languish in bed of a morning was considered to be truly *du bon ton*.[11] Molly, as many critics have observed, is a woman with middle-class pretensions, pretensions that are sufficiently well-known locally for Nosey Flynn, a habitual gossip, to remark later in the day to the barman in Davy Byrne's, "She's well nourished I tell you. Plovers on toast" (8.952). Both the contents of her tray—four slices of bread and butter—and how it is arranged speak eloquently to this. She will eventually rise around eleven o'clock, when Mrs. Fleming, the charlady, comes in to clean (6.237). That Bloom, instead of being the attentive husband, is playing the role of maid-of-all-work, the "slavey," to Molly's middle-class pretensions and "dancing attendance on her" is a further indication of the power politics of their marriage.

Molly has not trusted her husband with servants since 1898, when they lived in Ontario Terrace, where they had a heated row about his regard for Mary Driscoll, whom Molly promptly dismissed. As we will see in Chapter 5, Bloom is haunted by memories of his relationship with the former servant, who accuses him in the hallucinatory, phantasmagoric court world of "Circe" of propositioning her, assaulting her, and interfering with her clothing (15.885–88). Elsewhere in *Ulysses*, in a passage

[10] "Food Timeline," accessed 27 February 2015, http://www.foodtimeline.org/foodfaq7.html, and "About Irish Bread," accessed 23 July 2016, http://www.nationalbreadweek.ie/irish-bread/about-irish-bread/. I am indebted to Emeritus Professor Helen Leach and Mary Browne for this information. The irony of Bloom's breakfast order, however, is that Mrs. Beeton's recipe, if that is what he has in mind, is a recipe for two.

[11] Henry Handel Richardson, *The Fortunes of Richard Mahony: The Way Home*, ed. Clive Probyn and Bruce Steele (Melbourne: Australian Scholarly Publishing, 2007), 98.

modeled on early eighteenth-century social and political satire, Bloom is accused of attempting "illicit intercourse with a female domestic drawn from the lowest strata of society! Nay, had the hussy's scouring brush not been her tutelary angel, it had gone with her as hard as with Hagar, the Egyptian!" (14.922–25). Whether or not Molly's suspicions of her husband's sexual misbehavior are justified—Bloom after all admits to giving Mary Driscoll some "smart emerald garters" (15.876–77)—her prompt dismissal of the servant after only four months in the position is understandable given that contemporary court records show there were "a large number of cases" in Dublin "involving the sexual exploitation and abuse of servants" by the men of a household, and given that such cases were frequently reported in the newspapers.[12] In the case of *Harrison v. Harrison*, for example, which was heard in February 1904, the court reporter observed, "It seems that Mr Harrison had been guilty of misconduct with the maidservant [Minnie], and when he refused her an increase in wages she told his wife. Hence a *decree nisi* with costs for the petitioner."[13]

As the class, sexual, and gender politics of being served bread and butter and tea in bed begin to unfold, the reader might well come to suspect that 7 Eccles Street, the neighborhood, and for that matter Dublin itself, for all its material certainty and ritualized sociability, could prove to be a space where the conventional can unexpectedly turn on itself. The preparation of Molly's tray offers a case in point. Bloom is first shown "righting her breakfast things on the humpy tray." "Righting" is the "action of correcting something," "of making reparation," of returning something to "the proper, upright, or vertical position."[14] "Breakfast things" implies crockery and cutlery, not "breakfast" as the name for a morning meal. "Humpy tray" and the fact that Molly's cup does not have a handle suggest both tray and cup are well worn and perhaps shabby, even if they are much loved. "Righting" things—in this case ensuring nothing spills or falls—is characteristic of Bloom's desire for order, for having

[12] Diarmaid Ferriter, *Occasions of Sin: Sex and Society in Modern Ireland* (London: Profile Books, 2009), 81. Ferriter also points out that "in 1911, for example, there were 125,783 indoor servants [in Dublin], of whom 47 percent were under the age of 25, and 92 percent were unmarried."

[13] "Maidservant's Disclosure," *Daily Mail*, 13 February 1904, 3.

[14] *Oxford English Dictionary*, 3rd online ed., s.v. "righting."

things turn out right.[15] As Joyce once remarked to Frank Budgen, character reveals itself "not in the doing or not doing of grand action but in the peculiar and personal manner of performing a simple one."[16] Bloom then says to himself, "Another slice of bread and butter: three, four: right. She didn't like her plate full. Right." Repeating the word "right"—"as that which is considered correct, proper, or incumbent on someone to do"[17]—suggests Bloom is anxious to avoid disapproval. By limiting the amount of bread and butter, he will not have to field Molly's comment that her plate is too full, although four slices is generous. As we later learn, she is concerned about her weight.

But the repetition of "right" might also be read as expressing satisfaction with a special task correctly performed; that is, with Bloom mentally granting himself approval; or it might simply indicate the completion of a task in the sense of "now that's done." "Right" can also be seen as an uncertain temporal marker. Is "right" associated in his mind with checking items off a list, and if it is, how familiar is he with that list and where do the items come from? Does its repetition indicate that Bloom has brought Molly a tray with bread and butter and tea once before, on various occasions, frequently, or infrequently? Since he then says to himself, "thin bread and butter she likes in the morning," and then asks her softly from the bottom of the stairs if she would also like "something tasty," it would appear that the 16th of June is not the first time Bloom has brought his wife bread and butter and tea in bed, as unusual as that might be for an Irish husband in 1904. Yet his remark to himself—"still perhaps: once in a way"—suggests a sense of occasion, that there is something distinctive about this particular morning.

That Bloom continues to monitor himself, whether anxiously or reassuringly, is again evident in the way he hears himself ask Molly, "You don't want anything for breakfast?" after he has told her that he's about to go out for a minute, his use of the negative presupposing an ambiguous response. As it turns out, Bloom takes her "mn" to mean "no," but it is an expression that can also mean "yes," and it can also indicate that the

[15] Osteen, *Economy*, 72, suggests that "righting" here "literally…means that [Bloom] is balancing objects by upending them," though this is not a reading supported by the *Oxford English Dictionary*, 3rd online ed., s.v. "righting."

[16] Budgen, *Making of "Ulysses"*, 74.

[17] *Oxford English Dictionary*, 3rd online ed., s.v. "right."

person is noncommittal. If he did get her "something tasty" to add to the bread and butter and tea—a combination originally devised by the Duchess of Bedford around 1840 to stave off hunger between meals[18]—that "something tasty," whether it was meat or fish, would mean he was getting Molly a conventional Edwardian breakfast. Interpreting her "mn" as "no" confirms his role as a maid-of-all-work, a "slavey," rather than a breakfast-cook or house-husband. However, as we subsequently learn, Molly actually "prefers yesterday's loaves turnovers crisp crowns hot" (4.82–83). Is using yesterday's loaf a sign of her thrift? Is it because yesterday's loaves, being slightly stale, are crisper than fresh bread when toasted? Is it indicative of her desire to maintain appearances by transforming day-old bread into a delicacy? Does she enjoy the *cachet* of eating a type of bread that in Edwardian Dublin was traditionally bought from St. Catherine's Bakery in Thomas Court?[19]

By mid-morning it is clear that Bloom himself has begun to reframe the narrative of the morning's tray. When McCoy innocently asks, "Who's getting it up?" referring to the Belfast concert for which Molly is engaged, Bloom thinks to himself, "Marion Bloom. Not up yet. Queen was in her bedroom eating bread and. No book. Blackened court cards laid along her thigh by sevens. Dark lady and fair man. Letter. Cat furry black ball. Torn strip of envelope" (5.153–56). Such thoughts are as replete with suspicions as they are with ironies. "Marion Bloom" and "Torn strip of envelope" are now linked as clues that suggest an assignation. "The Queen was in her bedroom," from "Sing a Song of Sixpence," memorializes the way the eighteenth-century pirate Blackbeard drew passing ships to their doom by pretending that his own ship, the Queen Anne's Revenge, was in distress. By about half past ten in the morning, the thought that the marital bed will prove irresistibly enticing to Boylan seems to have firmed in Bloom's mind. While he has obviously played the part of the maid in the parlor bringing up the tray, and while the nursery rhyme had popped into

[18] Jane Pettigrew, *A Social History of Tea* (London: National Trust Enterprises, 2001), 102. A preference for bread and butter as indicative of good taste was popularized by Oscar Wilde's *The Importance of Being Earnest.* Julie-Ann Robson, e-mail message to author, 30 July 2016.

[19] John Kirkland, *The Bakers' ABC: An Encyclopedic Dictionary for Bakers, Confectioners, and Caterers* (London: Gresham, 1927), 358.

his mind on the way to the jakes (4.473–74; 4.498–99), whether or not "The Queen" will snare her prey remains a matter for the cards.

The most revealing interpretative context for Bloom's and Molly's "breakfasts," however, is the breakfast Bloom orders in the early hours of 17 June 1904, once he has discovered sufficient evidence to convince himself that a sexual relationship has taken place. I examine Bloom's "Sherlockholmesing" of the matrimonial bed in Chapter 7; for the present, it is sufficient to scrutinize Molly's indignity bordering on outrage at being ordered to bring her apparently complacent husband "breakfast in bed with a couple of eggs" (18.2). The order, we subsequently learn, is actually for "eggs and tea and Findon haddy and hot buttered toast" (18.930–31), with the further instruction that the toast is to be buttered on both sides and that the eggs must be new-laid (18.1243–44). Findon haddy is haddock from Findon in Scotland. According to Mrs. Beeton, the correct way to prepare a breakfast of Findon haddy and eggs is to steam the haddock for about ten minutes, remove the bone, place the fish on a hot dish, spread on a little butter, sprinkle with pepper, and then place the two poached eggs on top of the fish. "Time taken: 10 to 15 minutes."[20] To prepare such a breakfast and bring it upstairs, Molly will need to rise no later than twenty-to-eight for Bloom to be out the door by eight. That she is more than a little irritated by his demand and the reversal of their roles is evident from her next thought: "I suppose well have him sitting up like the king of the country pumping the wrong end of the spoon up and down on his egg wherever he learned that from" (18.931–32). Thinking of the eggs as boiled rather than poached probably has less to do with her ignorance of the recipe and more to do with the way that her husband's method of breaking open an eggshell has persistently annoyed her. As many have observed, failing relationships tend to become littered with trivial irritations.

Irritation, however, is just one of her reactions. With the immediate urgency of her body satisfied by her affair and Bloom asleep after making his demand for breakfast in bed, she begins to think about what she might lose as a consequence of her adultery: the comfort of the cat coming to curl up on the bed; the sound of Bloom "falling up the stairs of a morning with the cups rattling on the tray" (18.933–34). Musing about her

[20] Beeton, *Everyday Cookery*, 526. Findon haddy is also included in one of the menus "for a simple breakfast" (711). Findon haddies could be purchased from Scotch Fish Stores, 20 Upper Liffey Street.

husband's insistence that the toast is to be buttered on both sides and that the eggs are to be new-laid, Molly thinks to herself, "I suppose Im nothing anymore" (18.1245). But this self-pity and self-denigration soon gives way to a self-assertion that is as class-conscious as it is disdainful: "Im to be slooching around in the kitchen to get his lordship his breakfast while hes rolled up like a mummy will I indeed" (18.1431–32). Should she be defiant, or should she pretend nothing has happened?

She decides that she will "go about rather gay" but "not too much," and that once she has thrown "him up his eggs and tea in the moustache-cup" that Milly has given him, she will begin

> singing a bit now and then *mi fa pieta Masetto* then Ill start dressing myself to go out *presto non son piu forte* Ill put on my best shift and drawers let him have a good eyeful out of that to make his micky stand for him Ill let him know if thats what he wanted that his wife is fucked yes and damn well fucked too up to my neck . . . if you dont believe me feel my belly unless I made him stand there and put him into me Ive a mind to tell him every scrap and make him do it out in front of me serve him right its all his own fault if I am an adulteress. (18.1504–16)

The snatches of lyric that Molly proposes to sing are from "*Là ci darem la mano*" (Give me thy hand), which is the seduction duet from Mozart's *Don Giovanni*. This is the duet that Molly has told Bloom, after he has brought up her morning tray, she will be rehearsing with Boylan that afternoon. In the duet, Don Giovanni's attempts to seduce Zerlina are first met with hesitation, "*vorrei e non vorrei*" (I would and yet I would not); then with a suspicion that he might be deceiving her in order to shame her betrothed, "*mi fa pietà Masetto*" (I feel sorry for Masetto); to which the Don replies, "*Io cangierò tua sorte*" (I will change your lot); a promise that entices Zerlina to yield with "*presto non son più forte*" (suddenly I am no longer strong).

Molly's choice of "*la ci darem la mano*" suggests she intends to exploit the ambiguity of her situation, because the lyrics will not only acknowledge the game of patty-fingers that sealed her affair with Boylan when the three of them were walking by the Tolka on the 29th of May (8.588),[21] but they will also, she hopes, excite Bloom to have conjugal sex with her.

[21] Patty-fingers is a sexually suggestive furtive caressing of the hands. The most well-known use of the expression is in John Ford's *The Quiet Man* (1952).

Were she to succeed, she might be considered to have been legally granted condonation. As *Every Man's Own Lawyer* explains,

> Condonation is a bar to divorce; it means forgiveness and reconciliation, and a blotting out of the offence; and if the petitioner has condoned the adultery or cruelty complained of, the petition will be dismissed, on proof of the condonation. Condonation may be implied from facts and circumstances.[22]

Of course, whether or not her strategy is successful, and whether or not Bloom gets his breakfast in bed, remains uncertain. What is more certain is that the court, as with *Maguire v. Maguire* (1903), severely disapproved of attempts to resort to sexual enticement to secure condonation.[23] As we will see in Chapter 7, the way Bloom kisses Molly goodnight, when he eventually returns to the marital bed, seems deliberately intended to prevent any possibility of claiming condonation. Power resided with the husband. If it was the case that Bloom was guilty of a matrimonial offence, Molly's having sex with him would not necessarily confirm that she had granted him condonation. As a leading authority on Irish divorce explains,

> If a husband has sexual intercourse with his wife knowing that she has committed adultery, the husband's act in consenting to intercourse amounts to condonation. On the other hand, a wife's sexual intercourse with a husband after he has committed a matrimonial offence does not automatically establish that she condones his offence.[24]

In matrimonial matters, conjugal sex was the husband's right.

* * * *

There are two further incidents that take place during the Blooms' breakfasts that presage the future. The first has to do with the way that Bloom seems to act at a remove from himself throughout much of 16 June 1904, a remove that indicates he instinctively understands his sense of self is

[22] *Every Man's Own Lawyer*, 376.

[23] *Maguire v. Maguire*, NA J77/778/3700, Filed: 2 March 1903; Set Down: 23 April 1903; Dismissed: 23 November (1903?).

[24] Shatter, *Family Law*, 121.

about to undergo a significant transformation. Downstairs and pausing in the entrance hall on his way to Dlugacz's, the butcher's, it is reported that it is Bloom's "hand" that takes his hat from the peg. And though we are then told that "he peeped quickly inside the leather headband," the free indirect discourse that immediately follows restores that sense of self-appraisal and self-commentary that we are being encouraged to see as characteristic: "White slip of paper. Quite safe." The slip of paper, as we subsequently learn, authenticates another identity, an alternate secret self, called Henry Flower, who is engaging in a clandestine correspondence with a woman called Martha Clifford, though the "slip of paper" turns out to be not "a slip of paper" but a "card." Is the reader being misled? Is this a rare Joycean error? Or is the change from "slip of paper" to "card" indicative of Bloom's anxious and furtive state of mind or a signal to the reader that Bloom is becoming more purposeful?

Transferring the "card" from his hat to his waistcoat before he presents it at the Westland Row Post Office barely an hour later involves Bloom in even more performance and subterfuge than retrieving his hat from the peg at No. 7. It is now eleven o'clock, and it is warm but not hot. But by pretending it is "rather warm," Bloom devises a sequence of gestures that he hopes will conceal what he is actually doing—that is, transferring the card from his hat to his waistcoat. All his gestures become self-consciously choreographed. Having removed his hat with his left hand and used his hat partly to shield his face, he then sends "his right hand with slow grace over his brow and hair." His right hand then comes "down into the bowl of his hat" so that his "fingers found quickly a card," which they then transfer "to his waistcoat pocket." The card is now in a conventionally acceptable place so he can produce it inside the Post Office without drawing attention to what he is doing, but the subterfuge needs to be completed. "So warm," we are told. "His right hand once more more slowly went over his brow and hair. Then he put on his hat again, relieved" (5.21–28). What had been a quick and somewhat furtive action before breakfast has become, barely an hour later, a subterfuge that is as complex as it is self-consciously orchestrated, performed meticulously as it were before a wholly imagined audience.

And yet there is still an element of repetition according to the account given by the third-person narration. "Once more more slowly" reminds us of "right. Right" and other doublings, such as when Bloom enters the carriage to take him to Paddy Dignam's funeral and slams the door "twice till it shut tight" (6.9–10); or the "quickbreathing" he experiences walking past La Maison Clair in Grafton Street around half past one having recalled a remark Molly made about the full moon on the 29th of May and wondering if it was on that occasion, as the three of them were walking by the Tolka, that her assignation with Boylan was confirmed via "Touch. Fingers," when fingers seem to have instinctively orchestrated themselves as patty-fingers. The recollection causes Bloom a momentary upsurge of panic: "Stop. Stop. If it was it was. Must" (8.592). But does "must" mean inevitable in the sense that it relates to "it was it was"; or does "must" mean he must intervene and prevent what he suspects will happen in the sense that "must" actually relates to "Stop. Stop"? To prevent himself from giving way, Bloom thinks of his own secret correspondence with Martha Clifford: "With ha quiet keep quiet relief" (8.594). The suspicion is that if he is too robust in the way he questions Molly, he might find himself the subject of a much more confronting interrogation about his own peccadillos.

* * * *

It is through the rhetorical accumulation of resonant detail and the elaboration of what at first might appear incidental or even trivial actions, random associations, miscellaneous impressions, and fleeting, disconnected thoughts about something over which he seems to have little or no control that we come to know Bloom as he strives to know himself. It is through narrativizing his experience, as he projects himself as narrator and narratee in search of a temporality or a causality that might bring some coherence and meaning to what is taking place on 16 June 1904, that we are invited to read him reading himself as he encodes and decodes his world. For Joyce to usher Bloom through *Ulysses* in this way is to emphasize the degree to which Bloom is detached from himself, a detachment that can be anxious, shrewd, furtive, self-protective, panic-stricken, calculating, stressed, or forensic, depending on the situation and on the circumstances of the story-world. It is also to introduce uncertainty (what is meant by the "right" that Bloom repeats to himself as he prepares Molly's tray?) even while affirming various certainties (in this case, the "fact" that he is preparing Molly's tray). Above all it is to suggest that there are backstories to this story-world: that there are events and interactions, allusions and intertexts, gaps and silences that hover teasingly around the edges of *Ulysses* that might or might not illuminate Bloom's attempts to construct a narrative about his relationship with Molly and of and for himself.

He devises two such narratives on his way to the butcher's. The first has to do with Molly's sexuality read in terms of popular culture; the second with a shared vestigial Jewish heritage mediated by recollection, memory, and history into feeling and emotion. Responding to the heat of the sun as he rounds the corner at the top of Eccles Street, Bloom allows his imagination to journey East: "wander through awned streets. Turbaned faces going by. Dark caves of carpet shops, big man, Turko the Terrible, seated crosslegged, smoking a coiled pipe. Cries of sellers in the streets. . . . High wall: beyond strings twanged. Night sky, moon, violet, colour of Molly's new garters. String. Listen. A girl playing one of those instruments what do you call them: dulcimers. I pass" (4.88–98). While this imagined journey draws its color from pantomimes such as *Turko the Terrible* and *Sinbad the Sailor* that were frequently performed in Dublin, illustrated books Bloom has in his possession, and popular reproductions of paintings of seraglios,[25] it is also associated with Molly's desire to "get a nice pair of red slippers like those Turks with the fez used to sell" and Bloom's suspicion that the new "violet garters" he has recently given her might well feature in her image of herself as a seductress, which, as he eventually discovers, they do.[26] Although the image of Molly as an odalisque returns to haunt him after midnight, his immediate response to what he imagines on his way to the butcher's is to terminate his fantasy abruptly with "probably not a bit like it really. Kind of stuff you read" (4.99). Having drifted into a narrative about her desire and how it might enact itself, Bloom suddenly opts for foreclosure once the memory of the garters occurs to him. He will not permit his suspicions to develop, at least "not now." Similarly, the newspaper advertisement he reads on his return from the butcher's describing the Turkish government's willingness to cede land for a Jewish settlement initially prompts him to think, "Nothing doing. Still an idea behind it" (4.200). But then imagination, recollection, and memories of failed hopes gather in his mind. "A barren land, bare waste," he thinks to himself; the chosen people wandering "far away over all the

[25] Mid- to late-nineteenth-century paintings of seraglios, such as the Odalisques of Leon-Comerre, Francisco Masriera, and Pierre-Auguste Renoir, and Gilbert and Sullivan's light operas provide further examples (e.g., *Mikado*); as does the lingering fashion for Chinoiserie and Japonisme that influenced the design of everything from crockery to gardening. Frederick Diodati Thompson, *In the Track of the Sun: Readings from the Diary of a Globe Trotter* (New York: D. Appleton, 1893), https://archive.org/details/intrackofsunread00thom.

[26] *U*18.1495; *U*13.800; *U*17.2093–94.

earth, captivity to captivity, multiplying, dying, being born everywhere. It lay there now. Now it could bear no more" (4.225–27). As Bloom turns into Eccles Street, his image of his ancestral homeland acquires a horrifying realism: "cold oils slid along his veins, chilling his blood: age crusting him with a salt cloak" (4.231–32). Has his failure as a Jewish husband doomed him to suffer the fate of Lot's wife, who, because she flouted a divine command, was transformed into a pillar of salt? Haunted by fears of fate, usurpation, and retribution, he abruptly folds "the page into his pocket" and hurries "homeward."

Central to the construction of these and other narratives in which Bloom imagines himself participating is the temporal marker "not now." It is a locution that postpones rather than terminates a situation, a response that can express itself in thought, emotion, word, or action. For instance, when he returns to 7 Eccles Street after buying his pork kidney, Bloom finds the post has been delivered. There are two letters and a card lying on the hall floor.

> He stooped and gathered them. Mrs Marion Bloom. His quickened heart slowed at once. Bold hand. Mrs Marion.
> —Poldy!
> Entering the bedroom he halfclosed his eyes and walked through warm yellow twilight towards her tousled head,
> —Who are the letters for?
> He looked at them. Mullingar. Milly.
> —A letter from Milly, he said carefully, and a card for you. And a letter for you.
> He laid her card and letter on the twill bedspread near the curve of her knees.
> —Do you want the blind up?
> Letting the blind by gentle tugs halfway his backward eye saw her glance at the letter and tuck it under her pillow.
> —That do? He asked, turning.
> She was reading the card, propped on her elbow. (4.243–58)

As the tray with buttered bread and teacup is still in the kitchen and as the kidney is still in Bloom's pocket, bringing up the post is the first time that husband and wife see one another again since they have woken. As the narrative indicates, it is an encounter replete with separateness, surveillance, and "not now." What is retrieved from the hall is eloquent of the state of the Blooms' marriage. Milly has written a letter to her father. Her correspondence is private. She has written a card to her mother; a card can be read by anyone who picks it up. As Molly muses to herself early in the morning of 17 June, "see she wrote a letter to him who did I get the last letter from" (18.717–18). Apart from a letter from a school friend, the most she has received are the "few" she posted to herself when she was young (18.698–99). The second letter is addressed familiarly as Mrs. Marion Bloom rather than a respectful Mrs. Leopold Bloom. Bloom's reaction to this assumed familiarity, evidenced by the way his quickened heart slows, announces the way his body will respond every time he detects more evidence of Molly's and Boylan's intentions, and every time he recollects or hears more about Boylan or sees him.

But Bloom conceals his emotional reaction to the way his wife has been addressed. He does not immediately respond to Molly's enquiry from the bedroom, and, when he does, he is careful to distinguish between his mail and hers. What is more he places her mail on the bed rather than in her hands. Although he notices that she conceals the letter under her pillow, he does not immediately ask her to reveal who has written to her. In fact, he does not ask her until after he has brought up the tray while his kidney is cooking downstairs, and after he has seen "a strip of torn envelope" peeping from "under the dimpled pillow." His question is direct: "Who was the letter from?" But when she deflects the force of his question with the response, "O! Boylan," and with the normalizing explanation that "He's bringing the programme," Bloom yields to her evasiveness with "What are you singing?" Instead of questioning whether or not she will invite him in or confronting her with the impropriety of having a single man visit their home while her husband is out, he acquiesces. In part, it is the directness and apparent openness of her response that effectively preempts further enquiry. But in part it is also his implied choice of "not now," of deciding not to seize the moment. As *Bennett v. Bennett and McKay* (1901) makes clear, postponement does not necessarily constitute condonation, and it does not necessarily prejudice a petitioner's application for a *decree nisi*. Although Thomas Bennett had refrained from attempting to discover the identity of the person who it was alleged had committed adultery with his wife "from about 1895 until the present time" and who wrote regularly to her between 1896 and 1900, he was still granted a *decree nisi* with costs of £161-1-11 awarded against the co-respondent, even though he did not file for divorce until 5 October 1901.[27] However, in *Robinson v. Robinson and Dearden* (1903), Justice Bucknill presiding, His Honour ruled that

> Where in a petition for divorce by the husband on the ground of his wife's adultery, it appeared that he had taken no steps beyond mere verbal remonstrances to terminate a course of conduct on the part of his wife and the co-respondent which, if it did not bring about actual adultery at the time, eventually resulted in it:—*Held*, that the petitioner was not entitled to relief, and the petition should be dismissed.[28]

As *Every Man's Own Lawyer* points out, "Connivance is also a peremptory bar to divorce. By connivance is meant, that the complaining party was aware of the adultery or impropriety at the time it was committed, but shut his eyes to it, and took no steps to prevent it."[29]

"Not now" is thus double-edged: it can be interpreted as conniving in and perhaps even conducing adultery; or it can be interpreted as a genuine desire to ensure that the evidence obtained is free of supposition and conjecture, is grounded in fact, and will withstand cross-examination. It can give free passage to assertion and evasion, but it can also ameliorate tension and create time for assessment and reflection. It can be seen as prudent, generous, kind, and empathetic; but it can also be interpreted as sly, distant, and manipulative. "Not now" is also characteristic of probabilistic inductive reasoning as opposed to deductive reasoning in that space and time are necessary for collocations of evidence to form into possible interpretations. Above all it is a psychologically convincing response to a complex situation whose outcome has yet to be revealed. As Kimberly Devlin has persuasively argued, "Joyce understood the ambiguities of agency: *Ulysses* shows through many examples that agency or

[27] "Probate, Divorce and Admiralty Division," *Times* (London), 1 February 1902, 5. *Bennett v. Bennett and McKay*, NA J77/730/2193, Filed: 5 October 1901; Set Down: 31 December 1901; Decree Nisi: 31 January 1902; Final Decree: 11 August 1902.

[28] *Law Reports Digest 1901–1910*, col. 950. *Robinson v. Robinson and Dearden*, NA J77/763/3213, Filed: 26 September 1902; Set Down: 3 March 1903; Petition Dismissed: 6 May 1903. Cruelty also a factor; P 155; 72 LJP 63; 89 LT 74.

[29] *Every Man's Own Lawyer*, 376.

mastery is usually desired, but that passivity—or paradoxically, the choice of passivity—is psychologically complex and cannot simply be dismissed as 'negative'."[30] From the moment he delivers the letter from Boylan, Bloom seems instinctively to understand that if Molly and Boylan are sufficiently determined to have sex, they will find a way.

His immediate circumstances appear to reinforce this sense of inevitability. Milly's letter, which is affectionate, nevertheless asks him to tell Boylan that "silly Milly" sends her "best respects," both message and nickname signaling a level of intimacy that suggests Boylan is at least an acquaintance if not a friend of the family. The news that she has met a young student prompts Bloom to think of his son's early death and his daughter's first experience of sex. In retrospect and prospect both seem freighted with the inevitable. He recalls that the midwife "knew from the first poor little Rudy wouldn't live" and that she tried to console him with "Well, God is good, sir." And he realizes that there is little to gain from worrying about Milly: "Wait in any case till it does." The life force that compels her also compels Molly. "Will happen, yes. Prevent. Useless: can't move. Girl's sweet light lips. Will happen too. He felt the flowing qualm spread over him. Useless to move *now*" (4.447–50; emphasis mine).

As we will see, Bloom registers the conflict between the temporality of "now" and the motion of "qualm" (which means "a sudden fit, impulse, or pang of sickening fear, misgiving, despair") in his body.[31] This sickening fear recurs every time he hears a reference to Boylan and every time he accidentally encounters him in public. "Not now" provides one way of coping with these irruptions of panic because it enables Bloom to engage in avoidance activity, seek solace in memory, or retrieve hints and guesses from the past that, assembled as a narrative, might furnish a consoling explanation. It is also paradoxically empowering because it privileges strategy over intervention and seeming rationality over impulsive reaction. Not to act "now" is to reserve the right to act once what is being reacted against is more completely understood. Yet the unintended consequences of not acting might prove dire, particularly if not

[30] Kimberly J. Devlin, "En-Gendered Choice and Agency in *Ulysses*," in *"Ulysses" in Critical Perspective*, ed. Michael Patrick Gillespie and A. Nicholas Fargnoli (Gainesville: University Press of Florida, 2006), 79.

[31] *Oxford English Dictionary*, 3rd online ed., s.v. "qualm."

acting results in an outcome that has much wider ramifications than what was anticipated.

* * * *

The most significant "not now" that has become a "so now" has to do with Rudy's death. Reading Milly's letter over breakfast prompts Bloom to begin to piece together memories that affirm his sense of inevitability. But what they also reveal are the dire consequences of postponement. On at least two occasions during the day, Bloom explicitly blames himself for his son's death. When a child's mourning coach passes him on his way to Paddy Dignam's funeral, he thinks to himself, "Our. Little. Beggar. Baby. Meant nothing. Mistake of nature. If it's healthy it's from the mother. If not from the man. Better luck next time" (6.326–30). And later, as the time of Molly's assignation approaches, he thinks to himself, "Well, my fault perhaps. No son. Rudy. Too late now. Or if not? If not? If still?" (11.1066–67).

Bloom is again prompted to think further about Rudy's death after hearing about Mrs. Purefoy's confinement from Josie Breen when they meet in Westmoreland Street after the funeral. Josie, it emerges, was once a rival for his affections. The accidental meeting provokes memories of Molly and Milly that again confirm the way inevitability accompanies loss. "I was happier then," he muses to himself. "Or was that I? Or am I now I?' Twentyeight I was. She twentythree. When we left Lombard street west something changed. Could never like it again after Rudy. Can't bring back time. Like holding water in your hand" (8.608–11).

Molly also acknowledges that their sexual relationship has significantly changed following the death of their only son. While she shares Bloom's awareness that "they were never the same since," she has determined not to think herself "into the glooms about that anymore" (18.1449–50). However, it is only Bloom who speculates about a possible cause for Rudy's death. In the middle of thinking about the risks of childbirth after he has left Josie Breen, he suddenly asks himself, "Suppose he was consumptive," the "he," as his subsequent thoughts reveal, referring to Rudy. Bloom recalls Molly's pregnancy during the Lombard Street West days: "Funny sight two of them together, their bellies out. Molly and Mrs. Moisel. Mothers' meeting. Phthisis retires for the time being, then returns. How flat they look all of a sudden after. Peaceful eyes. Weight off their mind" (8.391–94). He then recalls how Mrs. Thornton, the midwife, used to put the "spoon of pap in her mouth before she fed" babies and how she would say, "O, that's nyumnyum" (8.394–95).

The telling word here is "phthisis," which, while broadly referring to wasting, is particularly applied to the wasting caused by tuberculosis. It was well known in Dublin in 1904 that tuberculosis had reached epidemic proportions; it is now well known that the neonatal morbidity rate for infants born to a mother who has contracted tuberculosis is some 23 percent compared with a general population rate of 3.8 percent. Subsequent medical research has also established that tuberculosis can "retire for the time being" and that, although neonatal infection is rare, infants born to tubercular mothers can die within weeks of birth, having displayed symptoms of weight loss, failure to thrive, jaundice, and respiratory distress.[32] The tragedy is that the mother, if her tuberculosis had "retired for the time being," would not be aware that she had fatally infected her baby. As C. N. Mnyani and J. A. McIntyre point out, "TB infection in pregnancy may present with diagnostic challenges, mainly because of the often nonspecific nature of the early symptoms of the

[32] I am indebted to Liz Barrett for the following: Victoria State Government, "Tuberculosis (TB) in Neonates," accessed 19 July 2016, https://www2.health.vic.gov.au/hospitals-and-health-services/patient-care/perinatal-reproductive/neonatal-ehandbook/infections/tuberculosis, referencing C. N. Mnyani and J. A. McIntyre, "Tuberculosis in Pregnancy," *BJOG: An International Journal of Obstetrics and Gynaecology* 118, no. 2 (2011): 226–31; S. Graham, "Treatment of Paediatric Tuberculosis: Revised WHO Guidelines," *Paediatric Respiratory Reviews* 12 (2011): 22–26; and E. Whittaker and B. Kampmann, "Perinatal Tuberculosis: New Challenges in the Diagnosis and Treatment of Tuberculosis in Infants and the Newborn," *Early Human Development* 84, no. 12 (2008): 795–99. Victoria State Government, "Tuberculosis (TB) in Neonates": "Clinical features may be present at birth or delayed until eight weeks of age. The mean time of onset is two to four weeks. Clinical features of tuberculosis include: respiratory distress, fever, hepatosplenomegaly, irritability, poor feeding and lethargy, lymphadenopathy, failure to thrive, jaundice." Kathleen Ferris, *James Joyce and the Burden of Disease* (1995; Lexington: University Press of Kentucky, 2010), 58–65, argues that both Bloom and Molly have been infected with venereal diseases, though she notes, "the question of whether Molly has been infected is crucial, because if she has not, then Rudy's death would have to be attributed to causes other than venereal disease" (62).

infection, such as malaise and fatigue, which may be attributed to pregnancy and not raise the suspicion of TB infection."[33]

But Rudy might also have been unwittingly infected by the midwife as a consequence of her habit of putting the pap in her mouth before feeding it to a baby. Rudy's respiratory distress, if he has been born with tuberculosis, would provide a partial explanation for Bloom's memory of his son's appearance: "A dwarf's face, mauve and wrinkled like little Rudy's was. Dwarf's body, weak as putty" (6.326–30). And when Rudy reappears in vision at the end of "Circe," Bloom again finds himself gazing into unseeing eyes set in a "delicate mauve face" (15.4965). The "mauve" appearance points to a lack of oxygen associated with respiratory distress. The wrinkling indicates a catastrophic loss of muscle and subcutaneous fat known as cachexia that is associated with tuberculosis. Bloom's memory would also explain his recollection of the midwife's instinctive diagnosis: "She knew from the first poor little Rudy wouldn't live" (4.418–20). When Bloom fantasizes about his ideal house, "Flowerville," it is noteworthy that he wants to have it built either in Dundrum or Sutton, "both localities equally reported by trial to resemble the terrestrial poles in being favourable climates for phthisical subjects" (17.1516–18). Rudy dying from tuberculosis might further explain Molly's grief-driven, harshly pragmatic "what was the good in going into mourning for what was neither one thing nor the other the first cry was enough for me I heard the deathwatch too ticking in the wall" (18.1308–9). That Bloom blames himself for Rudy's death and that Molly thinks his mourning is excessive and sentimental—"hed go into mourning for the cat" (18.1310)—suggests that the likely cause of Rudy's death is not something they have discussed in detail or at length. And Molly, as readers subsequently discover, is clearly in denial. In "Oxen of the Sun," she is depicted as "wondrous stricken of heart for that evil hap and for his burial did him on a corselet of lamb's wool, the flower of the flock, lest he might perish utterly and lie akeled (for it was then about the midst of the winter)" (14.268–71). It is also highly plausible, regardless of when the thought of Rudy's contracting tuberculosis first occurred to him, that Bloom might well postpone such a discussion as being too uncertain, too painful, and potentially too confronting, as a topic that ought to be discussed but "not now." He might well have postponed talking about his fears on the

[33] Mnyani and McIntyre, "Tuberculosis in Pregnancy," 226.

grounds that no good and perhaps even greater harm might result from trying to attribute blame, and as a consequence postponed it so effectively that it needed a crisis to refresh his memory.[34] In Bloom's mind Rudy's death has become one of those things "that had to be" (8.633).

But the Blooms' evident failure to reconcile themselves to their son's death and to one another has significantly harmed their sexual relationship. Bloom's thought that he "could never like it again after Rudy" is a euphemism for the fact that he has not participated in penetrative sex with Molly for ten years. Rudy's death also seems to have made him pathologically anxious that he might be a purveyor of malformation or morbidity. I will return to look at the Blooms' sexual difficulties and how these compound their other problems in more detail in Chapter 5. For the present it is sufficient to reiterate that Bloom's failure to fulfill his marital obligations for the past ten years and his failure to make adequate provision for his wife furnish her, in the first instance as a Catholic and then in both instances as a Jewess, with grounds for petitioning her Bishop or her Rabbi for a divorce. Such a divorce, as we have seen from Chapter 1, might calm consciences, but it would not permit the "divorcees" to remarry until the appropriate civil court had passed judgement.

* * * *

Bloom has two minor tasks to perform before he joins the funeral procession conveying the body of Paddy Dignam from the Dignam family home in Sandymount to the cemetery in Glasnevin. The first is to check if there has been a response to his clandestine correspondence with Martha Clifford, one of forty-four respondents to an advertisement he had placed in the *Irish Times*: "Wanted smart lady typist to aid gentleman in literary work" (8.326–27). Not being an Irish speaker and perhaps wishing to present himself as an Edwardian gentleman, he has chosen the English alias Henry Flower rather than the Irish *Anraí Bláth*. The second is to call at Sweny's in

[34] In *Chapman v. Chapman*, in *Times* (London), 15 March 1919, 4, the respondent's proposed defence that his tuberculosis was so advanced as to constitute a health threat to his wife was abandoned, the petitioner's counsel remarking that he doubted "whether the defence would have been an answer in law." *Chapman v. Chapman*, NA J77/1368/1909, Filed: 9 July 1918; Set Down: 19 December 1918; Decree rescinded: 14 March 1918.

Lincoln Place to ask the chemist to make up a skin tonic for Molly. By conducting a clandestine correspondence with Martha Clifford and keeping three of her letters in a drawer in 7 Eccles Street (17.1796–98), Bloom and Molly (if she keeps Boylan's letter) would be equally compromised in terms of court proceedings regardless of whether or not she had committed adultery with Boylan. With incriminating letters as evidence, neither Molly nor Bloom could come to court with "clean hands."

As many court records show, it was often difficult to secure evidence that adultery had taken place, if the guilty parties denied it—that is, evidence (including confession) that was untainted by fraud, fabrication, perjury, or collusion. As Mr. Justice Gorell Barnes, in summing up *Palgrave v. Palgrave and Lutifer* (1904), pointed out,

> in ordinary cases . . . direct evidence of misconduct was not often forthcoming. Evidence of familiarity had to be tendered and a true inference deduced from it. For a man to be alone with a woman was not sufficient. Otherwise men would never be safe, nor would their daughters be allowed to take music lessons from male artists. For such evidence of familiarity a totally different class of facts was necessary in order to justify a finding of misconduct.[35]

In many hearings, letters, whether covert *billets-doux* or normal correspondence and whether between the parties or about them, provided that "class of facts." As remarked in *Methofer v. Methofer and Bain* (1903), "Whenever there [is] wrongdoing . . . there are always letters."[36] Even though Martha Clifford's letter to Bloom indicates that their correspondence is comparatively recent and even though the letter itself might seem relatively innocuous, it nevertheless chimes with correspondence tended as evidence in contemporary divorce hearings. Counsel, whether for petitioner or respondent, were particularly alert to passages containing pet names, pseudonyms, and thinly veiled innuendos that could be read aloud, frequently to the merriment of the court. What would be bound to

[35] *Times* (London), 15 July 1904, 14. For Court Minutes, see *Palgrave v. Palgrave and Lutifer*, NA J77/806/4512 consolidated with *Palgrave v. Palgrave*, NA J77/811/4669.

[36] *Daily Mail*, 28 July 1904, 3. *Methofer v. Methofer and Bain*, NA J77/800/4343, Filed: 4 November 1903; Set Down: 21 March 1904; Decree Nisi: 27 July 1904; Final Decree: 6 February 1905.

provoke a quip at Martha Clifford's expense would be her warning, "So now you know what I will do to you, you naughty boy, if you do not wrote" (5.241–59). As unlikely as it seems, the word laughter (in parentheses) appears regularly in newspaper reports of divorce hearings. Bloom is painfully aware of this.

A crucial decision for him on 16 June 1904 is whether or not to respond to her urgent request that he "write *by return* to your longing Martha" (5.255–57; emphasis mine). If he does, he runs the risk of incriminating himself on three counts. Molly's counsel could use the reply against him in a hearing for divorce; Martha Clifford could use the reply against him to threaten him with blackmail or with breach of promise. What the prosecution in a suit for breach of promise would characteristically seize upon would be phrases such as "I do wish I could do something for you"; "I often think of the beautiful name you have. Dear Henry, when will we meet?"; and "Do tell me what kind of perfume does your wife use. I want to know." Martha's knowing Henry Flower (aka Bloom) is married might complicate her suit for breach of promise, although she might attempt to claim that she did not know he was married. As *Every Man's Own Lawyer* citing *Wild v. Harris* (1849) advises, "If a person already married promise to marry another who knew not of the existing marriage, an Action may be maintained against such a person for breach of promise of marriage."[37] It is possible that Bloom keeps the incriminating letters to protect himself against such an eventuality.

When he comes to respond, Bloom writes his reply by hand. Martha is more strategic. She types the envelope and presumably her letter,[38] thereby, as we will see in Chapter 4, making it difficult but not impossible to use her handwriting to establish authorship (5.61). This might seem an unnecessary caution, but it was not unknown for men to sue for breach of promise.[39]

As we will also see, approximately six hours pass before Bloom decides to reply. For example, as he walks by the Molesworth Street Post Office at about half past one, Bloom recalls her demand for an immediate response but checks himself with "Wait. Think it over" (8.1134). It is only after he

[37] *Every Man's Own Lawyer*, 365. *Wild v. Harris* [1843–60] All ER Rep 413.

[38] The three letters from her that Bloom keeps in the second drawer are all typed, as is the fourth (*U*17.1840–42).

[39] "Man's Action for Breach of Promise," *Times* (London), 14 December 1901, 15.

has heard Boylan leave the Ormond Hotel in a jaunting car for his four o'clock rendezvous with Molly that Bloom calls for pen and paper and thinks about adding a postal order for two shillings and sixpence. Is the two shillings and sixpence designed to prevent Martha Clifford from claiming that while she responded to an advertisement for secretarial assistance in good faith she was never paid? But the fact that Bloom has replied and that he has kept three of her letters continues to haunt him. As we will see in Chapter 6, in the account he gives Stephen of the way trials are conducted in the Probate, Divorce and Admiralty Division of the King's Bench in London, Bloom not only knowingly remarks the damning evidence contained in the "usual affectionate letters that passed between" the illicit lovers "full of sweet nothings" but also emphasizes that such letters are "made public" (16.1363–64). By midnight, Bloom's fear about Martha Clifford suing him in a civil action has grown into a fear that her letters might be used as evidence for breach of promise or in *Bloom v. Bloom and Boylan.*[40]

[40] Since Bloom has advertised for a smart lady typist to assist with literary work, Martha Clifford would most likely be advised to threaten Bloom with a suit for failing to fulfill a contract to hire. See *Every Man's Own Lawyer*, "Contracts of Personal Service," 78; "Contracting under an Assumed Name," 83–84; and "Contract by Letters Sent by Post," 84.

CHAPTER 3

Bloom in the Sexualized City

Because most of his morning has been devoted to Paddy Dignam's funeral, Bloom does not begin his day's work until noon. His first task is to visit the offices of the *Freeman's Journal and National Press* in "the heart of the Hibernian metropolis."[1] He needs to renew an advertisement for Alexander Keyes, a local tea, wine, and spirits merchant. If he is successful, he will collect a small commission. Passing through the case-room where the type is stored, Bloom sees old Monks, the head steward, and thinks to himself, "Queer lot of stuff he must have put through his hands in his time: obituary notices, pubs' ads, speeches, *divorce suits*, found drowned" (7.197–99; emphasis mine). This is the first time since leaving 7 Eccles Street that the word "divorce" has crossed his mind. That it occurs to Bloom in the offices of a pro-Catholic national newspaper and that he mentally includes it in a list of items and events which routinely provide copy suggests to the reader that "divorce suits" were as much a commonplace in Dublin newspapers as pubs' ads, speeches, and death notices. An electronically assisted search of the metropolitan broadsheets on sale in Dublin in 1904 confirms this. It reveals the majority carried some reference to "divorce" almost every day. So it is not surprising that from "Aeolus," which is devoted to the press, allusions to divorce and

[1] Also the offices of the *Weekly Freeman and National Press* and the *Dublin Daily Express*.

P. Kuch, *Irish Divorce / Joyce's Ulysses*,
DOI 10.1057/978-1-137-57186-1_3

implicit and explicit references to famous divorce cases begin to intrude more and more on the narrative.

Neither is it surprising that an episode whose technique Joyce described as "enthymemic" should be the one where divorce is first mentioned and where divorce is shown to be an aspect of the *mentalité* of 1904 Dublin, even though divorce was not sanctioned, acknowledged, or, for that matter, mutely accepted as an inevitable consequence of modernity. In logic, an enthymeme "is a syllogism in which one of the premises is only implicit, or is based on probability, instead of [being] true in all cases; an enthymeme thus resembles a syllogism but is more rhetorical than logical."[2] As a stylistic technique, "enthymemic" is eminently suited to representing the probabilistic inductive reasoning that Bloom and in many cases divorce court juries were obliged to employ in their attempts to establish proof of infidelity that would result in a verdict in divorce proceedings.[3]

* * * *

The Dublin Bloom enters at noon seems to be a whirl of activity with trams departing for the suburbs, mailcars and brewery floats being loaded and unloaded, shoeblacks crying their services, Davy Stephens collecting his daily supply of newspapers from the *Freeman's* offices,[4] and newsboys rushing through the streets with the latest racing special. But what the reader soon learns is that all this activity—which entails distribution and consumption rather than production—is being carried out under the aegis of the British Empire and the controlling eye of the Catholic Church. The frantic pace of activity suggests a society under stress; the fact that some of the vehicles in "Aeolus" and elsewhere are represented as horse-drawn

[2] Gifford with Seidman, *"Ulysses" Annotated*, 128.

[3] "Consider the kinds of inferences members of a jury are supposed to make based on the evidence presented at a murder trial. The inference to probable guilt or innocence is usually based on a patchwork of various sorts of evidence. It almost never involves consideration of a randomly selected sequences of past situations when people like the accused committed similar murders." James Hawthorne, "Inductive Logic," Stanford Encyclopedia of Philosophy, revised 29 October 2012, http://plato.stanford.edu/entries/logic-inductive/.

[4] Davy Stephens, *The Life and Times of Davy Stephens: Told by Himself* (Dublin: Cahill, 1912).

implies an economy not yet fully equipped for modernity,[5] the more so since the trams which arrived and departed from Nelson's Pillar in the historical Dublin of 1904 were all electrified.[6]

Bloom's status in this workday world of Dublin, at once the second city of the British Empire and the seventh city of Christendom, is equally ambivalent. His association with advertising and with the insurance industry (his next task will be to meet Martin Cunningham to check on the status of Paddy Dignam's life assurance) and the apparent ease with which he navigates the mechanized printing works of a major national newspaper,[7] uses the telephone, conducts a library search, and proposes a design for an advertisement suggest a modest Edwardian man technologically at ease in the modern world. The fact that he is merely a canvasser, that he seems to have appointed himself as the Dignam family's insurance advisor, that he has a checkered history of employment, and that he is periodically identified as a Jew by a society known for bouts of virulent anti-Semitism should remind the reader that Bloom's social and financial status is uncertain. The word "divorce" will occur to Bloom again shortly after he leaves the *Freeman's* offices in search of somewhere to have lunch. Recalling the way a tramcar had denied him a view of an elegant silk-stockinged leg, he tries to associate the wearer with someone he might know. "O yes!" he says to himself. "Mrs Miriam Dandrade that sold me her old wraps and black underclothes in the Shelbourne Hotel. Divorced Spanish American" (8.349–51).[8]

[5] Bloom et al. go to the funeral in a horse-drawn cab, and when they reach the Dolphin they halt to allow the ambulance car to gallop past them (*U*10.504–5).

[6] Gifford with Seidman, *"Ulysses" Annotated*, 128. They also note that "Many of the final destinations were near one another (as Sandymount Green and the tower), but the trams followed different routes in a system that in 1904 was regarded as the most efficient and 'modern' in Europe." The Guinness "drays" that are being unloaded and reloaded, for example, were still largely horse-drawn in 1904.

[7] See David Pierce, *Reading Joyce* (New York: Routledge, 2014), 254–57 for images of the composing room, the stone room, and foundry of the *Freeman's Journal*.

[8] Joseph Allen Boone, *Libidinal Currents: Sexuality and the Shaping of Modernism* (Chicago: University of Chicago Press, 1998), 161, points out that Mrs. Miriam Dandrade's "short trunkleg naughties" feature in "Circe" as "a cover for Bloom's taboo desires and a vehicle for the cross-dressing masquerade" (*U*15.2993–94). These desires include fantasies about seduction and penetration.

That Bloom was at one time buying and selling second-hand clothes and that a "demimondaine" (15.2997) would be reduced to selling her wraps and underwear provides further evidence of how precarious life could prove and how pervasive prostitution was in 1904 Dublin.

Bloom's interactions, as we have seen from the previous chapter, until he gets into the carriage to go to Paddy Dignam's funeral, have been limited to his cat and to his wife; to phatic communication with a publican, a butcher, a postmistress, and a chemist; and to desultory conversations with McCoy and then Bantam Lyons, acquaintances who happen to come across him in the street.[9] Most of the reader's time has been spent with Bloom's thoughts, feelings, emotions, imaginings, fantasies, and memories. And though, as we have seen, his interactions with Simon Dedalus, Jack Power, and Martin Cunningham and the other mourners at the funeral suggest that there is still much for the reader to learn about him, it is not until he emerges from the comparatively circumscribed worlds of home, neighborhood, and funeral that the reader is able to bring Bloom's private worlds into creative tension with the reactions of other characters and their worlds and the fictional social imaginary of 1904 Dublin.

What these interactions reveal is an acculturated denial of adultery and divorce that nevertheless perpetually speaks in spite of being placed under ban. At play here is Foucault's critique of the "repressive hypothesis":[10] that the more sex is sublimated and subjugated, the more it finds avenues and occasions for expression. Though the actual words "adultery" and "divorce" are rarely uttered, they constantly erupt in conversation and social intercourse in the guise of allusion, reference, suggestion, irony, innuendo, and ribaldry—forms of confession that are generated by a plethora of discourses. There is a demand to talk about sex, to treat it as the core of one's being. The most forthright statement and, as we will see, the most relevant to understanding early twentieth-century Irish attitudes to divorce is Buck Mulligan's quip that Shakespeare's bequeathing Ann Hathaway his "secondbest bed" suggests they were divorced, "*separatio a*

[9] Bloom's exchange with Hornblower, the Porter at the Lincoln Place entry to Trinity College, takes place in his mind.

[10] Michel Foucault, *The History of Sexuality*, trans. Robert Hurley (1976; London: Penguin, 1990), 1: 17–49. Such repression is "emblematic of what we call the bourgeois societies" (17).

mensa et a [sic] *thalamo*" (9.716). Mulligan offers this comment during the later stages of the discussion about Stephen Dedalus's theory of Shakespeare's creativity that is taking place in the National Library while Bloom is examining back copies of the *Kilkenny People*. Equally significant for the reader are Father John Conmee's thoughts about the moral implications of the legal definition of adultery—*eiaculatio seminis inter vas natural mulieris* (ejaculation of semen within the natural female organ)—that crosses his mind in "Wandering Rocks" as he thinks about the book he is considering on the life of Mary, first Countess of Belvedere, who was accused of committing adultery with her brother-in-law.

And while Mulligan's quip is presumably uttered well outside Bloom's hearing and Father Conmee's thoughts are not shared with anyone but the reader, both become part of the reader's understanding of Irish attitudes toward divorce as *Ulysses* is read sequentially from "Aeolus" to "Wandering Rocks." The legal implications of Mulligan's quip, the significance of Mulligan uttering it, and the significance of Father Conmee's thoughts about what constitutes adultery will be examined later in this chapter. But for the moment it is worth noting that both Shakespeare's desertion and the Belvederes' divorce are relevant to the Blooms only to the extent that they draw attention to the fact that despite matrimonial causes being treated as a civil matter in the Scottish jurisdiction since the Reformation and in the English jurisdiction since 1857, Ireland rigorously retained its adherence to ecclesiastical law with respect to adultery and divorce.

Yet adultery, and to some extent divorce, refused to be silenced. What gave them voice were the various imperial monuments that dominated the inner city. Associated with each was an unofficial history, circulated as local lore via anecdote, gossip, and legend that delighted in naming infidelity.[11] So it is not surprising that adultery is on Bloom's mind as he goes about his business; and it should not surprise the alert reader to find an association between adultery and divorce begin to emerge as Bloom traverses a cityscape that memorialized sexual liberation.

[11] W. B. Yeats drew attention to the O'Connell, Parnell, and Nelson monuments when he delivered his speech on divorce to the Senate on 11 June 1925. *The Senate Speeches of W. B. Yeats*, ed. Donald R. Pearce (London: Faber and Faber, 1971), 97–102.

This chapter will show how Bloom's anxiety about Molly's appointment with Boylan in "Aeolus," "Lestrygonians," and "Wandering Rocks" is periodically intensified by stories of adultery, associated with the various people he encounters, recalls, or glimpses. Some of these resonate with divorce. The chapter will also show how the intensity of allusions to adultery and the association with divorce relates to the various statues and buildings he passes, the more so since he has to foot it round the city in an unrewarding and stigmatized job. It will propose that Bloom's much criticized indecisiveness is in fact a predictable response of a colonial subject committed to probabilistic inductive reasoning in a Catholic society that paradoxically gave covert license through confession and contrition to what it sought most rigorously to suppress. Bloom's indecisiveness, in fact, chimes with the current state of divorce proceedings. As evidenced by reports in the Irish press, the English jurisdiction was still coming to terms in 1904 with the ways "presumption of innocence," "evidential burden," and "legal burden" pertained to divorce proceedings.[12]

So each time Bloom recovers from a bout of anxiety about his marriage, as he crosses and re-crosses the city from Sackville Street to Ormond Street in the course of his work, and each time he begins to explore memories of happier times with Molly and Milly, some allusion to adultery or divorce so discombobulates him that he becomes anxious or has a panic attack.

* * * *

"Aeolus" opens with trams destined for the suburbs being marshaled before Nelson's Pillar and closes with Stephen Dedalus's *A Pisgah Sight of Palestine* or *The Parable of the Plums* with its quip that Nelson should be known as the "onehandled adulterer."[13] Devising such soubriquets continues to be a traditional Dublin pastime. As today's visitor soon discovers, the Oscar Wilde statue in Merrion Square is known as the "fag on the crag," the

[12] Claire Hamilton, *The Presumption of Innocence and Irish Criminal Law: "Whittling the Golden Thread"* (Dublin: Irish Academic Press, 2007), 2–5.

[13] Michael Groden, "Genetic Joyce: Textual Studies and the Reader," in *Palgrave Advances in James Joyce Studies*, ed. Jean-Michel Rabaté (London: Palgrave Macmillan, 2004), 227–31, gives a list of interpretations of Stephen's parable other than the above.

Anna Livia fountain as the "floozy in the jacuzzi," the statue of Joyce himself as "the prick with the stick," and so on. Stephen's parable, however, is multi-layered. Literally, it refers to Nelson losing an arm during an unsuccessful assault on Santa Cruz de Tenerife in July 1797. "Onehandled" rather than "onehanded" seems to be a rather jejune attempt to perpetuate the masturbation imagery that runs through Stephen's jibes at Imperialism. "Adulterer" literally refers to Nelson's extra-marital affair, which began in September 1798, with Emma Hamilton, the young wife of Sir William Hamilton, the British envoy to Naples. The newspapers of the day made much of her living openly with Nelson in a *ménage à trois* and having two children by him after she refused to divorce her elderly husband.[14]

Politically, Nelson's pillar symbolizes the imperial gaze. To obtain the best view of Dublin, the two old women, Stephen's "vestal virgins," must climb to the top. What they achieve, however, is not a vista of the seventh city of Christendom but *A Pisgah Sight of Palestine*, an allusion to the Biblical story that God denied Moses the right to enter the Promised Land because of his failure to rebuke the Israelites for their idolatry.[15] In terms of Ireland's now parlous economy, Stephen's parable also satirizes the eagerness with which Dubliners subscribed to the commemoration of Nelson's 1805 defeat of the Franco-Spanish fleet so soon after the event. The pillar, which dominated Sackville (now O'Connell) Street, was designed, funded by public subscription, and erected in 1808–1809, several decades before its better-known namesake in Trafalgar Square.[16] The inference is that the rush to commemorate the defeat of Ireland's traditional allies, Catholic France and Spain, by a notorious adulterer so soon after the 1798

[14] Joyce had a copy of E. Hallam Moorhouse's *The Story of Lady Hamilton* (London: T. N. Foulis, 1911) in his library. Ellmann, *Consciousness of Joyce*, 120.

[15] See AV, Numbers 20:12; Deuteronomy 32:51. The "promised land" also alludes to the Zionist ambition for a Jewish homeland. Note advertisement for the "model farm at Kinnereth" that Bloom reads that morning in the butcher's (*U*48.154–55). For Kinnereth as a successful socialist experiment, see Isaiah Friedman, *Germany, Turkey, and Zionism, 1897–1918* (Oxford: Clarendon Press, 1977), 134–35.

[16] Yvonne Whelan, "Monuments, Power and Contested Space: The Iconography of Sackville Street (O'Connell Street) before Independence (1922)," *Irish Geography* 34, no. 1 (2001): 15–20.

Rising and the enforced Union of Hearts of 1800–1801 is so craven as to merit the old women spitting their plum stones on the city below. And it offers a riposte to Professor MacHugh's assertion, made earlier in the conversation, that the Irish "are liege subjects of the catholic chivalry of Europe that foundered at Trafalgar" and to Myles Crawford's dismissing Stephen's Dubliners as "two old trickies" (7.566; 7.1009). Not so! Stephen's parable insists: the Irish are in fact liege subjects to the British Empire and the Roman Catholic Church. The two old women are not prostitutes but "vestal virgins." The analogy that Stephen draws with Moses affirms that Nelson's Pillar is Ireland's golden calf, an expensive idol to a foreign god that has distracted the nation from its true goal of self-realization.

The extent to which adultery permeates the *mentalité* of the city is further illustrated by the allusion to Davy Stephens's popular nickname, "the king's courier." The nickname derives from a conversation Stephens was alleged to have had when Edward VII purchased a newspaper from him at Kingstown in July 1903. It mischievously aligns Stephens with M. Fehr, the "King's courier," the royal agent personally responsible for making all of the King's travel arrangements and famous for attending to all of his needs.[17] Although Edward VII, true to his soubriquet of "Edward the Peacemaker," made several efforts to placate nationalist outrage that his visit, so soon after the Boer War, coincided with the Emmet centenary, his reputation as a philanderer would later prompt the Citizen to remark in Bloom's presence that there is "a bloody sight more pox than pax in that boyo" (12.1400–1). So, whether Bloom walks by Nelson's Pillar, which it would be difficult for him to avoid as it commanded Sackville Street, or whether Davy Stephens aka "the king's courier" walks past him, he is being alerted, whether consciously or subliminally, to intimations of adultery. But it is not quite as simple as that.

[17] "When the King came to Town," *Galway Advertiser*, 12 May 2011, http://www.advertiser.ie/galway/article/39668/when-the-king-came-to-town; Cóilín Owens, "July 1903: Edward VII, the Gordon Bennett Cup and the Emmet Centennial," *History Ireland*, accessed 19 July 2016, http://www.historyireland.com/20th-century-contemporary-history/july-1903-edward-vii-the-gordon-bennett-cup-and-the-emmet-centennial/.

While the reader can be certain that Stephen Dedalus is aware of Nelson's associations with adultery and divorce (after all, he conjures a parable about it), it is uncertain whether the same associations occur to Bloom. It is even more uncertain whether Bloom, or Stephen for that matter, will recall Edward VII's philandering even if he thinks of Davy Stephens as "the king's courier." The same is true of Bloom's memory of Ned Lambert's family connection to "the right honorable Hedges Eyre Chatterton" (1819–1910), the Vice-Chancellor of Ireland. Bloom associates Chatterton with influence and money and wonders whether or not Ned Lambert will benefit from a "windfall" when the old Judge dies. But, in 1904 Dublin, the Judge was also renowned for the dubious honor of having Temple Street, infamous for prostitution, officially renamed Chatterton Street, purportedly in his honor. It was suspected locally that the renaming was actually in revenge for the Judge's granting an injunction against the Dublin Corporation and then unwisely attacking them when they attempted to rename Sackville Street as O'Connell Street.[18]

Thus, reading the Dublin that Bloom encounters involves relating Stephen's Dublin and Bloom's Dublin to all the other images of Dublin in *Ulysses* in order to reach an understanding of the fictional city. As Cheryl Herr pointed out in her pioneering work on *Joyce's Anatomy of Culture* many years ago, one of the challenges but also one of the delights of reading *Ulysses* is to discover details of how the vast network of cultural allusions relate to one another. Again, Hugh Kenner and many others since have remarked the significance of "parallax," a word whose meaning temporarily bothers Bloom, as a "key organizing (or disorganizing) motif" in the book.[19] While several of the allusions to adultery and divorce in "Aeolus" occur when Bloom is not present, their occurrence nevertheless alerts the reader to the ways in which these issues haunt the Dublin that Bloom traverses in the course of his working day and the way they contribute to the construction of Bloom and to the book's multiperspectivity.

[18] W. N. Osborough, *Law and the Emergence of Modern Dublin: A Litigation Topography for a Capital City* (Dublin: Irish Academic Press, 1996), 49, 181–84. Subsequently renamed Hill Street.

[19] Kenner, *"Ulysses"*, 73–76. See also Luke Gibbons, "Spaces of Time through Times of Space: Joyce, Ireland and Colonial Modernity," *Field Day Review* 1 (2005): 79–82.

For example, behind the reference to Archbishop Walsh's two telephone calls that are reported in Bloom's presence is the Editor's undisguised preference for the pro-Parnellite Cardinal Logue and hence his willingness to overlook Parnell's adulterous relationship with Katharine O'Shea. But by the time Stephen gives the Editor Deasy's letter and the Editor calls Deasy an "old pelters" (archaic: a whoremonger) and makes a crude joke about Deasy's estranged wife, Bloom has left the group to telephone Alexander Keyes. During the conversation that ensues between Stephen and the newsmen in Bloom's absence, there are further allusions to adultery: to Hamlet's "beast with the two backs" and to the unrepentant Francesca da Rimini's adultery with her brother-in-law, Paolo Malatesta, for which Dante condemned them to the second circle of Hell, a circle reserved for the lustful. Lines are quoted from Friedrich von Flotow's light opera *Martha* (discussed in detail in Chapter 4) and from a popular song where a young widow asks her son to accommodate her fancy man: "Tommy, make room for your uncle, /I want him to sit here" (7.264–65). And Stephen Dedalus privately recalls his own encounter with a prostitute in Fumbally's Lane off Blackpitts: "Damp night reeking of hungry dough. Against the wall. Face glistening tallow under her fustian shawl. Frantic hearts.... Quicker, darlint!" (7.927–29).

The conversation in the newsroom is also interlaced with mythical and historical allusions to deception, sexual liaisons, adultery, and divorce. There are references to Pyrrhus, who was reputedly killed by a prostitute in Argos; to Helen of Troy, "the runaway wife of Menelaus" (7.536–37); and to Derbforgaill or Dervorgilla (1108–1193), whose clandestine correspondence with and subsequent abduction by Diarmait Mac Murchada, King of Leinster, in 1152, was popularly believed to have brought the Anglo-Normans to Ireland. Napoleon's courting of Marie Josèphe Rose Tascher de la Pagerie, a divorcee with a reputation, whom he married and then divorced, is recalled as "Madam, I'm Adam. And Able was I ere I saw Elba" (7.683). But the most famous divorce case alluded to in "Aeolus" (7.741–45) is *Brooke v. Bushe* (49 & 50 Vict., c.181). As Justice Adrian Hardiman explains,

> In 1886 a wealthy Dubliner, Mr Gerald Brooke, obtained a parliamentary divorce from his wife, formerly the Honourable Kathleen Maude, daughter of Viscount Hawarden, on the grounds that on 2 October 1885 she did "elope with Seymour Bushe, of Ely Place, Dublin, Barrister-at-Law, with whom she has since lived and cohabited in a state of adultery." The private

> divorce bill which became Brooke's Divorce Act 1886 chronicles the extraordinary rapidity with which, between October 1885 and the following June, Brooke obtained a divorce *a mensa* from his wife, a decree for a £1000 damages for criminal conversation against Bushe the very next day, and subsequently a parliamentary divorce.[20]

Later in the conversation, Stephen's pun on "poor Penelope Rich" refers to the wife of Lord Rich (ca. 1581), a favorite of Sir Philip Sidney, who formed a liaison with Lord Mountjoy (ca. 1594), by whom she had several children. When Lord Rich divorced her after the execution of her influential brother Robert Devereux, the second Earl of Essex, she admitted her adultery, and though her divorce was granted, she was forbidden to remarry or to retain custody of her children because, this being 1601, she was subject to ecclesiastical law. Notwithstanding, she and Mountjoy persuaded William Laud, afterwards Archbishop of Canterbury, to marry them in 1605 in a private ceremony. Their marriage, however, was short-lived, Mountjoy dying the following year and Penelope two years later.[21] Stephen will refer to her again as he develops his theory that Shakespeare's art derived its complexity from adultery, sex, and betrayal (9.639). For the reader, it is worth observing that both cases are alluded to in Bloom's absence and that while both cases involved parliamentary divorces that provoked scandal and led to ostracism and financial hardship, the respondents in both cases were also accorded a measure of understanding as time passed.[22] This would be small comfort to Bloom, because he is not privy to the conversation. But what is revealed by the allusions to adultery and divorce that emerge in his absence is that both topics are firmly lodged within the *mentalité* of the city in terms of Ireland's continued adherence to the principles of

[20] Hardiman, "Law, Crime and Punishment," 61–62. As Hardiman points out, the recitals to 49 & 50 Vict., c.181 provide the history of events leading up to the divorce.

[21] Joyce had a copy of Maud Stepney Rawson, *Penelope Rich and Her Circle* (London: Hutchinson, 1911) in his library. Ellmann, *Consciousness*, 125.

[22] "It is true she spun many a web, that she was faithful—though not to her lawful Ulysses. But she had not the full reward of the faithful. Neither was her lord a fit Ulysses. That role fell to another man." Rawson, *Penelope Rich*, 1, https://archive.org/details/cu31924027985427.

ecclesiastical law. Finally, Mr. O'Madden Burke's quip that Madam Bloom was "Dublin's prime favourite" (7.610), also uttered in Bloom's absence, is sufficiently ambiguous to signal to the reader that Molly might have something of a reputation, even if it is only street gossip circulated among the male "bladderbags" of the newspaper office.

Allusions to adultery continue to intrude on the narrative, though with increasing complexity, as the reader passes from "Aeolus" to "Lestrygonians" to rejoin Bloom. He is now on his way to the National Library in Kildare Street. While still in Sackville Street, he is handed a "throwaway" by a YMCA youth advertising a meeting by the visiting American evangelist Alexander Dowie. Bloom immediately thinks "polygamy" and notes, "His wife will put the stopper on that" (8.17–18). Shortly after, musing on the Roman Catholic prohibition of birth control, he yields to the sectarian commonplace that priests are able to advocate chastity because housekeepers cater for their sexual needs. Arriving at the Liffey, he sees an advertisement for off-the-peg trousers, which prompts him to think of the way a local quack, Dr. Hy Franks, illegally advertises his clinic for the treatment of venereal diseases by placing posters in urinals.[23] Hy Franks is purportedly based on Henry Jacob Franks, who arrived in Dublin in 1903, having deserted his wife and four children in Manchester. The association causes a moment of panic. Does Boylan have venereal disease? Will he infect Molly? And though Bloom immediately counters the thought—"No, no. I don't believe it. He wouldn't surely? No, no"—the thought clearly disturbs him. While the willful and deceitful transmission of venereal disease was

[23] "Whoever affixes to or inscribes on any building, hoarding, gate, fence, pillar, board, tree, or any other thing whatsoever, so as to be visible to a person passing along any street, highway, or footpath, and whoever affixes to or inscribes on any public urinal, or delivers or attempts to deliver, or exhibits, to any person in any street, public highway, or footpath, or throws down the area of any house, or exhibits to public view in the window of any house or shop, any picture or written matter of an indecent or obscene nature (including any advertisement relating to syphilis or the like) will be liable to a penalty of 40s, or to imprisonment for a month, with or without hard labour. (52 & 53 Vict. c.18, §§3,5)." *Every Man's Own Lawyer*, 577.

considered very serious, as is evident in *Slater v. Slater* (1902),[24] *Bennett v. Bennett* (1902),[25] and *Curl v. Curl* (1902),[26] it was deemed an act of cruelty rather than an assault, with the consequence that an action for damages could not be brought. In *Hegarty v. Shine* (1878),[27] the court ruled that

> the concealment alleged to have vitiated the plaintiff's consent, as having been fraudulently obtained, did not consist of deceit as to the nature of the act to be done, and no duty of disclosure was imposed by the relations of the parties to each other as being legally enforced. *Held*, further, that an action of such a character was not maintainable or fit to be tried in a court of justice, because the injury complained of was directly consequent of willful immorality, and, though founded in tort, came within the maxim—"*ex turpi causâ non oritur actio.*"[28]

While it would be unreasonable to expect Bloom to know the legal consequences of Molly's liaison, the fact that he has a French letter concealed in one of his pockets indicates that he has taken care to protect himself.[29] As Catherine Heffernan has argued, given that "social fears about 'the great scourge' (syphilis and gonorrhea)" had, by the turn of the twentieth century, "escalated into a panic that syphilis was at the root of all diseases," preserving "oneself from venereal disease became the mark of a good citizen who took personal

[24] *Slater v. Slater*, NA J77/753/2912, Filed: 9 June 1902; Set Down: 19 September 1902; Decree Nisi: 8 December 1902; Final Decree: 13 July 1903.

[25] *Bennett v. Bennett*, NA J77/753/2920, Filed: 11 June 1902; Set Down: 24 October 1902; Decree Nisi: 19 January 1903; Final Decree: 27 July 1903.

[26] *Curl v. Curl*, NA J77/753/2926, Filed: 12 June 1902; Set Down: 4 July 1902; Decree Nisi: 24 October 1902; Final Decree: 4 May 1903.

[27] *Hegarty v. Shine* (1878) 4 LR Ir 228.

[28] *Irish Law Times Digest of Cases*, cols. 2 and 3, §2.

[29] David Fitzpatrick, *The Two Irelands 1912–1939* (Oxford: Oxford University Press, 1998), 227, points out that while advertising contraceptive devices was illegal from 1929, their importation and sale did not become illegal in Ireland (Free State) until 1935.

responsibility for his own sexual health and the health of the nation."[30] Rates of infection in Dublin in 1904 were very high;[31] there were no effective cures, the resumption of a normal marital relationship was severely compromised. But that Bloom so quickly abrogates his moral and connubial responsibility for cautioning his wife about sexually transmitted disease is disturbing, the more so since he does this by resorting to a memory about her request for information. In an attempt to banish his fear, he smiles to himself as he recalls Molly's protestation of "O rocks... Tell us in plain words" when he tried to explain the meaning of metempsychosis to her that morning (4.343). Yet he himself still feels vulnerable.

As he crosses Westmoreland Street, he calls to mind the happy times when he, Molly, and Milly were living in Lombard Street West.

> Happy. Happier then. Snug little room that was with the red wallpaper. Dockrell's, one and ninepence a dozen. Milly's tubbing night. American soap I bought: elderflower. Cosy smell of her bathwater. Funny she looked soaped all over. (8.170–73)

But even then there were shadows. "What was the name of that priesty-looking chap was always squinting in when he passed?" Bloom asks himself (8.176–77). Recalling that it was "Pen something," he first thinks of Pendennis, Thackeray's mollycoddled protagonist whose imprudent love affairs almost brought about his ruin, but then he remembers that the name was Penrose. As if to confirm his suspicions, hours later, lying awake in bed, Molly recalls Penrose "nearly" catching her "washing" her engorged breasts at the time she was still breast-feeding Milly (18.573–75).

As Bloom passes the offices of the *Irish Times* at 31 Westmoreland Street, his reveries about Molly and Milly are abruptly brought to an end by Josie Breen's greeting: "O, Mr Bloom how do you do" (4.203). As

[30] Catherine Heffernan, "Sexually Transmitted Infections, Sex and the Irish" (D. Phil. diss., Oxford University, 2002), 55. See also *Royal Commission on Venereal Disease: Final Report of the Commission* (London: His Majesty's Stationery Office, 1916).

[31] Heffernan, "Sex and the Irish," 37, 58–60, 65–71, 105–7, 109–15, 118–20; Ferris, *Burden of Disease*, 83.

Josie once competed with Molly for his affection, Bloom reflects kindly on the ways she has been affected by an unfortunate marriage, though he cannot suppress a ribald image of her as "rhubarb tart with liberal fillings, rich fruit interior" (8.273). She appears exhausted by childbearing, and this prompts him to pass from thinking sympathetically about the way drugs might ease childbirth to a crude comparison with Queen Victoria: "Nine she had. A good layer" (8.379). His recollection of the divorced Spanish American Miriam Dandrade is even more ribald: "Want to be a bull for her. Born courtesan. No nursery work for her, thanks," the final thought a fantasy about Miriam Dandrade's imagined preference for obligation-free sex (8.356–57). Moments later, when he sees a flock of pigeons wheel past the Bank of Ireland, he recalls his school friends nicknaming him "Mackerel" (8.405; 15.3331), which is Dublin slang for a pimp. The question of whether or not he has turned pander for his own wife, as we will see, continues to trouble him for the rest of the day.

Reaching College Green, Bloom "crosses over under Tom Moore's roguish finger" and thinks of the irony of erecting a monument to the poet who wrote "Meeting of the Waters" over a public urinal. The contrast between Moore's "fragile eroticism" and the methods employed by the Castle and the Nationalists to gather intelligence about one another's activities crosses his mind. He imagines the way flash plain-clothes policemen use sexual advances to extract intelligence from young female servants—"maul her a bit"—and compares it with the milder but equally insidious approach of the young Nationalist who sidles up to the kitchen maid with the line "there are great times coming, Mary" (8.454). In Grafton Street, the sight of John Howard Parnell prompts memories of his brother's infamous divorce. Because Parnell had chosen not to defend the proceedings or, according to his brother, had been "persuaded . . . not to do so," witnesses were not cross-examined, and evidence was not tested, with the result that the newspapers felt free to publish whatever was presented in court.[32] It has been claimed that "the evidence rendered

[32] John Howard Parnell, *Charles Stewart Parnell: A Memoir by His Brother John Howard Parnell* (New York: Henry Holt, 1914), 233. See also Katharine O'Shea, *Charles Stewart Parnell: His Love Story and Political Life* (New York: Doran, 1914), 147; F. S. L. Lyons, *The Fall of Parnell, 1890–91* (London: Routledge and Kegan Paul, 1960), 65–70; Paul Bew, *Enigma: A New Life of Charles Stewart Parnell* (Dublin: Gill and Macmillan, 2011), 164–67.

Parnell ludicrous as well as dishonourable."[33] Bloom then thinks about the scandals attached to surgeon McArdle, a notorious womanizer, and the rumors about the poet and literary mentor AE's alleged affair with Susan Mitchell.[34] Speculating about how he can finesse an introduction to the present Astronomer Royal, Professor Charles Jasper Joly (1864–1906), Bloom wonders whether he should do some research on the Professor's ancestry in the belief that great men always feel complimented when you know something about their rise to fame. And though his mind runs on to "Flattery where least expected. Nobleman proud to be descended from some king's mistress. His foremother. Lay it on with a trowel" (8.375–77), it is uncertain whether Bloom is mentally debunking influence or innocently confusing Charles Jasper Joly with the first Astronomer Royal, John Mortimer Brinkley (1763–1835), the illegitimate son of Sarah Brinkley, a butcher's daughter from Woodbridge, Suffolk.[35] The keyword here is "foremother," because a bastard technically remains fatherless unless legally acknowledged. It was a common belief in Dublin at the time that Brinkley's father was not John Toler but the 1st Earl of Norbury (1745–1831), for some twenty-seven years Chief Justice of the Irish Common Pleas and the Judge responsible for sentencing Emmet to death.

Passing "La Maison Claire," the court dressmaker at Number 4 Grafton Street, Bloom is seized by a momentary panic as he recalls walking by the Tolka with Boylan and Molly about a fortnight before, hearing Molly humming a line from Moore's "The Young May Moon" and Boylan responding with the answering line, all the while suspecting they were playing patty-fingers. As with his fear that Boylan might have a venereal disease, Bloom immediately imposes an iron grip on himself: "Stop. Stop. If it was it was. Must" (8.592). I will examine these and other panic attacks shortly and how they might be read in the light of Bloom's consideration, "divorce, not now." But for the present, it is sufficient to remark two of the thoughts that help to calm him. The first, depicted as "With ha quiet keep quiet relief" (8.594), signals Martha Clifford as a compensatory

[33] Frank Callanan, *The Parnell Split 1890–91* (Cork: Cork University Press, 1992), 9.

[34] George Moore threatened to "out" Russell until Russell threatened him with a lawsuit. See Adrian Frazier, *George Moore, 1852–1933* (New Haven, CT: Yale University Press, 2000), 368, 558 n. 236.

[35] John Venn, "John Brinkley," in *Biographical History of Gonville and Caius College 1349–1897* (Cambridge: Cambridge University Press, 1898), 2:107–8.

fantasy, while the second, about Bob Doran maintaining a sober demeanor by indulging himself once a year with "streetwalkers," points to a strategy that Bloom himself seems to have experimented with at least once. But he banishes this thought with a searching recollection of what he suspects has caused the change in his relationship with Molly: the death of their only son Rudolph, Rudy, when he was only eleven days old. "I was happier then. Or was that I? Or am I now I?" he asks himself. "Twentyeight I was. She twentythree. When we left Lombard street west something changed. Could never like it again after Rudy. Can't bring back time. Like holding water in your hand" (8.608–11). As we have seen, this is one of the most incisive and revelatory comments that Bloom makes about his marriage, though sexual indifference is not the only cause of their problems. Paradoxically, what most calms him is the realization that he cannot prevent Molly and Boylan from having an affair. They are free agents with desires, appetites, and drives. At that time of the day, the possibility that they will have sex seems as inevitable as the urgency of "the stream of life" that flows round him in the street. All the merchandise on display, from the flimsy China silks in Brown Thomas's to the perfume worn by the women he passes, insist on sensuality and assert sex.

That a light lunch might prove diverting turns out to be delusory. The masses of men gobbling their food in the Burton repels him, and so he orders a gorgonzola cheese sandwich garnished with mustard and a glass of burgundy in Davy Byrne's, but the palliative effect is compromised by Nosey Flynn's enquiries about Molly and the proposed concert in Belfast; his enquiry about the latter phrased as "who's getting it up?"

> —Ay, now I remember Nosey Flynn said, putting his hand in his pocket to scratch his groin. Who is this was telling me? Isn't Blazes Boylan mixed up in it?
>
> A warm shock of air heat of mustard haunched on Mr Bloom's heart. He raised his eyes to stare at the bilious clock. Two. Pub clock five minutes fast. Time going on. Hands moving. Two. Not yet.
>
> His midriff yearned then upward, sank within him. Yearned more longingly, longingly.
>
> Wine.
>
> He smellsipped the cordial juice and, bidding his throat strongly to speed it, set his wineglass delicately down.
>
> —Yes, he said. He's the organiser in point of fact.
>
> No fear: no brains. (8.786–98)

The extent of Bloom's anxiety can be gauged by the fact that in attributing "no fear" to Nosey Flynn, he is assuming that Flynn must know something about Boylan and Molly, but is so insensitive he feels he can talk about them openly. Though Flynn's seemingly innocent remark, his food-stained clothing, and the way he snuffles up the drips from his nose repel Bloom, he nevertheless momentarily wonders whether women like cold noses and prickly beards, as he will shortly wonder what sex is like for a blind person.

Out in the street, such musings are interrupted by the sight of Sir Frederick Falkiner K. C., a character based on the Recorder of Dublin, a renowned anti-Semite, entering the Freemason's Hall in Molesworth Street. In 1902 Falkiner had addressed Henry Kahn, a tobacconist who was a Polish Jew, when he sentenced him to a year in prison for breaking windows in retaliation for persecution: "You are a specimen of your nation and your race that cause you to be hunted out of every country."[36] Bloom remembers it as a "strawcalling," Dublin slang for an excessive tongue lashing, though he attributes the incident to Reuben J. Dodd, the subject of an anecdote related in the carriage on the way to Paddy Dignam's funeral.[37] Though the Judge's remarks prompted a question in the House of Commons,[38] Falkiner was not censured, the trial was not deemed a miscarriage of justice, and the sentence was permitted to stand.[39] Having been sharply reminded that Jews were not always regarded kindly in Ireland, Bloom is even more disconcerted when he glimpses "a straw hat in sunlight" once he enters Kildare Street from Molesworth Street. His immediate reaction is one of extreme anxiety. It is as if all the allusions to adultery that he has encountered since he left the

[36] Sir Frederick Falkiner was the Recorder of Dublin from 1876 to 1905. See Hardiman, "Law, Crime and Punishment," 73–74 for a more positive account of Falkiner.

[37] As Robert Boyle, "A Note on Reuben J. Dodd as 'a dirty Jew,'" *James Joyce Quarterly* 3, no. 1 (1965): 64–66, points out, Dodd was not a Jew, but his activities as a money-lender led him to be described as one. According to Ellmann the Joyce family blamed Dodd for their financial plight.

[38] "Dublin Recorder and Prisoner: HC Deb 23 January 1902 vol 101 c689," http://hansard.millbanksystems.com/commons/1902/jan/23/dublin-recorder-and-prisoner#S4V0101P0_19020123_HOC_238.

[39] "Dublin Recorder and Prisoner."

Freeman's offices for the National Library, allusions that have persistently disrupted his memories of happier times, now come to rest in the one person—Boylan.

That Bloom should react as strongly as he does might, on first reading, seem somewhat surprising, because this is the second time that coincidence has brought him into proximity with Boylan. The first, when "the straw hat flashed reply" to Jack Power's greeting on their way to the funeral, was comparatively easy for him to ignore, partly because the carriage concealed Boylan and partly because his view of Boylan and Boylan's view of him was obstructed by Simon Dedalus leaning across Bloom in the carriage. The coincidental meeting in Kildare Street, however, is potentially much more confronting. It promises to be face-to-face, something Bloom understandably wishes at that point to avoid. At various times between Sackville Street and Kildare Street, he has deliberately refused to surrender to panic attacks. On two occasions he has consciously decided against returning to 7 Eccles Street on a pretext. The first is when he recalls the three of them walking by the Tolka (8.592). The second is when he is momentarily overcome by the eroticism of "gleaming silks, petticoats on slim brass rails, rays of flat silk stockings" (8.631–32). Having steeled himself against intervening in something he strongly suspects is about to happen, he has no wish at that point in the day to be given the impression, by Boylan's demeanor, dress, speech, or body language, that the affair will inevitably take place. There are still two hours to go before Boylan's proposed meeting with Molly.

In part, Bloom is a victim of his predilection for "Sherlockholmesing," with its investigative technique of probabilistic inductive reasoning. As someone who will eventually consider divorce as a possibility, he seems more interested in building a case than forcing an issue to a conclusion, even if circumstances would seem to favour such a course of action. There is enough of Hamlet in his makeup to ensure that he is the type of person who hesitates more than once before "taking arms against a sea of troubles."[40] There is no doubt that Molly's concealing Boylan's letter from him when he brings her breakfast in bed arouses his suspicions, but it seems that he prefers not to intrude on her privacy or to assume the right to question her. Though her concealing

[40] *Hamlet*, 3. 1. 58.

the letter under the pillow while leaving "a strip of torn envelope" in view is something he observes, it is simply allowed to remain one piece of evidence that must wait for other pieces of evidence to emerge before any conclusion can be drawn and actions taken. Bloom prefers explanations that remain probable. That the letter is addressed to Mrs. Marion Bloom is something that strikes him as "bold," but he suspects that others might not see it like that. Ambiguities that emerge during the few conversations that Bloom has during the morning and early afternoon might not be windlestraws but false inferences drawn from his own insecurity and anxiety. What he first glimpses in Kildare Street, "Straw hat in sunlight. Tan shoes. Turnedup trousers.... Yes, it is. The walk," at best indicates a stylish dresser and perhaps a sense of confidence bordering on bravura.[41] But it does not constitute evidence that Boylan is determined on adultery, though in 1904 to wear "turned up trousers," or trousers with cuffs, was to imitate Edward VII, well known in Dublin as a philanderer. But Bloom is too much a hostage to emotion to persist beyond the minimum markers of recognition. What we next read is that his "heart quopped softly." It is uncertain whether or not his palpitations cause him to blush, but if they do, Bloom himself believes it will reveal the effect of the glass of burgundy he drank in Davy Byrne's about half an hour before. "Wine in my face. Why did I? Too heady." Arguably, what emerges from this defensive self-appraisal is more a sense of inadequacy than cowardice, a sense that causes him to take "long windy steps" towards the museum and hurry inside so he can feel safe.

His avoidance behavior is also a result of the extent to which Bloom has become absorbed in his own plans. While he is in Davy Byrne's, he observes the pub clock, is aware that it is five minutes fast, and thinks, "Time going on. Hands moving. Two. Not yet" (8.791). About to leave, he reflects on his gorgonzola cheese sandwich and glass of burgundy as "just a bite or two" and thinks "then about six o'clock I can. Six. Six. Time will be gone then. She" (8.852–53). But Bloom's

[41] See Sonya Glyn Nicholson, "A Second Look at Trouser Turnups (Cuffs)," Parisian Gentleman, 24 July 2013, http://parisiangentleman.co.uk/2013/07/24/a-second-look-at-trouser-turnups-cuffs/; and Xavier Paoli, *My Royal Clients*; trans. Alexander Teixeira de Matos (London: Hodder and Stoughton, 1911), 210–11, https://archive.org/details/myroyalclients00paoluoft.

planned future is as selective as his reconstructed past. For at least two hours, his memories of Lombard Street West and his fantasies about Martha Clifford—memories and fantasies he has been able to rekindle each time they have been challenged by encountering references to adultery or divorce—have reconstituted themselves in a desired present. Now, when he least expects it, Boylan, who embodies an anticipated future, unexpectedly appears. Since it is between three-thirty and four in the afternoon and Boylan's office is in D'Olier Street, just the other side of Trinity, and since Bloom suspects Boylan will call at Number 7 Eccles Street at four, it is perhaps not surprising that Bloom would encounter him, even if he thought Boylan was not the type of person to visit libraries and museums.

The encounter with Boylan is also congruent with a sense of meaninglessness that had threatened to overwhelm him as he was passing the front of Trinity College. As Brian Cosgrove has remarked of Bloom, though in another context, "the contradictoriness inherent in the world is a matter not just of the world's bewildering plenitude, but of the recurrent incongruities of our experience."[42] The rush of traffic, the press of people in the street, the remorselessness of movement and of time's cycles of birth and death all threaten to bear down on him like a juggernaut. "Dignam carted off," he thinks.

> Mina Purefoy swollen body on a bed groaning to have a child tugged out of her. One born every second somewhere. Other dying every second. Since I fed the birds five minutes. Three hundred kicked the bucket. Other three hundred born, washing the blood off...
>
> Cityful passing away, other cityful coming, passing away too: other coming on, passing on. Houses, lines of houses, streets, miles of pavements, piled up bricks, stones. Changing hands. This owner, that. Landlord never dies they say. Other steps into his shoes when he gets the notice to quit. They buy the place up with gold and still they have all the gold...
>
> No-one is anything. (8.479–93)

* * * *

Having scampered into the Kildare Street Museum to avoid Boylan, Bloom then makes his way across the front of Leinster House to the

[42] Cosgrove, *Joyce's Negations*, 93.

National Library so that he can consult the *Kilkenny People* about Keyes's ad. He enters the Upper Reading Room just as T. W. Lyster, the head librarian, makes a remark to a group who have gathered around Stephen Dedalus to listen to his argument that Shakespeare forged his plays from his own life and times, whether it was loss, betrayal, revenge, sexual conquest, or financial success; that "all events brought grist to his mill" (9.748). Shakespeare's "myriadmindedness" is thus a reflection of the cosmopolitanism of his age and the breadth of his personal experience. Summoned, Lyster then momentarily leaves the group in his office to attend to Bloom's enquiry.

Though Bloom and Stephen are now in the same building, they are a room apart. The father who has lost a son has still to meet the son who, while purportedly in search of a father, is nevertheless still questioning whether paternity is a fiction riddled with complexities and fatherhood a myth militantly perpetuated by patriarchy. That morning, when Haines had asked what he meant by having to serve an Italian master, Stephen had replied that he was referring to the "holy Roman catholic and apostolic church" (1.644). Recalling to himself the Church's brutal suppression of heresies that had challenged the doctrine of the Trinity, Stephen suspects that defending patriarchy has served both British Imperialism and the Church militant with a time-honored way of exercising power, of maintaining hegemony. Returning to what he had earlier given a passing thought, Stephen now begins to use his knowledge of Shakespeare to advance various arguments about the ways patriarchy and creativity might relate to one another. Ostensibly for the purposes of his own aesthetic, these arguments nevertheless raise two issues that are foremost in Bloom's mind—adultery and the death of a son.

The "Scylla and Charybdis" episode is thus significant for understanding the extent to which sex and divorce color the *mentalité* of 1904 Dublin and for understanding the ways in which Stephen's desire to forge an aesthetic critiques and parallels Bloom's desire to come to terms with Rudy's death and the increasing possibility that Molly will commit adultery. Though the discussion generated by Stephen's theories is initially not quite as ribald as the morning's conversation in the *Freeman's* office, it becomes mockingly scatological once Buck Mulligan appears. But before Mulligan joins the four representatives of the Dublin literary establishment who have been drawn into the discussion—AE, John Eglinton, Richard Best, and T. W. Lyster—Stephen seizes the opportunity to develop his argument that Shakespeare's sole stage appearance as the Ghost in

Hamlet, as well as the play itself, should be interpreted in terms of the poet's response to his son's death and his wife's adultery with his brother, Richard Shakespeare. His argument is not that the plays were therapeutic or that art simply imitated life but that experience and creativity are coeval. Somehow, and this is what Stephen struggles to theorize, the play *Hamlet* and the death of Shakespeare's son Hamnet share a common origin, as do the role of Gertrude's and Ann Hathaway's adultery. To simply attribute such a process to fate is to deny the inexplicable plenitude of human existence and to leach creativity of its spontaneity. To label the common origin the "void" is to remove the corporeal from creativity. To privilege the body as the site of creativity is to place spirituality under erasure.

Stephen thus faces two significant problems. The first is to understand the nature of patriarchy; the second is to pursue an argument that does not become entangled in paradox. But in trying to develop a masculine counterpart to the feminine typology of the word becoming flesh in the virgin womb of the imagination, where word as λογος encapsulates both the spiritual and the linguistic, Stephen finds himself increasingly drawn to dealing with the prohibitions and prescriptions culture places on patriarchy, particularly incest and adultery, and what is permitted as revenge or retribution. Arguing that the Christian commandments merely amplify Jewish law and custom, with the implication that Jewish husbands exercised much more power over adultery than their Christian counterparts, Stephen queries,

> Whether these be sins or virtues old Nobodaddy will tell us at doomsday leet. But a man who holds so tightly to what he calls his rights over what he calls his debts will hold tightly also to what he calls his rights over her whom he calls his wife. No sir smile neighbour shall covet his ox or his wife or his manservant or his maidservant or his jackass. (9.787–91)

The most powerful counter to patriarchy, he further argues, is paternity: "The son unborn mars beauty: born, he brings pain, divides affection, increases care. He is a new male: his growth is his father's decline, his youth his father's envy, his friend his father's enemy" (9.854–57).

Stephen's theories provide a critique of Bloom's predicament in that Stephen tries to forge an aesthetic from the very experiences that Bloom is about to live through. Stephen's idea that experience and creativity are coeval and yet independent of fate, causality, or coincidence, even though they coexist in a symbiotic relationship, mirrors Bloom's recurrent concern that he is responsible in some unknown way for Rudy's death and that he has perhaps unwittingly facilitated Molly's affair with Boylan or that it is fated. Stephen's insistence on paternity as a mystical estate, a biological fact, and a cultural fiction offers a sharp corrective to Bloom's sentimental attitude to fatherhood and his unresolved grief. Finally, Buck Mulligan's boisterous interjection that creativity as parturition is merely a masturbatory fantasy and that onanism is the only way to achieve sexual consummation not only effectively subverts Stephen's arguments but is also proleptic of Bloom's compensatory encounter with Gerty MacDowell later that evening.

* * * *

In the meantime, "The Wandering Rocks" returns both Bloom and Stephen to the streets of Dublin. It is now 3 p.m., barely an hour before Boylan's meeting with Molly. Adultery and divorce continue to figure in the life of the city and its people. As he sets out to read his breviary in the countryside, Father John Conmee allows his mind to wander to a book he is contemplating on Mary Rochfort, first countess of Belvedere, accused of adultery in one of the most infamous divorce cases of the eighteenth century. In 1743 Robert Rochfort, the Earl of Belvedere, was informed that his attractive twenty-three-year-old wife, Mary, was involved in a liaison with his married younger brother, Arthur. Relations between the Belvederes had become strained, though they had only been married for seven years. Mary preferred to remain at Gaulstown House with their three children, while Robert, highly regarded by George II, pursued his political career in London. Mary is said to have first admitted and then denied the adultery, though it is uncertain whether she did so under duress or in the mistaken belief that a guilty plea would facilitate a divorce.[43] Arthur also denied the accusation,

[43] A. P. W. Malcomson, *The Pursuit of the Heiress: Aristocratic Marriage in Ireland 1740–1840* (1982; Belfast: Ulster Historical Foundation, 2005), 148. See also John Charles Lyons, *The Grand Juries of the County of Westmeath… [1727–1853], with an Historical Appendix* (Ledestown: privately printed, 1853), 273–85, http://www.askaboutireland.ie/aai-files/assets/ebooks/129_Grand-Juries-of-County-Westmeath/129%20Grand%20Juries%20of%20County%20Westmeath%201727-1853.pdf.

but when a case for *crim. con.* for the almost unprecedented sum of £20,000 went against him, he fled the country.[44] Faced with transportation, Mary appealed to her father, but he is alleged to have denounced her as illegitimate, with the result that she was handed over to her husband.[45] Instead of proceeding with a divorce, Robert, now Viscount Belvedere, promptly confined his wife to Gaulstown House. After several years she contrived to escape, but she was betrayed, returned to Gaulstown, and for the most part confined to a single room. When her husband eventually died in November 1774, it is claimed that Mary, taken on a restorative tour of Europe by one of her sons, sought refuge in a French convent where she converted to Catholicism, though this claim has been vigorously refuted. What is certain is that she returned to Ireland to live with her son, who had inherited the title, and then with her daughter. It is also claimed that on her deathbed, "after partaking of the communion," she "confirmed, with the most solemn oath, her perfect innocence of the crime for which she had been made to suffer."[46]

Father Conmee, however, seems unmoved by what one contemporary described as "cruelty unparalleled in the annals of domestic life." Instead, he fantasizes about himself as "Don John Conmee," "humane and honoured," the guardian of "secrets confessed," and imagines the Countess as "listlessly walking in the evening" alone on "the shore of lough Ennel." In fact, before her escape the Countess was confined to the demesne; after, she needed her husband's permission to leave her room and then only on condition that she was guarded by a bell-ringing servant shouting obscenities at her. But what at that moment engages the Jesuit priest are issues of testimony and evidence. "Who would know the truth?" he asks himself. "Not the jealous lord Belvedere"; because he had not sued for divorce after winning his suit for *crim. con.*, whether or not adultery had been committed had not

[44] Malcomson says £2,000; Lyons £20,000. The "action of Viscount Bellfield against his brother Mr Rochfort in 1740, in which the Viscount was awarded the totally unprecedented damages of £20,000, which in the end put his brother in gaol for the rest of his natural life." Lawrence Stone, *The Road to Divorce* (Oxford: Oxford University Press, 1990), 269.

[45] Malcomson, *Pursuit of the Heiress*, 148–49.

[46] See Denis O'Neill, "The Earl of Belvedere," Rochfortbridge, accessed 23 July 2016, http://rochfortbridge.wikidot.com/the-earl-of-belvedere.

been tested in court. "Not her confessor," Conmee goes on to think. If she had confessed after she allegedly converted, her confessor would be bound by the confidentiality of the confessional. Would that confession, he wonders, drawing on his own experience of hearing confessions, have been truthful, and would it have been a full confession? Would "she half confess if she had not all sinned as women did?" At issue here is the legal definition of adultery: "*eiaculatio seminis inter vas natural mulieris*" (ejaculation of semen within the natural female organ). Since the Countess's adultery is alleged to have taken place while she was a Protestant, she might have engaged in sexual activity other than full consummation as legally defined. For a Catholic, however, such activity, even if only contemplated, would still constitute a mortal sin.

Having opened his breviary, Father Conmee is about to begin reading *nones* when he encounters a young man followed by a young woman emerging from a gap in the hedge. The young man is "flushed" but raises his cap "abruptly," while the young woman, who is carrying some "wild nodding daisies," stops and abruptly detaches a "twig" from her "light skirt." Despite the indications of something illicit, Father Conmee, still indulging himself with an image of the power to forgive, simply blesses them both gravely and walks on. The young man, it later emerges, is Stephen's friend Lynch, who, much later in the company of drunken medical students, boasts that he had propositioned the young woman, Kitty, for sex (14.784–98; 14.1495–96). But, as with the Belvedere case, what actually took place on the other side of the hedge bordering the Malahide Road remains uncertain. Lynch's flushed appearance on seeing the priest, Kitty's "light skirt," and the knowledge that "twig" in Dublin slang means "do you understand" point to an assignation, as does Lynch's reputation as a womanizer; but Lynch is very drunk when he makes the claim; the daisies Kitty carries denote "innocence"; detaching a twig from a skirt hardly amounts to rearranging one's clothing; and the two have not emerged from the hedge in a way that would indicate intimacy. The juxtaposition of the historical case and the contemporary incident serves to remind the reader about the twin perils of applying *post hoc, ergo propter hoc* reasoning and unleashing revenge when faced with "evidence" purporting sexual indiscretion, perils that Bloom will face throughout the day.

While Father Conmee continues to read his breviary, Bloom arrives at the bookstalls by the Liffey Bridge, also known as the "Metal Bridge." Originally named the Wellington Bridge (the Iron Duke is known to have "sought solace elsewhere" during his marriage), it is now known as the Ha'penny Bridge, the name honoring the original toll after all the fees were suspended in 1919. Molly has asked Bloom to look for something slightly more salacious than the novel she has just finished, *Ruby: The Pride of the Ring*, which, as she has assured him, "has nothing smutty in it."

At the same moment that Bloom begins leafing through *The Awful Disclosures of Maria Monk* (1836) before turning to examine some of the plates in Aristotle's *Masterpiece* (1694), Father Conmee reaches the 21st section of Psalm 119 in his breviary: "*Sin:—principes persecute sunt me gratis: est a verbis tuis formidavit cor meum*" (Princes have persecuted me without a cause: but my heart standeth in awe of thy word, Psalm 119:161). This contrived simultaneity, even while sexualizing Father Conmee, positions the priesthood as defenders of the sacrament of marriage despite the scurrility of sectarianism and the secularist commodification of sexuality. The *Disclosures* were said to be Maria Monk's personal account of sexual exploitation and ritual infanticide during her novitiate with the Black Nuns of Montreal. Though the book was immediately discredited as a hoax, as just another lurid Gothic horror, it rapidly became an international best-seller, appealing as it did to the heightened sectarianism generated by Catholic emancipation in the United Kingdom, increased Catholic emigration to Canada and America, and militant turn-of-the-century Evangelical Protestantism. In fact, the more rabid the sectarianism, the more *Disclosures* was given credence. The *Masterpiece*, which Bloom lingers over, was "apparently the most widely circulated work of pseudosexual and pseudomedical folklore in seventeenth and eighteenth century England."[47] After rejecting Leopold von Sacher Masoch's *Tales of the Ghetto* (1885) and a flagellation novel by James Lovebirch, *Fair Tyrants*, Bloom is aroused by *Sweets of Sin*, which he buys with the assurance from the bookseller that it is a "good one" (10.641).

[47] Gifford with Seidman, *"Ulysses" Annotated*, 271. See also H. M. Hatch, *Popery Unmasked: Showing the Depravity of the Priesthood and the Immorality of the Confessional; Being the Questions Put to Females in Confession Extracted from the Theological Works now Used by Cardinal Wiseman, His Bishops and Priests, as Quoted in "The Confessional Unmasked," together with Extracts from Dowling, Hogan, and Maria Monk; Showing the Crimes Committed in the Black Nunnery and a Description of the Horrid Inquisition Rooms, with Notes* (Lowell, MA: H. M. Hatch, 1854), 29–33, 48–50, https://ia600401.us.archive.org/21/items/poperyunmaskedsh00hatc/poperyunmaskedsh00hatc.pdf.

To read *Ulysses* sequentially from "Aeolus" to "Wandering Rocks" is to be made aware that there are significant reasons why Bloom feels increasingly anxious about his marriage. As a socially stigmatized Jew in colonial Dublin, a city mapped as intensively by commodified sexuality and memorialized adultery as it is by Imperialism, Bloom has a limited number of choices available to him. As the time approaches four o'clock in the afternoon, the time when Boylan is supposed to arrive at 7 Eccles Street, those choices are diminishing. To be present just before Boylan arrives might simply delay what is inevitable. To confront Molly with or without Boylan is to act on assumptions that might be unwarranted and might well prove alienating and destructive. He can't attempt to surprise them *in flagrante* by himself as this could be dismissed as his word against theirs, although as in *Jolly v. Jolly and Fryer* (1919), a "decree of divorce founded on adultery can be made although on medical evidence there can only have been partial intercourse."[48] He can't stage a discovery because one or the other or both might accuse him of complicity. Yet to discount his premonitions is to ignore those shadows that coming events seem to cast, shadows that he has encountered a number of times during the day.[49] Though memory can furnish him with a narrative, it is powerless to take him beyond the present. None of his social interactions seem to offer anything decisive. They all appear to be honeycombed with ambiguities.

Several divorce cases from 1904—which is not to claim that they were known either to Bloom or to Joyce—reveal how important it was for the petitioner not to act precipitately, because "the burden of proof lay on the petitioner."[50] In *Mendoza v. Ruben* (1901), the Judge, who seems to have enjoyed fly-fishing, denied a request for a retrial on the grounds that the petitioner had "struck too early."[51] In *Rogerson v. Rogerson and Drummond* (1904), the petition was dismissed on the grounds that, even though the petitioner had employed a private detective, the evidence to

[48] *Jolly v. Jolly and Fryer* (1919) 63 SJ 777.

[49] Shelley, "A Defence of Poetry," affirms that "poets are . . . the mirrors of the gigantic shadows which futurity casts upon the present."

[50] Mr. Justice Gorell Barnes reported summing up *Palgrave v. Palgrave and Lutifer*, *Times* (London), 15 July 1904, 14.

[51] *Times* (London), 14 December 1901, 15.

prove his case was inadequate, and his petition was dismissed. Costs of £46-19-11 and £6-10-6 were awarded against him.[52] *Palgrave v. Palgrave and Lutifer* (1904) and *Abrahams v. Abrahams and Neuberger* (1903) also show the consequences of acting precipitately or acting on suspicion rather than evidence.[53] *Evans v. Evans* (1902), however, cautions against proceeding where the respondent can cite misconduct. In this case a *decree nisi* granted to the petitioner on 29 July 1902 was rescinded with costs in January 1904 on the grounds that the petitioner's "willful neglect and misconduct on his part . . . had conduced to the adultery of the respondent."[54] Finally, as pointed out in Chapter 1, in *Roberts v. Roberts* (1904), which was reported in the *Freeman's Journal* on 11 August 1904, "His Lordship, in giving judgment, found that the charge of misconduct against the respondent had been proved, but that the counter charge against the petitioner was also true. The petition of the husband must therefore be dismissed."[55]

As committed as he is to probabilistic inductive reasoning, Bloom's only realistic alternative is to continue to "Sherlockholmes" in the hope that he will acquire sufficient evidence to substantiate adultery beyond the bounds of probability. But he remains uncertain that this is what he actually wants

[52] "Musician as Co-Respondent," *Daily Mail*, 2 June 1904, 3 and "Fond of Detective Work," *Daily Mail*, 1 June 1904, 3. *Rogerson v. Rogerson and Drummond*, NA J77/800/4341, Filed: 4 November 1903; Set Down: 2 June 1904; Dismissed: 1 June 1904.

[53] *Palgrave v. Palgrave and Lutifer* (1904), NA J77/806/4512. See *Times* (London), 14 July 1904, 3–4; "Art and Divorce," *Daily Mail*, 14 July 1904, 3; "Wife Exonerated," *Daily Mail*, 15 July 1904, 3. *Abrahams v. Abrahams and Neuberger* (1903), NA J77/798/4289.

[54] "*Evans v. Evans and Wilson*—The King's Proctor Showing Cause," *Times* (London), 23 January 1904, 4. In delivering his judgment, Sir Francis Jeune cited *St Paul v. St Paul* (1 P&D 739) and *Cunnington v. Cunnington and Noble* (1859) 164 ER 820. See *Evans v. Evans and Wilson*, NA J77/744/2629, Filed: 25 February 1902; Set Down: 6 April 1903; Decree Nisi: 29 July 1903; Rescinded and Dismissed: 22 January 1904.

[55] "The Roberts Divorce Suit Judgment," *Freeman's Journal*, 11 August 1904, 3. *Roberts v. Roberts and Sanlon and Nixon*, NA J77/794/4147, Filed: 10 August 1903; Set Down: 31 December 1903; Decree Nisi: 10 August 1903; Dismissed: 10 August 1904.

to do. As he leaves the bookstall on Aston Quay and begins to walk down Wellington Quay, Bloom spots Boylan's hat in the distance. He immediately decides: "Follow. Risk it. Go quick. At four. Near now" (11.305). Though this is one of his most purposeful actions since he had left his house that morning, the place he will enter will prove to be just as impregnated with stories of adultery as the cityscape through which he has just passed.

CHAPTER 4

"Bloowho" and Silence

"Sirens" dramatizes the final opportunity Bloom has to engage Boylan before Boylan visits Molly at four o'clock on 16 June 1904. So it is not surprising that Bloom remains conflicted and on edge for the hour he is in the Ormond Hotel. "Sirens" is also the episode that departs most markedly from the mimetic realism of the episodes that precede it. Reading Bloom becomes a matter of responding to the interplay of text, context, intertext, and metatext as he endeavors "to persist" in his own being.[1] It is in "Sirens" that the reader moves from encountering "Bloo . . . Me? No." (8.8), which the narrator of "Lestrygonians" quickly identifies is a misunderstanding, to "Bloowho" (11.86), where the implied interrogative "who" subverts the truncated proper noun "Bloo" to signal a sequence of fluid reconfigurations of identity.

What has not been recognized to date is that the episode marks the first time Bloom begins to entertain thoughts about the legal implications of his predicament. This chapter will examine two of these thoughts as they relate to the seductive power of operetta and popular song as it attempts to persuade him to allow its lyrics to speak for him and its melodies to acculturate his attitude to adultery. Should he or should he not respond to Martha Clifford's *billet-doux*? His initial response to her suggestion that they "Could meet one Sunday after the rosary" is "Try it anyhow. A bit at

[1] Spinoza, *Ethica Ordine Geometrico Demonstrata*, Part III, On the Origin and Nature of the Emotions, Proposition VI.

P. Kuch, *Irish Divorce / Joyce's Ulysses*,
DOI 10.1057/978-1-137-57186-1_4

a time" (5.270; 5.274). But if he does agree to meet her, would he be encouraging a relationship that might unexpectedly turn into a civil suit for breach of contract or a suit for breach of promise? His advertisement, even if it is a thinly disguised way of seeking a partner for erotic correspondence, is nevertheless couched as an offer of employment. Surely, if his request for secretarial help is genuine, and he wished to avoid suspicion, he would have gone through an agency. Is he in danger of entrapment, of being set up for blackmail, or could he be furnishing material evidence that might prove damaging if he was to proceed with a divorce? There were a sufficient number of breach of promise cases reported in the Irish and British press between 1900 and 1904 for them to lodge in Bloom's mind. For example, the *Freeman's Journal* of 17 June 1904, the next day as it were, published a long article on *Delaney v. Burke*, a Gaelic Leaguer's trial for breach of promise.[2]

* * * *

Despite his soubriquet "slyboots," Bloom writes his letters to Martha Clifford by hand, although he attempts to disguise his authorship by substituting Greek "e's" for the Roman ones he usually employs (11.889). That this ruse is almost certain to fail is evident from *Evans v. Thomas* (1903), where the petitioner and her friend fabricated a correspondence about the respondent only to have their deceit exposed by an expert graphologist, with the result that the petitioner had her case dismissed while her friend was sentenced to prison with hard labour.[3] As we will see, Bloom's additional attempts to disguise his correspondence with Martha Clifford echo several breach of promise cases reported in the newspapers in the early 1900s.

Martha Clifford takes the precaution of typing her letters and typing the address on the envelope, so it might be difficult but would not be impossible to identify her as the author, should the letters be subpoenaed as evidence. In an 1891 story, "A Case of Identity," Sherlock Holmes obtains a note composed on a typewriter he suspects has been used for

[2] Collier, *Modernism on Fleet Street*, 130. See Hardiman, "Law, Crime and Punishment," 69–70 for a discussion of the case.

[3] "South Wales Circuit—*Evans v. Thomas* for Breach of Promise," *Times* (London), 2 December 1903, 10.

producing all the typewritten correspondence in a breach of promise case and by comparing the correspondence with the typed note is able to identify the typewriter and the culprit.[4]

Letters were not the only source of evidence. While it was not "necessary that a promise of marriage be in express words, or in writing," as *Every Man's Own Lawyer* points out, "it may be proved by the conduct of the parties, and by a definite understanding between them and their friends that a marriage is to take place."[5] But in a number of cases letters proved to be the sine qua non. In *Mendoza v. Ruben* (1901), counsel's argument that the plaintiff and defendant lived so close to one another that it was not necessary for them to communicate by letter was dismissed.[6] In *Owen v. Moberly* (1900), despite the defendant supporting the plaintiff to the value of £300, promising marriage, and having a child by her, Mr. Justice Darling ruled that because all the correspondence between them had been retrieved and destroyed, paragraphs 32 and 33 Vict., c. 68, section 2 provided that

> "no plaintiff in any action for a breach of promise of marriage shall recover a verdict unless his or her testimony shall be corroborated by some other material evidence in support of such promise." If therefore the plaintiff's testimony was not corroborated by some other material evidence the case must be withdrawn from the jury. The only evidence in this case rested upon the statement of the plaintiff herself, and, therefore, the learned Judge said that there was no other material evidence except that of the plaintiff, and he was bound to withdraw the case from the jury.[7]

Damages could prove punitive. In *Roberts v. Scott*, where Scott was a doctor practicing in Kingstown, Dublin, the evidence contained in 348 letters confirmed an award of one thousand pounds for a broken engagement.[8] In *Ricketts v. Gaskell*, the plaintiff was awarded one thousand pounds and

[4] Arthur Conan Doyle, "A Case of Identity," *Strand Magazine* 9 (September 1891): 248–59; republished in *The Adventures of Sherlock Holmes* (New York: Harper, 1892), 38–50.

[5] *Every Man's Own Lawyer*, 365. See *Wiedemann v. Walpole* [1891] 2 QB 534; 60 LJQB 762; 40 WR 114; 7 TLR 722, CA.

[6] *Times* (London), 14 December 1901, 15.

[7] *Times* (London), 2 February 1900, 15; *Owen v. Moberly* (1900) 64 JP 88.

[8] *Times* (London), 17 July 1901, 10.

then a further one thousand five hundred pounds in a consolidated suit. It was reported that she had kept all his letters, even the undated ones.[9] *Allen v. Chivers* was decided in favor of the plaintiff on the evidence of seventeen letters,[10] while an undisclosed number of letters proved crucial in the plaintiff securing damages of four thousand pounds in *Mavro v. Craven.*[11]

Then there was the embarrassment of having the letters read out in court, with the juiciest extracts published in the press. Had Bloom opened the *Times* on 22 July 1901, he would have read that in *Thomas v. Young*, "A number of letters from the defendant to the plaintiff were read which were of a most amusing and amorous description."[12] *Frasier v. Spindelow*,[13] where the plaintiff sought damages of six hundred pounds, was even more fully reported:

> Mr Justice Darling asked if they could not have something different.
> Mr Gill read a letter in which the defendant said: . . .
> "Sweetheart, you gave me life, this worldly guest
> Fires both of us, yet our love is not depressed
> There is a garden somewhere in our years
> And when we reach it, oh, how we will rest."
> (Laughter) The letter concluded with 40 million kisses.
> Mr Justice Darling—What puzzles me is how anyone can keep such rubbish.
> Mr Gill—I am told there is a time in everybody's life when they keep such things.
> Mr Justice Darling—What age was your client when she received these letters?
> Mr Gill—About 40. It is a susceptible age, my Lord. (Laughter)[14]

That Bloom is aware of the practice of reading incriminating passages aloud in court is clear when he thinks to himself, "Chorusgirl's romance. Letters read out for breach of promise. From Chickabiddy's owny

[9] *Times* (London), 31 March 1903, 3.

[10] *Times* (London), 31 March 1900, 17.

[11] *Times* (London), 6 September 1900, 13.

[12] *Times* (London), 22 July 1901, 12.

[13] *Frasier v. Spindelow*, in "Forty Million Kisses; Widow's Action for Breach of Promise," *Daily Mail*, 19 March 1904, 3.

[14] *Times* (London), 19 March 1904, 4, continued 21 March 1904, 2.

Mumpsypum. Laughter in court. Henry. I never signed it. The lovely name you" (11.1078–80).[15]

Bloom's decision whether or not to reply is further complicated because, by following Boylan into the Ormond, he finds himself surrounded by music about love, sex, betrayal, forgiveness, and revenge. As a narratee in search of a narrative, Bloom must negotiate the sentimental lyrics and plots offered by popular song and comic opera as he fluctuates between constructing himself and being constructed. Will he allow music to speak for him, to determine his response? Employing a rhetorical device that will come to characterize his psychological and emotional turmoil in "Circe," the librettist advises the reader that it is "the bag" of the legal firm of Collis and Ward that leads Bloom into the hotel restaurant (11.390).

That Joyce claimed to write Bloom's and Boylan's intersecting trajectories as a "*fuga per canonem*," or using "all the eight regular parts of a *fuga per canonem*," or as a "fugue with all musical notations" is well known and has been much debated, as has "Sirens" read as an opera, an operetta, or a musical comedy.[16] However, I propose that "Sirens" has less to do with Joyce's use of a particular style of musical composition in which "three or four voices (more rarely two) enter imitatively one after the other, each 'giving chase' to the preceding voice,"[17] and more to do with the iteration that characterizes the *fuga per canonem* and the antagonism that characterizes the *fugue*. The two forms, though sometimes confused, are quite different. As Henriette Power has argued, "the songs within the narrative" of "Sirens" "make explicit not only the fictive nature of the text that frames them, but also the disjunction between voice and words."[18] "But most significantly," as Andrew Gibson has

[15] According to the *Times* (London) digital archive, there were some 250 breach of promise suits that came to court between 1900 and 1920.

[16] Susan Brown, "The Mystery of the *Fuga per Canonem* Solved," *Genetic Joyce Studies* 7 (2007), http://www.antwerpjamesjoycecenter.com/GJS7/GJS7brown.html. Jürgen E. Grandt, "'Might be what you like, till you hear the words': Joyce in Zurich and the Contrapuntal Language of *Ulysses*," *Joyce Studies Annual* 14 (2003): 74–91.

[17] *The Oxford Companion to Music*, ed. Alison Latham (Oxford: Oxford University Press, 2002), 493.

[18] Henriette Lazaridis Power, "Pantomime Songs and the Limits of Narrative in *Ulysses*," in *Picking Up Airs: Hearing the Music in Joyce's Text*, ed. Ruth H. Bauerle (Urbana: University of Illinois Press, 1993), 58.

emphasized, "Sirens" "is made of language, the English language warped, distorted, even brutalized, twisted out of true by the countervailing pressure of music."[19] Were he to petition for divorce, Bloom would find a comparable loss of voice and a comparable appropriation of his narrative by the court, as his plea would be required to be framed by rules of procedure and would be interpreted by legal precedent and Legislative Act.

* * * *

In "Sirens," the fictive nature of the text is foregrounded via iteration (as repetition, circularity, allusion, and quotation) and antagonism (as conflict, opposition, and resistance). Both describe ways in which popular music threatens to acculturate Bloom, to subsume and interpret his situation as just another aspect of human experience. Iteration describes the verbal patterning of the episode, particularly the way that Bloom's thoughts persistently return to Molly. As Sebastian Knowles has persuasively demonstrated, "all the songs serve to underscore the centrality of Molly Bloom."[20] Antagonism characterizes the tension that exists for Bloom between the lyrics he overhears, the feelings and emotions they arouse, and the siren promise that they will ease or explain his predicament. What all the lyrics express are feelings of estrangement, acceptance, forgiveness, reconciliation, deception, betrayal, loss, and revenge.

Each piece of music Bloom calls to mind or overhears contains at least two or three of these expressions arranged in a pattern. Deception, for example, might be allied with estrangement and loss in one piece of music and with forgiveness and reconciliation in another. The cumulative effect of these different but recurring combinations is to dramatize, momentarily seduce, and then offer to sentimentalize what is an intensely personal experience. Music for Bloom turns out to be not the "food of love" but an appetizer, whose flavors leave him unsatisfied to the point where he walks out before the end of Ben Dollard's "deepsounding" rendition of "The Croppy Boy." "Get out before the end," he thinks to himself; and

[19] Andrew Gibson, *Joyce's Revenge: History, Politics and Aesthetics in "Ulysses"* (Oxford: Oxford University Press, 2008), 106.

[20] Sebastian D. G. Knowles, "A Form Endearing: A Performance of Siren Songs; or, 'I was only vamping, man,'" in *Joyce in the Hibernian Metropolis: Essays*, ed. Morris Beja and David Norris (Columbus: Ohio State University Press, 1996), 217.

then, on reflection, "Glad I avoided" (11.1122; 11.1145). Though he had been moved some fifteen minutes earlier by Simon Dedalus's rendition of a popular version of "*M'appari*" from *Martha*, Bloom resists its siren call to sentimentalize his situation: "Too poetical that about the sad. Music did that. Music hath charms. Shakespeare said. Quotations every day of the year. To be or not to be. Wisdom while you wait" (11.904–6).

Silence and surveillance, if the critical literature on the "Sirens" episode is an indication, are not aspects the reader immediately associates with Bloom's response to the increasing certainty of Molly's pending adultery. Yet they are at the core of the episode, as they are in all of Joyce's work, in which, as Maud Ellmann shrewdly notes, "the rival modalities of ear and eye are constantly competing for supremacy."[21] The classical parallel that informs the episode should also alert the reader to the significance of silence and surveillance. In Book 12 of *The Odyssey*, Odysseus fashions beeswax earplugs for his crew,[22] and he then has himself lashed to the mast so that he will not yield to and his crew will not hear the "enchanting sounds" of the Sirens' song: what Robert Fagles has memorably translated as their "urgent call."[23] What the beeswax earplugs ensure is that Odysseus's ship is a site of sound and silence. What the triangular relationship between the Sirens, the crew, and Odysseus ensures is multiperspectivity. What the passage of the ship past the island ensures is a discrete experience. And what the ropes ensure is that Odysseus is prevented from following the Sirens' "honeyed voices" with their promise that

> We know all the pains that the Greeks and Trojans once endured
> On the spreading plain of Troy when the gods willed it so—
> All that comes to pass on the fertile earth, we know it all.[24]

[21] Maud Ellmann, "The Music of Joyce's Vernacular Voices," *Modernism/Modernity* 16, no. 2 (2009): 383.

[22] The advice is given to him by Circe. The deafened crew is ironically echoed by bald Pat, the waiter, "hard of hearing," and Miss Kennedy's plugging "both two ears with little fingers" so she will not hear Miss Douce's anecdote about "that old fogey in Boyd's" (*U*11.129–30; *U*11.124–25).

[23] Homer, *The Odyssey*, trans. Robert Fagles (New York: Viking Penguin, 1997), 12.215.

[24] Homer, *Odyssey*, 12.205–7.

As we have seen from the previous chapter, Bloom has deliberately avoided confronting Boylan even though their paths have crossed. With the time approaching four o'clock, he now seizes the opportunity to follow his rival to the Ormond, though for what purpose beyond surveillance remains uncertain. Bloom's conflicted selection of his point of vantage is represented as "Aimless he chose with agitated aim ... a table near the door" (11.391). What remains uncertain throughout the episode is the extent to which Bloom is in command of his feelings and emotions, despite his evident intention to conceal them from Richie Goulding. What he thinks about what he feels and the ways his emotional experiences affect him remains private.[25] What is certain is that he does not say anything to Boylan and that he does his best to stay out of sight. What is also certain is that the siren-call of music, with its rhythms, cadences, and lyrics, whether popular, vaudevillian, light classical, operatic, or nationalist, is something he eventually walks away from.

* * * *

The Ormond is full of sociable sound—of drinking, eating, talking, giggling, laughing, singing, and applauding; of glasses clinking, cups rattling, beer pulls gushing, corks popping, the dinner bell going "tink," coins ringing, the cash register clanging, the clock clacking, and Miss Douce's garter going "thwack"; all punctuated by the ambient sounds of the city street—yet Bloom keeps to himself. Though it is doubtful whether he joins in the applause for Simon Dedalus's rendition of Lionel's song from *Martha*, it is clear that he does not join in the singing or in the sociability that follows.[26] When he does sing, it is to himself and in his head: "Lionel Simon, singer, laughed. Father Bob Cowley played. Mina Kennedy served. Second gentleman paid. Tom Kernan strutted in. Lydia, admired,

[25] Antonio Damasio, *Looking for Spinoza: Joy, Sorrow, and the Feeling Brain* (Orlando, FL: Harcourt, 2003), 28: "Emotions play out in the theater of the body. Feelings play out in the theater of the mind." See also Antonio Damasio, *Self Comes to Mind: Constructing the Conscious Brain* (New York: Vintage, 2010), 116: "Emotion and feeling, albeit part of a tightly bound cycle, are distinguishable processes." I am indebted to Kerri Haggart for drawing my attention to Damasio's work and to the distinction he draws between feelings and emotions.

[26] "Lionel's air in *Martha M'appari*, which, curiously enough, he had heard or overheard, to be more accurate, on yesterday" (*U*16.1756–60).

admired. But Bloom sang dumb" (11.774–76). It is a moot point grammatically whether "dumb" is to be read as transitive or intransitive; that is, whether Bloom's singing in his head renders him "silent or unheard" (*OED* transitive; Bloom as agent), or whether he becomes "speechless or silent" as a result of a spontaneous singing in his head that has begun by itself (*OED* intransitive; Bloom as acted upon). Though the distinction will become significant for the way we read Bloom reading himself as he responds to musical cues about how he might react to Molly's pending adultery; as far as the patrons of the Ormond are concerned, Bloom is as silent as he is inconspicuous. No one, apart from deaf Pat the waiter and Richie Goulding, appears to be aware that he is in the restaurant.

Even his nervous "looped, unlooped, noded, disnoded" playing with the "elastic band" that he removes from the packet in his pocket makes almost no contribution to either the music or the social buzz of the Ormond Hotel. The memory of Martha Clifford's question, "Are you not happy in your?" proves too much for his distracted performance, and the elastic band simply yields a despairing "Twang" before it snaps (11.811). Instead of sound, as we will see, Bloom's "teasing" of "the curling catgut line" provokes him into thinking about how much sex and music rely on intervals of silence (11.830–46)—the post-coital and the dying fall. These musings are sequences of observations that follow what he remembers, overhears, or is prompted to hear: "That voice was a lamentation. Calmer now. It's in the silence after you feel you hear. Vibrations. Now silent air" (11.793–94). Again, the reader is not sure whether Bloom thinks that it is in the silence after you feel, you hear, or whether it is in the silence after, you feel you hear—feel in the first case meaning feeling that you have felt or in the second case meaning you gain the impression, perhaps misleading, that you hear.

Either way, were the situation to be recorded for sound, Bloom's presence would hardly register a decibel. In an episode that comprises some 12,340 words, the narrator, who is best thought of as a librettist, attributes only twenty-two spoken words to Bloom and accords him only twelve words (three sets of four) of indirect speech. It is what Bloom experiences in the Ormond and gains from that experience rather than what he contributes that is the key. Granted his *monologue intérieur*, the dialogue of the mind with itself,[27] comprises some 3,400 words or slightly

[27] Dorrit Cohn, *Transparent Minds: Narrative Modes for Presenting Consciousness in Fiction* (Princeton, NJ: Princeton University Press, 1978).

more than a quarter of the episode, but this is mediated by the librettist who relates it in what Emile Benveniste famously denominated "the middle voice," where, grammatically, "the verb indicates a process centering in the subject, the subject being inside the process."[28] For example, the librettist characterizes Bloom's listening as "Instance he's playing now. Improvising. Might be what you like, till you hear the words. Want to listen sharp. Hard. Begin all right: then hear chords a bit off: feel lost a bit" (11.838–40).

The clause "hear chords a bit off" suggests Bloom is mentally performing the piece in anticipation of its actual performance; yet, when the actual performance does not chime with his expectation, he no longer continues to be, as it were, "inside" it. What this means is that we spend at least a quarter of the episode silently reading Bloom's musings, musings that are characterized by multiperspectivity, as he responds to a range of references, allusions, ironies, and memories. And, as if to remind us that we should not take this privilege or Bloom or ourselves as readers too seriously, the librettist concludes "Sirens" with a sequence of farts, heard apparently only by the reader and, naturally, Bloom. Although rhetoric and poetry, as we have already seen in "Aeolus," and music, as we see in "Sirens," evidence the divine afflatus, there are more ways of expressing air, as the librettist reminds us, than through the mouth.

Unlike Odysseus's crew, whose ears have been stopped with beeswax, it is the bar patrons and bar staff of the Ormond who hear and respond to the siren song of light opera, political ballad, practiced sociability, and the ritualized flirtatiousness of the barmaids. As Allan Hepburn has persuasively argued, "the operatic in *Ulysses* assumes its place within a general acoustic environment that defines the shared, dynamic unconscious of Joyce's Dubliners. What they cannot think, they convert into music, so that music stands as the Freudian *Unbewusste*, or 'unknown', component of identity that colors individual subjectivity and human interaction."[29]

[28] Cited in Denis Donoghue, "Is There a Case against *Ulysses*?" in *Joyce in Context*, ed. Vincent J. Cheng and Timothy Martin (Cambridge: Cambridge University Press, 1992), 27, citing Emile Benveniste, "Active and Middle Voice in the Verb," in *Problems in General Linguistics*, trans. Mary Elizabeth Meek (Coral Gables, FL: University of Miami Press, 1971), 145–51.

[29] Allan Hepburn, "*Ulysses*, Opera, Loss," *James Joyce Quarterly* 38, nos. 1–2 (2000–2001): 63.

Though Bloom, like Odysseus, allows the siren sounds of music to affect him, he is not seduced by its claim to encompass "all that comes to pass on the fertile earth." While he appears lost in his own thoughts, distracted, switching between one mood and another, thinking himself sad and lonely, and either unfamiliar with or ill at ease with the acculturated bonhomie of the bar, he nevertheless takes time to review what has happened that morning and what it seems is almost certain will take place shortly at his own home at 7 Eccles Street. Yet none of the memories, allusions, or associations prompted by the lyrics, the music, or the conversation enable him to narrativize his own situation. For Bloom, all remains uncertain, fragmented, partial, and frustratingly inconclusive.

The Ormond, however, is not the first time that we have seen Bloom elsewhere in company or found his social interactions punctuated by silences. McCoy, for instance, receives only half his attention when they meet in Westland Row around ten o'clock (5.82–194). Bloom chooses Davy Byrne's for lunch—"Moral pub. He doesn't chat" (8.732)—and is evasive when Nosey Flynn, who is already there, tries to strike up a conversation (8.737–936). He is distracted in his dealings with the bookseller on the Quays when he buys Molly a copy of Paul de Kock's *Sweets of Sin* (10.593–641).[30] And he does not even seem to acknowledge Simon Dedalus, who is already in the Ormond, even though he has shared a cab with him and with Martin Cunningham and Jack Power on their way to Paddy Dignam's funeral that morning. His interaction with Richie Goulding, who fortuitously invites him to join him in the Ormond for "something to eat" (11.356), is desultory at best.

> *Hello.* Where off to? Something to eat? *I too was just.* In here. *What, Ormond?* Best value in Dublin. *Is that so?* (11.356–57)

While elements of this exchange could be attributed to either Bloom or Goulding, the truncated syntax echoes the style of Bloom's fragmented musings, even though these musings do not have the energy that is derived from the way the librettist attributes the interrogative to an interlocutor in the few passages of recorded pre-speech that occur in the

[30] See Michael Crumb, "*Sweets of Sin*: Joyce's *Ulysses* and Swinburne's 'Dolores,'" *James Joyce Quarterly* 28, no. 1 (1990): 239–45. I am indebted to Tony Thwaites for drawing this article to my attention.

episode. To render these few exchanges in the same fragmented form as Bloom's musings suggests that even his limited social interactions occur largely in his mind rather than in the social story-world of the Ormond. The same is true of the single person Bloom associates with in the episode: Richie Goulding. The librettist characterizes their dining together as "Bloom with Goulding, married in silence, ate" (11.523); Goulding, of course, being Richie Goulding,[31] Stephen's uncle, himself the imperilled head of a house "of decay," is likewise removed the bonhomie of the occasion (3.105).[32]

In part Bloom's state of mind has to do with his intimation of inevitability, his sense of fate. Like his Homeric counterpart, his course of action is limited to what fate—as coincidence or destiny or the willpower of others—leaves open for choice, for that ingenuity that earns Odysseus the soubriquet of "wily and cunning" and Bloom the nickname "slyboots" (15.3586; 18.297).[33] What partially reconciles Bloom during his time in the Ormond to the seeming inevitability of Molly's affair is silence. It is not music or sociability or the assessment of feeling and the adjustment of emotion, or even actively calming his conflicting thoughts, but it is a silence that allows him to acknowledge that above and beyond whatever he does or does not do, there is some form of inevitability, some play of the hand of fate, some exercise of human will or urgency of the body against which he seems powerless.

Ever since leaving 7 Eccles Street that morning, the question of how to respond has proved as troubling as the question of whether or not Molly and Boylan will have sex. Returning unannounced, on however flimsy a pretext, might forestall an affair, but for how long? Attempting to spy on her might prompt Molly to become secretive. It might also provoke her to continue to act on what is being suspected as a way of affirming agency. Discovering Boylan and Molly *in flagrante delicto* would prove definitive,

[31] *U*6.56–62; *U*15.499–503.

[32] As Bloom is aware, Richie Goulding has already been openly disparaged by Simon Dedalus.

[33] For example, Circe informs Odysseus as he is about to leave:

> But once your crew has rowed you past the Sirens
> a choice of routes is yours. I cannot advise you
> which to take, or lead you through it all—
> you must decide for yourself. (Homer, *Odyssey*, 12.61–64)

but unless they were prepared to acknowledge their liaison, it would simply be his word against theirs.

In fact, his decision to go into the Ormond for a meal just before four o'clock, even though he has had a light lunch (8.697–98; 8.731–45; 8.936),[34] is the result of a double coincidence. Making his way along Wellington Quay after buying Molly a copy of *Sweets of Sin* from a bookseller on Aston Quay opposite the "halfpenny bridge," he spots Boylan's hat "from afar" as his "jaunting car" is crossing Essex Bridge.[35] Bloom decides, "Follow. Risk it. Go quick. At four. Near now" (11.305). Yet this decisiveness gives way to other feelings and emotions when he arrives at the entrance to the Ormond, minutes after his quarry: "Between the car and window, warily walking went Bloom, unconquered hero. See me he might. The seat he sat on warm" (11.341–42). Such proximity seems threatening, but by a second coincidence, Bloom catches sight of Richie Goulding, and his confidence immediately returns: "Black wary hecat walked towards Richie Goulding's legal bag, lifted aloft, saluting" (11.342–43). That it is the "legal bag" that salutes him suggests the law rather than the person is the preferred ally. In responding to Goulding's invitation to join him for a meal—even though he had earlier intended to dine at six o'clock (8.852–53)—Bloom reasons, "Diningroom. Sit tight there. See, not be seen. I think I'll join you" (11.357–58).

What follows is not evasion, cowardice, or a type of culpable voyeurism as some critics aver,[36] but it is very much in keeping with Bloom's strategy of assessment rather than intervention. Not that the restaurant at the Ormond proves to be the best point of vantage, even though he chooses a table by the door that opens onto the bar. By ordering a meal of liver and bacon and a bottle of cider from Pat the deaf waiter and eating and

[34] "He stood at Fleet street crossing. Luncheon interval. A sixpenny at Rowe's? Must look up that ad in the national library. An eightpenny in the Burton. Better. On my way" (*U*8.368–70); "Just a bite or two. Then about six o'clock. I can. Six. Six. Time will be gone then. She" (*U*8.852–53).

[35] Now Grattan Bridge.

[36] For example, Alan W. Friedman, *Party Pieces: Oral Storytelling and Social Performance in Joyce and Beckett* (Syracuse, NY: Syracuse University Press, 2007), 95: "contrasting with Bloom's passivity and sense of fatefulness, Boylan is in nearly constant motion"; and Peter Francis Mackey, *Chaos Theory and James Joyce's Everyman* (Gainesville: University Press of Florida, 1999), 161, who points to "Bloom's passivity in such a moment of opportunity."

drinking with Richie Goulding,[37] Bloom turns out to be as constrained spatially as Odysseus was physically. The internal arrangement of the Ormond, like hotels that held smoking concerts (11.277–78),[38] was one where the dining room and the saloon were separated from the bar in a manner that allowed the exclusively male audience at such events to overhear musical items in the restaurant and listen to them in the saloon without being unduly disturbed by noise from the bar.[39]

Bloom's spatial remove also signals his psychological distance from the bar. Concerned that his wife might well be about to have sex with Boylan, he is neither psychologically nor socially prepared to engage in the suggestive innuendo and flirtatious banter that characterizes the bar. Bloom is neither a gossip nor a raconteur. Even though his ready quips have got him into trouble with employers, his expressions of sexism are ocular rather than oral. His one notable attempt to socialize with Simon Dedalus, Jack Power, and Martin Cunningham on their way to Paddy Dignam's funeral by contributing an anecdote about "Reuben J and the son" conspicuously fails, as Simon Dedalus interrupts him and Martin Cunningham, fearing that the tale will be lost in the telling, thwarts "his speech rudely" (6.277). So it is hardly likely that Bloom would want to brave the public bar, even though it would enable him to engage if not confront Boylan. But like the "wily and cunning Odysseus," his choice is strategic, in Bourdieu's sense of someone possessing "*le sense du jeu*,"[40] even though it still leaves him prey to observation and supposition.

Ironically, as it turns out, Bloom's strategy of "see, not be seen" does not ensure invisibility. It would be possible for Simon Dedalus to see

[37] A meal that contrasts sharply with his earlier one of a glass of burgundy and a gorgonzola cheese sandwich.

[38] Jenny, "An Impromptu Smoking Concert was Held," *Endless Streams and Forests*, 30 July 2010, https://streamsandforests.wordpress.com/2010/07/; and FR, "Ireland, Charles Coborn and London's Smoking Concerts," John Ireland, accessed 23 July 2016, http://johnirelandmusicpeopleplaces.wordpress.com/2013/10/23/ireland-charles-coborn-and-londons-smoking-concerts/.

[39] For a detailed account of the history and layout of the Ormond, see Harald Beck, "Joyce's Ormond Hotel," James Joyce Online Notes, accessed 2 August 2016, http://www.jjon.org/joyce-s-environs/ormond.

[40] Lamaison and Bourdieu, "From Rules to Strategies."

Bloom when he returns to the bar to collect his pipe (11.478). While he is at the bar, Ben Dollard and Father Cowley gossip about the Blooms' domestic arrangements. Ben Dollard, recalling a time when they had gone searching for Bloom so he could borrow a pair of dress trousers, confides to Father Cowley,

> —I knew he was on the rocks, he said. The wife was playing the piano in the coffee palace on Saturdays for a very trifling consideration and who was it gave me the wheeze she was doing the other business? Do you remember? We had to search all Holles Street to find them till the chap in Keogh's gave us the number. Remember? (11.485–89)

Such gossip, that their financial situation was so straightened that the Blooms were trading second-hand clothes or that Molly was "doing the other business" (prostitution? /giving singing lessons? /modeling?), provides a further reason why Bloom would not want to confront Boylan or make Boylan conspicuously aware of his presence. To confront Boylan or even be pointedly seen by him, particularly in sight of Simon Dedalus, Ben Dollard, and Father Cowley, might see gossip become news and hearsay yield to the apparent confirmation of an eyewitness account.

Supposition continues to dominate his thoughts as he responds to the music he overhears as he dines with Richie Goulding.[41] "Sirens" is crammed with musical allusion. Zack Bowen has meticulously identified some 158 references to 47 songs.[42] But the pieces that exercise the strongest siren call for Bloom, in that they recur several times during his meal at the Ormond, are "Goodbye, Sweetheart, Goodbye";[43] Friedrich von Flotow's romantic comic opera *Martha, oder Der Markt zu Richmond* (1847),[44] especially

[41] "Sighing Mr Dedalus came through the saloon, a finger soothing an eyelid" (*U*11.440); "—*M'appari*, Simon, Father Cowley said. / Down stage he strode some paces" (*U*11.587–89).

[42] Zack Bowen, *Bloom's Old Sweet Song: Essays on Joyce and Music* (Gainesville: University Press of Florida, 1995), 128.

[43] Lyrics by Jane Williams (1806–1885) and music by John L. Hatton (1809–1886).

[44] "Martha: or, The Fair at Richmond by Flotow, Carle, Friedrich, and Baum," http://www.gutenberg.org/cache/epub/38597/pg38597.txt. Bowen, *Bloom's Old Sweet Song*, 27, points out that "Love's Old Sweet Song" and "*M'appari*" are mentioned thirty-two times in "Sirens."

Lionel's aria "*M'appari*" and its relationship to Vincenzo Bellini's *opera semiseria*, *La Sonnambula* (1831); and the 1798 nationalist ballad "The Croppy Boy."[45] Bellini's *La Sonnambula* and Flotow's *Martha* premiered in Dublin on 28 June 1837 and 9 April 1859 respectively, and both were frequently performed, ranking eighth and third respectively in the top ten operas staged in Dublin between 1840 and 1870.[46]

As Zack Bowen has observed, "Goodbye, Sweetheart, Goodbye" is being played by Simon Dedalus on the piano in the saloon as Boylan, followed moments later by Bloom, arrives at the Ormond. Though the song is not being sung, its significance is emphasized by the fact that seven fragments of lyrics from both stanzas are quoted during Boylan's short visit to the public bar. That Boylan is associated with the melody rather than the lyrics and that one of the lines from the song is misquoted is noteworthy. Instead of "And morn to floral lips doth hie," from the second verse, the misquote "*to Flora's lips did hie*" occurs at the point when Lenehan, with Boylan present, is urging Miss Douce to "sonnez la cloche." *Flora* is just one instance of the floriography that informs the episode; the carnation that Boylan wears, for example, represents health, vitality, and the fascination of the flesh (Latin: *carnatio*, fleshiness, corpulence).[47] After Miss Douce has surreptitiously performed for the two men, she rescues whatever dignity remains by directing "a smilesmirked supercilious" rebuke at the man she regards as her seducer. "You're the essence of vulgarity," she says to Boylan (11.416–17). Like the barmaid of late Victorian, early Edwardian culture, she possesses what Peter Bailey has termed "parasexuality"—a "sexuality that is deployed but contained."[48]

[45] The 1845 version by William B. McBurney (pseudonym of Caroll Malone).

[46] Rachel Cowgill and Julian Rushton, eds., *Europe, Empire, and Spectacle in Nineteenth-Century British Music* (Farnham: Ashgate, 2006), 110.

[47] *Oxford English Dictionary*, 3rd online ed., s.v. "carnation" gives three forms: carnation as an abbreviation of incarnation; carnation as flesh color, flesh tints, or a variety of cherry; and carnation as the name for the cultivated varieties of the clove-pink *Dianthus caryophyllus*. The *OED* also notes that the reason for these three forms is unexplained.

[48] Peter Bailey, "Parasexuality and Glamour: The Victorian Barmaid as Cultural Prototype," *Gender and History* 2, no. 2 (1990): 148.

What the italicized lyrics and the misquotation of "Goodbye, Sweetheart, Goodbye" imply is that Molly will be just another fleshy conquest in a series that has already seen Boylan flirting "gallantly" and "roguishly" with "the blond girl in Thornton's" when he was buying the potted meat, pears, and peaches to be delivered to 7 Eccles Street (10.327–29). Now, at the precise time he has agreed to meet Molly, he is again charming another woman to his will. That Bloom is in the street and then in the restaurant when all of this takes place and that he hears some of the melody but does not recall the lyrics or form any association with them introduces the way he will eventually need to "Sherlockholmes" the evidence of what is about to take place at 7 Eccles Street.

Two pieces of music that do exert a siren influence on Bloom are Lionel's aria "*M'appari*" and the way it becomes temporarily confused with "*Tutto è sciolto*" from Bellini's *La Sonnambula*. Snatches of *Martha* have been on his mind since midday when he first called at the *Freeman's Journal*, particularly the lines from Lionel's lament freely translated in a popular version as "Co-ome thou lost one, /Co-ome thou dear one!" (7.59–60), although these lines, as Bloom subsequently recognizes when he is in the restaurant with Richie Goulding, are not the ones that usually go with Flotow's melody. Briefly, the context of *M'appari* is that Lady Harriet Durham, a maid-of-honor to Queen Anne, becomes so irritated by the foppishness of the court that she retires to the country with her maid Nancy. As a lark, the two hire out themselves as maids at a country fair in Richmond, England, where they attract the attention of two local farmers, Lionel and Plunkett. The farmers contract them to work for a year, but Harriet and Nancy prove so incompetent that they contrive to escape, thereby breaking their contracts. Lionel, who has fallen in love with Harriet, is particularly distraught, and when he catches sight of her with a royal hunting party, he protests his love and demands that his contract be honored. She spurns him and, after persuading the Queen that he is mad, has him committed to prison. He produces a ring that was left to him when he was orphaned. The ring establishes his nobility. Lady Harriet Durham is filled with remorse at the way she has treated him. Lionel realizes that he is still in love with her. They embrace and agree to marry.

While Lionel's aria was originally composed in German, "*Ach! so fromm, ach! so traut*," the Italian translation was favored, particularly after the 1906 production at the New York Metropolitan Opera when the great Enrico Caruso sang the role of Lionel in the Italian version, which is as follows, "M'appari tutt' amor; il mio sguardo l'incontró" ("She appeared to me, full of love, my eyes caught sight of her").[49] Father Cowley tries to persuade Simon Dedalus to sing the Italian version by launching into the first two lines: "*M'appari tutt'amor: /Il mio sguardo l'incontr*" (11.594–95), but Simon Dedalus protests his inadequacy, which becomes apparent as soon as he begins to accompany himself on the piano.

> No, Simon, Father Cowley turned. Play it in the original. One flat.
> The keys, obedient, rose higher, told, faltered, confessed, confused.
> Up stage strode Father Cowley
> —Here, Simon, I'll accompany you, he said. Get up. (11.602–5)

Meanwhile, Richie Goulding, who is dining with Bloom, apparently tipped off by Father Cowley's Italian that Simon Dedalus is about to sing a tenor aria, confidently announces to Bloom,

> Most beautiful tenor air ever written, Richie said: *Sonnambula*. He heard Joe Maas sing that one night. Ah, what McGuckin! Yes. In his way. Choirboy style. Maas was the boy. Massboy. A lyrical tenor if you like. Never forget it. Never. (11.610–13)

Both Joseph Maas (1847–1886) and Barton McGuckin (1852–1913) were tenors who began life as choristers; both went on to train in Italy; and both, at one time or another, sang with the Carl Rosa Opera Company, which began annual tours that took in Dublin, Belfast, and Cork from 1873,[50] though I have not been able to find any evidence that either tenor performed in *La Sonnambula* or sang *Tutto è sciolto* at any time in Dublin.[51]

[49] "M'appari tutt' amor, Lionel's Aria from Martha," trans. Rogelio Aguilar, accessed 23 July 2016, http://www.aria-database.com/translations/martha15_mappari.txt.

[50] Laura Williams Macy, ed. *The Grove Book of Opera Singers* (Oxford: Oxford University Press, 2008), 292. See also Theodore William Moody, W. E. Vaughan, Francis X. Martin, and Francis John Byrne, eds., *A New History of Ireland* (Oxford: Oxford University Press, 2010), 6:512.

[51] Maas first achieved success in London in 1871, becoming principal tenor in the Carl Rosa Opera Company in 1878. Since Goulding claims he heard Maas in the Old Royal, the performance should have taken place between 1878 and 1880. I have not been able to find any record of Maas singing in Dublin from 1871 to 16

At first Bloom is generously aware of Richie Goulding's bad memory and tendency to exaggerate: "Tenderly Bloom over liverless bacon saw the tightened features strain. Backache he. Bright's bright eye. Next item on the programme. Paying the piper" (11.614–16). Apparently indifferent to Bloom's assessment of him, Richie Goulding continues to claim that the most memorable performance he had ever heard was when he and "little Peake" had got seats in the Gods in the "Old Royal" (11.624). But when Bloom asks, "which air is that?" and Richie Goulding prepares to whistle the tune from a performance that must have taken place twenty-four years before—the "Old Royal" burnt down in 1880—Bloom's attitude hardens: "Coming out with a whopper now. Rhapsodies about damn all. Believes his own lies. Does really. Wonderful liar. But want a good memory" (11.626–27). Though this might sound uncharacteristically harsh, it is a view shared by Richie Goulding's nephew. One of the reasons Stephen Dedalus offers himself for not calling on his uncle that morning is that he does not want to be subjected to his error-ridden enthusiasm for opera (3.99–103).[52]

Having established a context of error, a line from *La Sonnambula* is then introduced: "—*All is lost now*" (11.629). As with the fragments from Boylan's song, "Goodbye, Sweetheart, Goodbye," the first entry of the line is italicized to alert the reader to the fact that the opening line is sung and then the melody is whistled. Bloom, however, soon identifies the lyrics and begins to yield to the siren call of the plot: "Bloom bent leopold ear, turning a fringe of doyley down under the vase. Order. Yes, I remember. Lovely air" (11.637–38). The despairing "All is lost" is a free translation of the cry uttered by Elvino, a young landowner who has entered into a nuptial contract with Amina, a beautiful orphan who suffers from somnambulism. That night, while she dreams of coming to Elvino, she sleepwalks into another man's room at the local inn. The man, Count Rodolfo, recognizes she is sleepwalking and generously leaves the room, but Lisa, who has been engaged to Elvino, brings him to where Amina is still asleep

January 1886, when he died of gout, nor have I been able to find evidence of McGuckin singing at the Old Royal.

[52] Both Bowen, *Bloom's Old Sweet Song*, 40–41, and Chris Ackerley, "'Tutto è sciolto': An Operatic Crux in the 'Sirens' Episode of James Joyce's 'Ulysses,'" *James Joyce Quarterly* 38, nos. 1–2 (2000–2001): 198, have suggested this connection between "Proteus" and "Sirens."

in Rodolfo's bed. Elvino, not believing that she has sleepwalked, disavows the nuptial contract, his subsequent misery prompting the aria:

Tutto è sciolto. Oh dì funesto! Più per me non v'ha conforto. Il mio cor per sempre è morto alla gioia ed all'amor.[53]	All is lost now, By all hope and joy am I forsaken. Nevermore can love awaken Past enchantment, no, nevermore.[54]

Initially, Bloom is tempted to identify with Elvino and to wonder why Amina was not woken: "Call name. Touch water," the latter being a folk belief that a sleepwalker could be gently woken by having them dip their hand in water. But as the scene begins to take control of his feelings, he comes to associate Elvino's plight with his own and to attribute the sleepwalking to an urgency of the body that eventually proves irresistible: "Jingle Jaunty. Too late. She longed to go. That's why. Woman. As easy stop the sea. Yes, all is lost" (11.640–41). "Jingle Jaunty" are the notes associated with the leitmotif of the jaunting car that is bearing Boylan inexorably towards 7 Eccles Street and Molly.

Some critics have tended to emphasize "all is lost" and to advance it as proof of Bloom's despairing acceptance, but to do so is to ignore the context of misattribution that frames the phrase. "*Tutto è sciolto*" certainly sends out a siren call, and Bloom is temporarily seduced into allowing it to speak for him, but the phrase is brought to his attention by a person he knows has a faulty memory and is given to exaggeration. Besides, the phrase initially has a dubious provenance attributed to it, and it is not what Simon Dedalus is about to sing.

What Simon Dedalus does begin to sing is Charles Jeffrey's English version of "*M'appari*" from Flotow's *Martha* as arranged by Charles W. Glover.[55] As Zack Bowen points out, the arrangement is in two sharps (D major), a minor third below the original key. So what Bloom hears

[53] "La Sonnambula," accessed 23 July 2016, http://imslp.org/wiki/La_sonnambula_(Bellini,_Vincenzo); and "Bellini's Opera La Sonnambula," accessed 23 July 2016, https://archive.org/stream/bellinisoperalas00bellrich#page/4/mode/1up.

[54] Bowen, *Bloom's Old Sweet Song*, 41.

[55] Bowen, *Bloom's Old Sweet Song*, 40. Charles Jeffreys (1807–1865).

is a popular version rearranged to accommodate Simon Dedalus's voice. I have reproduced the complete text of Jeffrey's version with the fragments that evoke a response in Bloom italicized. Variants, as they appear in "Sirens," are printed in italics to the right of Jeffrey's text.

> *When first I saw that form endearing;*
> *Sorrow from me seem'd to depart:*
> Each graceful look, each word so cheering
> Charm'd my eye and won my heart.
> Full of hope, and all delighted, —*Full of hope and all delighted*
> None could feel more blessed than I;
> All on Earth I then could wish for
> Was near her to live and die:
> *But alas! 'twas idle dreaming,*[56]
> And the dream too soon hath flown;
> Not one *ray of hope is* gleaming;

It is at this point in Simon Dedalus's rendition that Bloom recognizes that the lyrics are from *Martha* (11.713). This strikes him as a coincidence because he is just about to ask Pat the waiter for pen and paper so he can reply to Martha Clifford: "Martha it is. Coincidence. Just going to write. Lionel's song. Lovely name you have. Can't write. Accept my little pres. Play on her heartstrings pursestrings too. She's a. I call you naughty boy. Still the name: Martha. How strange! Today" (11.713–16). All the while Simon Dedalus continues to sing:

> When first I saw that form endearing
> Sorrow from me seem'd to depart:

[56] Ackerley claims dreaming in "Sirens" text is Beaming, but Beaming is in roman and is not necessarily attributed to Bloom (*U*11.711). "Bloom hears '[b]eaming,' and his misapprehension is the more ironic since he has just criticized Simon for '[s]inging wrong words' (*U*11.711, *U*11.696). This constitutes a small Freudian slip, since the likely echo is that of '[t]he young May moon she's beaming, love'— the song Molly was humming as she walked with Bloom and Boylan down by the Tolka (*U*8.589). The error contributes, in a tiny yet not insignificant way, to the complex emotional experience that follows." "Tutto è sciolto," 200. But beaming is a musical expression that signifies notes joined visually; hence the Joycean pun on the fact that the song is joining Molly and Boylan.

> *Each graceful look*, each word so cheering
> *Charm'd my eye* and won my heart.
> Martha, Martha, I am sighing —*Martha! Ah, Martha!*
> I am weeping still; for thee;
> Come thou lost one, —*Co-ome, thou lost one!*
> Come thou dear one, —*Co-ome thou dear one!*
> Thou alone can'st comfort me:
> Ah Martha return! Come to me![57] —*Come . . . !* —*To me!*

Although the song is almost halfway through before Bloom recognizes it, what he does not identify with, in terms of the metatext, is arguably as telling as what he does. He does not identify with Lionel's claim that "sorrow seem'd to depart" or that Martha "won his heart." Neither does he identify with Lionel's "weeping" and "sighing" or his plea that "thou alone can'st comfort me." What he does identify with, once he has recognized the song, is that "Each graceful look . . . Charm'd my eye." I will return to the complexities of the closing four lines of the song shortly, but the "graceful look" that "charm'd" his eye reminds him of the first time Molly appeared to be as attracted to him as he was to her: "Singing. Waiting she sang. I turned her music. Full voice of perfume of what perfume does your lilactrees. Bosom I saw, both full, throat warbling. First I saw. She thanked me. Why did she me? Fate. Spanishy eyes" (11.730–34).

The phrase "what perfume" echoes Martha Clifford's question, while, in floriography, "lilactrees" (Bloom's substitution for Molly in the question Martha asks) are harbingers of spring and symbolic of first love. As Simon Dedalus sings the closing lines, Bloom's feelings, thoughts, and emotions about Molly ("*Co-ome, thou lost one*") and Martha ("*Co-ome thou dear one*") coalesce in a moment of epiphanic transcendence that is nevertheless depicted as being aware of its performativity:

> It soared, a bird, it held its flight, a swift pure cry, soar silver orb it leaped serene, speeding, sustained, to come, don't spin it out too long long breath he breath long life, soaring high, high resplendent, aflame, crowned, high in the effulgence

[57] Bowen, *Bloom's Old Sweet Song*, 44–45.

> symbolistic, of the ethereal bosom, high, of the high vast irradiation everywhere all soaring all round about the all, the endlessnessnessness. (11.745–50)

While Bloom has apparently been "consumed" by the song, his return to the sociability of the Ormond is different from the other patrons. It seems that both "*Tutto è sciolto*" and "*M'appari*" continue to sound in his head as self-critical performances, because the reader learns that, despite the sociable clatter and clutter that surrounds him, "Bloom sang dumb." As the moments pass, he begins progressively to disengage from both operas as the similarities and differences between his plight and those of Lionel and Elvino work themselves through his mind. As Zack Bowen points out, "Elvino made a mistake regarding the innocence of his fiancée, but there is no mistake on Bloom's part in this regard. Lionel has been duped, but certainly not cuckolded, as [Bloom] has. Furthermore, both Elvino's and Lionel's predicaments end with happy reconciliations."[58] The most significant parallel, however, is the legal one: Amina has contracted to marry Elvino; Harriet has contracted to serve for a year as Lionel's maid. Both women, whether unconsciously or consciously, break those contracts—as Molly is about to break or has already broken her marriage contract. Now that the performance is over and the social life of the Ormond has returned to normal, Bloom realizes that "It's in the silence after you feel you think. Vibrations. Now silent air." What the silence prompts him to consider is the likely breach of his own marriage contract.

His first thought is that everything he has heard since he came into the Ormond has had a common theme: "Thou lost one.... Cruel it seems. Let people get fond of each other: lure them on. Then tear asunder" (11.802–4). This leads Bloom to wonder whether or not the sexual encounter between Boylan and Molly will lead to a liaison that eventually results in her leaving him. Bloom suspects he will soon be forgotten—until perhaps one day, when having grown tired of Molly, Boylan will simply abandon her. She will "suffer then," he fantasizes, as he constructs a stereotypical late Victorian image of the fallen wife:[59] "Snivel. Big spanishy eyes goggling at nothing. Her wavyavyeavyheavyeavyevyevyhair un comb:'d" (11.807–9). The allusion to an abundance of uncombed hair suggests the barely repressed desire disclosed

[58] Bowen, *Bloom's Old Sweet Song*, 44.

[59] For a pictorial representation of such scenes, see the triptych *Past and Present* (1858) by Augustus Leopold Egg, RA (1816–1863), Tate Gallery, London.

by Amina's somnambulism,[60] the tragically thwarted desire of Shakespearean heroines such as Ophelia, particularly as she is depicted by Millais, or the psychosexual symbolism of hair in W. B. Yeats's *The Wind among the Reeds* (1899) and in pre-Raphaelite paintings such as Rossetti's *Lady Lilith* (1873),[61] Millais's *The Martyr of the Solway* (1871), Leighton's *Iphigenia* (1884), or Waterhouse's *Windswept* (1903).

Bloom's next thought is considerably more generous. Although it echoes a headline about a divorce that was reported in the *Daily Mail* on 29 August 1904, "Tame Husbands a Weariness,"[62] its recollection suggests that despite his emotional turmoil Bloom still believes he is able to think objectively about marital relationships. At the suspicion that perhaps "too much happy bores" and a recollection of the question that Martha Clifford had asked, "Are you not happy in your," the rubber band, on which Bloom has been improvising his own tune, snaps.

It is then that he decides to sign to Pat the deaf waiter to bring him a pen, some ink, and a blotting pad, so he can respond to Martha Clifford's letter. But before Pat brings the writing material, Bloom recalls a happy memory of Milly playing Gustav Lange's "*Blumenleid*," the flower song, a happy memory that, given his refiguring of the notion of happiness, immediately prompts him to recall his encounter with the young prostitute by the door of the stables in Celia Street as he was making his way home to Milly and Molly.[63] Was his opportunistic sex also a reaction to domesticity, a consequence of the possibility that "too much happiness bores"? And what would be the consequences for his marriage if Molly

[60] Towards the end of the first Act, when he is protesting about Count Rodolpho's attentions, Elvino declares, "*Son geleso del zefiro amante / Che ti scherzo col crine.*"

[61] First painted in 1866–1868 using Fanny Cornforth as a model and then repainted in 1872–1873 using Alexa Wilding.

[62] "Tame Husbands a Weariness," *Daily Mail*, 29 August 1904, 3.

[63] Crispi, *Creative Process*, 101, points out that the encounter took place in Hatch Street and that Bridie Kelly was originally called Bridie Cullen, an ironic affirmation that "name and memory solace thee not" (*U*14.1074). In "Eumaeus," Bloom cautions Stephen against "women of ill fame," although he adds, "barely permissible once in a while though not as habitual practice" (*U*16.63–65). He also points out that "fast women of the *demimonde* ran away with a lot of £.s.d. into the bargain" (*U*16.87–88).

discovered his resort to sex with prostitutes, though the reader comes to realise that this is something Molly already suspects (18.36).

An illicit correspondence with a woman he is yet to meet, regardless of the extent to which it titillates him with its suggestions of naughtiness, offers only a small compensation for the potential loss of his marriage. Reverting to some conventional thinking about gender roles, Bloom wonders, "Folly am I writing? Husbands don't. That's marriage does, their wives" (11.874–75). Perhaps there is a justification for what he is about to do: "Because I am away from. Suppose." But this seems far less plausible than what might excuse Molly's sexual adventure: "She must. Keep young" (11.875). About to write to Martha, he decides that even if Molly discovers what he is doing, he will not make a full confession: "If she found out. Card in my high grade ha. No, not tell all. Useless pain" (11.876). Having resisted the plots and lyrics of comic opera and popular song to provide him with a narrative for his own dilemma, Bloom now reverts to the proverbial commonplaces of "If they don't see" ("what the eye doesn't see, the heart doesn't grieve over") and "Sauce for the gander" ("what's sauce for the goose is sauce for the gander"). He won't tell if she asks, and he won't ask so she doesn't have to tell; yet he still wants to know what has happened, even if she pretends she doesn't. As the reader discovers, Molly has already detected that Bloom is doing something that he is trying to conceal from her (18.48–50).

That he believes he has to be secretive leaches some of the excitement from what he is doing. Now, with most of the music having been performed, writing his *billet-doux* to Martha seems as extemporized as the tune that Father Cowley is improvising on the piano in the saloon. Bloom devises Greek "e's" as a way of disguising his handwriting, gives a thought to punning on Martha's use of the word punish, and finally decides to include the present of a postal order for an amount that is sufficiently generous to elicit a grateful reply. And when Richie Goulding's eyes ask what he is doing, Bloom pretends he is answering an advertisement in the *Freeman's Journal* for a job as a "town traveller."[64] Having written his letter to Martha, Bloom addresses the

[64] *Irish Times*, 16 June 1904, 1, carried an advertisement for "Agents required for unrepresented districts for Railway Passengers' Assurance Co., Established 1849." Applicants were advised to contact "Resident Secretaries for Ireland. Messrs J. Stewart, Kincaid and Sons, 7 Leinster Street, Dublin."

envelope and then uses the blotting pad in such a way that it will not be possible to decipher the address from the imprint of the dried ink.

Still thinking of himself as a writer, he wonders whether he could use what he is doing as the basis for a short story to sell to the magazine he read on the jakes that morning: "Right. Idea prize titbit. Something detective read off blottingpad. Payment at the rate of one guinea per col" (11.901–3). Although having a detective discover incriminating evidence from a blotting pad became something of a cliché in the Edwardian crime novel—for example, Sherlock Holmes resorts to it in "The Adventure of the Missing Three-Quarter," first published in the *Strand Magazine* in 1904—there were three newspaper reports in 1904 of divorce cases where blotting pads were tended as prima facie evidence. In *Mansford v. Mansford*, reported in the *Daily Mail* on 18 February 1904, Captain Mansford was able to decipher the words "My own precious darling sweetheart" on his wife's blotting pad.[65] In *Rosenthal v. Rosenthal* in the *Daily Mail* for 30 June 1904, it was reported that "owing to an impression which she found upon" a blotting pad, "Mrs. Amelia Rosenthal learned that her husband, Mr. James Herman Rosenthal, was visiting a woman in London."[66] In *Ryan v. Ryan*, heard on 14 June 1904, the "petitioner had found on a blotting-pad the tracing of letters from the respondent to a Miss Smith. In consequence she had left the respondent's house, and had entered into a deed of separation with him. One condition had been imposed, and that had been the return of the blotting pad."[67] In countering her evidence, counsel for Mr. Ryan produced letters Mrs. Ryan had written to her mother-in-law that in word and tone appeared to contradict what she claimed the blotting pad evidence inferred. As further evidence in defense of Mr. Ryan, counsel produced letters Mr. Ryan had written to his wife.[68]

[65] "Tell-Tale Blotting-Pad," *Daily Mail*, 18 February 1904, 3.

[66] "Blotting-Pad Disclosure," *Daily Mail*, 30 June 1904, 3.

[67] *Times* (London), 15 June 1904, 3. At the hearing on 15 June 1904, it emerged that the petitioner's lawyers had kept copies of the tracings and wished to tender them as evidence, though this was contested.

[68] "These letters corroborated the account [the respondent] had given in the witness-box of the petitioner's hysterical temper." *Times* (London), 22 June 1904, 3. In the event a judicial separation was granted rather than a divorce on the grounds that the petitioner could not establish "cruelty" beyond reasonable doubt. *Times* (London), 24 June 1906, 4. *Ryan v. Ryan*, NA J77/793/4126,

That Bloom is concerned about the legal implications of what he is doing, even while he is fantasizing about himself as a potential prize-winning author, is evident from his momentary recollection of Denis Breen's quest for legal redress for receiving a postcard marked with what he believes is an insult: "U.P.: up" (11.903). Secret correspondence that hinted at unhappiness in marriage, such as the letter that Bloom receives from Martha Clifford, was a common source of evidence in divorce proceedings, as illustrated by *Roberts v. Roberts and Whitaker*,[69] *Smith v. Smith and Barnes* (which survived a challenge by the King's Proctor),[70] and *Pollard v. Pollard*, all of which were heard between February and April 1904, though in the last of these cases the letters were discovered to have been forged.[71]

These thoughts signal Bloom's awareness of two issues. By replying to Martha's letter, he is supplying her with "material evidence" that could be used against him should he decide to divorce Molly. The thoughts that occur to him as he composes his reply and his suggestive "it will excite me. You know how" signal that he is aware that Martha's letter is equally risqué: "P.S. How will you pun? You punish me? P.P.S. . . . I feel so sad today . . . So lonely" (11.788–94). Yet neither the contents nor the tone of Boylan's letter to Molly is revealed to the reader. And what Molly does with it after she has hidden it under her pillow is not disclosed. But letters, it seems, had a way of implicating litigants. In the case of *Harraden v. Harraden and Bohan—The King's Proctor Showing Cause* (1902), all the correspondence

Filed: 4 August 1903; Set Down: 12 October 1903; Decree Nisi: 23 June 1904. Note, file closed until 2022.

[69] *Roberts v. Roberts and Whitaker*, in "Newspaper Wrapper leads to a Divorce," *Daily Mail*, 9 March 1904, 3. *Hodgson-Roberts v. Hodgson-Roberts and Whitaker*, NA J77/798/4300, Filed: 21 October 1903; Set Down: 11 November 1903; Decree Nisi: 8 March 1904; Final Decree: 14 September 1904.

[70] *Smith v. Smith and Bothera and Barnes*, in "Lover's 'Flashing Eyes'; Lady's Secret Pockets for Love Letters," *Daily Mail*, 29 April 1904, 3. One of Mrs. Smith's letters contained the following: "Everyone tells me I am naughty. I certainly am naughty." Martha Clifford uses the word "naughty" several times in her letter to Bloom (*U*5.241–59). *Smith v. Smith and Bothera and Barnes: The King's Proctor Shewing Cause*, NA J77/798/4275, Filed: 13 October 1903; Set Down: 16 February 1904; Decree Nisi: 28 April 1904; King's Proctor: 7 March 1905; King's Proctor Dismissed: 5 June 1905; Final Decree: 8 June 1905.

[71] "Private Detective's Plea," *Daily Mail*, 27 April 1904, 3.

proved decisive in one way or another, and the *decree nisi* was rescinded.[72] The petitioner was obliged to admit that he had been living with a woman in Belfast. The respondent was obliged to admit that a letter she claimed had been written and posted by her sister without her knowledge was actually in her handwriting.[73] The co-respondent was obliged to admit adultery with the respondent.[74] Costs were determined at £147-11-0. Despite this web of deceit, the presiding Judge, Justice Gorell Barnes, permitted the proceedings to continue *in formâ pauperis* on 11 February 1905 "if a satisfactory Affidavit" could be filed. When neither sureties nor affidavit were tended, the case was dismissed.[75] Who ended up living with whom and under what circumstances remains unknown.

* * * *

"Done anyhow," Bloom thinks to himself as he prepares to leave the Ormond for an appointment with Martin Cunningham in Barney Kiernan's to discuss the life assurance policy that Paddy Dignam had taken out. Though it is a duty he has generously assumed, Bloom is not looking forward to the emotional stress of consoling and advising a broken family. "Wish they'd sing more," he thinks to himself. "Keep my mind off." Other things distract him, however.

Catching sight of Miss Douce talking to George Lidwell, a solicitor, he sees her show him a large seashell that she has brought back from her summer holidays. Watching them listen to the sounds the shell seems to make, he imagines that "he heard more faintly that that they heard, each for

[72] *Harraden v. Harraden and Bohan*, NA J77/753/2932, Filed: 13 June 1902; Set Down: 19 September 1902; King's Proctor's Intervention: 19 October 1903; Decree Nisi Rescinded: 2 June 1904; Case Dismissed: 26 October 1905.

[73] *Times* (London), 3 June 1904, 3.

[74] As both respondent and co-respondent were registered as living in Glasgow and Alfred Harraden as having lived in Glasgow when the respondent committed adultery, it seems Alfred Harraden moved to 113 North Street, Wandsworth, Surrey, either as a consequence of deserting the respondent or so he could bring his case before the English court or both.

[75] *Harraden v. Harraden and Bohan*, NA J77/753/2932, note dated 26 October 1905: "Affidavit filed for non-compliance of Petitioner with Order of 1st of July 1905. Whereby Petition is dismissed."

herself alone, then each for other, hearing the plash of waves, loudly, a silent roar" (11.934–36). Memories of Molly come to mind as he thinks about the seeming omnipresence of sound and the extent to which music needs to be distinguished from noise. In the meantime Father Cowley, who is still at the piano, begins to play a minuet from *Don Giovanni* which Bloom recognizes is from act 1 where Don Giovanni, who has discovered Masetto's fiancée, Zerlina, with a group of peasants outside his house, tempts her inside and with the help of his servant tries to distract Masetto, who remains outside, so he can proceed to seduce her. As tempting as it might prove for him to identify with Masetto, who while witness to his bride's seduction is unable to act, Bloom nevertheless resists the siren call of the music to dramatize his own predicament to that extent.[76]

It is at this point in the episode that the reader learns that Boylan has reached 7 Eccles Street and is knocking on the door, or so Bloom imagines must by now be the case.[77] Meanwhile in the saloon of the Ormond, Father Cowley calls out "*Qui sdegno*," from the opening line of the High Priest's aria from act 2 scene 3 of Mozart's *The Magic Flute*, in an attempt to persuade Ben Dollard to sing it. While the aria, in which the High Priest asserts that only true love rather than revenge can redress wrong, prompts Bloom to more pleasant memories of Molly, the High Priest's aria in *The Magic Flute* is preceded by the Queen of the Night's aria, which dramatically advocates revenge. But when the men who have gathered around the piano press Ben Dollard to sing "The Croppy Boy" rather than the Mozart aria, Bloom finds the mix of deception, pathos, and nationalist sentiment in the ballad increasingly alienating. The ballad tells the story of a devout young man who dutifully goes to confession before throwing in his lot with the 1798 rebels only to discover that the priest who hears his confession is actually a British soldier who promptly turns him over to be hanged. Ben Dollard's increasingly sonorous performance has two major

[76] Bloom also associates his plight with the dramatic image of peasants dying of hunger who, during the Great Famine, crowded the windows of the big houses to gaze distractedly on the lavish dining that was taking place within.

[77] "All of the passages detailing Boylan's movements after he's left the Ormond have been saturated with Bloom's fixated fantasy, perhaps culminating in the wonderfully funny and obscene 'aria' of 'One rapped on a door, one tapped with a knock, did he knock Paul de Kock with a loud proud knocker with a cock carracarracarra cock. Cockcock.'" Tony Thwaites, e-mail message to author, 11 August 2016.

effects on Bloom. The first is to remind him of the legal implications of his illicit correspondence with Martha Clifford. Though the Croppy Boy's motives are pure and his innocent desire for absolution is profoundly moral, his joining the rebels, as far as the law is concerned, makes him a felon who must be hanged to preserve imperial power. Likewise, Bloom's correspondence with Martha, as compensatory and as innocent as it might be deemed to be, nevertheless places him within the ambit of the court should it be tendered as evidence.

The second effect is to make Bloom even more impatient with sentimentality as a social bond and as a refuge from emotion that imprints itself on the body, and with music in its various forms as having the potential to leach individual experience of its specificity. His hour in the Ormond has been characterized by a recurring cycle of feelings aroused by the lyrics and/or the music he has heard, overheard, or recalled. Each feeling is reviewed in silence until it is overtaken by an emotion; and then each emotion is subsequently followed by silence until a new feeling intervenes, when the process begins again.[78] This goes on until Bloom, sensing that he will not be able to endure what Ben Dollard's rendition of "The Croppy Boy" evokes, gets up and leaves. "Bloom in the Ormond hallway heard the growls and roars of bravo, fat backslapping, their boots all treading, boots not the boot boy. General chorus off for a swill to wash it down. Glad I avoided" (11.1142–45). "Very sad thing," he thinks to himself about the parallels between himself and the Croppy Boy and what the ballad advises him against. "But had to be" (11.1121).

* * * *

In Homer, the music of the Sirens is said to be as prophetic as it is enthralling because "they know all that has happened." By lashing himself to the mast and keeping his ears open, Odysseus allows himself to be seduced into thinking he will acquire a knowledge of the future because it is grounded in what purports to be a comprehensive account of the past.

[78] Bloom associates his feelings for Milly with Gustav Lange's (1830–1889) "Blumenlied" (*U*11.844). Lange also composed "Edelweiss." Bloom immediately associates this with Bridie Kelly: "the girl. Door of the stables near Cecelia Street" (*U*11.845–46).

But as readers of the *Odyssey* know, Odysseus does not foresee that his crew will disobey his orders about slaughtering the herds of the Sungod or that Zeus will drive his ship back into Charybdis's maw or that all his crew will be drowned or that he himself will be cast up on Ogygia.[79] Bloom is also seduced into thinking that the music he hears not only expresses and explains his feelings and emotions but might also verify what has happened and guide him as to a future course of action.

Coincidence appears to substantiate this. In the course of replying to Martha Clifford's *billet-doux*, he overhears Simon Dedalus singing Lionel's song from Flotow's light opera *Martha* and is struck by the double coincidence that the opera and the person he is writing to have the same name and that his own name, Leopold, is similar to the name of the character who sings the song. That it takes him some time to recognize these coincidences indicates how distracted he is. And the anxiety he feels that his covert correspondence might be detected reveals how conflicted and furtive he has become. Yet the knowledge of what has happened and the insights into the future that Bloom is promised by the Siren lyrics of light opera, popular song, and patriotic ballads that he overhears in the Ormond prove illusory.[80] "All that has happened," he comes to realize, as memorable as music might make it, does not necessarily reveal what will happen.

It is worth recalling that "Sirens" closes with Bloom remembering Robert Emmet's promised epitaph, and that while it unambiguously signals what has happened (viz. his execution), it remains unwritten because Emmet cannot know the future. It is a blank space, a silence. Bloom strongly suspects that Molly has committed adultery, but he has yet to convince himself of this, and he has yet to obtain substantive proof. Now that the "Siren" music of the Ormond is a memory and the ambient sounds of the street have become internalized, Bloom realizes, "*It's in the silence after you feel /you hear.*" What that silence brings is the realization that, like Emmet's epitaph, until Bloom "takes his place," the epitaph of his marriage is yet to be and might never be written.

[79] Homer, *Odyssey*, 12.61–491.

[80] Miss Douce sings a line from the light opera *Floradora* (1899) as Boylan enters the bar.

CHAPTER 5

Sex, Pleasure, Guilt, and Divorce

Having refused to have his fears about Molly acculturated by the lyrics of operetta and popular song, Bloom now faces the possibility in Barney Kiernan's pub of being devoured by virulent, opinionated talk about justice and the law. The greatest challenge he faces, like his heroic counterpart, is to his identity, his sense of himself. "Is he a jew or a gentile or a holy Roman or a swaddler or what the hell is he?" demands Ned Lambert, one of the barflies. "Or who is he?" (12.1631–32). Bloom arrives at the pub as "Bloowho," but once he is drawn into the bar, he must meet the challenge of being stigmatized as ομτις (no one) by employing μετις (craft, cunning) to ensure that he is not με τις (just anyone).[1] He meets with mixed success. As indicative of the melee of discourses that characterize the episode's multiperspectivity,[2] Bloom, as ben Bloom Elijah, is eventually whisked aloft like Euripides' Medea. He survives, though like his Homeric counterpart he is severely buffeted.

What this chapter will show is that Bloom survives, albeit barely, because he has a better understanding of the law than has so far been

[1] Homer, *Odyssey*, 509–10.

[2] I am indebted to Marianna Gula, *A Tale of a Pub: Re-Reading the "Cyclops" Episode of James Joyce's "Ulysses" in the Context of Irish Cultural Nationalism* (Debrecen: University of Debrecen Press, 2012), for this insight.

P. Kuch, *Irish Divorce / Joyce's Ulysses*,
DOI 10.1057/978-1-137-57186-1_5

recognized,[3] despite the ineffectiveness of his intermittent performances as defendant, counsel for prosecution, and counsel for defense. And it will endorse Andrew Gibson's reading that the "Cyclops" episode is strewn "with all kinds of references to matters English,"[4] by comparing and contrasting Bloom before the bar in Barney Kiernan's with Bloom's arraignment in "Circe," where, in a desperate attempt to secure a fair hearing, it is asserted he is a "Britisher" and then an "acclimatized Britisher" (15.794; 15.909). As Fritz Senn has rightly emphasized, "what is dimly adumbrated in 'Cyclops' [is] resonantly re-enacted in 'Circe.'"[5]

Barney Kiernan's is "close to where Dublin's legal business is conducted and to the area of the courts." Lawyers and clerks "were known to frequent the actual pub in its time."[6] Typifying the Homeric *Kyklopes* is the Citizen, a concatenation of competing discourses for whom justice has to do with grievance and redress, of wrongs righted by recourse to his own version of "natural law."[7] While the title of Citizen has been critically associated with revolutionary republicanism, it is worth remarking that within the timeframe of *Ulysses* as far as British law was concerned "citizenship" could not be removed, renounced, or revoked.[8] Even in name, in 1904, the Citizen is inalienably British. In Homer, the *Kyklopes* are said to be "lawless brutes," to

[3] Fritz Senn, "Arguing about Law: Cyclopean Language," *James Joyce Quarterly* 37, no. 3–4 (2000): 427, characterizes Bloom as a "blundering advisor."

[4] Gibson, *Joyce's Revenge*, 117.

[5] Senn, "Arguing about Law," 426.

[6] Senn, "Arguing about Law," 425.

[7] It is noteworthy that "'Citizenship' is not a term of English law at all." "Extract from a Memorandum on Nationality and Citizenship," Documents on Irish Foreign Policy, accessed 21 July 2016, http://difp.ie/docs/Volume3/1929/1355.htm.

[8] The important distinction here is between "citizenship" and "nationality" because The Naturalization Act, 1870 (33 & 34 Vict. c. 14.) was "the first Act to provide for the renunciation of British nationality by means of a declaration of alienage." See H. S. Q. Henriques, "Historical Survey," in *The Law of Aliens and Naturalization including the Text of the Aliens Act, 1905* (London: Butterworth, 1906), 1–61, https://archive.org/stream/lawofaliensnatur00henruoft/lawofaliensnatur00henruoft_djvu.txt.

"have no meeting place for council, no laws either," but to be "each a law to himself."[9] Joining the Citizen is "a lawyer and a clerk from a sub-sheriff's office."[10] Even the principal consciousness of the episode—designated by Joyce as "the nameless one" but now generally known as the I-narrator—is working for the law as a "collector of bad and doubtful debts" (12.24–25).

A legal issue is also the reason for Bloom's presence. He is to meet Martin Cunningham around five o'clock to assist Dignam's widow with problems associated with her late husband's life assurance; Bloom's experience in the field and his supposed cunning being considered assets. But before Martin Cunningham arrives, Bloom is drawn into the bar. In the melee of talk that ensues, "cases, actions, suits are discussed freely. Lawsuits are mentioned, playacted, interpolated, and parodied. Exaggerated legal metaphors abound."[11] For the first time in the *Ulysses* text, mention is made of legal terms associated with divorce: "*Decree nisi*" and "*gets*" (12.1199; 12.1159); the first uttered by J. J. O'Molloy, a solicitor who, as we have seen from the Buffalo manuscript discussed in Chapter 2, wanted to advise Molly to sue Bloom for "specific performance" for his failure to fulfill his marital obligations; the second, uttered by the Citizen, is a slur on Bloom's Jewishness, a "get" being a sum of money deposited by a Jewish bride before her wedding and redeemable on divorce according to her husband's pleasure.[12]

A significant aspect of justice and the law that underpins the episode and yet seems to have been overlooked has to do with the relationships between "comity of nations" or "conflict of laws" and violence. According to Dicey, Morris and Collins,

> The branch of English law known as conflict of laws is that part of the law of England which deals with cases having a "foreign element." By a "foreign element" is meant simply a contact with some system of law other than English

[9] Homer, *Odyssey*, 9.120, 125, 127.

[10] Senn, "Arguing about Law," 425.

[11] Senn, "Arguing about Law," 425.

[12] The Chief Rabbi of England, Rev. Dr. Hermann Adler, provides a detailed description of the "get" in his *Minutes of Evidence*, 3:407, §41,384.

> law. Such a contact may exist, for example, because a contract was made or to be performed in a foreign country, or because a tort was committed there, or because property was situated there, or because the parties are not English.... From the point of view of the conflict of laws, Scotland and Northern Ireland are for many purposes as much foreign countries as France or Germany.[13]

Given the suppression or rejection of a country's laws once it is dominated by an imperial power, it is inevitable that colonization produces a "conflict of laws" whenever imperial domination is being challenged. As a marginalized "other" in a colonial society, Bloom finds himself at odds in a boisterous and ribald discussion that randomly invokes aspects of British Law, Irish Law, Canon Law, Jewish Law, Natural Law, and nationalist interpretations of ancient codes such as Brehon Law.[14] Each code, with the exception of the last, impinges in one way or another on the situation Bloom suspects he now finds himself in. All differ from one another in the way they regard divorce and matrimonial causes. A number offer a course of action he can adopt should it prove that Molly has committed adultery. All challenge his ethnicity, his nationality, his sexuality, his marital status, and his financial integrity. The problem for Bloom, as for Dignam's widow, is what can be achieved "nominally under the act" (12.764). For Dignam's widow, the relevant act is the Policies of Assurance Act, 1867 (30 & 31

[13] Dicey, Morris, and Collins, *Conflict of Laws*, 14th ed., 1.008–1.023, 1.071–1088. Senn perhaps comes closest in "Arguing about Law" when he points out that the *Kyklopes* in the *Odyssey* "have no courts or acknowledgement of the law.... They are introduced as 'overweening and lawless' (*hyperphailos, athemistos*). A cluster of words built around *themis*—defined variously as 'custom, usage, that which is laid down or established... by old law, what is right'—is used to characterize them negatively'" (427).

[14] Extensively parodied in the case of *Halliday v. Livingstone and Another* heard before "sir Frederick Falconer" (Sir Frederick Falconer, the Recorder of Dublin). The other Judges mentioned are "master Courtney" (Col. Arthur H. Courtney, master of the High Court of Justice in Ireland, King's Bench Division, 1904) and "master Justice Andrews" (William Drennan Andrews, Judge of the Probate and Matrimonial Bench of the King's Bench Division in 1904) (*U*12.1111–40). The "Canada swindle" case ("James Wrought alias Saphiro alias Spark alias Spiro" [*U*12.1086–87]) was not heard in Falkiner's court but in the "Southern Divisional Police Court before Earnest Godwin Swifte, divisional police magistrate." Gifford with Seidman, *"Ulysses" Annotated*, 346–48.

Vict., c.144);[15] for Bloom the act that privately concerns him is An Act to Amend the Law Relating to Divorce and Matrimonial Causes in England, 1857 (20 & 21 Vict., c.85) and subsequent acts and amendments.

While Bloom attempts to explain the intricacies of the Policies of Assurance Act to the I-narrator, he simply stigmatizes the Citizen's recourse to violence as hate. In opposing hate with love, he nevertheless refuses to be cowed, though the I-narrator cynically subverts his protestations. As the reader discovers, when Bloom confides to Stephen as they discuss English divorce procedure in the cabman's shelter, his rebuttal of the Citizen restores his confidence in himself. But his immediate delivery from Barney Kiernan's is fortuitous. What is facilitated is a strategic retreat. Whisked away by a jarvey, as if by a *deus ex machina*, he still has to negotiate the perils of Sandymount Strand, the Lying in Hospital, and Nighttown before he can return to 7 Eccles Street to see whether or not what he suspects has actually happened.

* * * *

The Dublin to which the reader is introduced in "Cyclops" is a city addicted to litigation and in thrall to legalese and gossip about legal matters. Unlike the preceding episodes, "Cyclops" is introduced by a "controlling consciousness"—an I-narrator, whose recourse to slang, breezy self-confidence, and ready opinion mark him as street-wise and cynical. Offered a drink, he thinks/says to himself: "I was blue mouldy for the want of that pint. Declare to God I could hear it hit the pit of my stomach with a click" (12.242–43). A collector of bad and doubtful debts, he has contacts in the Dublin Metropolitan Police and is only too ready to enlist their aid should he consider himself wronged. Obliged to dodge a Sweep's brooms and brushes, he confides to Joe Hynes, a drinking companion, that he ought to have the Sweep summonsed for obstruction. He then regales Joe (and the reader) with his task in hand. Moses Hertzog, a Jewish merchant, has sold tea and sugar to a Michael E. Geraghty for the sum of "one pound five shillings and sixpence," the debt to be amortized in weekly installments of three shillings. As Geraghty has fallen into arrears, Hertzog has called in the I-narrator, who finds himself

[15] Hardiman, "Law, Crime and Punishment," 67, argues that the relevant act is the Policies and Assurance Act, 1867 (31 & 32 Vict., c.144), and cites *In the matter of R. F. Young, a bankrupt* (1890) 25 LR Ir 372, but according to *Every Man's Own Lawyer*, 186, the Stamp Act, 1891 (54 & 55 Vict. c.39), also applies.

faced with a legal conundrum. The agreement between Hertzog and Geraghty, quoted in full, is precise, comprehensive, and legally binding, but Geraghty has an "out" because Hertzog is not a licensed trader. Since legal redress is complicated, both parties have begun to resort to threats. Recourse to the law, the reader is reminded, is not always straightforward. It is at this point that the I-narrator suggests to Joe that they visit the Citizen.

The Citizen represents a challenge to the reader and to Bloom because, in addition to much else, he embodies a hybrid form of physical force nationalism with a nativist perspective on natural law. His sense of justice is as significantly colored by Hobbes as it is by Locke. In part, as Andrew Gibson has argued, he represents a discursive "reclamation" of a sanitized Anglo-Irish Protestant depiction of pre-Christian Ireland, a reclamation that restores its gigantism, heterogeneity, violence, vulgarity, grotesqueness, and prodigious bizarrerie;[16] and in part he reflects the awkward fact that it was an armed insurrection inspired by the ancient legends rather than the politics of Home Rule that secured Ireland a measure of freedom after 1916. The parodic lists, or "runs" as they were known in the ancient legends, that periodically disrupt the I-narrative are also challenging because their comic inclusiveness serves to critique the strident nativism and xenophobia that characterize the Citizen's pronouncements.

Bloom's first exchange with the Citizen and his bar room court concerns the physiology of erections. It so happens that Joe Hynes has a collection of letters from an English Master Barber who has offered his services as hangman to the High Sherriff of Dublin. Alf Bergin offers the information that hanging can produce an erection, at which Joe quips, "ruling passion strong in death" (12.463). But Bloom interjects with a medical explanation. Passion and erections are too close to what might have happened at 7 Eccles Street. But his attempted medical explanation is summarily dismissed by the Citizen's invocation of *Sinn fein amhain*, the I-narrator's contempt for Molly—"The fat heap he married is a nice old phenomenon with a back on her like a ballalley" (12.503–4)—and an interpolated parody about the phallic heroics of dying for Ireland. The assaults on Bloom's sexual competence continue with the I-narrator marshaling hearsay as evidence: "Pisser Burke was telling me," he confides to the reader, "the wife used to be in rivers of tears some times." He then speculates about Boylan's role in the concert tour: "That explains the milk

[16] Gibson, *Joyce's Revenge*, 118.

in the cocoanut and absence of hair on the animal's chest. Blazes doing the tootle on the flute" (12.996–97).

At this point J. J. O'Molloy enters, and the conversation immediately turns to Denis Breen's attempt to bring a libel suit for £10,000. Four aspects of the ensuing discussion prove discomforting for Bloom. The first is Breen's search for a private detective, a strategy much favored by wronged parties in matrimonial matters. The second is the advice that Breen should "get the handwriting examined first" (12.1034–35), advice that would remind Bloom of his recent attempt to disguise his own handwriting. The third is whether or not the alleged insult to Breen's sexuality is in fact a libel. The truth of what has been written is not at issue, for as J. J. O'Molloy, the lawyer, argues, "the truth of a libel is no defence to an indictment for publishing it in the eyes of the law" (12.1048–49). "In my opinion," he continues, "a postcard is a publication. It was held to be sufficient evidence of malice in the testcase [*sic*] Sadgrove v. Hole. In my opinion an action might lie" (12.1071–73).[17]

His opinion is certainly confirmed by cases that were heard within the *Ulysses* time-scheme, as with *Foley v. Faunt* (1903),[18] *Keers v. Kane* (1904),[19] *Field v. Field* (1905),[20] *Croghan v. Colter* (1909),[21] *Doherty v. Mullins* (1909),[22] and *à Beckett v. De Burgh* (1912).[23] In each, libelous postcards provoked successful legal actions, with convictions ranging from fines to imprisonment and compensation varying from a farthing to twenty-five pounds. In delivering judgment in *Croghan v. Colter*, for example, "His Lordship said that a postcard was one of the best modes

[17] *Sadgrove v. Hole* [1901] CA 2 KB 1. The I-narrator's retort, "Six and eightpence, please," is a direct quotation from the title page of early editions of *Every Man's Own Lawyer* justifying the expense of purchasing the book: "Six and eightpence saved at Every Consultation." The 54th edition published in 1919 does not contain the statement. This suggests that Joyce might have known editions earlier than the 54th or might have seen the phrase in an advertisement. Gifford with Seidman, *"Ulysses" Annotated*, 346, claim the phrase was well known.

[18] "Libel on a Postcard," *Irish Times*, 20 November 1903, 4.

[19] "Alleged Libellous Postcards," *Irish Times*, 22 November 1904, 3A.

[20] "Libel on a Postcard," *Irish Times*, 14 September 1905, 3.

[21] "Libel by Postcard," *Irish Times*, 20 March 1909, 5.

[22] "Alleged Postcard Libel," *Irish Times*, 15 May 1909, 3; 43 ILTR 174.

[23] "Officer's Libel Action: Anonymous Postcard," *Irish Times*, 29 February 1912, 4.

of publicly slandering a man."[24] In *Sadgrove v. Hole* (1901), which J. J. O'Molloy cites, the Judge observed, "the mere fact that a communication had been sent by a postcard instead of a closed letter would generally be evidence of malice."[25] What is also relevant for Bloom here are the ways documents can be interpreted by a skilled lawyer within an adversarial system of justice. His secret correspondence with Martha Clifford again comes to mind. What is also relevant is the alleged vulnerability of the Bench to manipulation. Alf Bergin claims of Sir Frederick Falkiner, the Recorder of Dublin, "Tell him a tale of woe about arrears in rent and a sick wife and a squad of kids and, faith, he'll dissolve in tears" (12.1197–99). The dismissing of *Dodd v. Gumley* is cited, though how much in this fictional case is due to sympathy and how much is due to the Recorder's virulent anti-Semitism is not canvassed. Finally, when Bloom attempts to elicit pity for Josie Breen, the Citizen retorts, "Pity about her ... Or any other woman marries a half and half ... A pishogue, if you know what that means" (12.1058). Bloom apparently doesn't, though "the word the Citizen should be using is *pithogue*, from the Irish *piteog*, which means 'an effeminate man,' 'a dandy,' 'a sissy' or (in modern usage) 'a homosexual.'"[26] The slur against Bloom is obvious.

Much of the ire against him to this point arises from the fact that he will not drink with the group or stand a round of drinks but accepts the hospitable gesture of a cigar; that he is suspected of concealing his winnings from Throwaway's victory in the Gold Cup; and that his explanation of Mrs. Dignam's problem, though apparently well informed, becomes, as far as the I-narrator is concerned, unnecessarily complicated. It appears that Dignam has borrowed money against his life assurance but the

[24] "Libel by Postcard," *Irish Times*, 20 March 1909, 5: "This postcard could not but tend to ruin the man who was struggling with misfortune and with the water rolling over his head. Every word said would crush and ruin him, and it was a cruel publication."

[25] *Sadgrove v. Hole* [1901] CA 2 KB 1. Hardiman, "Law, Crime and Punishment," 69.

[26] *Irish–English Dictionary Online*, s.v. "piteog," accessed 24 October 2016, https://glosbe.com/ga/en/piteog. The Citizen confuses *pishogue* with *piteog*. The irony is that the Citizen rails against those who cannot speak Irish (12.680).

required notifications have not been completed. According to Joyce's source of legal knowledge, *Every Man's Own Lawyer*,

> When, therefore, a person lends money on the security of a policy of assurance on the life of the borrower or other person, the lender should, in addition to having the custody of the policy, take care that *notice*, under the hand of the borrower, be given to the insurance office, to the effect that the loan has been made and the policy assigned as a security, and specifying the amount.[27] In the absence of such a notice, if the borrower become bankrupt, the lender will have no security for his money, but may be compelled to give up the policy for the benefit of the bankrupt's estate.[28]
>
> Further, by the Stamp Act, 1891 (54 & 55 Vict. c.39), no assignment of a life policy shall confer on the assignee or his assigns any right to sue for the insurance moneys, or to give a valid discharge for the same, unless duly stamped (§118).[29]

No duly stamped notification to the insurance company means that Mrs. Dignam and the Life Assurance Company cannot be sued to recover the debt. As Joe Hynes remarks, "So the wife comes out our top dog, what?" (12.766). The problem with applying the Act, however, is that it deals with bankruptcy not death and that Bridgeman, the person who has lent Dignam the money, "*may*" rather than "will" be "compelled to give up the policy for the benefit of the bankrupt's [deceased] estate." However, as soon as Bloom tries to explain these finer points, according to the I-narrator,

> he starts all confused mucking it up about mortgagor under the act like the lord chancellor giving it out at the bench and for the benefit of the wife and that a trust is created but on the other hand Dignam owed Bridgeman the money and if now the wife or the widow contested the mortgagee's right till he near had the head of me addled with his mortgager under the act. (12.770–75)[30]

[27] *Williams v. Thorp* 2 Sim 257.

[28] *Edwards v. Martin* 35 LJ Ch 186.

[29] *Every Man's Own Lawyer*, 185–86.

[30] It is likely the I-narrator's complaint in *Ulysses* is echoing *Every Man's Own Lawyer*, 182–83: "There are other interests, also, which give a right to insure: for instance, a wife may insure the life of her husband, upon whose income or exertions she is dependent (*Reed v. Royal Exchange Assurance Company* 24 LJ CPD 2)* [*sic*], and a

Ironically, it is Bloom's miscellaneous erudition and his working knowledge of the law that earn him the opprobrium of the bar, the I-narrator at various times describing him as a "bloody freemason," "Mr Knowall," and "as cute as a shithouse rat" (12.300; 12.383; 12.1761). But because this is the I-narrator's opinion, it remains uncertain whether or not Bloom is as knowledgeable and as opinionated as he is depicted or whether he is preeminently a textual construct in a satire on Dublin pub culture and beer-talk about the law or whether he is both. According to Michael Groden, "Joyce's earliest work on 'Cyclops' in mid-June 1919 may thus represent the precise chronological point at which he stopped writing one kind of novel—one basically concerned with Stephen and Bloom—and began to write another—one in which a succession of parody styles, and eventually a group of schematic correspondences, began to take over."[31] Groden's suggestion, I would argue, is confirmed by the melee of discourses that characterize the pub talk in Barney Kiernan's as populist interpretations of the law and street-wise notions about legality compete with one another in the cut and thrust of conversation. And yet, as we have already seen, multiperspectivity and the challenges to constructing narratives of the self posed by music and popular song have already assailed Bloom in "Sirens."

* * * *

Sexual scandal and divorce permeate the pub talk in Barney Kiernan's, to Bloom's further discomfort. Preoccupied with situating everything within a nationalist historiography, the Citizen segues from stigmatizing Denis

husband may insure the life of his wife (*Reed v. Key* Peake Add Cas 70; *Huckman v. Fernie* (1838) 3 M&W 501; 150 ER 1245)* [*sic*]; and the *Married Women's Property Act*, 1882, expressly provides that a married woman may insure her own life or that of her husband for her separate use (45 & 46 Vict. c.75, §11). And it has been held that a trustee has sufficient interest to enable him to insure the life of a person who has granted an annuity to the person for whom he is trustee (*Tidswell v. Angerstein* Peake Add Cas 151). Further, the mortgagee of a life estate having insured the mortgagor's life to the amount of the mortgage, it was held that the mortgagee was entitled to the policy moneys against the mortgagor's executor (*Preston v. Neele* 12 LR CP 760; alt cit. *Preston v. Neele* (1879) 12 ChD 760)." **Reed v. Royal Exchange Assurance Company* (1795) Peake Add cas 70.

[31] Groden, "'Cyclops' in Progress, 1919," 135.

Breen's sexuality (and by implication Bloom's) to Dermot MacMurrough's seduction of Dervorgilla, the wife of Tiernan O'Ruark, to MacMurrough's alliance with Strongbow, and the Norman presence in Ireland.

> The strangers, says the citizen. Our own fault. We let them come in. We brought them in. The adulteress and her paramour brought the Saxon robbers here.
> —Decree *nisi*, says J. J.
> And Bloom letting on to be awfully deeply interested in nothing, a spider's web in the corner behind the barrel, and the citizen scowling after him . . .
> —A dishonoured wife, says the citizen, that's the cause of all our misfortunes. (12.1156–64)

As if the reason for being granted a *decree nisi*—preparatory to being granted a divorce *a mensa et thoro* in the Irish jurisdiction or a divorce *a vincula matrimonii* in the English jurisdiction—was not immediately obvious, the pub talk then turns to the barman's and Alf's salacious enjoyment of the divorce court reports in one of the most sensationalist newspapers then in circulation in Ireland, the *Police Gazette*.[32] As Joseph Valente argues, "the *Gazette* was a quintessentially homosocial institution, connecting networks of loosely affiliated men in the expression of gender and class-conscious fantasy, resentment, and self-affirmation."[33] What the sequence of cartoon-like drawings, text, and speech bubbles depicts is "Misconduct of society belle. Norman W. Tupper, wealthy Chicago contractor, finds pretty but faithless wife in lap of officer Taylor. Belle in her bloomers misconducting herself, and her fancyman feeling for her tickles and Norman W. Tupper bouncing in with his peashooter just in time to be late after she doing the trick of the loop with officer Taylor" (12.1170–74).

Though Bloom's performance of detachment, his "letting on to be awfully deeply interested in nothing," echoes a long list of avoidance activities he has employed during the day, it also signals his desire to distance himself and his situation from tabloid press titillation. Despite suspecting

[32] Joseph Valente, "The Novel and the Police (Gazette)," *NOVEL: A Forum on Fiction* 29, no. 1 (1995): 8–18.

[33] Valente, "The Novel and the Police (Gazette)," 14, citing Elliott J. Gorn, "The Wicked World: The National *Police Gazette* and Gilded-Age America," *Media Studies Journal* 6, no. 1 (1992): 4.

that he has been cuckolded, Bloom refuses to see himself as a "Tupper," Molly as a "society belle," and Boylan as "officer Taylor." His distancing himself is not simply due to his disapproval of pornography—after all, he has a copy of *Sweets of Sin* in his pocket—but is representative of the type of self-censorship/self-indulgence of sexuality that Foucault argued was characteristic of the *petit bourgeois*.[34] But the consequence of refusing to engage with the *Police Gazette* further isolates Bloom from the aggressive homosociality of the pub, the more so when he tries to advocate tolerance and love as essential for personal, communal, and national relations.

When Bloom temporarily leaves in order to find out what has happened to Martin Cunningham, the rumor that he has actually gone to collect his winnings from the Gold Cup rapidly gains currency. In his absence, the bar buzzes with anti-Semitic and xenophobic gossip about Bloom as a Jew, about his claim to be Irish, about his advocacy of a dual monarchy for Ireland based on the Hungarian model and its influence on *Sinn Fein*, and about his father's suicide. By the time Martin Cunningham arrives, the conversation has intensified to the point where Bloom's sexuality and paternity are up for ridicule:

> —O, by God, says Ned, you should have seen Bloom before that son of his that died was born. I met him one day in the south city markets buying a tin of Neave's food six weeks before the wife was delivered.
> —*En ventre sa mère*, says J. J.
> —Do you call that a man? says the citizen.
> —I wonder did he ever put it out of sight, says Joe.
> —Well, there were two children born anyhow, says Jack Power.
> —And who does he suspect? Says the citizen.
> Gob, there's many a true word spoken in jest. (12.1650–58)[35]

What brings matters to a head, however, is an argument about residence, domicile, and nationality—all key concepts in determining jurisdiction

[34] Foucault, *History of Sexuality*, 17: "Such repression is emblematic of what we call the bourgeois societies."

[35] Note that according to *Gordon v. Gordon and Gordon* (1903), "In the case of a child born in wedlock, as to whose paternity questions are raised upon an application as to the child's custody, if the husband could, from circumstances of time, place, and health, have had nuptial intercourse with his wife, the mother of the child, and it be not proved that he did not have such intercourse, he must be

for matrimonial causes. Earlier, when challenged to define his nationality, Bloom has legitimately claimed *jus soli*—that he is Irish by birth.[36] The Citizen counters with his own sectarian interpretation of *Lex soli*—that it is only practicing Christians who can assert the right of *jus soli*. But when Bloom retorts, "Your God was a Jew. Christ was a Jew like me" (12.1808–9), pandemonium breaks out, and all the self-instructed, street-wise, quasi-legal argument erupts in violence.

* * * *

Cast up on Sandymount Strand after he has advised Mrs. Dignam about her husband's life assurance and wondering if it is too early to return to 7 Eccles Street, Bloom encounters his Nausicaa in the person of Gerty MacDowell. At least that is the proper noun attached to "as fair a specimen of winsome Irish girlhood as anyone could wish to see" (13.80–81). The words "wish" and "to see" have significant implications for interpreting the episode, for reading Bloom, and for understanding the ways readers themselves might be affected. Having just escaped the blind prejudice assembled piecemeal from unionist and nationalist representations of the heroic and a farrago of street-wise notions about the law, Bloom is seduced by a commodified sexuality in the form of an artfully dressed young woman who briefly exposes her underwear. As Patrick McGee has pointed out, "After 'Sirens' where Bloom notes that music is a language of love, after 'Cyclops' where he combats nationalistic *ressentiment* with the message of love, 'Nausicaa' arrives to repeat and displace the frame of 'romance' ideology and to remind us that no word, no discourse, is wholly determinate as to its political effects in every context."[37] What I will argue is that critics, including McGee, have overlooked some of the legal implications of these "words" in their analyses of the scopic eroticism shared by Gerty and Bloom and for that matter the

considered the father of the child, even if she were shown to have committed adultery with any number of men."

[36] He could also have claimed *jus sanguinis* (right of blood) as his mother was Irish. See Barry McCrea, "Secrets of Szombathely: The H.E.L.Y.'S Sandwichmen and Irish Citizenship," *James Joyce Quarterly* 41, no. 3 (2004): 398–99.

[37] Patrick McGee, "Joyce's *Nausea*: Style and Representation in 'Nausicaa,'" *James Joyce Quarterly* 24, no. 3 (1987): 307.

reader, particularly for the narrative that Bloom is attempting to construct for himself.

* * * *

In contrast to what has taken place at 7 Eccles Street at about half past four that afternoon, the legal implications of what takes place on Sandymount Strand are uncertain. The essential difference between Boylan's encounter with Molly and Bloom's encounter with Gerty, as Bloom himself is said to realize, involves penetration. At issue here is the legal definition of adultery: "*eiaculatio seminis inter vas natural mulieris*" ("ejaculation of semen within the natural female organ"). Observing that his watch has stopped at half past four, just as he is about to recompose his wet shirt, Bloom is represented thinking, "was that just when he, she? O, he did. Into her. She did. Done. Ah!" (13.848–50). The key phrase, in a legal sense, is "into her." Sexual connection, as distinguished from "acts of gross indecency," whether heterosexual or homosexual, is legally deemed to have taken place only on penetration followed by emission.[38] The fantasy in "Circe" that Boylan will invite him to apply his "eye to the keyhole and play" with himself while he "goes through" Molly "a few times" arises from Bloom's recurrent fears about collusion and connivance and his perverse need to be convinced that sexual connection has actually taken place (15.3788–89). Gerty's awareness that "there was absolution so long as you didn't do the other thing before being married" reveals that even fair specimens of "winsome Irish girlhood" were aware of the distinction between sexual connection and indecency (13.708–9). What brought this aspect of the law to public attention was the publicity surrounding the Criminal Law Amendment Act, 1885 (48 & 49 Vict. Cap. 69),[39] specifically section 11,

[38] The exception here is *Reg. v. Marsden* [1868] CCR 131; [1891] 2 QB 149: "To prove the offence of carnally knowing a girl under the age of thirteen, under s. 4 of the Criminal Law Amendment Act (48 & 49 Vict. 69) 1885, it is not necessary to prove emission." Current sexology now distinguishes between emission and expulsion.

[39] *The Criminal Law Amendment Act, 1885: With Introduction, Notes and Index*, ed. Frederick Mead and Archibald Henry Bodkin (London: Shaw, 1885), 11–18, https://archive.org/stream/criminallawamen00bodkgoog#page/n30/mode/2up.

which became known as the Labouchere Amendment. The intention and effect of the Amendment was to distinguish between sex acts involving penetration, such as sodomy, the penalty for which was life imprisonment, and sex acts deemed "gross indecency," the penalty for which was two years' imprisonment with hard labour. A further intention was to remove the distinction between "public" and "private," a distinction that had proved troublesome for prosecutions under the previous Act. Gross indecency in the Amended Act of 1885 was defined as "such conduct as is at common law, if public, the subject of an indictment."

One problem with the Labouchere Amendment was the way the wording focused on male sexual behaviour; especially since one of the cases tried under the Act, *R. v. Elliott* (L&C 103), as Mead and Bodkin point out, involved a man and a woman.[40] A further problem was that the Amendment did not address "acts of gross indecency" committed in public. The previous Act had stated that

> Every one commits a misdemeanor who does any grossly indecent act in any open or public place in the presence of more persons than one; but it is uncertain whether such conduct in a public place amounts to a misdemeanor if it is done when no one is present, or in the presence of one person only. A place is public within the meaning of this article if it is so situated that what passes there can be seen by any considerable number of persons if they happen to look.[41]

Following the 1885 Act, prosecution of sexual offences committed in public was generally conducted under the Town Police Clauses Act, 1847 c. 89 (*regnal.* 10 and 11 Vict.), specifically section 28, which stated that it was an offence for anyone to "willfully and indecently expose his Person in any Street." To do so was to attract "a fine not exceeding forty shillings or imprisonment for a period not exceeding fourteen days," the circumstances of the offence determining the severity of the penalty.[42] The term "indecently expose" seems to have included masturbation and other "such conduct as is at common law, if public, the subject of an indictment." As with the Labouchere Amendment, the wording was gendered.

[40] *Criminal Law Amendment Act*, 69.

[41] Quoted in *Criminal Law Amendment Act*, 68.

[42] "Town Police Causes Act, 1847," accessed 23 July 2016, http://www.legislation.gov.uk/ukpga/Vict/10-11/89/enacted.

My argument is that Bloom has opportunistically sought sexual relief in circumstances that would maximize the frisson of transgression and minimize the illegality of his action. There is no doubt that Sandymount Strand would qualify as a public place under both the old and the new Acts and under the Town Police Clauses Act. But it is after sunset, and, regardless of the duration and intensity of the twilight, visibility has been reduced, though to what degree is a moot point.[43]

There is also little doubt that what occurs takes place "in the presence of one person only." Gerty is said to be alone, acutely conscious of Bloom's gaze, because she has refused to join her friends for a better view of the fireworks (13.683–88): "At last they were left alone without the others to pry and pass remarks and she knew he could be trusted to the death, steadfast, a sterling man, a man of inflexible honor to his fingertips" (13.692–94). Since they are alone, it is "uncertain" in legal terms whether Bloom could legally be said to commit a misdemeanor. This is not to claim that he knows the law and so has taken advantage of the uncertainty, but it is to affirm that the uncertainty exists.

A further uncertainty relates to the seemingly consensual nature of the event. According to the Gerty narrative, "she saw that he saw," and "she wasn't ashamed that he wasn't either to look in that immodest way" (13.726; 13.730). However, the "visual markers signifying the erotic" in her narrative, as Dominika Bednarska has observed, are "often euphemized or implied rather than explicitly stated . . . what is seen and the way it differs from previous glances" remains uncertain.[44] Consequently, the evidential value of the statement that "His hands and face were working and a tremor went over her" is doubtful because of the extent to which Gerty has commodified herself or been commodified by advertising, women's magazines, and the penny novelette. Does she actually see Bloom masturbate? Or does she merely imagine a sexual act that she has heard about from Bertha Supple that is said to be associated with men looking at pictures of skirt dancers or moving images in mutascope parlors? Given that it is physiologically possible for men who are experiencing

[43] See http://www.timeanddate.com/sun/ireland/dublin for calculating twilight.

[44] Dominika Bednarska, "A Crippled Erotic: Gender and Disability in James Joyce's 'Nausicca,'" *James Joyce Quarterly* 49, no. 1 (2011): 88 n. 27. See also Thomas Richards, *The Commodity Culture of Victorian England: Advertising and Spectacle, 1851–1914* (Stanford, CA: Stanford University Press, 1990), 205–48.

anxiety, panic, or psychological stress to ejaculate spontaneously,[45] the sight of "hands and face working" attributed to her may have more to do with phallocentricism than what she supposedly sees. What remains uncertain is whether Gerty seeks refuge in patriarchy or is constructed by patriarchy to the extent that she requires an image of male sexuality to endorse what she herself is experiencing sexually.

Bloom appears to convince himself that Gerty knew what he was doing and that it was her desire that aroused his desire. "Yours for the asking," he thinks. "Because they want it themselves. Their natural craving" (13.785–90). He is also convinced he has been close enough to her to read her eyes: "Fine eyes she had, clear. It's the white of the eye brings that out not so much the pupil. Did she know what I? Course. Like a cat sitting beyond a dog's jump" (13.906–9). For women, the extent of *mydriasis*, dilation of the pupil, is physiologically associated with their degree of sexual arousal. But complicating Bloom's reason for assuming her strategic complicity are the facts that Gerty's pupils would naturally dilate in the twilight and that if there was sufficient light for him to read her eyes, there was also sufficient light for others to see what he was doing.

A key question, since it has legal consequences and it is something that is said to concern Bloom, is whether he has accidentally exposed himself. As *Every Man's Own Lawyer* makes abundantly clear, "Obscene exposure of the person renders the offender punishable as a rogue and vagabond."[46] Wondering if women are sexually attracted to neatly dressed men or to men whose tie, *pace* Freud, is left undone, Bloom thinks, "Trousers? Suppose I

[45] Y. Sato, "Silodosin Improved Spontaneous Ejaculation Induced by Mental Strain," *International Journal of Urology* 21 (August 2014): 841, doi: 10.1111/iju.12439. In "Circe," Virag, Bloom's father, prescribes "lycopodium" (*U*15.2366) for his son, a herbal remedy traditionally used to treat premature ejaculation, impotency due to sexual excess, and loss of erection during coition.

[46] *Every Man's Own Lawyer*, 572. Offenders could be prosecuted under The Vagrant Act, 1824 (5 Geo IV c. 83). For application of the Criminal Law Amendment Act to Ireland, see *Criminal Law Amendment Act*, 80–90 and Fitzpatrick, *The Two Irelands 1912–1939*, 230. Bloom's misdemeanor pales into insignificance compared with the successful prosecution of Alfred E. Carson by the Kingstown Urban District Council in 1906 ([1906] 40 ILTSJ 287) for swimming naked at the Forty Foot after 9 a.m. See Osborough, *Law and the Emergence of Modern Dublin*, 155–57.

was when I was. No. Gently does it. Dislike rough and tumble. Kiss in the dark and never tell. Saw something in me. Wonder what" (13.831–32). His concern recurs with a recollection of Wilkins, who had become so engrossed in drawing Venus in an art class that he had exposed himself without apparently being aware of it (13.909). But that too is dismissed. That he might have spontaneously ejaculated as a result of anxiety and frustrated voyeurism crosses Bloom's mind: "Damned glad I didn't do it in the bath this morning over her silly I will punish you letter. Made up for that tramdriver this morning" (13.786–88); but that thought is also dismissed.

A second key question, "Should a girl tell," is said to occur to them both (13.750). The reader is made aware of Gerty's response but not Bloom's. Her "No, a thousand times no" is not communicated to him as they do not speak (13.750). In fact, Bloom is relieved they haven't spoken: "Suppose I spoke to her. What about? Bad plan however if you don't know how to end the conversation... Wonderful of course if you say: good evening, and you see she's on for it" (13.862–66). But he then recalls a "dark evening in the Appian way" when he nearly propositioned "Mrs Clinch" for sex, thinking she was a prostitute; and the time he paid a girl in Meath Street for dirty talk and how embarrassed he felt when he tipped her and she thanked him as "sir" (13.866–73). He is momentarily worried that the woman on the strand might be Martha, is relieved when he hears her called Gerty, but then wonders if this is a "false name" (13.944–45). Not speaking to Gerty after the others have left also ensures that he does not discover she is lame until she gets up to leave: "Glad I didn't know it when she was on show. Hot little devil all the same" (13.775–76). Sometime later he is shown thinking to himself, "Sad about her lame of course but must be on your guard not to feel too much pity. They take advantage" (13.1095–97). The decision not to talk and the advantages of not talking mean that Bloom is not able to complete the "message" in the sand that he thinks of leaving for Gerty. Like onanism, sand is not fertile. As he realizes, "Hopeless thing sand. Nothing grows in it. All fades" (13.1266–67). Bloom's inability to complete the ostensive definition of himself, "I AM A...," has been read in several ways; what has not been emphasized is that, despite his desire to write "*The Mystery Man on the Beach*, prize titbit story by Mr Leopold Bloom" (13.1060), he cannot define himself, even imaginatively, to someone he has objectified or via an eroticism that has been mass produced for male consumption.

This is not to say that Bloom has not achieved a measure of relief, despite the legal consequences of strategically performing an act of "gross indecency" in public. Thoughts such as "Thankful for small mercies. Cheap too" (13.789–90), "Anyhow I got the best of that" (13.785–86), and "This wet is very unpleasant. Stuck. Well the foreskin is not back. Better detach. Ow!" (13.979–81) are counteracted by "Did me good all the same. Off colour after Kiernan's, Dignam's. For this relief much thanks" (13.939–40), "The strength it gives a man. That's the secret of it.... Makes you want to sing after" (13.859–60), and "Chance. We'll never meet again. But it was lovely. Goodbye, dear. Thanks. Made me feel so young" (13.1271–73).

The most important consequence of the encounter with Gerty, however, is his decision not to go to Belfast to be with Molly while she is on tour with Boylan. Catching sight of Howth in the fading light, he recalls the time when Molly first gave herself to him. Feeling that Gerty has "drained all the manhood out of [him], little wretch" (13.1096), he seems to surrender to the inevitable consequences of Molly's affair, an affair he has yet to confirm has actually taken place. Bloom is shown saying to himself, "And she can do the other. Did too. And Belfast. *I won't go.* Race there, race back to Ennis. *Let him.* Just close my eyes a moment" (13.1275–77; emphasis mine).

* * * *

While Bloom has difficulty communicating his knowledge of the law to the *Kyklopes* and does not break the law in his encounter with Gerty, he is hard pressed to defend himself against charges of voyeurism, breach of promise, molestation, sexual assault, attempted rape, acts of indecency, solicitation, and procurement in the phantasmagoric court world of "Circe." As Finn Fordham has argued, "a distinguishing feature of the 'Circe' episode is the existence of multiple parallel worlds each one an 'alter' of the real one, or of some posited 'realistic level' of the episode."[47] The "realistic level" that underpins and frames all the others is the state of prostitution in Dublin in 1904. Dublin's red light district was notorious.

[47] Finn Fordham, "'Circe' and the Genesis of Multiple Personality," *James Joyce Quarterly* 45, nos. 3–4 (2008): 511.

It had the reputation for being "the worst in Europe for streetwalking prostitutes."[48] While the statistics for arrest, which went from 431 in 1900 to a high of 1,067 in 1912, would seem to indicate that law enforcement was effective, it was well known that the police permitted "open brothels confined to one area, but carried on more openly than in the south of Europe or even in Algiers."[49]

Having ventured into a world of sex for sale, Bloom dramatizes rather than narrativizes himself. Following a fantasy procession of accusers that range from Molly (the odalisque), to Bridie Kelly (the cyprian), to Gerty MacDowell (the mutascope skirt dancer), to Josie Breen (the married woman as potential adulteress), Bloom is arrested by the Watch and committed for trial. As a fantasy persona, Jimmy Henry, announces, "The Court of Conscience is now open" (15.1629). What legally is at issue for Bloom is the fear that, according to the Matrimonial Causes Act, 1857 (20 and 21 Vict. c.85) s. 31, he might be found guilty of misconduct conducive to or of collusion in her adultery. As I have shown in earlier chapters, Bloom is represented as being justifiably haunted by the fear that he has not fulfilled his contractual obligations as a husband—that he has not provided Molly with the comfort and protection she deserves and the sexual satisfaction she desires. The "world" that is most closely associated with this "realistic level" of legality is the world of the Law in the Kantian sense of *Lex justi* (maintaining one's own worth in relation to others), *Lex juridica* (doing wrong to no one), and *Lex justitiæ* (entering into a state in which everyone can have what is their own secured against the action of every other).[50] Bloom's is an existential fear compounded by a fear about what might be revealed about his own sexuality.

Hence, the "trials" that take place after Bloom has been arrested are psychological enactments of the cross-examination he fears he would be subjected to if he brought an action for *criminal conversation* against Boylan in the Irish jurisdiction or if he entered a petition for a divorce from Molly in the Probate, Divorce and Admiralty Division

[48] Maria Luddy, *Prostitution and Irish Society* (Cambridge: Cambridge University Press, 2007), 157.

[49] Luddy, *Prostitution and Irish Society*, 158.

[50] Kant, *Philosophy of Law*, 54–55.

of the King's Bench in London. Though his sexual "crimes" would be more likely to influence the legal outcome of the latter, there is little doubt that embarrassing publicity would follow both actions. For a petition for divorce to succeed, it was necessary for both petitioner and defendant to present themselves to the court with "clean hands."

Bloom's situation is also Kafkaesque. Aware that it is more than likely that Molly has committed adultery, Bloom feels accused—but, like Joseph K in Kafka's *The Trial*, he is not certain what he is accused of because he fears he is already guilty. The trial scenes that follow his arrest dramatize his attempt to define his guilt and ameliorate his fear. In the threatening, threatened, and sexually clamorous world of Dublin's notorious red-light district, he is forcefully made aware that whatever narrative he tries to construct for himself, regardless of its "truth," might or might not prove to be "the truth," despite his sincere belief in its veracity. Regardless of jurisdiction, his story will be tested against rival stories, all of which will be molded to the language of the law and framed within the procedures of the court in order for the Bench to adjudicate and the jury to deliver a verdict, with the possibility that whatever story emerges might be further reconfigured in a Court of Appeal. Trials for *criminal conversation* in the Irish jurisdiction were comparatively straightforward in the sense that adultery was deemed as injury to property; the husband's morality was not at issue. In the English jurisdiction, however, the verdict in a divorce case could turn on the husband's or wife's morality when it was discovered that both were guilty of misconduct, as in *Wyke v. Wyke* (1902), *Moyst v. Moyst and Wilcox and Essling* (1902), *Anderson v. Anderson and Rising* (1903), and *Rogerson v. Rogerson and Drummond* (1903). Though Bloom, "blushing furiously all over from frons to nates, three tears falling from his left eye," pleads with "A Deadhand," a "Crab," a "Female Infant," and a "Hollybush" to "spare my past" (15.1880–81), it is his past that persistently returns to haunt him.

* * * *

Bloom's first court appearance involves allegations that he has propositioned Mary Driscoll, a live-in domestic servant. He is alleged to have "made a certain suggestion," to have held her so forcibly she was "discoloured in four places," and to have "interfered twice" with her clothing. Bloom pleads "not guilty," advancing in his defense his intention to reform occasioned by random insights into British-inspired domestic bliss. Cross-examined as to whether or not he has defecated in public, after interjections from the press that they cannot hear him, Bloom attempts to present himself as foreign, destitute, and a victim of circumstance. The Gallery promptly howls him down. His counsel, J. J. O'Molloy, enters a plea for leniency on the grounds that "intimacy did not occur and the offence complained by Driscoll, that her virtue was solicited, was not repeated" (15.948–49); but his rhetoric collapses under the weight of its own eloquence. What further complicates J. J. O'Molloy's argument is his transformation into Seymour Bushe, as renowned for his appearance as co-respondent in the divorce proceedings—*Brooke v. Bushe* (49 & 50 Vict., c.181) discussed in Chapter 3—as for his court room eloquence.

Bloom's second appearance involves allegations that he has sent sexually offensive material to several society ladies through the post with the intention of inciting them to commit adultery with him. He neither admits nor rebuts the allegations beyond claiming that illicit correspondence titillates him (shades of his correspondence with Martha Clifford) and that he was secretly hoping for a birching or some other form of masochistic punishment. At one point the "sluts and ragamuffins" interject with screams of "Hurrah there, Bluebeard. Three cheers for Ikey Mo!" (15.1040). The allusion is not only to "the legendary character who murdered a succession of wives before he was finally exposed and slain,"[51] but also to a notorious divorce case and murder enquiry that was widely reported in the French and English press while Joyce was writing "Circe." A certain Mme Landru, from Vernouillet, a village in France, lodged a petition for divorce in the French courts on the grounds that police enquiries into allegations that her husband had killed eleven of the ninety-seven women who had responded to advertisements inviting them to meet him had made her life unbearable.[52]

The third appearance arises from an allegation made collectively by Davy Stephens, a "timepiece," the "quoits" on the matrimonial bed at 7 Eccles Street, and "the nameless one" (the I-narrator in "Cyclops") that Bloom has colluded with Boylan or conspired with him to "sell" Molly into adultery.

[51] Gifford with Seidman, *"Ulysses" Annotated*, 466.

[52] "Bluebeard's 97," *Daily Mail*, 21 May 1919, 8; "Bluebeard Divorce Case," *Daily Mail*, 20 November 1919, 9, reports ten women and one boy. See also "Bluebeard Divorce," *Daily Mail*, 2 December 1919, 5.

After the "Timepiece" is heard to call "Cuckoo" and "The Quoits" to go "Jigjag. Jigajiga. Jigjag," a jury emerges comprised of the faces of "Martin Cunningham, foreman, silkhatted, Jack Power, Simon Dedalus, Tom Kernan, Ned Lambert, John Henry Menton, Myles Crawford, Lenehan, Paddy Leonard, Nosey Flynn, McCoy and the Featureless face of a Nameless One" (15.1140–43). It is the Nameless One who makes the allegation linking Bloom's supposed winnings at the Gold Cup with the allegation that he has prostituted his wife, "Bareback riding. Weight for age. Gob, he organised her" (15.1145). Arraigned before Sir Frederick Falkiner, the Dublin Recorder, Bloom is committed for trial and sentenced to death on the grounds that he has engaged in "white slave traffic" (15.1167). Instead of being hanged (perhaps producing an erection), Bloom is invited to "play with himself" while he watches Boylan enjoy vigorous sexual intercourse with Molly. Her reaction is to echo the Citizen and label her husband a "pishogue" and then to accuse him of being a pimp (15.3778). To satisfy Bloom's need of masochistic punishment, one of the prostitutes threatens to send him to the bearded woman for a whipping that "will raise weals out on him an inch thick" (15.3779–80). In British law, any husband who prostituted his wife could not obtain a divorce. In *Burdon v. Burdon; The Queen's Proctor Shewing Cause* (1900),[53] and *Wilkins v. Wilkins and McCoy; The King's Proctor Shewing Cause* (1904),[54] two cases contemporary with the time-scheme of *Ulysses*, *decrees nisi* that had been granted by the court were challenged because of accusations that the husbands had prostituted their wives.

To prostitute, as the Nymph infers, who speaks from the *Photo Bits* print that Bloom has had framed above the bed, is also to "defile, dishonor, or profane."[55] "What have I not seen in that chamber?" she protests. "What must my eyes look down on?" (15.3285–86). Bloom tries to deflect her inferences by confessing that he snores and by apologizing for Molly's soiled

[53] *Burdon v. Burdon; The Queen's Proctor Shewing Cause*, NA J77/663/176, Filed: 14 March 1899; Set Down: 15 April 1899; Decree Nisi: 5 June 1899; Queen's Proctor: 13 November 1899; Further Particulars: 15 December 1899; Further Particulars: 12 January 1900; Further Particulars: 24 April 1900; Final Decree: 30 April 1900; For ruling see *Burdon v. Burdon* [1901] P 52; 69 LJP 118.

[54] *Wilkins v. Wilkins and McCoy; The King's Proctor Shewing Cause*, NA J77/822/5005, Filed: 13 July 1904; Set Down: 8 August 1904; *Decree Nisi*: 14 November 1904; Decree Rescinded: 26 June 1905.

[55] *Oxford English Dictionary*, 3rd online ed., s.v. "prostitute."

underwear and remarking her weight, but the Nymph persists with "Worse, Worse," until Bloom relents. He confesses to adolescent explorations of sex, to fetishizing the female body, to purchasing condoms, and to insisting that Molly permit him to perform oral sex (15.1740–41; 15.3424–27; 18.1245–50). But when he attempts to interfere with the Nymph, after she has morphed into the image of a Nun from one of his pornographic postcards, she explodes like the Siren in Book 19 of Dante's *Purgatorio*.[56] Her self-destruction completes a cycle of innuendo and allegation that had assumed patriarchal authority when Virag, Bloom's father, began by enquiring whether or not "glimpses of lingerie appealed to you in virtue of its exhibitionisticicity" (15.2324–25)—the woman leaving the Grosvenor, the girl in Eustace Street, Lotty Clarke, and Gerty MacDowell—and concluded that his son's voyeurism was symptomatic of an anal eroticism that sought relief in pornography and incitement to illicit sex.

It is the whoremistress Bello/Bella who most panders to Bloom's masochism, via a bewildering sequence of gender reversals, to placate the Law. As Amber Musser has argued, the masochist is a subject most often male who, according to Deleuze,

> disavows the Law of the Father and attempts to recreate the pre-Oedipal maternal world by enlisting a cold, cruel woman to dominate. In Deleuze's analysis, the masochist oscillates between submission and domination, rendering reality (and binaries) absurd in favour of fantasy. The masochist uses his/her power to simulate powerlessness through the contract, which simulates, but cannot replace the law. The fantasy of a relation of absolute submission is approximated by the fetishistic reiteration of objects that symbolize domination (such as fur, high heels, and whips) and disavowal of his or her agency. The masochist receives pleasure from the material symbols of submission while continually producing desire for the impossible—absolute submission.[57]

Before she/he submits him to punishment, the whoremistress reassures Bloom, "What you long for has come to pass. Henceforth you are unmanned and mine in earnest, a thing under the yoke" (15.2964–66). She/he grinds her high heels into his/her neck and threatens to torture

[56] Gifford with Seidman, *"Ulysses" Annotated*, 509.

[57] Amber Musser, "Masochism: A Queer Subjectivity?" *Rhizomes* 11–12 (Fall 2005–Spring 2006), http://www.rhizomes.net/issue11/musser.html.

him/her with "the nosering, the pliers, the bastinado, the hanging hook, [and] the knout" and to corset and costume him/her while periodically subjecting him/her to repeated humiliations (15.2891–92). Each cruel act of subjection is accompanied with a taunt: "What was the most revolting piece of obscenity in all your career of crime? Go the whole hog. Puke it out! Be candid for once" (15.3042–43); "What else are you good for, an impotent thing like you?" (15.3127); and "You are down and out and don't you forget it, old bean" (15.3199–20).

What begins to unravel this interplay of power is Stephen Dedalus's incoherent gibes that what Bello/Bella flaunts as masochistic, perverse, and exotic pales in comparison with what is offered in the bordellos of Paris. His drunken ramblings and then his terrified reaction to his mother's ghost, who appears to plead on behalf of his soul, begin to awaken Bloom to Stephen's spiritual turmoil. And when Bloom asks, "What?" and Stephen shouts out in rage, "*Non serviam*!"—and in a Nietzschean gesture of defiance wields his ashplant and smashes the chandelier—Bloom is moved to cry, "Stop." While it is Lynch who seizes Stephen's hand and cautions him "don't run amok," it is Bloom who calmly and authoritatively pays for the damage—not what Bella demands, but what he estimates. And then when Stephen gets knocked down by two English Tommies, it is Bloom who once again comes to the rescue, controlling the crowd with "Get back, stand back!" and enforcing his version of the assault: "You hit him without provocation. I'm a witness. Constable, take his regimental number" (15.4768; 15.4788–89). Having taken charge of Stephen's hat, money, and ashplant and persuaded the Watch, who had previously arrested Stephen, not to report him, Bloom has an intense momentary vision of his dead son as he contemplates how to take care of Stephen.

But what Bloom's aroused paternity engenders is a contradictory symbology of authority and betrayal. Stephen's face calls to his mind "the dark wood" from Book 1 of Dante's *Inferno*, where the poet reports that in the "middle journey of life" he "came to himself." What it also calls to mind is "the white breast" from Yeats's lyric "Who Goes with Fergus?"—a poem about patriarchal treachery that admonishes the reader to "no more turn aside and brood /Upon love's bitter mystery." But the reader also sees that Bloom is advised by the stage directions of the closing scene to adopt "the attitude of a secret master," that is, the "fourth degree in the Ancient and Accepted Scottish Rite of Freemasonry," requisite for contemplating "the Ineffable Name [of the Deity]" or absolute Patriarchy. The vision of the dead son that is achieved is itself ambiguous. As Joan Kiernan has argued,

Rudy's apparition can be seen as symbolizing Hermes, whose gift of moly to Odysseus protected him from Circe's enchantment; or his apparition can be read as symbolizing the paschal lamb of the Pentateuch, where the lamb represents innocence, peace, and ultimate reconciliation, and the "violet bowknot" on his ivory cane, penitence and authority. That the apparition is "unseeing" suggests the legend of Homer's blindness and the ability to "foresee all" attributed to the blind prophet Tiresias.

While Bloom emerges from the animality of Nighttown with his humanity scarred but intact, he still has to endure the final interrogation of the self that will come with his return to 7 Eccles Street. Will there be any evidence that Molly has committed adultery? Will it be "such as would lead the guarded discretion of a reasonable and just man to the conclusion" that adultery has been committed? And if there is incontrovertible evidence, what will he do with it?

CHAPTER 6

Money and Divorce

When poverty walks through the door, love flies out the window.

—Proverb

While Bloom retains and at various times during the day revives happy memories of his life with Molly, it is Molly's early morning thoughts about their finances and about her husband's checkered history of employment that provide the reader with several insights into why their marriage is in the state that it is, why she has embarked on an affair, and why divorce is being considered by both of them. This thought is not surprising. Money, particularly when it is linked to income, household expenses, discretionary spending, and security, figures in most divorce cases. There are three reasons, I suggest, why money and the sexual empowerment of wealth have not been thoroughly investigated for their impact on the Blooms.

First, there seems to be a consensus that the Blooms' finances are fundamentally sound,[1] despite some heated debate about Bloom's book-keeping and his spotty employment record.[2] It is the documents kept in the second drawer of the walnut bureau in Number 7 Eccles Street that

[1] Osteen, *Economy*, 71, 91–92.

[2] See Keith Warnock, "Auditing Bloom, Editing Joyce: Accounting and Accountability in *Ulysses*," *Accounting, Business & Financial History* 18, no. 1 (2008): 81–95; Michael D. Rubenstein, "'The Waters of Finance': Moneyed States in *Joyce's 'Ulysses'*," *Novel: A Forum on Fiction* 36, no. 3 (2003): 289–306.

P. Kuch, *Irish Divorce / Joyce's Ulysses*,
DOI 10.1057/978-1-137-57186-1_6

appear to support this view (17.1855–67). At face value, these documents are reassuring. However, there is a significant difference between what the documents state, what the stock markets reported they were worth in the weeks preceding 16 June 1904, and what they meant at the time Joyce was drafting the *nostos* episodes of *Ulysses*. On the day, securities are only as comforting as the markets deem them to be.

Second, it might be that Molly's adultery will be ignored or forgiven and that life at Number 7 will continue. Despite her irritation with Bloom's financial schemes, his refusal to take a steady job, and his monitoring of her expenditure, Molly's vivid memory of how she persuaded him to marry her when they were courting on the Hill of Howth convinces her (and some readers) that she will be able to seduce him again. For Molly, immediate, illicit sexual satisfaction has become more important than the security considered to be provided by traditional marriage. Speculating about the psychological impulse driving the erotic, Bataille observes, "We want to feel as remote from the world where thrift is the rule as we can:– that is hardly strong enough; we want the world turned upside down and inside out. The truth of eroticism is treason."[3] Only after Molly has seduced Boylan does she begin to commodify her sexuality in terms of money, presents, travel, and a career. That she has not been able to entice her husband into having conjugal sex with her for ten years does not seem to have seriously dented her belief in her powers of seduction. It could be that Bloom thinks that the money Molly will earn from her concert tour with Boylan will benefit their domestic economy. While he worries at various times during the day that he might be pimping for him, he also is sensitive to Molly's fears that she is losing her sexual attractiveness. Perhaps a brief affair with Boylan might help her to restore belief in herself and empower her financially.

In essence, while Molly's dilemma is about risk versus gain, Bloom's is about balancing risk, income, and expenditure. Fundamental to Joyce's work, as Mark Osteen has convincingly demonstrated, is a view of domestic economics which is governed by the necessity of making ends meet, of reconciling the ideal or imaginary function of money (something that has a stated value and can be accumulated—saving) with its symbolic function (something that needs to be circulated and therefore needs to be disbursed—spending).[4]

[3] Georges Bataille, *Eroticism*, trans. Mary Dalwood (1957; London: John Calder, 1962), 170–71.

[4] Osteen, *Economy*, 77–81.

A third view is that Molly's "autonomous monologue" implies that she has the final word,[5] that Joyce intended Penelope to serve as the "coda." Although he told Frank Budgen that he wanted the reader of "Ithaca" to "know everything and know it in the boldest and coldest way," he intended that "the last word (human all-too-human)" would be "left to Penelope."[6] But he also told Budgen, "to understand Penelope you should have an idea of Ithaca," and advised Harriet Shaw Weaver that the "Ithaca episode . . . is in reality the end as Penelope has no beginning, middle or end."[7] In responding to Joyce's statements of intention, Karen Lawrence has shrewdly observed that

> perhaps it makes sense to say that in "Penelope" Joyce provides a powerful ending for one "story" of *Ulysses* and not another: he completes the archetypal plot of the *Odyssey* by giving us Penelope, and he fleshes out the naturalistic plot as well by showing us the very human Molly Bloom, whom we have waited to see throughout the day. Joyce called "Penelope" the "indispensable countersign to Bloom's passport to eternity"—he felt the chapter was necessary to provide thematic and structural balance . . . [but] the whole book has cautioned us not to trust one version of things more than another, even one so apparently formless or "natural" as this one.[8]

My argument is that the style and story-world of "Ithaca" and the style and story-world of "Penelope" provide this balance because they are characteristic of the dialogic relationship between petitioner and respondent in divorce proceedings: the petitioner (Bloom) relying on questions that are intended to elicit answers that will disclose what has happened (something that can never be fully known); the respondent (Molly) constructing a narrative that she hopes will withstand questioning or, if it is dismantled, will justify her actions (often a forlorn hope, as many court cases attest). In offering a reading of "Ithaca" and "Penelope" in terms of the role played by money in the breakdown of the Blooms' marriage, this chapter will show that while it is certain that Molly feels financially

[5] Cohn, *Transparent Minds*, 218.

[6] James Joyce to Frank Budgen, end of February 1921, in *Letters of James Joyce*, ed. Stuart Gilbert (London: Faber, 1957), 159–60.

[7] James Joyce to Frank Budgen, 6 September 1921, in *Letters of James Joyce*, 172.

[8] Karen R. Lawrence, *The Odyssey of Style in "Ulysses"* (Princeton, NJ: Princeton University Press, 1981), 207.

insecure and is chafing under Bloom's checks on her spending,[9] and while it is certain that Bloom has provided gilt-edged security for Milly rather than Molly, it is also certain that Molly's "suppose I divorced him" and Bloom's "divorce, not now" are both inextricably bound up with money.

* * * *

Bloom first suspects that Boylan's money will prove attractive to Molly while he is still sitting on the jakes after breakfast. Having contemplated writing a sketch to rival "Matcham's Masterstroke"—and thereby potentially earning himself three pounds thirteen shillings and sixpence—Bloom recalls May's band playing Ponchielli's *Dance of the Hours.* He wonders if this was the first time Molly and Boylan were attracted to one another. "Is that Boylan well off?" he asks himself. "He has money. Why? I noticed he had a good rich smell on his breath dancing" (4.528–30).[10] Boylan, it seems, has been on Bloom's mind ever since he got up that morning. While waiting to be served in the butcher's, the thought "wonder if I'll meet him today" crosses his mind (4.215–16). And as he is just about to enter the jakes, he is struck by the coincidence of hearing Drago's shopbell ring, recalling Boylan's "brillantined hair," and thinking about having a bath in Tara Street, all three thoughts first occurring to him almost simultaneously as he was about to pick up the mail from the floor of the entrance hall, mail that includes a letter from Boylan (4.488–89).

For Bloom to meet Boylan face-to-face,[11] if only in passing, at any time during the 16th of June 1904, is to risk being reminded of his own financial situation. Boylan, as we learn in "Wandering Rocks" and elsewhere, owns an advertising business, has an office in town with a secretary,

[9] Anon, "Defects of Laws Relating to Married Women," *Irish Law Times and Solicitors' Journal* 28 (28 May 1904): 181–84, gives a detailed account of the difficulties that could be faced by shop owners and tradesmen to recover payment for goods and services because of loopholes in the Married Women's Property Act, 1882 (45 & 48 Vict. c.75) and subsequent acts. Bloom's monitoring of Molly's domestic expenditure may well relate to the problem of irrecoverable household debt associated with the1882 Act.

[10] Molly is sure Boylan has "plenty of money" (*U*18.411).

[11] As Bloom enters Kildare Street from the Molesworth Street end, it is quicker for him to rush into the Museum than to enter the Library.

and employs a number of casual staff. Successful advertising agencies in 1904 Dublin were lucrative. As Elisabetta d'Erme has pointed out, advertising was big business, with some two million people employed in the industry in the United Kingdom in 1904 and firms like Cadbury or Pears spending up to £125,000 per annum on advertisements.[12] So it is not surprising that Boylan would plunge "20 quid" on a "certainty" in a horse race or spend an estimated ten shillings on a basket of fruit, a jar of Plumtree's Potted Meat, and a bottle of port to be delivered to 7 Eccles Street in anticipation of his affair with Molly (18.424–25).[13] Bloom, by contrast, is one of the lowest paid and most highly stigmatized members of the advertising business: a canvasser, who, with door-to-door salesmen, were a favorite butt of social satirists and cartoonists.[14]

Molly is particularly dismissive of her husband's "pretending to be mooching about after advertisements"; "he ought to chuck that *Freeman* with the paltry few shillings he knocks out of it and go into an office or something where he would get regular pay or a bank where they could put him up on a throne to count the money all the day" (18.503–6). The telling word here, given its endorsement of wealth and power, is "throne." While

[12] Elisabetta d'Erme, "Mr Canvasser Bloom," paper presented at the 17th Trieste Joyce School, Trieste, 29 June–5 July 2014.

[13] "Plumtree's Potted Meat," accessed 23 July 2013, https://thefloatinglibrary.com/2009/05/03/what-is-a-home-withoutplumtrees-potted-meat-incomplete/: Plumtree's Potted Meat seven pence ha'penny. "Plumtree's Potted Meat," accessed 23 July 2013, https://thefloatinglibrary.com/2009/05/03/what-is-a-home-withoutplumtrees-potted-meat-incomplete/: Gilbey's Invalid Port two shillings and sixpence per bottle, W. & A. Gilbey, 46–47 Upper Sackville Street and Branch Depots in Dublin, "It is a soft matured wine, not medicated, free from excess of acidity and sugar, and therefore of a kind which is of service to the medical man when he considers that Port can be prescribed with advantage as a stimulant and restorative." See also John Smurthwaite, "A Joycean Price Guide," James Joyce Online Notes, accessed 23 July 2016, http://www.jjon.org/joyce-s-environs/joycean-price-guide; and "Prices in 1904 Dublin," *"Ulysses" Page-by-Page*, 2 March 2016, http://ulyssespages.blogspot.co.nz/2014/03/prices-in-1904-dublin.html.

[14] Donald Nicoll, *Publicity: An Essay on Advertising, by an Adept of 35 Years' Experience* (London: Office of the Parliamentary, Patent and Advertising Agency, 1878), 26–27.

Boylan is able to calculate his income in tens and hundreds of pounds, Bloom is obliged to reckon his in shillings and pounds. Shortly after leaving Davy Byrne's, following his light lunch of a glass of burgundy and a gorgonzola cheese sandwich, Bloom thinks to himself, "Keyes: two months if I get Nannetti too. That'll be two pounds ten about two pounds eight. Three Hynes owes me. Two eleven. Prescott's dye-works van over there. If I get Billy Prescott's ad: two fifteen. Five guineas about. On the pig's back" (8.1057–60). Though the predicted total is a shilling clear of five guineas, the money still has to be collected, and, even if it is, there is no guarantee of renewal. Molly admits she has grown tired of "always listening to" Bloom talk about "Billy Prescotts ad and Keyess ad and Tom the Devils ad," and she knows only too well that "if anything goes wrong in their business we have to suffer" (18.1342–44).

In fact, the rough budget for 16 June 1904, either compiled for Bloom by the unreliable "arranger" or disingenuously drafted as evidence should Molly question him, reveals a "credit" of two pounds fourteen and six, and only four shillings and nine-pence as "cash in hand," a result that appears to confirm Molly's fears rather than substantiate Bloom's predictions (17.1458–60).[15] Four shillings and nine pence as "cash in hand" is actually one penny less than what Stephen Dedalus's "vestal virgins" prise out of their money box so they can enjoy a picnic at the top of Nelson's column (7.932–34). If Bloom has compiled a list of income and expenditure to counter Molly's suspicions, then he has forgotten to include the cost of the "performance by Mrs Bandmann Palmer of *Leah*" he assures Molly he's been to (17.2256–57).[16] Likewise, as Osteen has argued, Bloom has not included a commission of one pound seven shillings and sixpence that he can collect from the cashier at the *Freeman's Journal*;[17] but this assumes that the advertisement is being printed and the commission is ready to be collected. Bloom's nod to Hynes, who owes him three shillings, might equally indicate that Bloom has requested an advance on obtaining the commission rather than payment in full of the entire sum.

[15] Note that the budget does not reconcile in the way that the creative balance of "£2-19-3" makes it seem. Osteen, *Economy*, 412, 449–50, provides a "Revised Budget" that gives a balance of "£2-19-2" with cash in hand plus earnings of "£1–12–3."

[16] Tony Thwaites, e-mail message to author, 12 August 2016.

[17] Osteen, *Economy*, 91, 411, 450.

To understand further why Bloom would not want to meet Boylan on the street and why Boylan represents an attractive proposition to Molly, it is worth comparing what the two men are prepared to spend on her and what that spending reveals. Boylan is youthful, confident, wealthy, and calculating; Bloom is approaching middle age, is anxious and insecure, and is comparatively less well off. Alf Bergin ventures that Boylan made "a cool hundred quid" out of the Keogh-Bennett boxing match that he promoted (12.942), and Molly has fond memories of the "fish supper" Boylan paid for to celebrate his winnings (18.1420–22). She surmises it was done to impress her, which suggests that Boylan might have taken them to somewhere like the Bailey, the Red Bank, or the Dive.[18] From his £100 winnings and whatever else he has made from his advertising business, Boylan is prepared to spend an unknown sum on a fish supper, approximately ten shillings on a basket of fruit containing a bottle of port and a jar of Plumtree's Potted Meat, and wager twenty pounds on Sceptre in the Gold Cup on the understanding that Molly will receive half the winnings. Bloom, on the other hand, has recently given Molly a present of half a dozen handkerchiefs, some violet garters, and a second-hand copy of the *Sweets of Sin*. But he persistently irritates her by asking how much things cost and, having reckoned on earning five guineas (actually five shillings and two pence for that week), is fantasizing about buying her a red satin petticoat for five pounds.[19] Boylan's pattern of spending suggests a shrewd operator who is prepared to spend a small sum to create a good impression and to risk a comparatively large sum, if the odds favor him, to be considered a lucky person. Molly, who is superstitious in her own way, places a high value on luck (18.140). Bloom's spending suggests someone who is so justifiably anxious to create a good impression that he will spend money he does not yet have on something that is just as likely to provoke a protest about its cost as it is to elicit gratitude. He will later remark to Stephen that "everybody gets their own ration of luck, they say" (16.240). To draw such a contrast is not to imply that Molly can be bought—that

[18] Leo Burdock's did not open until 1913, whereas the Bailey Fish Restaurant, the Red Bank Oyster Restaurant, and The Dive Oyster Restaurant at 8 Duke Street were all operating in 1904.

[19] He has also rather generously donated five shillings to the fund for Paddy Dignam's widow and will spend the rest of the afternoon ensuring that Mrs. Dignam can collect her late husband's life assurance.

she is crudely materialistic[20]—but it is to show that while Boylan delivers in person and well within his means, Bloom makes promises to himself in secret, promises he might or might not be able to keep were they to prove beyond his means.

Boylan would also appear attractive because he has agreed to enter into a business arrangement with Molly and her fellow artists for a concert that is to be held in Belfast in a week's time—a "swagger affair" in which there are "part shares and part profits"—and he has agreed to join her in a duet (5.151; 5.163). To be regarded as a financial asset rather than a dependent would doubtless be flattering to any wife whose husband did not hold a steady job, hung about the house, got under her feet, and periodically questioned her about her spending. As Mark Osteen has pointed out,

> if the figures Boylan recites on the phone to his secretary—£1.7s.6d (£2.15. for the two)—are Molly's fees for the concerts, then her earning power is excellent, especially considering that many male labourers in Dublin supported families on a pound a week (she does not earn this much every week). The symmetry between this figure and Bloom's commission for the day (17.1459) implies that the Blooms' earning power is comparable.[21]

So it is not surprising that Molly would think of the Belfast concert in terms of elopement or divorce (18.373–74). The Belfast venture not only provides a sharp contrast to the financial strictures which the Blooms faced in Holles Street, when she had to sing for next to nothing or when it was suggested she pose naked for a photographer or when she was reduced to selling her clothes to supplement the family budget (18.560–63). The concert tour, by contrast, promises the possibilities of first-class train travel, a good hotel, an expensive present, and the frisson of forbidden sexuality (18.367; 18.404).[22]

[20] Osteen, *Economy*, 425: "One of Joyce's notes to 'Penelope' reads, 'MB avarice,' *Notesheets*, 515."

[21] Osteen, *Economy*, 428.

[22] In *Wisdon v. Wisdon and St Vincent Parker-Jervis* reported in *Daily Mail*, 23 January 1920, 4, the defendant stated, "I have had a much better time with Parker-Jervis, who is a rich man with plenty of money."

Molly's feelings of financial insecurity, however, are more deep-seated than her irritation with Bloom's surveillance of their domestic economy or his proven inability to hold a steady job. What troubles her most are the various schemes that Bloom has either ventured in the past or imagines undertaking in the future. Haunting her is the fact that his father has committed suicide, apparently over a failed business venture, and that Bloom himself was once at considerable risk of being arrested over an illegal Hungarian Lotteries scheme that might well have seen him, but for the intervention of his fellow Masons, enjoying a custodial sentence at His Majesty's pleasure (18.1224–25). Though Bloom thinks of 7 Eccles Street as "My house down there. Big place" (6.376), Molly regards it as "a gesabo [*sic*]" (18.1493), a "big barracks of a place" (18.978). She worries that her husband's fantasies about opening a musical academy or a private hotel might mean that he will "go and ruin himself altogether the way his father did down in Ennis" (18.982–83). Even though she replaces the sign advertising "*Unfurnished Apartments*" in the bedroom window after the sign has fallen when the one-legged sailor stops in the street and calls for charity (10.250; 10.524), she is not happy about taking in "lodgers off the street" (18.1492–93). And if Bloom has ventured a lease on the whole building in the hope that at least the income from the two empty rooms will defray expenses, the collateral he holds is not as gilt-edged as it might seem.

It is the "certificate of possession of £900, Canadian 4% (inscribed) government stock" yielding four percent interest that is problematic (17.1864–65).[23] A reader would not be surprised that Bloom holds Canadian stock. As the arranger of "Ithaca" points out, "To Daniel Magrane and Francis Wade in 1882 during a juvenile friendship (terminated by the premature emigration of the former) he had advocated during nocturnal perambulations the political theory of colonial (e.g.

[23] Danis Rose, "The Source of Mr. Bloom's Wealth," *James Joyce Quarterly* 25, no. 1 (1987): 129, notes that "'The most valuable of Bloom's assets, the Certificate of possession of £900, Canadian 4% inscribed government stock (free of stamp duty)' was added to the text (and placed in the 2nd drawer) on a gathering of page proofs dated 27 January 1922. This last minute insertion, I submit, was a hasty compromise reached after several months of indecision occasioned by Joyce's knowledge of Bloom's past." See also Joyce, *Manuscript and First Printings Compared*, 675.

Canadian) expansion" (17.1640–44).[24] Neither would a reader be surprised that such stock was risky. As Osteen has extensively illustrated, Bloom's approach to spending and saving is governed by the strategy of covering risk with security.[25] As we will see later in this chapter, the £900 Canadian stock, in terms of the Blooms' overall finances, is partly offset by "an endowment assurance policy of £500 in the Scottish Widows' Assurance Society, intestated Millicent (Milly) Bloom," a financial institution that was and still is regarded as impeccably sound.[26] Not so the Canadian stock. Throughout the early 1900s, Canada was the market of choice for high-yield investment, particularly following the numerous bank failures and the catastrophic collapse of the Australian stock market in the 1890s,[27] and the prolonged "bear" phase of the London Stock Market following the end of the Boer War.[28] Even the American markets were in a "bear" phase

[24] See *The Empire and the Century: A Series of Essays on Imperial Problems and Possibilities by Various Writers* (London: John Murray, 1905), 351–420, for analysis of the importance of Canada to the Empire. For the Canada swindle lawsuit (*U*12.1984), see Gifford with Seidman, *"Ulysses" Annotated*, 135–36.

[25] Osteen, *Economy*, 72–74.

[26] Dorian Mormont, "Performance and Analysis of the Oldest Mutual Fund, the Scottish Widows' Fund from 1815 to 2000," *Memoire Presente en vue de l'obtention du Master en Sciences Economiques, Finalement Management Sciences* (MS thesis, Solvay Brussels School of Economics and Management, 2011–2012). *Every Man's Own Lawyer* carried advertisements for the Scottish Widows. The amount for Milly was raised from £100 in the *Little Review* to £500 for the first edition; also "coming into force at 21" raised to "coming into force at 25." Joyce, *Manuscript and First Printings Compared*, 675.

[27] David Tolmie Merrett, "The 1893 Bank Crashes and Monetary Aggregates," Research Discussion Paper 9303 (Sydney: Reserve Bank of Australia, 1993), 16: "a monetary contraction of unparalleled proportions in Australian history." See also David Tolmie Merrett, "Australian Banking Practice and the Crisis of 1893," *Australian Economic History Review* 29, no. 1 (1989): 60–65 and David Tolmie Merrett, "The Australian Bank Crashes of the 1890s Revisited," *Business History Review* 87 (Autumn 2013): 407–29.

[28] "The seven years from July 1900, down to the present day have been to the City generally, and to investors in particular, a long series of disillusionments and disappointments." *The Bankers' Insurance Managers' and Agents' Magazine*, vol. 84 (London: Waterlow, 1907), 328.

at that time. On the last day of May 1904, the *Freeman's Journal* ruefully observed that "it is reported that the depression in Wall Street at the present time is more pronounced than it has been for some years past."[29]

By contrast, between 1896 and 1914, Canada had the world's fastest growing economy.[30] Vast sums of money poured into the country from the United Kingdom and from America. Even Australian investors were encouraged to buy Canadian stock on the assurance that "that is where the smart money was going."[31] But high yield invariably involves high risk. While the interest on Bloom's "£900, Canadian 4% (inscribed) government stock" was "guaranteed," the principal, as events subsequently proved, was not. In *Ulysses Annotated* Gifford and Seidman propose that "according to calculations based on Moody's *Manual of Corporate Securities* [*sic*] (New York, 1904), Bloom can expect 'an annual income from the interest on the book value of his holdings [of] £36.'"[32] But Moody's, even in the unlikely event that Bloom could consult a copy (neither the British Library nor the National Library of Ireland presently hold it), would provide cold comfort given what was being reported in the newspapers of the day. Besides, Bloom's stock is not listed on the New York exchange, as *Ulysses Annotated* implies, but on the London exchange. Another problem with Gifford and Seidman's calculation is that it assumes the stock regularly yields a four percent return. *The Stock Exchange Official Intelligence*, published annually by the London Stock Market, shows that this "book value" was rarely if ever achieved. As Davis

[29] "Commercial News," *Freeman's Journal*, 30 May 1904, 3.

[30] Lance E. Davis and Robert E. Gallman, eds., *Evolving Financial Markets and International Capital Flows: Britain, the Americas, and Australia* (Cambridge: Cambridge University Press, 2001), 379–83.

[31] "Australians in Canada," *Brisbane Courier*, 9 November 1904, 4.

[32] Gifford with Seidman, *"Ulysses" Annotated*, 597; Osteen, *Economy*, 92. For problems in 1904 with Canadian Railway management and investment, see "All Aboard: The Board of Railway Commissioners, 1904 to 1938," Canadian Transportation Agency, accessed 23 July 2016, https://www.otc-cta.gc.ca/eng/publication/100-years-heart-transportation-historical-perspective#chapter1. See also Leslie T. Fournier, "Present Railroad Problems in Canada," *The Annals of the American Academy of Political and Social Science* 187, no. 1 (1936): 151–52; Railway Inquiry Commission 1916; and The Drayton-Acworth Report (1917).

and Gallman point out, "Canadian government 4 per cent stock offered British investors a return of 3.1 per cent."[33] The *Freeman's Journal* for the 9th of March 1904, which is the most likely source for Joyce's and Bloom's information, provides a very detailed and tempting description of the Canadian 4 percent (inscribed) government stock and why it appears to be an attractive investment. It is listed as number 38 in a list of supposedly high-yield investments published by the newspaper in March 1904.

> No. 38 Canadian Four Per Cent Loan:—
> Amount £4,000,000 present yield per percent per annum £3-17-9.
> This is a Four per Cent stock of the Canadian Government, registered and inscribed, issued in June, 1885, and redeemable at any time between 1st January 1910 and 1st January 1935, at the option of the Government on giving six months' notice. The dividends are payable twice annually in January and July. £3,499,900 of the stock is inscribed and registered, and can be transferred in any amount free of charge except a small stamp duty of 2s 6d per £100 stock, in the transfer books kept by the Bank of Montreal in London. The balance of £500,100 was issued in bearer bonds of £100, £500 and £1000 each, which can be transferred or converted into registered stock free of any charges. In 1902 this stock stood at £108-10s, while last year it had fallen to £102-15s, and now figures at about £103 for each £100 stock. The bonds are about the same price. The amount of this security being rather large admits of extensive dealings, and transactions are recorded daily. No doubt it has depreciated in sympathy with others, but like them it also remains eligible for a substantial increase in its present value in case of an early recovery in the markets. The annual fluctuations are a little over three points, deduced from the statistics of the past two or three years. This is an authorized trustee investment.[34]

However, in a long and very detailed article in the *Freeman's Journal* published on 30 May 1904, Lord Dunraven, castigated the newspaper

[33] Davis and Gallman, *Evolving Financial Markets*, 556.

[34] *Freeman's Journal*, 9 March 1904, 5. See also "Lord Dunraven on the Land Act," *Freeman's Journal*, 30 May 1904, 5: "The Canadian Guaranteed 4 per Cent are not a trustee security at all, as they are redeemable in 1908, 1910, 1913, and are always above par; also the three classes yield respectively £2-10s-9d, £3-1s-6d, £3-6s-9d according to Coates's list."

for publishing inaccurate and misleading advice. "You must bear in mind," he told readers,

> what the *Freeman* entirely ignores—the effect of such large sums of money as about five millions a year seeking investment. Everything is subject to the law of supply and demand, but nothing is so sensitive as the Stock Exchange, especially in good securities bearing so high a rate of interest as 3½% . . . What the object of the *Freeman* is in publishing this long and misleading list, I do not pretend to say. The effect is plain enough. . . . [People] who have neither the time nor the money to enquire into the matter themselves are deluded into believing [they] can get four or five or six per cent for their money.[35]

If Bloom has bought his Canadian stock on the advice of his own newspaper, then he has been seriously ill-advised. The *Economist* for 4 June 1904 reported significant problems with the Grand Trunk and the Canadian Pacific, two of the major infrastructure projects financed by government bonds.[36] As one investment analyst noted in 1908, "the lowest price at which its 4% guaranteed stock has sold in four years was 95½ in 1904."[37] That Bloom has chosen to invest in risky stock, even if it is to cover his rent at Number 7, rather than purchase a house for himself and Molly in town or in one of the new suburbs, is not a decision that generates confidence in Bloom's financial acumen or in his commitment to Molly.

Equally problematic is the origin of the £900. It is hardly likely that Bloom inherited it from his father, as his father's suicide appears to have been associated with a failed business venture. It is also unlikely that Bloom could have saved such a large amount of money since he started working twenty-five years ago, in jobs ranging from door-to-door salesmanship to being employed as a tally clerk in the cattle yards.[38] To include

[35] "Lord Dunraven on the Land Act," 5.

[36] *The Economist*, 4 June 1904, 947.

[37] Carl Snyder, *American Railways as Investments: A Detailed and Comparative Analysis of All the Leading Railways, from the Investor's Point of View, with an Introductory Chapter on the Methods of Estimating Railway Values* (New York: Moody, 1907), 329.

[38] To save £900, Bloom would have had to put aside £36 per year for every year since he began working, assuming that he bought the Canadian stock in 1903.

the £900 in a statement of assets, as Osteen does, is to assume that Bloom has saved the entire sum; he might equally have borrowed some or all of it at a lower interest rate. If there was a call on borrowings—something not unknown in the stock market debacles of the 1890s and early 1900s—then selling his Canadian stock could also prove problematic. Authoritative sources, such as *The Canadian Annual Review of Public Affairs*, and financial columns, such as the London *Times's* "Finance and Commerce" and the *Daily Mail's* "Chat on Change," record the extreme volatility of the Canadian market throughout the first half of 1904, with reports employing phrases like "severe disappointment" (12 January), "dull and idle" (20 January), "market remained weak" (1 February), "shocking" (1 March), "heavy in tone" (28 March), and "dividend outlook anything but cheering" (6 June). In fact, investors were so nervous that while the April report was being delivered to the London Exchange at the end of May, "there was unbroken silence until one man raised an hysterical cheer," which "broke the spell and a few bids were made."[39]

According to the narrator of the section of "Oxen of the Sun" modeled on the style of the eighteenth-century Irish satirist *Junius*,[40] Bloom shares this anxiety. Like many investors in the stock market, the value of his stock was influenced by the fluctuating fortunes of the Russo-Japanese war fought between 8 February 1904 and 5 September 1905. One view in Dublin, recalled by Bloom as he passes Larry O'Rourke's, is that the "Russians, they'd only be an eight o'clock breakfast for the Japanese" (4.116–17). Another, that if the "markets are on the rise," "foreign wars is the cause of it," given "the Russians wish to tyrannise" (12.136–40). Though Japanese victory would not come until the battle of Tsushima on 27 and 28 May 1905, a succession of victories between February and April 1904 clearly signaled their superiority. *Junius*'s satirical portrait of Bloom's shifting allegiances arraigns his sympathies with Sinn Fein against his capitalist concern that his stock will be adversely affected. "During the recent war," the narrator questions, "whenever the enemy [Japan] had a temporary advantage with his granados [silk] did this traitor to his kind [Bloom] not seize the moment to discharge his piece against the empire [England] of which he is a tenant at will while he trembled for the security of his four per cents" (14.908–12)?

[39] "Chat on Change," *Daily Mail*, 31 May 1904, 2.

[40] Most likely the pseudonym of Sir Philip Francis (1740–1818).

The reason for this nervousness lay in the nature of the stock itself. From the mid-nineteenth century, Canada's economic development depended on investment in railways financed by British and American "entrepreneurs through the issuance of bonds, preferred shares, and other instruments that required the payment of annual interest, rather than common shares."[41] As early as the fiscal year of 1870, for example, "all of the net operating income of £358,058" generated by The Grand Trunk Railway, Canada's first "system" road, went "towards the payment of bond interest and lease payments."[42] That the debt-financing of interest and lease payments was still causing problems in 1904 is evident from two extracts from a run of market reports in the *Daily Mail*:

> Saturday, May 28, 1904: The most interesting market on Monday will be Grand Trunks. When the dealers arrive they will find waiting for them the statement for the month of April. To every one of them it will mean a great deal; whether it will be a "bull" or a "bear". If it shows a gain of £10,000 over the last year, it will not only be considered a good statement, but will be regarded as the turning point in a long run of bad luck. The first quarter of the year—January to March inclusive—was simply disastrous. It imperilled not merely the Preference dividends, but the Guaranteed as well.[43]
>
> Tuesday, May 31, 1904: While the Grand Trunk crowd were revelling in their April gain of £43,000, the Canadian Pacific statement for the same month was quietly posted. It drew no joyful "bulls" round it, for it showed a loss of $81,000. But such contradictions between the two roads are nothing new. In fact it is very seldom they publish good results simultaneously. When the Canadian Pacific is in luck the Grand Trunk is likely to be the other way, and vice versa.[44]

By 1905 the Grand Trunk, the Canadian Pacific, and the Canadian Northern had emerged as the major players, but fluctuating commodity prices,

[41] *The Canadian Encyclopedia* (Toronto: McClelland and Stewart, 2000), 1001–2.

[42] "Grand Trunk Railway System," accessed 21 July 2016, http://www.railwaybob.com/Constituents/GTRConstituents.htm. See also, "Grand Trunk Railway," canada-rail, accessed 2 July 2016, http://www.canada-rail.com/ontario/railways/GTR.html#.WBPPWKNh3Hc.

[43] "Grand Trunks," *Daily Mail*, 28 May 1904, 2.

[44] "Chat on Change: Canadian Pacifics," *Daily Mail*, 31 May 1904, 2.

unseasonable weather, labor problems, and poor management and then the outbreak of the First World War saw the Grand Trunk, then the Canadian Northern, and finally the Canadian Pacific effectively nationalized by the Canadian government in 1920—with no compensation for British and American investors.[45] It has been said that British investors "never forgave" the Canadian government for stealing their property.[46] Come July 1922, Bloom would have lost his entire principal, his investment of £900.

This is not to argue that Joyce deliberately set a trap for the unwary reader; what I wish to propose is that given the nationalization of the railways at the time Joyce was drafting the *nostos* episodes, Canadian bonds, known as risky, provided the speculative counter to the proven security of the Scottish Widows' Assurance Society; a counter, as I have already mentioned, that was quintessential to the way Bloom thought about money. Furthermore, the poor performance of Canadian stocks, particularly during the early months of 1904, might partly explain why Bloom would not feel confident confronting Boylan and why he chose to avoid him throughout the day.

* * * * *

In addition to granting Bloom's financial situation more security and certainty than is warranted, what also appears to have been overlooked is the fact that Bloom's balance sheet for the day is associated with his undressing, his "divestiture." It is immediately followed by his fantasy of acquiring his

[45] "Judicial Committee of the Privy Council," *Times* (London), 12 July 1922, 5; 14 July 1922, 4; 29 July 1922, 4. *The Accountant*, 6 May 1922, 616, and 5 August 1922, 194. I am indebted to Katy Davies, Librarian at the Institute of Chartered Accountants of England and Wales for these references from *The Accountant*. The process of nationalization followed the establishment of a commission under Prime Minister Robert Borden headed by Sir Henry Drayton and W. M. Ackworth in May 1917. See "Drayton and Ackworth Favor Nationalization," *Toronto World*, 28 March 1917, 6, accessed 15 July 2016, https://news.google.com/newspapers?nid=hqOjcs7Dif8C&dat=19170328&printsec=frontpage&hl=en.

[46] "Grand Trunk Railway," Canada-Rail, accessed 23 July 2016, http://www.canada-rail.com/ontario/railways/GTR.html#.V29qHN5UN0A. See also Leslie T. Fournier, *Railway Nationalization in Canada: The Problem of the Canadian National Railways* (1935; New York: Arno Press, 1981), 49–73.

ideal home, "Flowerville," a fantasy he also subsequently divests by realizing that the only way he might be able to realize such an extravagant fantasy is to make "an independent discovery of a goldseam of inexhaustible ore" (17.1753). This is a fantasy, like the Canadian stock, that is equally impervious to the economics and politics of war, nationalization, and the fluctuation of the stock markets. What also seems to have been overlooked is that £900 in 1904, assuming it is money Bloom actually has, would provide a substantial deposit for "Flowerville," although perhaps not for the "additional attractions that the grounds might obtain" (17.1551). Again, as with his fantasy gift for Molly of a red silk petticoat, he has opted for the unrealizable as against the achievable. Bloom, we are informed, does not want to acquire or inherit a country estate or buy "a terracehouse or semidetatched villa" in Dublin or in the suburbs (17.1499–506).

His fantasy is to "purchase by private treaty in fee simple a thatched bungalowshaped 2 storey dwellinghouse of southerly aspect" on five or six acres in either Dundrum or Sutton (17.1504–5). He wants "freehold" title (the meaning of "fee simple"), and he does not want to buy the property through a real estate agent, such as H. F. Norman, whose office at 110 Grafton Street Bloom passes on his way to the National Library to check on the Keyes advertisement. Were Bloom to look in the window, or were he to consult the property pages of the *Irish Times*, he would find that his £900 would enable him to buy a three-story Victorian Villa in Putland Road, Bray, for example, "at reduced price of £700, to effect immediate disposal, an excellent house, lease 1000 years, only subject to £10: £300 spent on house within recent years: immediate possession."[47] Or if he wished to hedge some of his Canadian stock, assuming he himself has saved the whole £900, he could opt for something more modest but more central, such as a terrace house in Seville Place: "Capital House in this desirable position. Close to Amiens Street and Clontarf tram line. 7 rooms in perfect order: new sewerage, back garden. Price only £460; immediate possession."[48] But his dream residence, "Flowerville," whether in Dundrum or Sutton, is far more elaborate. If it was written up for sale in 1904, it would most likely be advertised as "Freestanding two-story

[47] *Irish Times*, 26 September 1903, 10. Agent: James H. North & Co., 110 Grafton Street. Presently, the Offices of the Dublin Trading Company.

[48] *Irish Times*, 16 September 1903, 10. *Every Man's Own Lawyer*, 17, contains a comprehensive list of "Solicitors' Costs for Sales, Purchases, and Mortgages."

thatched villa: nine rooms plus modern kitchen, three bathrooms. Fully furnished. Gas heated and carpeted throughout. Situated on five acres containing outbuildings, a tennis court and gardens. Pasture suitable for grazing stock. Extensive views."

In the fair copy of this section of "Ithaca," Bloom is shown financing "Flowerville," which is estimated to cost £1,200, by taking out a loan with the Irish Civil Service Building Society (incorporated 1874) for £800 to be repaid over twenty years at 5 percent interest. To qualify, he would need a deposit of £400 and an assured income of £360 per annum (17.1657–71). According to Danis Rose, the original "Flowerville" was "intended" to be a "perfectly realistic and realizable plan for the eventual move out of Eccles street and the beginning of a new phase of life."[49] But, by the final draft, "Flowerville" has become an unrealizable fantasy. The historically known Irish Civil Service Building Society (incorporated 1874) is now the fictional "Industrious Foreign Acclimatised Nationalised Friendly Stateaided Building Society (incorporated 1874)," while the mortgage calculations went north as the project morphed into unreality.

Danis Rose has offered a biographical explanation for these revisions, but I contend that, as a fantasy, "Flowerville" is not only more in keeping with Bloom's attitude to money but that it also chimes with Bloom's need to narrativize his situation. As the "arranger" explains, "For what reason did he meditate on schemes so difficult of realisation? It was one of his axioms that similar meditations *or the automatic relation of himself to a narrative concerning himself* or tranquil recollection of the past when practised habitually before retiring for the night alleviated fatigue and produced as a result sound repose and renovated vitality" (17.1754–58; emphasis mine).

* * * *

It is the "endowment assurance policy of £500 in the Scottish Widows' Assurance Society, intestated Millicent (Milly) Bloom," held in the second

[49] Rose, "The Source of Mr. Bloom's Wealth." Andrew Gibson, "'Nobody Owns': *Ulysses*, Tenancy, and Property Law," *James Joyce Quarterly* 50, no. 4 (2013): 959, has convincingly argued that "Flowerville" raises "the question of 'how far modern legal agreements over property outdistance the feudalism that has so crippled Ireland.'" See also Mary Daly, *Dublin, the Deposed Capital: A Social and Economic History 1860–1914* (Cork: Cork University Press, 1984).

drawer of the walnut bureau in 7 Eccles Street that provides a realist narrative that counterbalances the fantasy narrative of "Flowerville" within the fictional story-world of Bloom's domestic economy. The assurance policy means that Bloom has made secure provision for his daughter, particularly in the eventuality of his death or if he decides to divorce Molly. Intestated (meaning in her name), the assurance policy provides her with a guaranteed sum of money that makes her independent.[50] As we have seen, the mail that Bloom collects from the hall floor of Number 7 at eight o'clock in the morning is eloquent of the shared affection between father and daughter. She calls him "Dearest Papli," signs herself "your fond daughter," and thoughtfully apologies for her bad handwriting. At various times during the day, he has warm memories of her counting his waistcoat buttons; of her running to the letterbox to collect notes he has written to her; of the funeral she conducts for a dead bird; of her "tubbing night" when they lived in Lombard Street West; of the quarrel they had in the XL café about her bracelet—"wouldn't eat her cakes or speak or look. Saucebox"; of her delight in the wind and the waves when they rounded the Kish lighthouse in choppy seas on a pleasure cruise on *Erin's King*; of the "breakfast moustachecup of imitation Crown Derby porcelain ware" she buys him for his twenty-seventh birthday; and of her maturing into an independent young woman. He also recalls Molly chasing her with an umbrella to chastise her and the growing tension between the two. And although Molly admits to boxing Milly's ears for impudence, and although she is irritated by what she sees as her vanity, laziness, and disobedience and her lack of respect for her privacy, Molly still wants her to remain at home and further her education at the Skerrys Academy, a professional commercial college. But Bloom insists that on her fifteenth birthday Milly accept a job as an assistant in a photography shop in Mullingar at twelve and sixpence a week—"pig headed as usual"

[50] *Kingham v. Kingham* [1897] 1 IR 170. Final judgment against wife at 29 ILTR 5: "Testator declared that any money to which any daughter should become entitled under his will should be settled free of any liabilities of any other person, and with full power of willing same on her decease. *Held*, that each daughter's share should be settled upon her for her separate use, with restraint on anticipation, and with power to dispose of same by will; and in default of such disposition to such daughter's next-of-kin as if she had died unmarried." See also *Hartford v. Power* (1868) 16 WR 822 (IR); affirmed on appeal 3 IR Eq 602.

(18.528), Molly thinks to herself—although it will mean Milly has to board, as Mullingar is some fifty miles from Dublin (18.1004–7). Doubtless Molly's preference reflects a class bias; a professionally trained secretary being considered a cut above a shop assistant.

But there are sound legal reasons why Bloom has insisted that Milly move out of home and why he has taken out a life assurance policy with the Scottish Widows' Assurance Society. The first has to do with Milly's recent habit of bursting in on her mother unannounced (18.1009–13), and both his and Molly's awareness of their daughter's burgeoning sexuality. In *Jenkins v. Jenkins* (1903),[51] the ten-year-old daughter on one occasion surprised her father *in flagrante delicto*; but when the mother proposed that her daughter be called as a witness, His Honour Justice Bargrave Deane demurred, remarking it would not be necessary.[52] Bloom would not wish Milly to have a similar experience. As Molly muses to herself as she thinks about his insistence that Milly work in Mullingar, "such an idea for him to send the girl down there to learn to take photographs…only he'd do a thing like that all the same *on account of me and Boylan thats why he did it Im certain the way he plots and plans everything out*" (18.1004–9; emphasis mine).

Yet Bloom's insistence that Milly move far enough away to prevent surprise visits might be interpreted as conducing adultery, as making it easier for Molly to have an affair with Boylan; the "he wants a divorce but is too frightened to make it happen himself" argument that had occurred to Molly when she thought about her husband's flirtation with Josie Powell before Josie married Denis Breen. That Milly is perhaps still innocent of anything between her mother and Boylan is evident from the Freudian slip she confesses to making when she admits in her letter to her father that she was "on the pop of writing Blazes Boylan's" (4.408).[53] It is unlikely that Bloom would have insisted that Milly go to Mullingar to protect her from Boylan, despite her burgeoning sexuality, as legally she is under age,[54]

[51] *Times* (London), 20 January 1904, 4.

[52] *Jenkins v. Jenkins*, NA J77/791/4064, Filed: 14 July 1903; Set Down: 19 January 1904; Final Decree: 2 August 1904.

[53] Molly uses the same expression: "he was on the pop of asking me" (*U*18.198).

[54] See *Criminal Law Amendment Act*, "Table of Offences," 102: "Unlawful carnal knowledge against girls above 13 or under 16: two years imprisonment. Reasonable belief that girl was above 16 a defence. Defendant and wife or husband

although the reader knows from Boylan's interaction with the shop assistant in Thornton's that he is adept at provoking sexual self-awareness in young women (10.327–36). And given the arguments about her working in Mullingar and his suspicions about Boylan's intentions regarding Molly, it is not something Bloom can discuss with his wife.

What Bloom doubtless does not realize is that insisting that Milly works in Mullingar while she is still a minor effectively removes her from his authority and consequently from his protection. In *Gladney v. Murphy*, the Court ruled, "A father's dominion and control over his minor daughter (in lieu of *animus revertendi*) is suspended during an actual service under contract of hiring entered into by her and with his consent."[55] But this is something, it seems, that Bloom has neither discussed with Milly nor sought legal advice about. In fact, it is not until he rescues Stephen from the phantasmagoric horrors and guilt of Nighttown and takes him to the Cabman's shelter for something to eat and drink that Bloom is able to talk about adultery and divorce, the two issues that have nagged at him since breakfast.

* * * *

The "Eumaeus" episode, as many critics have observed, is full of references to adultery and divorce. Not only do they alert the reader to the extent to which both adultery and divorce refuse to be silenced, but they also provide a sequence of nested narratives through which Bloom can discreetly explore his own concerns. As Leckie has convincingly argued, daily newspaper reporting of divorce court proceedings provided what Judith Butler has termed "the conditions of intelligibility."[56] Adultery and divorce, once taboo, could now be introduced into general conversation, even if it was

competent witnesses." Note, however, Keith Smith, "Offences against the Person," in *The Oxford History of the Laws of England: Volume XIII: 1820–1914 Fields of Development*, ed. William Cornish, J. Stuart Anderson, Ray Cocks, Michael Loban, Patrick Polden, and Keith Smith (Oxford: Oxford University Press, 2010), 406: "In relation to non-penetrative sexual assault, legal consent was set at 13 for both girls and boys in 1880 by the Assault of Young Persons Act, and at 16 by the Criminal Law Amendment Act 1922."

[55] *Gladney v. Murphy* 26 ILTR 651.

[56] Leckie, "Simple Case of Adultery," 734, citing Judith Butler, *Excitable Speech: A Politics of the Performative* (New York: Routledge, 1997), 134.

not something one did in mixed company, because they could be talked about using a vocabulary and a genre that legitimized them as belonging to the public sphere. In Stephen, Bloom has discovered someone he believes he can talk to, albeit indirectly, about what has been worrying him since he left home that morning and that in the world of Nighttown had come to assume Kafkaesque proportions. He can use terms like *liaison* and *decree nisi*, and he can refer to the King's Proctor. He can parody the Registrar's orders for "Further Particulars" ("she unbuttoned his and then he untied her" [16.1210–11]) and mock the love letters that were read out in court because these were terms, procedures, and functionaries of the court that were common knowledge to everyone who read the newspapers.[57]

Divorce Court journalism also licensed Joyce to fill "Eumaeus" with references to sex, adultery, and divorce as if they were naturally part of the consciousness of his characters and of the *mentalité* of Edwardian Dublin rather than the underworld of Nighttown. Present and past cases could be woven seamlessly into the narrative; comparisons and contrasts with the ways adultery and divorce were represented in high and low culture could be readily introduced, while the style of reporting itself, which overlaid everything with a veneer of decorum, provided an ideal vehicle for the tension between concealment and disclosure that was quintessential to the Homeric parallel.

* * * *

Because it has not been understood that Bloom is able to petition the Probate, Divorce and Admiralty Division of the King's Bench if he affirms English domicile, the world of the Cabman's shelter and his conversation with Stephen have not been read as purportedly real-world narratives through which Bloom can explore the information about Divorce Court procedure he has randomly acquired from the newspapers and from elsewhere. Bloom conducts this exploration by assessing the narratives even as he inhabits them. In essence, the cabman's shelter is an ur-court. Stories, which might or might not be true, are told to an audience of common people—a quasi-jury—by a person who affirms an identity which might or

[57] For example, "Letters to a Wife: Colonel's Discovery of a Friend's Intrigue," *Daily Mail*, 24 March 1920, 4, where extracts from a bundle of letters were read out in court and one letter was published.

might not be true and who produces evidence which might or might not be relevant about something which might or might not have happened.

All the stories in one way or another have as their principal motif a woman who has committed adultery. All of them engage issues of agency, circumstance, identity, evidence, and disclosure, and all of them explore closure. How is adultery detected? How is it proved? How should a wronged person respond? What happens to petitioners?

The first story that Bloom critiques has to do with the "redbearded sailor" they encounter in the shelter who goes by the name of D. B. Murphy of Carrigaloe. To confirm his identity Murphy produces a postcard, his certificate of discharge, and shows everyone his tattoos. Declaring name, address, occupation, and domicile—he asserts of Carrigaloe "that's where I hails from"—particularly following the introduction of Divorce Rule 220 in 1905, were mandatory for filing a petition. Murphy, as it were, is in court. What the jury will assess is his claim that "My little woman's down there. She's waiting for me, I know. *For England, home and beauty*. She's my own true wife I haven't seen for seven years now, sailing about" (16.418–21).

Bloom immediately challenges this Odyssean parallel by imaginatively relating a counternarrative to himself. This counternarrative is not a fantasy, as Barbara Leckie and others have claimed, but a satirical and somewhat cynical summary of the numerous petitions for divorce that were filed by mariners and by soldiers and sailors who had extended voyages in the merchant navy or long periods of active service during the Boer War and subsequently during the First World War. To take just four examples that were reported in the newspapers: *Milne v. Milne* (1902),[58] *Goodfellow v. Goodfellow and Keys* (1902),[59] *Roberts v. Roberts and Drew* (1902),[60] and *Roberts v. Roberts and Foulkes* (1901).[61] In the first case Milne was away for much of 1901 and

[58] *Milne v. Milne*, NA J77/754/2958, Filed: 24 June 1902; Set Down: 27 November 1902; Decree Nisi: 16 February 1903; Final Decree: 30 October 1905.

[59] *Goodfellow v. Goodfellow and Keys*, NA J77/754/2959, Filed: 25 June 1902; Set Down: 11 July 1902; Decree Nisi: 7 August 1902; Final Decree: 16 February 1902.

[60] *Roberts v. Roberts and Drew*, NA J77/754/2937, Filed: 13 June 1902; Set Down: 20 August 1902; Decree Nisi: 10 November 1902; Final Decree: 25 May 1903.

[61] *Roberts v. Roberts and Foulkes*, NA J77/733/2303, Filed: 8 November 1901; Set Down: 2 January 1902; Decree Nisi: 30 May 1905; Final Decree: 11 December 1905.

1902, having been called to his ship shortly after he was married. While the co-respondent could not be identified, the adultery could be proved. However, paternity was not an issue, as the Milnes remained childless. In the second case, Goodfellow was frequently away on voyages, but the adultery, though proved, did not correspond to his absences. In the third case, Roberts, who was a coppersmith, joined the Royal Navy after he and his wife had two children. While he was on active service in the Mediterranean throughout 1895 to 1899, she had two children by the co-respondent. In the fourth case, Roberts was a Chief Officer in the Mercantile Marine. His wife committed adultery with a person or persons unknown in 1901. In January 1902 he was appointed to a ship that was to sail from Cardiff to Port Elizabeth in South Africa. In the event, the ship received further commissions that took it to Australia, Canada, South Africa, Peru, and Belgium; in all an absence of nearly three years. As Roberts explained to the court, "When leaving I was not aware of the length of the voyage. The vessel is now lying at Ghent and I am under agreement for another voyage and have to leave Ghent for Cape Town in a few weeks time but am very desirous of having this petition disposed of before again leaving this country. During my absence the alimony of £36 per annum ordered by the Court to be paid to the said respondent has been regularly paid." The case was heard. The respondent's adultery was established, and the *decree nisi* was then made absolute as soon as the statutory period of six months had elapsed. There is no extant record of costs being awarded.

The cases that began to be presented to the Divorce Division of the King's Bench after the first two years of First World War and up to the time that *Ulysses* was published are too numerous to mention. In many of these, the co-respondents could not be identified. The Registrar of the Court would then request "further particulars" that either named the co-respondent or co-respondents or affirmed that the petitioner had exhausted all possible means of discovering their identity. Such orders for "further particulars" might be issued several times. In others, when the petitioner could produce witnesses or documented evidence that adultery had taken place or of the time when it was obvious it had taken place, because the respondent had conceived and given birth during the petitioner's absence, the case was allowed to proceed. With the latter, the birth certificate became part of the evidence. In cases where more than one co-respondent was cited, as in

Jones v. Jones and Saunders and Cook (1902),[62] each co-respondent was required to defend himself.

Again, Bloom's imagined account of the petitioner's response—"O! Bow to the inevitable. Grin and bear it. I remain with much love your brokenhearted husband D B Murphy" (16.438–40)—reflects a common reality. If co-respondents could be identified, they were generally condemned to costs, but such costs were in lieu of *crim. con.*, as damages were rarely awarded. To resort to the cliché that Bloom imaginatively attributes to Murphy, many "bowed to the inevitable." Only rarely, as in the case of *Kirk v. Kirk* (1902), who were married in the Registry Office in Dublin prior to his being ordered to South Africa in 1901, was the petition submitted to the Court but not prosecuted, even though the respondent had given birth to a son "of which the petitioner was not the father" while the petitioner was away.[63] Whether there was forgiveness or whether there was simply a parting of ways remains unknown.

To substantiate his voyages to exotic lands, D. B. Murphy produces a postcard depicting a group of women and children identified as "*Choza de Indios. Beni, Bolivia.*" Bloom, who has been skeptical of Murphy's identity, engages in his first foray into "Sherlockholmesing." He reverses the postcard and sees *Targeta Postal, Senor A Boudin, Galeria Becche, Santiago, Chile* as the address.[64] He observes that there is no message. This is the first of several references in the episode to the key role played by postcards, letters, and other written documents in divorce proceedings, a role to which I will return. What is pertinent for the present is the way Murphy's "sailing under false colours" and his allegedly first-hand account of how native women control their fertility remind Bloom of his "longcherished plan" of "travelling to London via long sea" (16.499–501).

[62] *Jones v. Jones and Saunders and Cook*, NA J77/755/2984, Filed: 4 July 1902; Set Down: 9 December 1902; Decree Nisi: 31 March 1903; Final Decree: 14 October 1903. Saunders was not guilty of adultery; Cook was. More sensational is *Sutton v. Sutton and Adams and Lloyd and Loveless*, NA J77/806/4520, Filed: 9 January 1904; Set Down: 16 June 1904; Decree Nisi: 23 January 1905; Final Decree 31 July 1905—where the petitioner was not only granted custody of the children but was permitted to take them with him to Canada.

[63] *Kirk v. Kirk*, NA J77/768/3378, Filed: 12 November 1902.

[64] Nicolas-Thomas Baudin (1754–1803). French explorer, cartographer, naturalist, and hydrographer. Between 1800 and 1803 he led an expedition to map the coast of New Holland (now Australia).

In contrast to his satirical narrative about Murphy's homecoming, Bloom's imagined sea journey to London begins with details about the best day to depart, whether or not he can "work a ticket," and how much a ticket might cost compared with the cost of a return journey to Mullingar to see Milly. His sense of the route is slightly inaccurate as ships called at Falmouth before Plymouth, but Falmouth–Plymouth–Southampton was a well-recognized route (16.512–13); and from there to London by train. Despite his disclaimer that "he had never travelled extensively to any great extent," Bloom thinks of himself as having been to London before; on his imagined voyage "he would doubtless see the greatest improvement, tower, abbey, wealth of Park lane to renew acquaintance with" (16.514–16). If he was in London previously, then it was only a fetal visit.[65] As an indulgence, this might be excused as another "Bloomism," a "factual near miss," but it marks the point where the narrative begins to morph into a compensatory fantasy about "sailing under false colours." Traveling to London, whether as Leopold Bloom or Henry Flower, would enable him to reconnoiter the large Jewish community that had established itself there should he wish to set up a business and establish English domicile. But his mind turns toward becoming an impresario for an imagined "Tweedy-Flower grand opera company," "with his own legal consort as a leading lady," engaged to tour the "first rate hydros and spas... which might prove highly remunerative." Perhaps this is a way of obtaining English domicile. Perhaps this is a way of making a fresh start. Perhaps this is to compensate for Boylan's promotion of the Belfast concert, or perhaps it is the way he might represent such a plan to Molly. But the fantasy implodes when he realizes that, unlike Boylan, he does not have the business contacts or the acumen to make it work (16.526–30).[66]

In the meantime, D. B. Murphy has regaled the shelter with a story about a fatal stabbing in a Triestine brothel. At first Bloom is skeptical. He confides to Stephen that the old sea dog is someone who "could spin those yarns for hours

[65] Bloom, while born in Dublin, was apparently conceived in London. See John Henry Raleigh, *The Chronicle of Leopold and Molly Bloom: "Ulysses" as Narrative* (Berkeley: University of California Press, 1977), 15–16.

[66] Even though Bloom might act as Molly's manager, any money she earned would remain hers. See *In re Simon* [1909] 1 KB 201; 78 LJKB 392; 100 LT 133; 53 Sol Jo 117; 16 Mans 96, CA: "A trade belonging exclusively to a married woman but managed by her husband on her behalf was a trade carried on by a married woman separately within Married Women's Property Act 1882 (c. 75)."

on end all night long and lie like old boots." But the idea haunts him, and he comes to acknowledge to himself that he has "a certain kind of admiration for a man who had actually brandished a knife . . . when the husband frequently, after some words passed between the two concerning her relations with the other lucky mortal (he having had the pair watched), inflicted fatal injuries on his adored one as a result of an alternative postnuptial *liaison* by plunging his knife into her" (16.1058; 16.1062–65). Bloom obviously has *Carmen* or *Rigoletto* in mind, because crimes of passion involving knives were generally associated with drunken rage rather than cool revenge. In almost all of the forty or so cases of uxoricide that were reported in the English press between 1900 and 1904, drunkenness was a major determinant.[67] The action of Mr. Mooney in *Dubliners*, "who went for his wife with a meat cleaver," given that Mr. Mooney has taken to the drink, is not as unusual as it might seem. In "Ithaca," Bloom will momentarily consider assassinating Boylan but just as quickly dismiss the idea with "two wrongs never make a right."

His apparent honesty with himself contrasts sharply with his retreat into cliché and platitude when a "streetwalker glazed and haggard under a black straw hat" peers into the shelter (16.704–5). Although Bloom recalls an occasion when she attempted to solicit him, he affects indifference, remarking to Stephen, "Unfortunate creature! Of course I suppose some man is ultimately responsible for her condition" (16.731–32). The "I suppose" reflects the impossibility of satisfactorily proving who was responsible, even while it echoes the allegation that features in many petitions for divorce that the husband "had knowingly and cruelly communicated a sexual disease," adultery and cruelty being the joint requirements for a woman to obtain a divorce.[68] The wording occurs as early as 1858 in *Durdin v. Durdin* and is repeated *ad pedem litterae* until well after *Ulysses* is published.[69] The nature of

[67] See Martin J. Weiner, *Men of Blood: Violence, Manliness and Criminal Justice in Victorian England* (Cambridge: Cambridge University Press, 2006), 151–69, particularly 164; N. Radojevic et al., "Multiple Stabbing in Sex Related Homicides," *Journal of Forensic and Legal Medicine* 20 (July 2013): 502–7.

[68] An exception is *Light v. Light and Evans and Perry*, where the husband unsuccessfully alleged that the wife had communicated a sexual disease. *Light v. Light and Evans and Perry*, NA J77/798/4297, Filed: 20 October 1903; Set Down: 1 July 1904. Struck Out.

[69] See "Rules and Regulations for the Court for Divorce and Matrimonial Causes," in *The Law Journal Reports for the Year 1866: Michaelmas Term 1865 to*

the sexual disease is almost never specified in either the affidavits or the Court Minutes and almost never mentioned in the newspaper reports. But the allegation still had to be tested, although this was done *in camerâ*. Because pathology was still in its infancy, the result could never be definitive; responsibility could only be established in terms "such as would lead the guarded discretion of a reasonable and just man to the conclusion."

Bloom's attempt to represent prostitution as a "necessary evil" and venereal disease as a public health issue tempts Stephen to quip that the consequences of illicit sex are best understood in terms of the scholastic distinction between "*corruptio per se* and *corruptio per accidens*" (16.759–60). Responsibility is not the issue; rather, it has to do with *per se* as opposed to *per accidens*. Are sexual diseases communicated because of inherent corruption? Or are they an unforeseen consequence of inherently corrupt acts? Although he is not aware of it, the distinction Stephen makes is germane to Bloom's dilemma. Momentarily calculating earlier in the day that Boylan would not "knowingly and cruelly communicate a sexual disease," Bloom had taken refuge in "think no more of that" (8.105–9). Better to allow Molly's adultery and its consequences to remain *per accidens* than conceive of it as *per se*. But when Stephen responds to Bloom's platitudes about sexually transmitted diseases with "Fear not them that sell the body but have not power to buy the soul. She is a bad merchant. She buys dear and sells cheap" (16.737–38), Bloom avoids the complex moral and ethical issues raised by illicit sex and immediately turns the conversation to issues of evidence and proof.

It is at this point that Bloom refers to *Crawford v. Crawford and Dilke* (1886)[70] and *O'Shea v. O'Shea and Parnell* (1890)[71] in terms of motive, gossip, evidence, court procedure, press coverage, and public reaction.

Michaelmas Term 1866, Forming Part V of Vol. LXIV, New Series, Vol. XXXV (London: Edward Bret Ince, 1866), 1–13, 14–21.

[70] *Crawford v. Crawford and Dilke* (1886) 11 P&D 150; 55 LT 305; 34 WR 677; 2 TLR 768, CA. For Dilke's disastrous pressure on the Queen's Proctor to secure the re-opening of the Crawford divorce, in which he had already been found not to be a co-respondent, see Roy Jenkins, *Victorian Scandal: A Biography of the Right Honourable Gentleman Sir Charles Dilke* (New York: Chilmark Press, 1965), chaps. 11–17. Dilke reckoned without the belligerent antagonism of the Queen's Proctor, Sir Augustus Stevenson.

[71] *O'Shea v. O'Shea and Parnell* (1890) 15 P&D 59; 59 LJP 47; 62 LT 713; 38 WR 374; 6 LTR 221; 17 Cox CC 107, CA. See also, Bew, *Enigma*, 164–88.

Talking about them with Stephen provides him with an opportunity to narrativize himself, to explore what might happen should he proceed with a divorce, or, alternatively, to persuade himself that divorce is a course of action he should not pursue. Both cases also function as cautionary tales. Parnell resolutely refused to appoint counsel with the result that none of the evidence tendered against him was subjected to cross-examination. The most damaging allegation, and it is one that Bloom relates to Stephen with skepticism, is "the unfounded surmise of a maidservant that Parnell to avoid Captain O'Shea must have on several occasions fled by a fire-escape from the house on Medina Terrace to reappear at the door asking for the Captain" (17.1375–79).[72] And while Bloom does not refer by name to the divorce proceedings that alleged Sir Charles Dilke as the co-respondent in *Crawford v. Crawford* (1886), Bloom's description of the activities of the King's Proctor suggest knowledge of the case. Like Parnell, Dilke refused to defend himself. Since the case against him was largely circumstantial, he was deemed innocent, but when an investigative journalist began questioning the verdict, Dilke decided to clear his name by requesting a retrial with the Queen's Proctor as an interested party. So vigorous and penetrating was the cross-examination and so extensive the newspaper coverage that he was utterly destroyed. That Bloom fears he might be undone by false evidence or caught out during cross-examination is evident from his account of both cases.

For the reader, however, his explanation of the processes and procedures of the Admiralty, Divorce and Probate Division of the King's Bench is limited by the language attributed to him. As Katie Wales points out, Bloom "no longer controls and plays with cliché at this hour of the night, but is controlled by them. . . . The result for the reader is the foregrounding of meaning in the 'tired' clichés of discourse, and the play of literalness and figurativeness."[73] It is as if Bloom's experience,

[72] Callanan, *The Parnell Split*, 9.

[73] Katie Wales, *The Language of James Joyce* (London: Macmillan, 1992), 125. Robert Byrnes, in "A Statistical Analysis of the 'Eumaeus' Phrasemes in James Joyce's "*Ulysses*"," contends that "Bloom operates from a broad base of 1478 tonally neutral clichés, then works up into ceremonious and formal zones 529 times, and down into informality, slang and vulgarity a further 554 times. The upper and lower zones of his range are almost exactly symmetrical." http://www.ledonline.it/ledonline/JADT-2010/allegati/JADT-2010-0289-0296_184-Byrnes.pdf.

which seems genuine, in struggling to find the appropriate means to express itself gives poignancy to his pronouncements such as the "eternal question of the life connubial… *Can real love, supposing there happens to be another chap in the case, exist between married folk? Poser*" (16.1384–86; emphasis mine).

So it is not surprising that the first aspect of the Parnell affair that he considers with Stephen is the attractiveness of a man secure in his masculinity or the surge of the hot blood of the south for the cool demeanor of the north: "It was just the wellknown case of hot passion, pure and simple, upsetting the applecart with a vengeance and just bore out the very thing he was saying as she also was Spanish or half so, types that wouldn't do things by halves, passionate abandon of the south, casting every shred of decency to the winds" (16.1406–10). The most telling phrase in terms of what it reveals about Bloom's identifying himself with Parnell is the mistaken parallel he draws between Molly and Katharine O'Shea—"she *also was* Spanish or half so."[74] He then implies a further parallel when he says to Stephen that it "was simply a case of the husband not being up to the scratch, with nothing in common between them beyond the name, and then a real man arriving on the scene, strong to the verge of weakness, falling a victim to her siren charms and forgetting home ties, the usual sequel, to bask in the loved one's smiles" (16.1380–84). At first, Bloom surmises, the attraction "was strictly Platonic till nature intervened and an attachment sprang up between them till bit by bit matters came to a climax and the matter became the talk of the town" (16.1364–66). Whether or not O'Shea knew about the liaison in its early stages is not considered; it is assumed in "Eumaeus" that he sues for divorce once the liaison becomes so well known that he can no longer ignore it.

What the Parnell narrative and by implication the Dilke enable Bloom to explore is the extent to which the injured party can ignore adultery before either condonation or connivance prevents legal redress and triangulates the parties in enduring complexity and unhappiness. The implication is that once the liaison is the "talk of the town," the injured party

[74] David Robbins, "Revealed: Secret Evidence in the Parnell, Kitty O'Shea Scandal," *Irish Independent*, 3 March 2013, http://www.independent.ie/lifestyle/revealed-secret-evidence-in-the-parnell-kitty-oshea-scandal-29104292.html, points out that O'Shea had, along with other liaisons, committed adultery with Maria Dominguez in Las Minas in Spain in 1877 and 1878.

cannot ignore it. For Bloom, the issue at this point is what and how much is already known around Dublin about Molly and Boylan. And how much of it is true? But seeking redress through the court, given the rapacity of the newspapers for reporting divorce proceedings, is equally hazardous because, as Bloom rightly explains to Stephen, illicit intimacy is gleefully amplified into scandal. As Sir George H. Lewis, a Judge in the Divorce Court, remarked to the 1912 Royal Commission on Divorce, "a great many people take up the paper and the first thing they do is to turn up and read about the Divorce Court.... I think they are spicy reading."[75] In *Duplany v. Duplany; Cohen Intervening* (1892), the petitioner's plea that the scurrilous reporting by *The Day's Doings* had prejudiced her case resulted in the publisher being cautioned and then imprisoned.[76] In his magisterial study *The Road to Divorce*, Lawrence Stone claims that "In 1909, respectable papers like the *Times*, the *Daily Telegraph*, and the *Daily Mail* devoted to divorce cases some 82 to 126 columns of print every year, while one Sunday paper, *The Umpire*, printed no fewer than 238."[77] As early as 1891 Oscar Wilde had protested: "the private lives of men and women should not be made public. The public have nothing to do with them at all. In France they manage these things much better. There they do not allow the details of trials that take place in the divorce courts to be published for the amusement and criticism of the public."[78] It was not until 1926 that Parliament, "spurred into action by the wide publicity given to all the details about a peculiarly scabrous divorce case (*Russell v.*

[75] Quoted in Stone, *Road to Divorce*, 295–96.

[76] *Duplany v. Duplany; Cohen Intervening*, NA J77/462/4065, Filed: 5 December 1890; Judicial Separation: 15 December 1891. See ruling of Sir Francis Henry Jeune, 9 June 1891: "the said Adolphus Rosenberg has given an undertaking not to repeat the said offence." Note, however, 28 February 1893: "Affidavit filed by Jeannie Rosenberg, Wife of Adolphus Rosenberg, to Release Adolphus Rosenberg from Prison (Contempt of Court)." *Duplany v. Duplany* [1892] P 53; 61 LJP 49; 66 LT 267; 8 TLR 169.

[77] Stone, *Road to Divorce*, 295, citing *Royal Commission on Divorce* (1912), 1:146.

[78] Oscar Wilde, "The Soul of Man under Socialism," *Fortnightly Review* 49 (1891), 305; *The Complete Works of Oscar Wilde*, ed. Josephine M. Guy (Oxford: Oxford University Press, 2007), 256.

Russell), at last passed legislation restricting the publication of such materials in the newspapers."[79]

For Bloom, the intrusion of the press and the fact that divorces are heard in open court and sometimes before a jury is not simply a violation of privacy but an unwarranted amplification and distortion of what has taken place. As he explains to Stephen, "An awful lot of makebelieve went on about that sort of thing with the usual splash of gutterpress about the same old matrimonial triangle alleging misconduct with professional golfer or the newest stage favourite" (16.1480–83). (Another subconscious allusion to Molly!) Whether knowingly or not, Bloom may be alluding to two notorious divorce cases that were widely reported in the press in 1919 and 1920. The 1919 case, *Beck v. Beck and Spittal*, involved a golf professional's affair with the wife of a Member of Parliament;[80] the 1920 case, *Bamberger v. Bamberger and Symonds and Leeson and Stephenson and Stein*, involved a woman who went by the name of Thelma Bamberger. Married when a Gaiety Girl of fifteen, she had divorced her first husband and while petitioning for a divorce from her second husband was successfully prosecuted for entrapping several men and subsequently obtaining money under false pretenses.[81] Whether or not Bloom is aware of the details, he protests to Stephen that since Parnell was Katharine O'Shea's "declared favourite, where was the particular necessity to proclaim it to the rank and file from the housetops" (16.1370–72). Furthermore, "it was no concern of theirs absolutely if he regarded her with affection, carried away by a wave of folly" (16.1386–88). The latter remark perhaps reflects his own hope that Molly's affair, unlike Katharine's, will be a ripple rather than a wave of folly.

What follows is a brief account of hearings in the divorce division of the King's Bench that is eloquent of Joyce's qua Bloom's knowledge of case history and procedure. First, there is the customary defense of inevitability: that the respondent and co-respondent "were fated to meet and an

[79] Stone, *Road to Divorce*, 295.

[80] "MP's Divorce Suit: Wife and Professional Golfer: Intercepted Letter," *Daily Mail*, 26 February 1919, 3.

[81] The case, *Bamberger v. Bamberger and Symonds and Leeson and Stephenson and Stein*, was reported in detail in the *Daily Mail* on 11 March 1920, 5; 12 March 1920, 5; 13 March 1920, 5; 18 March 1920, 5; 19 March 1920, 7; 20 March 1920, 5; 23 April 1920, 7; 24 April 1920, 3; 3 May 1920, 5; et passim.

attachment sprang up between the two so that their names were coupled in the public eye" (16.1484–86). As numerous Court Minutes show, many respondents and co-respondents claimed fate or coincidence as a way of mitigating intention and re-apportioning blame. Legally required in their affidavits to state the place, date, time, and circumstances of their first encounter, many lovers made it appear that they had met one another by chance and that their meeting was due to their husband's or wife's lack of attention.[82]

The next step was for the meetings to become more frequent until they led to intimacy. As Bloom explains to Stephen, evidence for intimacy was often submitted to the "court with letters containing the habitual mushy and compromising expressions leaving no loophole to show that they openly cohabited two or three times a week at some well known seaside hotel and relations, when the thing ran its normal course, became in due course intimate" (16.1486–90). While the discovery of letters, as I have shown in Chapter 4, often provided the evidence to proceed to court and frequently provided the basis for a successful outcome, Bloom has yet to discover Boylan's and Molly's correspondence. All he has at present is a glimpse of "a strip of torn envelope" when he was bringing up the tray that morning (4.308). That he includes letters in his account of adultery and divorce might reveal more about his concern about his own illicit correspondence than what he thinks he might discover about Molly. But including letters in his account shows that he is aware that proof of adultery requires either unambiguous material evidence or independent testimony free of collusion or connivance.

Once the injured party has sufficient evidence and once he or she can no longer ignore the liaison for fear of prejudicing their own case, they must approach the court. What Bloom next confides to Stephen reveals his understanding of the psychological state of the lovers and his awareness that adultery is a misdemeanor rather than a crime: "But as for that the two misdemeanants, wrapped up as they were largely in one another, could safely afford to ignore it as they very largely did till the matter was

[82] Katharine O'Shea's defense was that her husband was an adulterer who neglected her and encouraged her intimacy with Parnell. *William Henry O'Shea v. Katharine O'Shea and Stewart Charles Parnell*, NA J77/440/3419; 15 PD 59; 59 LJP 47; 62 LT 713; 38 WR 374; 6 LTR 221; 17 Cox CC 107, CA.

put in the hands of a solicitor who filed a petition for the party wronged in due course" (16.1493–96). In the English jurisdiction, petitions were framed in a style and language that remained unchanged from 1857 until 24 October 1905, when rule 220 was introduced requiring the additional details of the husband's occupation and domicile and the husband's and wife's place of residence. In terms of procedure, the petition was then lodged with a Court Registrar, who decided whether or not the matter should proceed to court. In some cases the preliminary hearing before the Registrar would result in extra particulars being required. These were meant to clarify claims about evidence in either the petition or in the respondent's affidavit.

Bloom does not canvas these details with Stephen, and he does not describe the hearing, even though, as Richard Brown has shown, Joyce possessed a copy of *Nouveau scandale de Londres*,[83] an anonymous account of the second part of *Crawford v. Crawford and Dilke* (1886), which detailed the examination of witnesses and the assessment of evidence. It is understandable that Bloom, whose visit to Nighttown has seen him arraigned before the court of his own sexual proclivities, might not want to reconstruct such a scenario for Stephen.

Two further aspects of Bloom's conversation with Stephen are eloquent of his anxiety about his own situation. The first comes to his mind as Stephen is looking at a slightly soiled photograph of Molly. Bloom links the soiling with the soiled underwear that he has retrieved from beside the chamber pot that morning until it suddenly occurs to him that "*suppose she is gone* when he" returns (16.1470). That it has taken him until early the following morning to even consider that Molly might have eloped reveals how involved he has become in his own "Sherlockholmesing," how reticent he is to return to 7 Eccles Street, and how deeply he has immersed himself in depicting and analyzing his own situation.

Bloom's account of the next step in divorce, as "the *decree nisi*" "and the King's Proctor tries to show cause why and, he failing to quash it, *nisi* was made absolute" (16.1490–92), clearly establishes that he is familiar with the English jurisdiction, even to the order of events, because, as *Jackson v. Jackson* (1910) established, the King's Proctor can only make

[83] Brown, *Joyce and Sexuality*, 37–38, 203; *Nouveau scandale de Londres: l'Affaire Crawford* (Paris: Libraire Illustreé, 1886); Ellmann, *Consciousness*, 121.

enquiries after the *decree nisi* had been granted regardless of how suspect the evidence in the affidavits might appear.[84] It was also not possible for an Irish petitioner domiciled in the island of Ireland to secure a *decree absolute* in the Irish jurisdiction. That Bloom represents the King's Proctor challenging the *decree nisi*, however, points to his own anxieties, because, until 1920, the King's Proctor only investigated those cases where collusion had "necessarily" been brought to his notice; even then he tested "the evidence" before he brought proceedings.[85] According to *Every Man's Own Lawyer*, "The King's (or Queen's) Proctor is the legal advisor of the Crown whose duty it is to intervene in divorce suits, after a *decree nisi* has been pronounced, and before the decree is made absolute, if he has reason to suspect collusion between the parties to the suit."[86] In fact, the Office was far more minatory than that. Though the King's Proctor was funded from Treasury, costs were determined according to success or failure. If the King's Proctor won his case, costs were awarded against the guilty party; if he lost, costs were awarded against him. As Cornish points out,

> The Proctor's office examined the papers for every undefended *decree nisi*, dealt with information from outsiders, sent inquiry agents out when there were suspicious circumstances and informed the Attorney-General where evidence of collusion or recrimination resulted. The Attorney might then intervene, causing the judge to refuse the decree absolute. Costs of the whole proceedings would then, in all likelihood, be awarded against the petitioner, and the couple would remain married. The husband who arranged that his wife's lover would pay for his divorce proceedings against her would fail, the adulterous pair would be left to live in adultery, and the husband would be unable to marry again. The wife who sought to escape from the domination of a cruel and adulterous husband would be left under his yoke, if it turned out that she had had sex with someone else. The Earl of Desart, formerly the King's Proctor, who would give evidence before the Gorell Royal Commission on Divorce of 1910–12, felt that his intervention "over and over again . . . has done more harm than good."[87]

[84] *Jackson v. Jackson* [1910] P 230; 79 LJP 82; 103 LT 79; 26 TLR 476.

[85] "The King's Proctor: Who is He and How He Works," *Daily Mail*, 22 March 1920, 5.

[86] *Every Man's Own Lawyer, Dictionary*, 19.

[87] Cornish, "Marital Breakdown," 795–96.

In 1904 the Office was combined with the Treasury Solicitor and the Public Prosecutor, but in 1909 the latter was detached and set up as a separate office.[88] By 1920 the President of the Divorce Court was sending all cases to the King's Proctor "for enquiry where successful petitioners did not apply to have the *decree nisi* made absolute within the usual period (six months) and there was no apparent reason for delay."[89] As various analyses have shown, the King's Proctor was generally successful in about sixty to sixty-five percent of cases.[90] That Bloom's account of divorce has the King's Proctor failing to "quash" the *decree nisi* is again eloquent of his hope that, if he does proceed, his case will not be investigated.

In essence, as he explains to Stephen, it is the publicity given to illicit love affairs that he finds most offensive. What incenses him, he emphasizes, are "the blatant jokes of the cabman and so on who passed it all off as a jest, laughing immoderately, pretending to understand everything" as soon as the Parnell case was mentioned. What he finds equally offensive is "the anonymous letter from the usual boy Jones" who happens to "come across" the errant couple "at the crucial moment in a loving position locked in one another's arms" (16.1534–36). Again, Bloom is reflecting discussions that were taking place in the newspapers of the day. In an article titled "Anonymous Letter Fiends," the writer notes that "anonymous letter writers have been very busy recently" and advises that "the worst of the anonymous letter is that once read . . . the mischief is done . . . what if it be true—in part or in whole? . . . for the private individual there is only one way. Refuse to read an anonymous letter."[91] The affairs of consenting adults, Bloom insists to Stephen, should remain private. They are not for speculation, commodification, and salacious consumption.

Bloom then ironically restages the confession and plea for forgiveness scenario that he had constructed for himself in the Ormond when he was listening to Lionel's song from Flotow's *Martha*:

[88] "The King's Proctor: Who is He and How He Works," 5.

[89] "Divorce Delays," *Daily Mail*, 27 July 1920, 4. Cornish, "Marital Breakdown," 794–95, points out that the change from three months to six months dates from 1866 as a consequence of the Divorce Court Act 1860, §7.

[90] Savage, "Divorce and the Law," 506; Latey, *Law and Practice*, "Interventions by the Queen's Proctor," 857–63, §4, 880–95; "King's Proctor Busy: 24 Divorce Decrees Rescinded," *Daily Mail*, 19 October 1920, 4.

[91] "Anonymous Letter Fiends," *Daily Mail*, 18 November 1920, 6.

> The erring fair one begging forgiveness of her lord and master upon her knees and promising to sever the connection and not receive his visits any more if only the aggrieved husband would overlook the matter and let bygones be bygones with tears in her eyes though possibly with her tongue in her fair cheek at the same time as quite possibly there were several others. (16.1537–42)

Such scenes, as Bloom suggests to Stephen, as much as they appeal to the restoration of power historically inherent in patriarchy, belong to popular culture and to the late Victorian iconography of the "errant wife," depicted in painting, popular song, operetta, verse, and the three-volume novel. Bloom, who represents himself to Stephen as "being of a more skeptical bias," offers an explanation of Katharine O'Shea's qua Molly's liaison that is more compassionate than insisting on a conditional reconciliation or proceeding to divorce. Again, whether he is aware of it or not, Bloom is not simply narrativizing his own situation; he is having it framed for him in terms of discussions about marriage failure that were being conducted in the newspapers at the time Joyce was writing the "Eumaeus" episode. For example, in an article titled "Divorce Year: Danger Ages in Married Life" published in the *Daily Mail*, an "official of the Divorce Law Reform Union" is quoted as saying "that the biggest total of divorces occurs between the tenth and twentieth year of marriage," that both "men and women tend to drift apart when they are about 30," and that "one way of avoiding the danger years altogether is for the woman to work—not housework, but to have a vocation of her own."[92] As Bloom explains to Stephen, he

> didn't make the smallest bones about saying so either that man or men in the plural were always hanging around on the waiting list about a lady, even supposing she was the best wife in the world and they got on fairly well together for the sake of the argument, when, neglecting her duties, she chose to be tired of wedded life and was on for a flutter in polite debauchery to press their intentions upon her with improper intent, the upshot being that her affections centred on another, the cause of many *liaisons* between still attractive married women going on for fair and forty and younger men, no doubt as several famous cases of feminine infatuation proved up to the hilt. (16.1543–52)

[92] "Divorce Year: Danger Age in Married Life," *Daily Mail*, 28 August 1920, 3.

That Bloom should then proceed to recommend marriage to Stephen as a way of achieving sexual satisfaction, avoiding "a nice dose that might last him a lifetime," and securing domestic comfort should strike the reader as ironic. But before Stephen is able to respond, the information that he has not eaten since "the day before yesterday" at once astounds Bloom and immediately prompts him to offer Stephen the hospitality of 7 Eccles Street.

CHAPTER 7

Bloom Enters the Bed

In the early morning of 17 June 1904, the imposing four-story Georgian terrace that is Number 7 Eccles Street, Dublin, is somewhat further from the "abode of bliss" than is indicated by the engorged full stop that closes "Ithaca" and the "Yes." that closes "Penelope." By the time the reader encounters Molly's "Yes." it is after three o'clock in the morning. Until then she has been upstairs, asleep after her vigorous sexual encounter with Boylan—singer, impresario, advertising agent, and boxing promoter, somewhat of a lad about town.[1] Bloom is downstairs in the kitchen, having farewelled a tired, semi-inebriated Stephen Dedalus whom he has attempted to protect and befriend in the course of the day. Despite some gentle encouragement, he has not been able to persuade Stephen to stay the night, even though Stephen is apparently homeless. As we have seen, Number 7 Eccles Street is a large terrace house, and there are spare rooms. As for Stephen, what Joyce "jocoseriously" described as the "mathematico-astronomico-physico-mechanicogeometrico-chemico sublimation of Bloom and Stephen" is now complete.[2] With

[1] See Margot Norris, "Don't Call Him 'Blazes': Hugh E. Boylan's Narrative Caricature," *James Joyce Quarterly* 48, no. 2 (2011): 229–49.

[2] Joyce, *Letters of James Joyce*, 1:164. See Richard E. Madtes, *A Textual and Critical Study of the "Ithaca" Episode of James Joyce's "Ulysses"* (Ann Arbor: UMI Research Press, 1983). See also James Joyce, *Joyce's "Ulysses" Notesheets in the British Museum*, ed. Phillip F. Herring (Charlottesville: University Press of Virginia, 1972); and Joyce, *Joyce's Notes and Early Drafts.*

P. Kuch, *Irish Divorce / Joyce's Ulysses*,
DOI 10.1057/978-1-137-57186-1_7

the after-touch of a departing handshake and the sounds of "the double reverberation of retreating feet on the heavenborn earth" and "the double vibration of a jew's harp in the resonant lane" (17.1243–44), Stephen disappears into the night.

But what of Bloom? The immediate effect, the reader is informed, is a sense of utter isolation. Stephen, a prospective surrogate son, has apparently walked out of his life. The Dubliners Bloom has met during the day, for whom he feels some affiliation, are fast asleep in their beds. "Alone" on the doorstep, we are told, Bloom experiences a "lonechill" engendered by "the cold of interstellar space" (17.1245–46; 17.1249). Memories of past friends and friendships come briefly to mind. He then re-enters his own home, inadvertently bumping his head on the doorpost of the front room in an instinctive effort to avoid some furniture that has been rearranged during his absence. Having cast about, he selects an incense cone and lights it to purify and reclaim the space; regards himself in the mirror; restores his books to their correct order; partly undresses; fantasizes about the ultramodern country mansion he would build were he to discover gold; recalls his father's suicide in terms of his own financial resources; and, before deciding whether or not to mount the stairs to the matrimonial bed, considers running away to the far corners of the world in the guise of "Everyman" or "Noman" accompanied by a "nymph" of "immortal . . . beauty" (17.2010–11), given the ways his rival seems to have made himself at home and taken his ease in his, Bloom's, kitchen and front room.

It is at this point that the "jocoserious" complexities of "Ithaca" pose a challenge for the reader (17.369). Despite its multisyllabic poly-vocal quasi-scientific verbosity, the episode is replete with a wry humor that parodies the preoccupation with verisimilitude that characterizes the realist novel of adultery in particular and realism, with its preoccupation with logic and empiricism, in general. Such humor has the effect of undercutting the solemnity and authority of the questions and answers that are provided by the patriarchal "arranger" who purportedly authors the episode. The humor also serves to evoke even while it deflates the compensatory self-indulgent fantasies that can be produced by deception and betrayal. Bloom, for example, is said to imagine the notice that "would" be published in the newspapers were he to run away:

> £5 reward, lost, stolen or strayed from his residence 7 Eccles street, missing gent about 40, answering to the name of Bloom, Leopold (Poldy), height 5ft. 9½ inches, full build, olive complexion, may have since grown a beard,

> when last seen was wearing a black suit. Above sum will be paid for information leading to his discovery. (17.2001–5)

To imagine that he would be sought for is touchingly human; but to have that imagining find expression as a £5 reward notice in the "Lost and Found" column of a newspaper as if he were a missing cat or dog is to draw attention to the immaturity and self-protective sentimentality that characterizes the compulsion to run away, however common that compulsion might be in the circumstances. Similarly, however rejected he might feel, however strongly he might desire to be restored to domestic bliss, and however much *Ulysses* parodies the realist novel of adultery, Bloom, as readers are aware by this point in the book, is undeniably more than the sum of his factually enumerated parts. Listing his height, weight, and appearance might identify Bloom, but it does not fully characterize "him," even if that were possible.

And yet, in order to detect whether or not he has been cuckolded, Bloom and the reader will need to employ those very techniques of forensic reading, of disinterested rational enquiry, of decoding the evidence that the "Ithaca" episode itself so effectively parodies. Here, it is worth recalling the implications of Bloom's response to Molly when she accused him of "having something on" with Mary Driscoll, a servant she suspected of stealing potatoes and oysters and encouraging Bloom to flirt with her. Molly's book of evidence of his alleged philandering amounts to "the long hair on his coat," his suggestion that they invite Mary Driscoll to dine with them on Christmas Day, and the emerald green "garters" she has discovered in Mary's room. Since two-thirds of this evidence is circumstantial, Bloom's response is a blunt "you have no proof" (18.65–66), a response that provokes Molly into immediately giving Mary "a week's notice" (18.70). That Bloom defends himself in terms of inconclusive evidence rather than outright denial suggests that, instead of confronting Molly, he will engage in his own version of "Sherlockholmesing" to determine whether or not she has had sex with Boylan; that is, he will employ the same probabilistic inductive reasoning that we saw him use on seaman Murphy in the previous chapter. Of the two methods for determining guilt, it is Bloom's rather than Molly's that is legally the more correct. In *Lagan v. Gibson* (1878),[3] the Court ruled that

[3] *Irish Law Times Digest*, col. 696, §4.

> A motion to compel the plaintiff in an action of seduction to furnish particulars of the time and place when and where the acts alleged in the summons and plaint were committed was refused. The defendant in an action of seduction will be allowed to traverse the seduction and also the service, if he shows by affidavit he has good grounds for doing so.[4]

Having found himself, as the patriarchal "arranger" expresses it, cast in the role of a "conscious reactor against the void of incertitude" (17.2210–11), Bloom will be just as keen to establish certainty as he is to avoid further uncertainty. Though some clues might appear to lead to a hypothesis, he does not want to commit himself until he is convinced that there is sufficient evidence to establish proof. But obtaining proof of adultery sufficient to satisfy the requirements of the divorce court was not as straightforward as it might seem. In what became the landmark case, *Lovedon v. Lovedon* (1810), the presiding judge, Sir William Scott, stated that "the only general rule that can be laid down is that the circumstances must be such as would lead the guarded discretion of a reasonable and just man to the conclusion."[5] The loaded words here are "discretion" and "reasonable and just." To be seen to exploit circumstance or to exaggerate trivialities was to risk a suspicion that one party was merely looking for any excuse to rid themselves of the other. As a leading authority on Irish law has pointed out, citing *Loveden v. Loveden* (1810) and *Allen v. Allen and Bell* (1893), "It has been said that 'the standard of proof' to establish adultery 'is more stringent than that required of a plaintiff in other civil actions,' which may be determined on a mere balance of probability, but less stringent than the standard of 'beyond reasonable doubt' which is required in criminal cases."[6]

Thus, there are significant legal issues for Bloom and emotional and epistemological issues for both Bloom and the reader. First, there is the natural desire to know what has happened. Having come thus far, both Bloom and the reader have an investment in trying to find out whether or not Molly has had sex with Boylan. Second, according to English and Irish law, in the absence of an independent witness, the bed was the most likely

[4] *Lagan v. Gibson* 10 ILTSJ 6.

[5] *Loveden v. Loveden* (1810) 2 Hag Con 1; 161 ER 648 (Consis. Court), quoted in Shatter, *Family Law*, 132. For *Allen v. Allen and Bell*, NA J77/512/15602, Filed: 18 March 1893; Decree Nisi: 15 March 1894; Final Decree: 26 September 1894.

[6] Shatter, *Family Law*, 132.

place to find evidence—as invasive and as melodramatic as that might seem.[7] This is tricky. What can be established beyond reasonable doubt is that Boylan has visited 7 Eccles Street. What both Bloom and the reader know for certain is that Boylan has left the Ormond in the direction of Eccles Street in a jaunting car. If necessary, the driver of the car can be called as a witness, assuming, of course, that Boylan had given 7 Eccles Street as the address and not a nearby number. But what has happened after Boylan arrived at 7 Eccles Street will need to be discovered. Bloom's preference for employing probabilistic induction means that not only will he engage in analytic and synthetic reasoning (that is, reasoning backward and reasoning forward), but he will also employ the processes of elimination and exclusion to evaluate the usefulness of what he discovers.

It would almost certainly prove a tactical mistake for him to advance the rearranged furniture in the front room as evidence of unacceptable intimacy. Unacceptable intimacy does not necessarily establish adultery. Rearranged furniture does not necessarily establish unacceptable intimacy. To argue his case on the basis of the rearranged furniture might well jeopardize his image as "a reasonable and just man" who had exercised "guarded discretion." As marked as he is by the impact of the doorpost, he must continue to observe and analyze. Since a divorce is something that it is reported Bloom will consider and a *decree absolute* is a course of action that is available to him only in the English jurisdiction, he will not only need to collect and interpret his evidence and frame it in such a way that it can withstand cross-examination, but he will also need to present evidence in a manner that does not advantage the defendant or arouse the suspicions of the King's Proctor.[8] *Barnett v. Barnett and Freakes* (1904) provides a case in point where the petitioner, having already obtained a separation order, subsequently sued for a divorce on the grounds that in "playing his own detective" he had observed his wife "walking out arm-in-arm with the co-respondent.... The petition was dismissed with costs."[9]

[7] The stained sheet from the bed that it was alleged Wilde and Douglas had used was accepted as evidence in the trial. See Merlin Holland, *Irish Peacock and Scarlet Marquess: The Real Trial of Oscar Wilde* (London: HarperCollins, 2003).

[8] For contemporary newspaper reports about the King's Proctor, see Chapter 6.

[9] "His Own Detective, Naval Pensioner's Divorce Suit Fails," *Daily Mail*, 23 November 1904, 3. *Barnett v. Barnett and Freakes*, NA J77/812/4694, Filed: 19 March 1904; Set Down: 11 May 1904; Dismissed: 22 November 1904.

The best Bloom can hope for is that his plea will not be contested. But if it is contested, he will be cross-examined by counsel for Molly, and he will most likely have to face Boylan's counsel too. If he opts for the Irish jurisdiction, since he must proceed with a suit for *criminal conversation* prior to proceeding to a plea for a divorce *a mensa et thoro*, his evidence will be subjected to rigorous investigation in each of the hearings. In the court proceedings for *criminal conversation*, he will be cross-examined by counsel for both Boylan and Molly, though, in a suit for "a divorce *a mensa et thoro*," he will only need to face Molly's counsel as "the only parties to the proceeding" in the Irish jurisdiction "are the two spouses."[10] In the English jurisdiction, however, if the case is contested, he might well have to face counsel for both Molly and Boylan should she decide to protest her innocence and play Bloom at his own game of "you have no proof."

Having had to resort to a "stratagem" to regain entry to 7 Eccles Street, because he had left his latch-key in the pocket of his other trousers, Bloom is now under even greater pressure to act strategically, to be the "slyboots" that Molly thinks he is or the "levelheaded individual who could give points to not a few in point of shrewd observation" as the narrator of the preceding episode, "Eumaeus," describes him (16.219–20). As readers, having reached a critical point in the trajectory of this modern novel of adultery—the determining evidence is about to be revealed—and having striven to interpret some 270 sets of questions and answers to get there or, to put it another way, some 600 pages of text, we now need to read Bloom as shrewdly as he reads the matrimonial bed.

It is here that either experience of or research into newspaper accounts of divorce proceedings comes to the aid of the reader because "Ithaca," I would argue, to employ Lubomír Doležel's term, possesses a "transworld identity." What emerges, despite the obfuscation, irony, parody, and misinformation, and the plethora of leading questions, is a convincing psychological account of a mind suddenly confronted with questions it does not want to answer and yet does. And even if it does arrive at answers, it is aware that such answers might well be interrogated, reinterpreted, denied, or just simply dismissed. Though the extent to which the question-and-answer form of the episode mirrors legal cross-examination has

[10] Shatter, *Family Law*, 132: "The person with whom a spouse is alleged to have committed adultery is never a party but will usually be called as a witness."

been remarked, not enough attention has been paid to Joyce's skillful marshaling of the affective power of the interplay between language and form that characterizes the episode. And not enough attention has been paid to the fact that most of the questions in "Ithaca" are leading questions. It is as if Bloom is being constructed through a method of cross-examination that would not be permitted in a court of law.

What we also read as we turn the pages is Bloom the husband reading Bloom the cuckold. This is highly effective, as it foreshadows what will take place in court, should Bloom proceed. As anyone who has experienced or attended a divorce court hearing and as marriage counselors and divorce lawyers will attest, what is frequently produced in a plaintiff is a feeling of estrangement, of a self-sundering that takes place once their version of events is cross-examined. This sundering occurs as their story is progressively molded to the court's story. Because petitioner and co-respondent may only answer questions directed to them, they progressively reinforce, modify, or might even abandon their account of what they believe took place.

Another of the affective aspects shared by both the episode and divorce proceedings is the way the petitioner's and respondent's case becomes generalized by the court even while it purports to judge its particularity. It is as if what the reader is invited to experience and what Bloom is represented as experiencing is simultaneously specific and general, local and yet universal, personal and yet typical of what happens when one party in a long-established relationship discovers evidence of adultery. And while the logical sequence of questions with their seemingly definitive answers that constitute "Ithaca" produces a sense of confidence that the reader is participating in Bloom's discovery of the truth, the orotund quasi-technical vocabulary and the digressions into elaboration—not all of them relevant—not only unsettle this confidence but also tend to remove both Bloom and the reader from the emotional immediacy of the situation. The reader is both with Bloom and removed from him, both sharing his discovery and yet having that discovery related in language that is at a chilling remove from common usage and via a method of questioning that presupposes the answers.

* * * *

Having mounted the stairs and quietly completed his undressing, Bloom prepares "the bedlinen accordingly" and enters the bed. The question

"What did his limbs, when gradually extended, encounter?" is then posed by the patriarchal "arranger." The answer that is provided points to, for the most part, the unmistakable evidence of a sexual encounter that both we and Bloom, as forensic readers, are challenged to interpret:

> New clean bedlinen, additional odours, the presence of a human form, female, hers, the imprint of a human form, male, not his, some crumbs, some flakes of potted meat, recooked, which he removed. (17.2122–25)[11]

For Bloom the new clean bed linen might be considered an ambiguous sign or something of dubious evidential value. It might mark the usual time of the week when the bed linen is always changed. It might indicate that Molly's period had started that morning and that she has simply changed the sheets.[12] But it might also constitute evidence that the bed has been prepared for sex, which is what we as readers subsequently discover toward the end of the next episode. But how is the word "new" to be read? Is the bed linen newly clean? Or is it new in the sense of having been recently purchased? The signs that follow, however, are arguably less ambiguous for Bloom than for the reader because for Bloom, in terms of the book, they come freighted with the day's accumulated meanings free of the formal and linguistic complexities that the reader encounters, complexities to which I will return. As far as the reader is concerned—whether or not Bloom is viewed as a character, a representation of a typical human response, or read as text—the range of emotions, feelings, and thoughts that are attributed to him seem as credible and coherent as they are logical and life-like.

[11] Eric Bulson, *The Cambridge Introduction to James Joyce* (Cambridge: Cambridge University Press, 2006), 88: "when he crawls into bed with [Molly] he notices some crumbs in the bed and a dry semen stain." Bulson appears to have confused *U*18.1512—"theres the mark of his spunk on the clean sheet"—with *U*17.1122–25. There is no textual evidence that Bloom sees the stain, even though Molly has made no effort to remove it. It would also be easy for Molly to attribute it to Bloom given his sexual predilection for masturbating on her (*U*18.1528).

[12] It seems Molly is in the habit of getting up sometime between 10.00 a.m. and 11.00 a.m. so her period could have begun after Bloom left the house to go to Paddy Dignam's funeral: "Mrs Marion Bloom. Not up yet" (*U*5.154). ("Lotus Eaters" time is 10.00 a.m.) "And *madame*. Twenty past eleven. Up. Mrs Fleming in to clean" (*U*6.237). On Molly's thoughts about the linen, see *U*18.1124–25.

Readers with an excellent memory or a reliable computer will not find it surprising that Bloom detects "additional odours" immediately after noticing the new bed linen because his day has been one of aromas, fragrances, scents, smells, and stenches—recalled, savored, or recoiled from—with many of them being associated with Molly. That morning, leaving Dlugacz's with a kidney for his breakfast, Bloom recalls the smell of citrons, which in turn recalls pleasant times with Molly (4.204–8); and when his reverie is interrupted by a cloud passing over the sun, he restores himself with the thought of smelling "the gentle smoke of tea, fume of the pan, sizzling butter. Be near her ample bedwarmed flesh. Yes, yes" (4.237–39). At home and upstairs, as she pours the tea, he glances at her "large soft bubs" as "the warmth of her couched body" rises in the air, "mingling with the fragrance of the tea" (4.304–7), though this sensory pleasure is brought to an abrupt end by the smell of the burning kidney downstairs. After breakfast Bloom recalls the time when Ponchielli's *Dance of the Hours* was played. And, as we have already noticed, he wonders whether that "was the first night" Molly was attracted to Boylan, having deduced that Boylan was probably "well off" because Bloom himself had "noticed he had a good rich smell off his breath dancing" (4.529–30). So it is not surprising that once he has remarked the new clean bed linen, Bloom should detect "additional odours," given the extent to which the olfactory has commanded his attention and stimulated his memory throughout the day, nor is it surprising that when he finally kisses Molly on the bottom it is a "melonsmellonous osculation" (17.2243).

"Form" also holds its measure of fascination for him. Bloom is a form conscious—whether human or animal—corporally aware person. Hearing the cat meow in the kitchen as he prepares Molly's breakfast, he watches "curiously, kindly the lithe black form" (4.21). Some hours later, talking to Josie Breen in the street, it is his intimation of Cashel Boyle O'Connor Fitzmaurice Tisdall Farrell's "bony form" that prompts him to alert her that she needs to "let this man pass" (8.294–95). But most of all, it is Molly's form that haunts him. In comparing her with all other women, he thinks to himself, "That's where Molly can knock the spots off them. It's the blood of the south. Moorish. Also the form, the figure" (13.968–69). And when he discusses the female body with Stephen in the cabman's shelter, he dismisses the "handsome" and the "pretty" by assuring his young companion that what he is "talking about is the female form," "the splendid proportion of hips, bosom" (16.892). So when Bloom detects "human form, female, hers," his perception could be said to constitute the embodiment of idealized desire; and when he observes "the imprint of a human form, male, not his," it could be said to mark a corporeal space in which Bloom is now obliged to re-examine his sexuality and review his marriage.[13]

Both the "crumbs" and the "flakes of potted meat, recooked," which he removes before he climbs between the sheets, are also resonant with coded meanings that have been accumulating throughout the day. The "crumbs" recall Martin Cunningham's discovery of "crust crumbs" in the carriage on the way to Paddy Dignam's funeral and the awareness shared between Simon Dedalus, Martin Cunningham, Jack Power, and Bloom that the carriage has probably been used by its previous occupants for a sexual liaison that was euphemistically known locally "as once round the Green" (6.95–104).[14]

Now, at the end of the day, there are crumbs in the matrimonial bed. How likely is it that they have been left over from Molly's breakfast of a pot of tea and slices of "thin bread and butter" (4.50–51)? And if that is the source of the crumbs, what is their relationship to the flakes of re-cooked Plumtree's Potted Meat, a delicacy that was not on the breakfast tray he had prepared for her that morning? What too is the relationship between the empty jar of Plumtree's Potted Meat and the "oval wicker basket bedded with fibre and containing one Jersey pear" that is resting beside it on the middle shelf of the kitchen dresser downstairs (17.304–5)? If not for Bloom, then for the reader, the flakes of Plumtree's Potted Meat recall the jingle that has been jangling in Bloom's mind since 10.00 a.m., with its promise that "Plumtree's Potted Meat" will complete the transformation of the "home" into "an abode of bliss." It is a jingle that replays itself whenever Bloom thinks about Molly's appointment with Boylan or whenever someone asks after her (5.144–47; 8.142–43; 17.304; 17.597–99).

[13] "Pillow Problem. Divorce Judge on Bedroom Evidence," *Daily Mail*, 18 December 1920, 5: "The Judge: I can never understand how you can tell that two persons have slept in the one bed. Counsel: Cannot your lordship understand that two bodies leave separate marks in a bed? The Judge: No, I cannot. A man might sleep on both pillows in the bed. Counsel: Then I can only say that my experience has been different. (Laughter) His Lordship pronounced a decree."

[14] Ferriter, *Occasions of Sin*, 152, explains how "girls and jarveys (hackney coach drivers) provided a 'once around the Green' service for gentlemen at the end of their evening."

To introduce the preliminary evidence of infidelity through Bloom's senses via a chain of signification that links sights and smells to memory and analysis is to entice the reader to interpret the scene in terms of the conventional novel of adultery. It is an invitation to the reader to read it as an objective account of what is actually occurring to "a character" or, for the naïve reader, "a person," at a certain time in a particular place—specifically, early in the morning of 17 June 1904, in the bedroom of the Bloom household at Number 7 Eccles Street, Drumcondra, Dublin, Ireland. Such objectivity is seemingly reinforced by the question-and-answer technique that distinguishes the "Ithaca" episode, with its linguistic and stylistic echoes of the catechism, legal cross-examination, and the maieutic method of textbooks of instruction such as Richmal Mangnall's *Historical and Miscellaneous Questions* and the Berlitz grammars.[15] Appropriate questioning, it is suggested, will yield all the relevant facts. Yet, as Wittgenstein has argued, employing the interrogative mode *per se* does not guarantee that a statement in that mode is either a valid question or a question for which there is a correct answer—or, for that matter, even an answer.[16] Like Bloom, the reader will need either to eliminate or exclude some questions and some answers as either marginal, incidental, or irrelevant in order to attempt to determine what has happened.

Bloom's response, as he "remove[s] the crumbs" and settles himself, and it is a response that is as plausible as it is considered, is framed by an apparently exhaustive list of men who have shown some sort of appreciative attention to Molly that culminates with Hugh E. (Blazes) Boylan, men who seem in Bloom's mind to have been on "the waiting list" (16.1545). It is here that we again see Bloom employing probabilistic induction as he uses the methods of exclusion and elimination combined with analytic and synthetic reasoning to form a preliminary hypothesis about Boylan. He first reflects on his rival's "vigour (a bounder), corporal proportion (a billsticker),[17] commercial ability (a bester), [and] impressionability (a boaster)" (17.2145–46). Suspecting that it has been Boylan's aggressive self-

[15] Litz, "Ithaca," 394–96; McCourt, *Years of Bloom*, 21–22.

[16] Ludwig Wittgenstein, *Tractatus Logico-Philosophicus* (London: Kegan Paul, Trench, Trubner; New York: Harcourt, Brace, 1922), 4.003, 4.1251–56, 4.1274, 5.551, 5.5542; note, however, 6.5, 6.51.

[17] Stephen, in passing on "Lord John Corley's" request for work to Bloom, refers to Boylan as a "billsticker" (*U*16.234).

confidence, his "impressionability" (17.2147–53), that has achieved the conquest to which all previous *soupirants* have only aspired,[18] Bloom is then reported to experience "antagonistic sentiments" that range from "envy,"[19] "jealousy,"[20] and "abnegation,"[21] to "equanimity" (17.2155).[22]

At least this is what the patriarchal "arranger" advances as a reliable, objective, comprehensive, and factual answer to the question that he has just provided—though as John Hannay and others have demonstrated, not all the answers in "Ithaca" are responses to the questions posed and not all of them always satisfy all the criteria they purport to endorse.[23] Yet, as anyone who has experienced the trauma, the psychological dislocation of self, that follows the apparent confirmation that what they thought was a monogamous relationship is no longer one—at that point where justifications no longer seem plausible and explanations no longer persuasive—what is offered in "Ithaca" convincingly dramatizes the turbulent rational and irrational conversations that people have with themselves in such crises.

For the moment, however, let us return to Bloom ensconced head to toe in the matrimonial bed. Being the "slyboots" that he purportedly is, Bloom ponders in turn each of the "sentiments"—"envy, jealousy, abnegation, equanimity"—that he initially experiences. Again probabilistic induction comes to his aid. First, his "envy" of Boylan's imagined sexual prowess—

[18] Bloom has already anticipated this in "Eumaeus" (*U*16.1543–52).

[19] The word "envy" is used eight times in *Ulysses*.

[20] James Joyce, *Exiles* (Hammersmith: Paladin, 1991), 163: "the scholastic definition of jealousy as a *passio iracibilis* (the passion of the irascible)."

[21] All occurrences of "abnegation" in *Ulysses* refer to Bloom: in "Circe" when "Rumbold" is on the scaffold; and the other three in terms of his emotional reaction to Boylan in "Ithaca."

[22] There are four uses of "equanimity" in *Ulysses*: three relate to the "equation" of Bloom's emotional reaction to Boylan; one relates to Bloom's patient cultivation of Mrs. Riordan.

[23] John Hannay, "Coincidence and Analytic Reduction in the 'Ithaca' Episode, *Ulysses*," *Journal of Narrative Technique* 13, no. 3 (1983): 141. See also James H. Maddox, *Joyce's "Ulysses" and the Assault upon Character* (New Bunswick, NJ: Rutgers University Press, 1978), 188–89: "there is enough error in 'Ithaca' to at least suggest the use of error as a motif," cited in Weldon Thornton, *Voices and Values in Joyce's "Ulysses"* (Gainesville: University Press of Florida, 2000), 200, where, in n. 24, Thornton lists over a dozen errors.

Boylan's supposed "energetic piston and cylinder movement"—is somewhat mitigated because he suspects that Molly is neither "passive" nor "obtuse," and that while her sexual needs are powerful, they are not crudely physical. In assuming this he is largely correct, as Molly's subsequent night thoughts reveal.[24] Second, the "jealousy" Bloom feels is to a degree offset by his realization that her exercise of freewill might confer freedoms on him, even though such freedoms might themselves become unpleasantly restrictive.

Third, "abnegation," as a "refusal" to take "a course of action" and as "a renunciation of a personal right,"[25] arises from Bloom's realization that Dublin is intricately networked; or so we as readers have been led to believe.[26] Both he and Boylan, for example, share the same tailor, "Robert Mesias, tailor and cutter of five Eden quay";[27] both have bought hats from "John Plasto of number one Great Brunswick Street." And both their lives now intersect intimately with Molly's. The Dublin of 16 June 1904 has seen their paths cross a number of times, much to Bloom's discomfort.[28] So, rash action would be ill advised in a city where everyone not only seems to know everyone and everyone's business, but also runs the risk daily of encountering one another about town. Besides, there is "an imminent provincial musical tour" in the offing, featuring Molly and organized by Boylan. Given the Blooms' present financial circumstances, as we have seen in the previous chapter, it would be foolish to jeopardize a venture involving "common current expenses, net proceeds divided" (17.2175–76).

Bloom's fourth "antagonistic sentiment" (of "equanimity") is more complex than the "sentiments" that have preceded it. In the cold light of reason or in the abstract, Bloom is reported to reflect that adultery is less "calamitous" than a host of violent crimes, large-scale natural disasters, or the possibility of cosmic catastrophe. Like eating and drinking and appetite and inclination and even disease, it is part of the human condition. Consequently,

[24] Norris, "Don't Call Him 'Blazes,'" 242.

[25] *Oxford English Dictionary*, 3rd online ed., s.v. "abnegation."

[26] Bloom's own speculations about Jack Power's ambiguous relationship with "another woman" provide a case in point (*U*6.244–45). Molly's thoughts about Power are at *U*636.1272–73.

[27] In "Circe" Bloom is arraigned over a debt of eleven shillings for payment for "alteration to one pair trousers" owing to Mesias.

[28] *U*6.196–97; *U*8.1168; *U*11.302–5; *U*11.357–58; *U*11.457–58; *U*11.761–66.

because adultery is "more than inevitable, irreparable" (17.2194), its occurrence becomes fact. If it has taken place, it has happened, and that is that.

However, as the patriarchal "arranger" of "Ithaca" informs the reader, none of these "antagonistic sentiments" exists in isolation: so "why more abnegation than jealousy, less envy than equanimity" (17.2195)? Formulating the comparisons in this way is problematic for the reader. Since one term of each pair is given only one value in *Ulysses*, the value of the other term has to be inferred. Though a reader might deduce, for example, that there are considerable grounds for envy—Boylan's youth as opposed to Bloom's middle age; his success as an advertising agent as opposed to Bloom's lowly status as a peripatetic "canvasser"; his wealth as opposed to Bloom's precarious finances—such comparisons and contrasts have to be inferred because the only explicit reference to Bloom's envy of Boylan is his envy of his rival's genetically evolved maleness (17.2157–61). The same is true of any abnegation Bloom might feel about his rival. Four of the five events that are said to demonstrate occurrences of abnegation need to be inferred as they are not represented in *Ulysses* (17.2170–76). Furthermore, abnegation, as we have seen, can mean both a "renunciation of a personal right" and a "refusal of a course of action." Since a satisfactory account of one half of the proposed comparison or contrast has to be inferred from the text and the meta-text, the value of the other half remains uncertain. While, according to the patriarchal "arranger," it is certain that Bloom's feeling of equanimity is greater than his feeling of envy, it remains uncertain what this means precisely, as it is just as likely that Bloom is not envious of some aspects of Boylan as it is that he is envious of just his physicality. Hence, the value to the reader that Bloom's "equanimity" is greater than his envy remains uncertain.

However, what might be probabilistically induced about "equanimity" is worth pursuing, particularly since it is a quality that is frequently attributed to Bloom. The *Oxford English Dictionary* defines "equanimity" as "fairness of judgement, impartiality, equity," a definition that chimes with Aquinas's contention that the good person "*æquanimiter tolerentur mala eis. Et ad hoc pertinent mansuetudo quæ cohibet iras*" ("bears with equanimity the evils done to them. To this pertains meekness or mildness, which restrains anger").[29] And this seems to be the definition favored by most Joyceans. But in light of the fact that it is possible for Bloom to obtain a divorce, more

[29] Thomas Aquinas, *The Gifts of the Spirit*, vol. 24 of *Summa Theologiæ*, ed. Edward D. O'Connor (Cambridge: Cambridge University Press, 2006), 74–75 (1a 2æ 70).

emphasis needs to be placed on the *Oxford English Dictionary* definition 2a: "Evenness of mind or temper; the quality or condition of being undisturbed by elation, depression, or agitating emotion; unruffledness," a definition that chimes with the Platonic contention that the good person "ἥκιστ᾽ ἄρα καὶ ὀδύρεσθαι, φέρειν δὲ ὡς πρᾳότατα, ὅταν τις αὐτὸν τοιαύτη συμφορὰ καταλάβῃ" ("should be the last to mourn, but bear it as resignedly as possible whenever such a disaster befalls him").[30] The emphasis here is on an even-mindedness that is a preparation for rational action, on Bloom as agent rather than victim. In classical Latin, according to the *Thesaurus Linguae Latinae*, the most frequent use of *aeqanimitas* is not just "even-handedness," "fairness," but "favor, beneficence." The second meaning is "tranquility," "ability to bear hardships." The third derived meaning is a "gentleness of soul, slowness to anger."[31] The opposites of *aeqanimitas* are "anger" and "jealousy" (*ira, invidia*).[32] As will become evident, Bloom not only reads the

[30] Plato, *Republic*, ed. and trans. Chris Emlyn-Jones and William Preddy, Loeb Classical Library (Cambridge, MA: Harvard University Press, 2013), 3:228–89 (387e). See also 10:433–34 (605d–e).

[31] Thesaurus Linguae Latinae (TLL) Online (subscription only), http://www.degruyter.com/databasecontent;jsessionid=90AABF5D208C5AFB62FE9B7C015C2B40?dbid=tll&dbsource=%2Fdb%2Ftll. Seneca, *Epistles* 66.13, lists as virtues: "tranquillity, simplicity, generosity, constancy, equanimity, tolerance." I am indebted to Haun Saussy and Theodor Harbsmeier for these references. As Haun Saussy points out,

> The most frequent meaning in classical Latin (and the first given here) is not just "even-handedness," "fairness," as we'd think, but "favor, beneficence." I think this indicates that the root metaphor is that of a flat surface (*cf.* "*aequor*," the surface of the sea), which is approachable and therefore "friendly" as opposed to a high and haughty person who would be like a steep upward slope. (Haun Saussy, e-mail message to author, 20 January 2015)

[32] *aequanimitās*, -ātis *f.* 1 *factum a* TER. *in prologis ex* aequo animo *i. iusto vel benigno, cf.* aequus *III B.* GLOSS. V 530, 35 favor vel aequitas. TER. Phorm. 34 quem . . . restituit locum bonitasque vestra . . . atque aequanimitas (*cf.* 30 adeste aequo animo, *item in prologis* Andr. 24 Heaut. 35, *sim.* Hec. 28). Ad. 24 facite aequanimitas poetae ad scribendum augeat industriam. *opposita*: ira, invidia. Detailed in Haun Saussy, e-mail message to author, 20 January 2015, with acknowledgment of assistance from Theodor Harbsmeier.

matrimonial bed impartially, or so the patriarchal "arranger" assures us, but he also governs his emotions and his responses in such a way as to keep open the possibility of forgiveness or to preserve his legal options should he become convinced that Molly has committed adultery (*U*17.497).

However, the attribution of "abnegation" by the patriarchal "arranger" threatens to unsettle Bloom's much vaunted "equanimity" because it raises the vexed issue of complicity. As readers will discover in "Penelope," one of the ways Molly rationalizes her affair is to blame Bloom for not being affectionate and not enjoying a conventional sexual relationship for some ten years of their sixteen-year marriage. Even more telling is the extent to which Bloom has absented himself from 7 Eccles Street on 16 June 1904 until well after midnight, even though he knows Boylan will be visiting. Pleas for divorce that were made because of adultery and were defended on the grounds of an abrogation of conjugal rights inevitably failed if it could be proved that the adultery had been staged. For example, in the case of *Pollard v. Pollard* (1904), the King's Proctor intervened on the grounds that the husband had been "caused" to commit adultery. Not only was the *decree absolute* withdrawn, but the solicitor and the private detectives involved in the apparent entrapment were also arrested.[33] Similar cases before the Probate, Divorce and Admiralty Division, such as *Moyst v. Moyst, Wilcox, and Essling* (1902), *Webb v. Webb and Mekin* (1903), and *Worsley v. Worsley* (1904) where the King's Proctor was able to establish that the adultery had been staged, led to the rescinding of the *decree nisi* and charges for perjury and conspiracy.[34] As we have seen in Chapter 5, Bloom is deeply troubled by the idea

[33] *Times* (London), 13 June 1904, 11 and *Times* (London), 26 October 1904, 9 et seq. For reports of the case in Australia and New Zealand, see, for example, *The Western Australian*, 25 April 1904, 5; and *The Auckland Star*, 28 May 1904, 5.

[34] *Worsley v. Worsley and Worsley* (1904) 20 TLR 171. The granting of the *decree absolute* was held over pending resolution of legal argument consequent on false evidence given by the detective, the intervention of the King's Proctor, and the fact that both the petitioner and the respondent had not abided by the orders of the Court (*Times* [London], 12 January 1904). The result of legal argument was that "an application by the respondent to be dismissed from the suit was granted" (*Times* [London], 19 January 1904, 7). But Florence Rebecca Redhead, aged twenty-nine, who appeared before Judge Rentoul, K.C. accused of "having three husbands living," although found guilty, was only sentenced to "five days imprisonment, and

that his abnegation might well have reduced him to the status of a procurer, that in the end he might have lived up to his high school nickname of "mackerel" (pimp). The issue now is whether or not his failure to intervene has severely compromised his chances of obtaining a divorce. The simple answer to the riddle of these conflicting emotions, we are assured (though the issue is in law anything but simple), is that Bloom realizes that he himself has not been physically "violated." But that is not the end of the matter.

Having established to his own satisfaction that Molly and Boylan have had sex, the question then arises, "What retribution, if any?" Bloom, who has already forcefully declared his pacifism during his confrontation with the Citizen in Barney Kiernan's pub, immediately rules out "assassination" on the ethical grounds that "two wrongs did not make one right." Duel by combat is also summarily dismissed, the reader is told, particularly as Bloom has already remarked the fate of Ferdinand Lassalles, a German Jewish lawyer who had been killed in a duel over a love affair.[35] By contrast, the third alternative "*divorce*" is held open as a possible course of action, although with the rider "*not now*" (17.2202; emphasis mine). Both the possibility and the feasibility of this course of action specifically for the Blooms is something to which I will return, for, as we have seen in Chapter 1, the only court in the United Kingdom where Bloom might realistically obtain a *decree absolute* was the Probate, Divorce and Admiralty Division that in 1904 sat only in London. And as we have also seen in the previous chapter, Bloom's mind, prior to returning to 7 Eccles Street in the early hours of the 17th of June 1904, has already turned to ways of traveling to London.

That obtaining a divorce appears attractive as an action that might be taken in the future is evident from what immediately follows: "Exposure by

was as a result at once discharged" (*Times* [London], 6 January 1904, 3). *Webb v. Webb and Mekin* (1903), NA J77/778/3690. In *Moyst v. Moyst and Wilcox and Essling*, NA J77/765/3284, Filed: 20 October 1902; Set Down: 15 January 1903; Decree Nisi: 30 April 1903; Rescinded and Dismissed: 11 January 1904. The King's Proctor established that the petitioner himself was a serial adulterer.

[35] Gifford with Seidman, *"Ulysses" Annotated*, 576–77. The career of Ferdinand Lassalles was fictionalized by George Meredith in *The Tragic Comedians* (1880). Note also "The Count and the Actress: Tale of a Duel and a Diamond Ornament," *Daily Mail*, 25 May 1904, 5; and "Erring Wife. Husband's Shots at Her and Her Lover," *Daily Mail*, 17 June 1920, 6.

mechanical artifice (automatic bed) or individual testimony (concealed ocular witnesses)," both of which are also to be held over with the cautionary thought of "*not yet*" (17.2203), as distinct from the decision to consider divorce, which has been qualified by "*not now.*" The first of these thoughts is mischievous fantasy. It is Bloom the scientist *manqué*, the deviser of eye-catching advertisements and graveyard gramophones. Though projecting the guilty pair out a second or third story window of Number 7 doubtless captivates his imagination, it is not something he can actually engineer however attractive it might seem to his sense of humor and his desire for retribution.

But the second thought, "ocular witnesses," was a recognized practice for gaining evidence of marital infidelity. However, the evidence needed to be independently obtained and free of the suspicion of connivance and/or collusion before it would be admitted, so Bloom's recourse to a "*concealed ocular witness*" (emphasis mine) would not constitute proof *per se*. As ruled in *Davidson v. Davidson* (1856), "it is not necessary to prove that the adultery with which a party is charged should have occurred at any particular time or place; ocular proof is very seldom to be procured; almost every case is a case of presumptive proof, though such proof varies in every possible shape and degree."[36] The voyeuristic fantasy that he entertains in "Circe," that Boylan would invite him to witness sex with Molly by peeping through a keyhole, has less to do with the law and more to do with Bloom's anxieties about obtaining incontrovertible evidence that penetration had taken place. Yet, as *Curtis v. Curtis* (1905) established, "As a general rule of practice the court will not act upon the uncorroborated evidence of a petitioner; but there is no rule of law which prohibits it from acting on such evidence if it is satisfied that the story put forward is a true one and that there is no collusion."[37] Additional witnesses could not be planted, though their intervention might be arranged in such a way as to appear accidental. Personal servants and hotel staff, particularly chambermaids, were often relied on as they generally satisfied these requirements.[38] But different rules applied to witnesses in different jurisdictions. If Bloom pursued a divorce in the Irish jurisdiction in 1904, he would need an independent witness—someone who would be willing to offer or to corroborate evidence and someone whose probity could withstand

[36] *Davidson v. Davidson* (1856) 164 ER 526.

[37] *Curtis v. Curtis* (1905) 21 TLR 676.

[38] Cornish, "Marital Breakdown," 793.

cross-examination. Using the testimony of a witness was not required in the English jurisdiction until the Divorce Committees of the Houses of Lords and Commons introduced a rule in 1906 "under which (parties) must have one witness to an adultery."[39] Until then it was not even a requirement, if the adultery had been observed, for the witness and, for that matter, for the respondent to be present at the hearing, as with *Lautour v. Lautour* (1905).[40] As neither Bloom nor Molly have siblings, they cannot trust family, even though the evidence from a purportedly impartial family member in some cases was considered admissible in the English jurisdiction.[41]

Here, as we have seen in the previous chapter, Bloom's insistence that Milly takes a job in Mullingar has proved far-sighted. Not that he would consider asking his daughter to spy on her mother, but he is doubtless aware of Molly's irritation at Milly bursting in on her. As we discover in "Penelope," Molly is convinced that Bloom's insistence on sending Milly away to work has to do with her and Boylan. However, by recruiting a "concealed ocular witness," Bloom might very well find himself in the same situation as *Narese v. Narese and Jones* (1902), where the King's Proctor successfully argued that a witness and the parties had colluded with the result that the *decree nisi* was rescinded and all the documents were impounded.[42] Even employing a private sleuth could be fraught with risk, as the 1904 case of Slater's Detective Agency proved, when their fabrication of evidence not only earned the solicitor and three staff

[39] Roberts, quoted in *Minutes of Evidence*, 3:465, §42,631. Regarding the Commons Committee, Roberts advised, "Generally the committee accepts as a rule the evidence given before the House of Lords with that of the petitioner and one other witness."

[40] Roberts, *Divorce Bills*, 44.

[41] See, for example, *Times* (London), 20 January 1904, 4.

[42] See *Times* (London), 19 February 1904, 13 for King's Proctor's evidence of condonation and collusion: "The jury found that there had been collusion by the petitioner with the respondent and co-respondent. The *decree nisi* was rescinded and all documents in the case were impounded." See also "Index," *Times* (London), 25 February 1904, 7. *Narese v. Narese and Jones*, NA J77/753/2905, Filed: 5 June 1902; Set Down: 8 July 1902; King's Proctor Shows Cause: 29 July 1902; Decree Nisi: 24 October 1902; King's Proctor Shows Cause: 11 June 1903; Set Down: 16, 17, 18, 22 February 1904; Decree Nisi Rescinded: 24 February 1904. Petitioner condemned to costs of £273-7-2.

prison sentences and nullified their current clients' cases, but also kept English and Irish newspaper readers agog for well over twelve months.[43] Not surprisingly, as committed as he is to probabilistic induction, Bloom quickly eliminates the idea, though this is not to suggest that he does so because he is abreast of all the relevant legislation and case law or has been following the case of *Narese v. Narese and Jones* even though it was widely reported.

Bloom's remaining strategies seem equally fraught. According to the law of the day, Molly is his "property," so it might be possible for him to bring a "suit for damages by legal influence,"[44] an "Ithaca" euphemism for *criminal conversation.* As Cornish has explained, prior to the passage of the 1857 Act, "thanks to *crim. con.* damages, the husband might come off more or less harmless, the adulterer footing the bill for the tri-partite process" involved in obtaining "a parliamentary divorce."[45] Subsequent to the 1857 Act, however, financial reparation in the English jurisdiction took the form of costs being awarded in favor of the petitioner should it become evident that the respondent or respondents had an intention to damage the finances as well as the reputation of the petitioner.[46] Should Bloom claim damages, Boylan might be unable to avoid payment, given *Rayment v. Rayment and Stuart* (1910) and *Chapman v. Chapman and Buist* (1910), where the court determined that while "a judgment following on a verdict for damages in a divorce suit in this Court could not be

[43] See, for example, "Charge against Inquiry Agents," *Ulster Herald*, 30 April 1904, 6; "Slater's Agency: Charge against the Accused," *Freeman's Journal*, 2 May 1904, 4; "Private Detectives; Sensational Sequel to a Divorce Suit; Astonishing Allegations of the King's Proctor; Inquiry Office Methods," *Daily Mail*, 17 March 1904, 3; "Slater's Agency; Five Arrests in the Private Detective Case," *Daily Mail*, 25 April 1904, 3; "Private Detectives; Slater Trial Opens at the Old Bailey; Huge Array of Documents," *Daily Mail*, 26 October 1904, 3; "Private Detectives; Principal of Slater's Agency Acquitted," *Daily Mail*, 3 November 1904, 3.

[44] Shatter, *Family Law*, 137.

[45] Cornish, "Marital Breakdown," 782.

[46] Shatter, *Family Law*, 93 n. 37: "In England the action of criminal conversation was abolished by the Matrimonial Causes Act, 1857, which substituted under section 33 of the Act a power in the Divorce Court to award damages for adultery to a petitioning husband. The right to claim such damages was abolished in 1970 by the Law reform (Miscellaneous Persons) Act."

enforced against a foreigner in a foreign country, it might possibly be enforced against a Scotsman or an Irishman, in Scotland or Ireland by means of the Judgements Extension Act, 1868."[47] As the controversy that followed Sir Francis Jeune's "remarkable utterance" about "unmarried men" indicates, the issue of wealthy bachelors seducing married women was not looked on with favor by the court, despite what unmarried men might think of themselves.[48]

But as *criminal conversation* remained a tort in the Irish jurisdiction, Bloom's passing thought of "a suit for legal damages by legal influence" is not only feasible but, if successful, also has the potential to provide a significant measure of redress, as evident from Justice McCardie's ruling in *Butterworth v. Butterworth* (1920), commenting on *Foster v. Foster* (1864).[49] In awarding damages to the petitioner, McCardie ruled that "the way in which the defendant's wealth was employed might have the most direct bearing on the question of damages."[50] Earlier in the day,

[47] *Law Reports Digest 1901–1910*, cols. 919–20. *Rayment v. Rayment and Stuart (otherwise Stewart)*, NA J77/1008/582, Filed: 19 May 1910; Set Down: 28 September 1910; Decree Nisi: 7 March 1911; Final Decree: 20 September 1911; *Chapman v. Chapman and Buist*, NA J77/1010/648, Filed: 14 June 1910; Dismissed on Summons: 18 October 1911.

[48] "Unmarried Men. Remarkable Utterance by Sir Francis Jeune," *Daily Mail*, 15 March 1904, 3. See also "Unmarried Men. To the Editor," *Daily Mail*, 16 March 1904, 4. The landmark case here is *Bell v. Bell and Anglesey* (Marquis) (1859) 1 Sw&Tr 565; Sea&Sm 110; 29 LJP&A 159; 1 LT 243; 8 WR 178; 164 ER 861.

[49] *Foster v. Foster* (1864) 33 LJCP 150; *Butterworth v. Butterworth* (1920) P 126.

[50] Note to Law Reform Commission, "The Law Relating to Criminal Conversation and the Enticement and Harbouring of a Spouse," Working Paper No. 5, 1978, 3–4, accessed 22 July 2016, http://www.lawreform.ie/_fileupload/consultation%20papers/wpHarbouringOfaSpouse.htm. This ruling was criticized by Diplock L. J. in *Pritchard v. Pritchard and Sims* [1967] P 195 at 212–13:

> The measure of... compensation for injury to the husband's feelings and pride must... take account of changing social norms. The test must be his rational resentment, not his mere idiosyncratic ire, and the factors to be taken into account in mitigation or aggravation are those which would affect the feelings of a reasonable man with an unfaithful wife in the social conditions of today.... When, however, J. McCardie in *Butterworth v. Butterworth* in 1920 accepted the use of wealth or station

Bloom has been prompted to link Parnell with "surgeon McArdle," who, according to Dublin lore, though "a damned good surgeon" was a "notorious womanizer," with the result that though he "made buckets of money," he "lost a lot" in actions for *criminal conversation* that aggrieved "husbands brought against him."[51] Wealth was seen as an aphrodisiac. For his part, Boylan is known about town to be well-off. Gossip about the origins of his wealth and the expensive basket of fruit he presents to Molly on his arrival at Bloom's house would tell against him, as would Molly's frequent complaints about her need to economize on everything, from the necessity to ration tea to the amount of household help she received (18.468–69; 18.1079–81), particularly if these points were argued by counsel with "legal influence." Nevertheless, as *Byrne v. Byrne and Helvoet* (1920) confirmed, "there is no absolute rule of practice that a co-respondent cannot be condemned in costs unless at the time of the first misconduct he knew that the respondent was a married woman. Costs are always at the discretion of the court."[52]

Bloom's next strategy, a suit for damages arising from a "simulation of assault with evidence of injuries sustained (self-inflicted)," is deemed "not impossib[le]." After all, Boylan is a boxing promoter, and so it might pass as plausible that he would resort to his fists if he had been surprised in a compromising situation. But Bloom abhors violence and self-harm, particularly given his father's suicide, so this strategy, consistent with his use of probabilistic induction reasoning, is dismissed. Similarly, an attempt to extort "hushmoney by moral influence," though it might "possibly" be successful, appears unlikely and is therefore eliminated. What purchase could "moral influence" have on a man who had committed an immoral act according to religion and a misdemeanor according to law? Bloom's remaining strategies for seeking retribution seem even more unlikely than the majority of those that have occurred to him at this point, the

by an adulterer as still being a factor in aggravation of damages, he was taking his psychology from the Victorian novelette and not from life in the 1920s.

51 Garvin, *James Joyce's Disunited Kingdom*, 76. See also *U*135.514: "Mad Fanny and his other sister Mrs. Dickinson driving about with scarlet harness. Bolt upright like surgeon M^c^Ardle."

52 *Burne v. Burne and Helvoet* [1920] P 17; 89 LJP 18; 122 LT 224; 64 Sol Jo 132.

fragmentation of the syntax of the patriarchal "arranger's" answer mirroring both the desperation and the fragmentation of Bloom's thoughts.

> If any, positively, connivance, introduction of emulation (material, a prosperous rival agency of publicity: moral, a successful rival agent of intimacy),[53] depreciation, alienation, humiliation, separation protecting the one separated from the other, protecting the separator from both. (17.2207–8)

As readers are by now aware, successful "emulation" of both a rival agency of publicity and a rival agent of intimacy seem most unlikely. While Bloom sees himself as press savvy, attuned to publicity and public relations, and a modern communicator,[54] it is doubtful that he would be able to rival the image of a confident, wealthy, well-dressed man-about-town that Boylan has achieved in the streets and pubs of Dublin.[55] It is also doubtful, given the tenor of his correspondence with Martha Clifford, that she will prove "a successful rival agent of intimacy."[56] Even though earlier

[53] See Cornish, "Marital Breakdown," 793:

> Collusion was particularly linked with the separate bar to divorce constituted by "recrimination"—conduct of the petitioner (most often adultery) which sullied his or her own hands.... The law itself offered only one possible accommodation: if the petitioner put the full truth of his or her own lapse before the court, it did have a discretion after all to order the divorce. But the judges soon announced that this discretion would be exercised only in exceptional cases. Within a decade they had spelled these out as: "accidental adultery," where there was no reason to believe that the other spouse was still alive; "unwilling adultery," where, for example, a husband forced his petitioner wife out to be a prostitute; and "condoned adultery," where the respondent had fully forgiven it. Doing the proper thing by throwing oneself on the court's mercy rarely had the desired effect.

[54] "The infinite possibilities hitherto unexploited of the modern art of advertisement" (*U*17.580–81).

[55] Molly admires the cut of his clothes, even though Bloom and Boylan buy their clothes from the same tailor. *U*18.422: "well off I know by the cut of his clothes."

[56] Note that Bloom might also be concerned about "breach of promise" or "contract of hire" issues should he get drawn into a relationship with Martha Clifford.

in the day Bloom has torn Martha Clifford's *billet-doux* into tiny pieces and scattered it to the four winds (5.300; cf. 17.840), the first drawer of the bureau in 7 Eccles Street, which is unlocked, contains

> 3 typewritten letters, addressee, Henry Flower, c/o. P. O. Westland Row, addresser, Martha Clifford, c/o. P. O. Dolphin's Barn: the transliterated name and address of the addresser of the 3 letters in reversed alphabetic boustrophedonic punctuated quadrilinear cryptogram (vowels suppressed) N. IGS./WI. UU. OX/W. OKS. MH/Y. IM. (17.1796–1801)

Though, as Gifford with Seidman point out, reversing Martha Clifford's surname makes what is a relatively simple code harder to break, it does not make it impossible to break.[57] Besides letters in code might well arouse suspicion. If the letters were tendered by Molly's counsel, Bloom might find himself in a quandary, as with *Brodrick v. Brodrick* (1903), where a letter written by a "friend" of the husband who had been granted a divorce proved decisive in the wife securing a judicial separation with costs of £74-6-11 awarded against him.[58] Even more sensational was the case of *Maxwell v. Maxwell* (1901) and a person known as "*Jenny Adair*," where the wife, suspecting infidelity, broke open the locked box where her husband kept their food only to find films which, when developed, substantiated her story and satisfied the court.[59]

Nevertheless, it would be a mistake to think that the significant problems attending all the strategies that Bloom contemplates in bed at Number 7 mean that he has entirely dismissed divorce as an option. Neither Molly nor Boylan have bothered to conceal their presence in the kitchen. Bloom not only bumps his head because the furniture has been rearranged, but the port and fruit that Boylan has brought Molly,

[57] Gifford with Seidman, *"Ulysses" Annotated*, 596. For an example of letters in code cited in divorce proceedings, see "Clergyman's Misconduct," *Daily Mail*, 3 February 1904, 3.

[58] *Times* (London), 26 January 1904, 4. *Brodrick v. Brodrick*, NA J77/783/3846, Filed: 27 April 1903; Set Down: 3 September 1903; Decree Nisi: 25 January 1904; Final Decree.

[59] "Secrets of a Locked Box," *Daily Mail*, 10 August 1904, 3. *Maxwell v. Maxwell*, NA J77/735/2351, Filed: 23 November 1901; Set Down: 18 January 1904; Decree Nisi: 9 August 1904; Final Decree: 27 February 1905.

complete with basket and tissue paper, and his betting tickets have been left exposed on the dresser.[60] But it is only when Bloom finds crumbs, remnants of Plumtree's potted meat, and the impression made by another male body in the matrimonial bed that he knows for certain that he has been cuckolded. What he does *not* discover, but what Molly thinks is conclusive evidence, is the "mark of [Boylan's] spunk on the clean sheet." "That ought to satisfy him if you don't believe me," she says to herself (18.1512). This brazen combative decision not to conceal damning evidence, and if necessary reveal it, is highly unusual, for as a leading authority on Irish family law has pointed out, "rarely will there be direct evidence of the fact of adultery . . . the fact is inferred from circumstances."[61] But there is, before the advent of modern forensic science, no conclusive way of establishing that the semen is Boylan's, unless he admits that it is his.

Bloom's next action is critical, as much for personal and psychological reasons as for its legal consequences. If he was to turn Molly out onto the streets, having secured what he now believes is absolute proof, she might be able to plead cruelty under the Summary Jurisdiction (Married Women) Act 1895, and he would then find himself legally required to maintain her.[62] If he were simply to walk out himself, he might find

[60] *U*17.296–319; *U*17.1279–1319.

[61] Shatter, *Family Law*, 132.

[62] *Read v. Legard* (1851) 6 Exch 636; 20 LJEx 309; 17 LTOS 145; 15 Jur 494; 155 ER 698. However, as the cases of *Close v. Close* and *Neligan v. Neligan, Times* (London), 5 February 1904, 13, illustrate, the question of alimony *pendente lite* could prove complicated. Note Cornish, "Marital Breakdown," 789:

> Nonetheless their condition was more hopeful than the wife found guilty as a respondent. For two decades [following 1857], she could expect nothing by way of maintenance. The discreet custom in parliamentary divorce had been for a "lady's friend" to ensure that the wife, for all her guilt, would not be left unprovided. Now the ethos was quite against any such intercession. Eventually, M. R. Jessel objected that the legislation was not meant to turn the wife out into the streets to starve (*Robinson v. Robinson* (1883) 8 P&D 94). This, it seemed, led to awards to her of very small amounts. It was extremely unlikely that she would be allowed access to her children, let alone custody. J. Cresswell said soon enough that this embargo was needed as "a salutary effect on the interest of public morality" (*Sedden v. Sedden and*

himself sued under the Married Women's Property (Ireland) Act 1865, an Act that enabled a wife, deserted by her husband, to sue him in tort. As one legal expert has explained, "These rights were further extended by the Act of 1870, by which she could bring an action to recover her separate property against anyone including her husband."[63] Desertion, as with *Dixon v. Dixon* (1858)[64] and *Duplany v. Duplany, Cohen Intervening* (1890),[65] was "not held to be a bar to a decree of judicial separation," though as Latey further points out, "in 1905 it was held that when the court found that the desertion of the husband petitioner had conduced to the adultery of the respondent, the petitioner was not entitled to a decree of judicial separation."[66] If, after deserting Molly, Bloom were to absent himself for a period of time, he might find himself served with an order for the restitution of conjugal rights, a strategy which, while often used against recalcitrant absent husbands, rarely restored marital harmony.[67] Were he to assert his conjugal rights, even though he and Molly have not experienced a conventional sexual relationship since the death of Rudy some ten years before, Molly would not have legal grounds for refusing to have sexual intercourse, as a woman's right to plead marital rape was

Doyle (1862) 2 Sw. & Tr. 640; cf. Lord Cairns' rather more sympathetic view in *Symington v. Symington* (1875) LR 2 Sc & Div 415).

[63] Shatter, *Family Law*, 111. Latey, *Law and Practice*, 319, §2.685, points out that the word "any" in section 17 of the 1883 Act has a very wide interpretation in that "title deeds, jewellery, and wedding gifts" may be deemed property. "After a divorce a sum paid by way of a Jewish dowry into a joint account of the husband and wife was held to be divisible among them (*Kellner v. Kellner* (1939)), but in the case of a nullity of a marriage *ab initio* the petitioning wife was held to be entitled to the whole amount of the dowry."

[64] *Dixon v. Dixon*, NA J77/13/D8. Court Minutes not digitized. *Dixon v. Dixon* (1859) LJP&M 96: "Where the court decrees a dissolution of marriage at the suit of the wife, costs follow the decree as a matter of course, if the court in pronouncing the decree, gives no directions as to costs."

[65] *Duplany v. Duplany* [1892], NA J77/462/4065; P 53; 61 LJP 49; 66 LT 267; 8 TLR 169.

[66] Latey, *Law and Practice*, 195, §2.345.

[67] See Shatter, *Family Law*, 88–90; Latey, *Law and Practice*, 199–202, §2.356–67.

not recognized in law in Ireland in 1904.[68] However, if he compelled her by such force that it was deemed an assault or an aggravated assault, he might be charged. Alternatively, she might be able to apply to a magistrate and, under the Matrimonial Causes Act 1878, be granted a protection order. *Dillon v. Dillon* (1842), however, states that the husband is the one who has to adjust where he lives until he has convinced himself that he has the evidence: "A husband receiving information, impugning his wife's fidelity, sufficient to induce him to investigate her conduct, is bound, pending the inquiry, to abstain from cohabitation, although not bound to remove her from his house."[69]

What is more crucial, legally, is that if she willingly assents to his urgings for sexual intercourse—and the thought of her infidelity causes him to have "an approximate" and then a "proximate erection" (17.2238; 17.2246)—Bloom might well be deemed to have granted "condonation." *Every Man's Own Lawyer* offers the following: "Condonation is a bar to divorce: it means forgiveness and reconciliation, and a blotting out of the offence; and if the petitioner has condoned the adultery or cruelty complained of, the petition will be dismissed, on proof of the condonation. Condonation may be implied from fact and circumstances."[70] The case of *Williams v. Williams* (1903) makes abundantly clear "the principle . . . that the moment a resumption of cohabitation took place there was an end of previous misconduct. This was a principle of law recognized not only in this division, but also in the Courts of equity and common law—'*Haddon v. Haddon* (18 QBD 778).'"[71] And as the President of the Divorce Division ruled in *Hyman v. Hyman and Goldman* (1904), "if a petition is dismissed by reason of condonation, it is dismissed for all purposes."[72] However, in *Rickhard v.*

[68] "By marriage a wife implicitly consents to having sexual intercourse with her husband. He cannot be convicted of raping her during the subsistence of the marriage." Shatter, *Family Law*, 109.

[69] *Dillon v. Dillon* (1842) 3 Curt 84; 1 Notes of Cases 415; 6 Jur 422; 163 ER 663.

[70] *Every Man's Own Lawyer*, 376.

[71] *Times* (London), 3 February 1904, 3. *Williams v. Williams*, NA J77/801/4378, Filed: 17 November 1903; Order of Justices to be Discharged: 2 February 1904.

[72] Jeune Pres. [1904] P 403. *Law Reports Digest 1901–1910*, cols. 920–21, citing *Long v. Long and Johnson* (1890) 15 PD 218.

Rickhard and Bowles (1902), heard before Justice Bucknell, where both petitioner and respondent had committed adultery, a divorce was granted on the grounds of the petitioner's (husband's) adultery, because the respondent (wife) successfully claimed condonation for her adultery, with the result that costs of £47-16-4 and alimony of one pound per week went against the petitioner (husband).[73] *Rickhard v. Rickhard and Bowles*, however, needs to be understood in terms of *Cramp v. Cramp and Freeman* (1918):

> Condonation, as applied to matrimonial offences, though frequently defined as conditional forgiveness, is not forgiveness in the ordinary sense, but would be more properly defined as conditional reinstatement of the offending spouse. It is always subject to the condition that the offence must not recur. Resumption by the husband of connubial intercourse with his wife, when he has full knowledge of her adultery, is conclusive proof of condonation. It cannot be rebutted by the fact that he never forgave her, though the fact is admitted by the wife.[74]

In returning to the marital bed so that he and Molly continue to sleep head to toe and by giving her a kiss on the bottom, which the "arranger" of "Ithaca" says produces in Molly an "incipient excitation" (17.2248),[75] Bloom might seem to be merely perpetuating a mildly perverse form of intimacy, but he is also protecting his legal right to pursue a divorce, even though this might not be his deliberate intention and is not something that he plans to do "*now*."[76] It is important to note, however, that "the

[73] *Rickhard v. Rickhard and Bowles*, NA J77/753/2925, Filed: 11 June 1902; Set Down: 3 November 1902; Decree Nisi: 10 February 1903; Final Decree: 23 November 1903.

[74] *Cramp v. Cramp and Freeman* [1920] P 158; All ER Rep 164. The Court Minutes, lodged at NA J77/1391/2680, have not been digitized at the time of this book going to press.

[75] Bloom's kiss on the bottom prompts Molly to think, "where we haven't 1 atom of any kind of expression in us" (*U*18.1403). Note, however, McCourt, *Years of Bloom*, 48, where melon is used in Triestine as a symbol for marriage: *Il matrimonio e un melone.*

[76] The case of *Wyke v. Wyke—The King's Proctor Showing Cause* before Mr. Justice Bucknill, *Times* (London), 29 January 1904, 13, is of interest here as the Judge had to decide whether or not "the discretion given to [him] by the 31st section of the Divorce Act of 1857" empowers him to "pronounce a *decree absolute* dissolving the marriage, notwithstanding the adultery of the petitioner."

limitations of activity and inhibitions of conjugal rights" observed by Bloom and Molly just before Bloom falls asleep and recorded by the "arranger" conform precisely to what is required to lodge an application for divorce that has a possibility of succeeding.

Having convinced himself that Molly has committed adultery and having refused to encourage any intimacy that might result in condonation, Bloom is now faced with several courses of action. The first and indisputably the kindest and most generous is to forgive and forget. The second, if cohabitation proves intolerable, is to obtain a separation order, which, as we have seen, is a course of action that was commonly adopted in late nineteenth- and early twentieth-century Ireland as a way of coping with marriage breakdown. The third, again resorted to not infrequently and for the same reason, was to migrate to Australia, New Zealand, or America, though not to every province in Canada.[77] A fourth, if Bloom decides he wants a *decree absolute*, is to become domiciled in a jurisdiction where a decree could be obtained without prejudice to comity of nations—preferably England. Again, this was a course of action that was adopted as early as 1888 in the matter of *McClintock v. McClintock* and as late as 1921 in the matters of *Sharpe v. Sharpe and Penny*, *Mills v. Mills*, *Laverton v. Laverton*, and *Irvine v. Irvine*. A fifth course of action is to wait for additional incontrovertible evidence but to do so in a way that does not give rise to allegations of connivance or collusion.[78] Time, if divorce case law is any guide, is not necessarily the essence of the contract here. For example, in the matter of *Fraser v. Fraser*, as reported on 25 April 1921 in the *Irish Times*, both petitioner and respondent gave Merrion Street, Dublin, as their address, the petitioner being granted a *decree nisi* from a marriage with the respondent at the Registry Office in Dublin in 1908 on the basis of the respondent's misconduct in Dublin several years previously with "a man unknown."[79] Some Irish, it seems, not only obtained a divorce in the

[77] Urquart, "Ireland and the Act of 1857," 314.

[78] Cornish, "Marital Breakdown," 792: "It was not connivance, however, on discovering the adultery, to let it continue in order to get evidence for a divorce petition." *Hunter v Hunter* [1905] P 217; 74 LJP 157; 93 LT 451; 53 WR 666; 21 TLR 602: "Concealment of facts is not a bar, either absolute or discretionary, unless the facts, if before the court, would have caused the court to withhold the decree."

[79] *Fraser v. Fraser*, *Irish Times*, 25 April 1921, 2.

English jurisdiction while domiciled in Ireland, but they did so thirteen years after the adultery had taken place.

So if Molly does decide to go to Belfast with Boylan or if she does decide to go on the stage, and if she is away for two years or more,[80] or if she and Boylan go to any place in England together, Bloom could simply initiate his "longcherished plan" of going to London, which he believes he has already visited at least once. Once there he could establish domicile through his connections with the significant Jewish community (16.499–538) and obtain his divorce by virtue of Molly's adultery and desertion,[81] the former charge not requiring to be proved as conclusively as if it were the only grounds for his petition. An uncontested divorce might cost him as little as £35 or it might not cost him anything if he was to succeed in having costs awarded against Boylan.

Of course, whether or not Bloom would move to London remains unknown. But, as Joyce himself well knew, exile can prove the most conducive place in which to establish a home.

[80] Note, however, Roberts, *Divorce Bills*, 11: "in Mrs. Lautour's case (1905) the grounds were adultery and desertion for twenty years, although the learned judge of the Court in Dublin was unable to declare desertion as a ground for the decree, as it is not a ground for divorce *a mensa et thoro*"; and again at 323: "In Mrs. Lautour's case, 1905, the divorce had been granted on the ground of adultery alone as the Court had no jurisdiction to grant it on the ground of desertion."

[81] For a discussion of the Jewish quarter in London and the Chief Rabbi's attitude to divorce, see Chapter 1. Note, however, Bloom's: "I mean Christ, was a jew too and all his family like me *though in reality I'm not*" (*U*16.1084–85; emphasis mine).

CHAPTER 8

Will They or Won't They?

My argument is that Joyce's fictional world mirrors the popular culture of 1904 Edwardian Dublin and that one of Bloom's reactions on discovering what he believes is convincing proof of Molly's adultery is to *consider* divorce. What he describes to Stephen during his conversation in the cabman's shelter indicates that he has begun to think in terms of the English jurisdiction—of the King's Proctor, of *decree nisi* and *decree absolute*—all functionaries and procedures of the Probate, Divorce and Admiralty Division of the King's Bench, which sat only in London. This is not to assume that he will petition the English court for a divorce; but it is to affirm that thinking about divorce points to his desire for agency.

Bloom's dilemma is also Molly's dilemma, for during the long night of 17 June 1904 she also considers divorce. Granting her the final episode of *Ulysses* emphasizes the significance Joyce attributed to the gender politics of the modern marriage, the emerging equality of the sexes under the law, and the extent to which the English jurisdiction was moving cautiously toward a more equitable process for divorce, a process comparable to what was already in existence in the Scottish and French jurisdictions.[1] Adultery, detection, and the possibility of divorce also furnished Joyce with sites of

[1] The Matrimonial Causes Act 1937 removed the tests of cruelty, incest, and sodomy that, in addition to adultery, had applied to women seeking divorce following the 1857 Act.

P. Kuch, *Irish Divorce / Joyce's Ulysses*,
DOI 10.1057/978-1-137-57186-1_8

contestation for dramatizing dialogue, exploring narrative conventions, experimenting with genre, and investigating the shaping power of social, sexual, cultural, religious, and political discourses, all of which were essential to his modernist project. Legal discourse, whether ecclesiastical or civil, could operate as a metatext that opened spaces for multiperspectivity. Whatever was represented in the story-world of the book could then be re-presented with reference to the world of pleas, affidavits, case law, legislation, advocacy, judgment, and the processes of appeal.

Within this "world" the contrast between the styles of Bloom's episodes ("Eumaeus"—"Ithaca") and Molly's episode ("Penelope") suggests that, regardless of whatever happens or is thought to happen, Molly is likely to succeed. As Katie Wales has persuasively argued, differences between the styles of their respective episodes enable the reader to construct "two different kinds of mindset, one deliberative, ponderous, the other quicker and smoother in flow."[2] As *Gaston v. Gaston* (1865) established, "An answer for a petition for dissolution of marriage must not necessarily be in conformity with a common law plea, either by way of traverse, or confession, or avoidance. It is intended to be a substantial statement of respondent's case, but should be within a reasonable degree of brevity."[3] Likewise, as many newspaper reports of divorce from the period show, given the adversarial nature of the proceedings, the bench was judiciously sympathetic to litigants who were lucid, frank, and honest; it could be quite sharp with pretense and periphrasis.

Whether Molly was petitioner or respondent, much would depend on the way her case was presented. Given that attack is sometimes the most effective form of defense, her counsel could submit a cross-petition arguing that it is Bloom who is the adulterer and that what he alleges about Molly and Boylan cannot be reasonably established. Grounds for alleging Bloom's adultery would require "The Watch" and "Mrs. Breen" to appear as witnesses and counsel to marshal case law following *Astley v. Astley* (1828), that "a married man going to a brothel, knowing it to be a house of that description, raises a suspicion of adultery necessary to be rebutted by the very best evidence."[4] That Bloom is depicted as being

[2] Wales, *Language of James Joyce*, 91–92.

[3] *Gaston v. Gaston* (1865) 13 LT 412.

[4] *Astley v. Astley* [1928] 162 ER 728.

acutely nervous about being discovered in Nighttown is evident when he imagines accidentally encountering Josie Breen there. His hasty excuse, "Short cut home here. Interesting quarter. Rescue of Fallen women. Magdalen asylum. I am the secretary," is summarily dismissed by her as, "Now, don't tell a big fib! I know somebody won't like that. O just wait till I see Molly! (*slily*) Account for yourself this very minute or woe betide you!" (15.401–6). And when he does return early the next morning to the marital bed, Molly is equally skeptical of his story about why he has stayed out so late: "either it was one of those night women if it was down there he was really and the hotel story he made up a pack of lies to hide it planning it Hynes kept me who did I meet ah yes I do remember Menton and who else who let me see" (18.36).[5] Even if Stephen could be persuaded to appear on Bloom's behalf should the matter go to court, the prostitutes Bloom spends time with, particularly those he has offended, might well support the aggrieved wife rather than the secretive husband.

In defending Molly against the charge that she has committed adultery, counsel could argue case law following *Evans v. Evans* (1844): "The proof of adultery, in a suit, depending upon the evidence of one witness alone, is insufficient to entitle the promoter to his prayer."[6] And allegations about her time in Belfast with Boylan could be countered, for example, with *Hunt v. Hunt* (1856): "When a young married woman goes with a man to an inn, and the blinds are pulled down, the room is in confusion, the door is locked, and they are there for a considerable time, these circumstances offer a case of very strong suspicion; they do not account to more than presumption (*per curiam*)."[7] And if Bloom had second thoughts about his "divorce, not now" and did proceed with a petition on the evidence of the marital bed on 17 June 1904, he might find himself confounded by *Alexander v. Alexander and Amos* (1860): "When a wife has conducted herself during a married life of twenty years with propriety, the court will not

[5] Note, Proust, *Swann's Way*, 2:84: "Swann could at once detect in this story one of those fragments of literal truth which liars, when taken by surprise, console themselves by introducing into the composition of the falsehood which they have to invent, thinking it can be safely incorporated, and will lend the whole story an air of verisimilitude."

[6] *Evans v. Evans* [1844] 163 ER 1000.

[7] *Hunt v. Hunt* [1856] 164 ER 522.

conclude that she has been guilty of adultery charged to have been committed without the slightest regard to decency or fear of detection, unless established by cogent evidence."[8]

Even after her time in Belfast, if Molly decides she will divorce Bloom but not marry Boylan, her counsel might well argue that Bloom is somewhat culpable because he failed to provide his wife with the emotional, conjugal, and financial security required by *consortium*. The divorce court did not consider adultery *in vacuo*. *Tulk v. Tulk* (1906) established that "to enable the court to exercise its discretion in favour of a wife who is petitioning for a divorce and who has herself committed adultery, she must show that her adultery was the necessary and reasonable consequence of her husband's conduct."[9] Furthermore, as ruled in *Boddington v. Boddington and Mossiter* (1858), "On proof of a petition for dissolution of marriage, by reason of the adultery of the wife, some evidence should be given of the conduct of the husband towards her previous to the adultery."[10] However, Bloom's spotty record of employment, financial misadventures, irritating behaviors, voyeurism, eccentricities, and sexual proclivities are not issues likely to influence the court, again given case law, no matter how persuasively they are presented. Neither it seems would his fixation with women's bottoms influence the court, as much as it offends Molly, as it has not led to sodomy or cruelty, either one being necessary for a woman to establish, in addition to adultery, if she wished to petition for a divorce in the English jurisdiction between 1857 and 1935. It might also prove difficult for Molly's counsel to argue a ten-year gap in conjugal relations as she is the sole witness, although not having another child after Rudy could be used to suggest that Bloom has not fulfilled his marital obligations following his son's death. As Cornish has noted, "there was a special distaste against a partner having to testify about his or her own sexual activity," although it was not until

[8] *Alexander v. Alexander and Amos* (1860) 2 Sw&Tr 95; Sea&Sm 153; 29 LJPM&A 56; 6 Jur NS 56; 8 WR 452; 164 ER 928.

[9] *Tulk v. Tulk* (1906) 23 TLR 120. See *Joseph v. Joseph and Wentzel* (1865) 34 LJP M&A 96; *Coleman v. Coleman* (1866) 1 P&D 81; *McCord v. McCord, Ogle and Coxton* (1875) 3 LR P&D 237; *Story v. Story and O'Connor* (1887) 12 PD 196; *Morgan v. Morgan and Porter* (1869) 1 P&D 644; *Symons v. Symons* [1897] P 167; TLR 353.

[10] *Boddington v. Boddington and Mossiter* [1858] 27 LJP&M 53.

the Law Reform (Miscellaneous Provisions) Act 1949 that it was ruled that questions, which partners had not been compelled to answer, should not even be put.[11]

However, even if it was established to the satisfaction of the court that Molly had committed a single act of adultery or had only embarked on an adulterous relationship after a considerable amount of time, *Brown v. Brown and Robey* (1869)[12] and *O'Shea v. O'Shea and Parnell* (1890) might be argued on the grounds that Bloom, like Brown and O'Shea, had not only deprived Molly of natural affection but had also encouraged the association with Boylan to the extent that it was almost inevitable it would end in adultery. Yet as *Shaw v. Shaw* [1904] indicates, such a defense needed to be mounted on reasonable grounds.[13] But if it was argued that Bloom's encouragement actually constituted connivance, then Molly's counsel could draw attention to *Adams v. Adams and Colter* (1867) with respect to Boylan that a "petition by a husband, and claiming damages from a co-respondent, was dismissed on the connivance of the petitioner and condonation, and petitioner was ordered to pay co-respondent his costs, although the adultery of the respondent and co-respondent was proved."[14] Counsel could also draw the court's attention to *Cox v. Cox and Warde* (1906), where it was determined that a husband who had "presented a petition for damages only and had himself been guilty of a matrimonial offence, which, in the exercise of the discretion vested in the court would lead the court to refuse to grant him a decree in a suit if a dissolution of the marriage was claimed by him, he was, on the like ground, debarred from recovering damages from the adulterer."[15] Regardless of what he does, "slyboots" Bloom, who, according to Molly, "plots and plans everything out," might well find himself wrong-footed by the law

[11] Cornish, "Marital Breakdown," 789.

[12] *Brown v. Brown and Robey* [1869] 21 LT 181; for *O'Shea v. O'Shea and Parnell* [1890], see Chapter 6.

[13] *Shaw v. Shaw* [1904] 20 TLR 795: "Held petitioner had failed to show that her husband's misconduct had directly conduced to her adultery, and therefore she had failed to make out any ground which would justify the court in exercising its statutory authority in her favour in granting her a decree of divorce."

[14] *Adams v. Adams and Colter* [1867] LR 1 P&D 333; 36 LJP&M 62; 16 LT 69.

[15] *Cox v. Cox and Warde* [1906] P 267; 75 LJP 75; 95 LT 546; 22 TLR 557.

should Molly transform her "suppose I divorced him" into a petition for divorce (18.297; 18.1008–9; 18.846).

Her plans, compared with Bloom's, seem more provisional. While there is much that Molly finds irritating about her husband, and while her memories of their courtship and marriage are less nostalgic and more energized by desire and occasion, she does argue herself into giving him one more chance. What remains uncertain for the reader is whether or not her strategies for restoring conjugal relations will succeed. Given the fluctuation of her feelings, it remains uncertain whether her memory of their commitment to one another on the Hill of Howth, like Bloom's fantasizing about "Flowerville," has become her version of a sedative, an avoidance technique necessary for constructing a consoling narrative that sets the past to rights.

* * * *

To speculate whether divorce is a likely, very likely, or highly unlikely outcome for the Blooms is to venture on the counterfactual and to impose closure on a text that intrinsically resists it.

To ignore the possibility of divorce is to deny ways of reading *Ulysses* that enhance both its uncertainty and its humanity, its truth to life.

What is worth speculating about are the reasons why Irish recourse to the English divorce court has been so comprehensively expunged from Joyce criticism, from Irish history, and from the Irish social imaginary between 1922 and 1986;[16] but that is a future project, one that will interrogate debates about how to read *Ulysses* that range from Leo Bersani's "Against *Ulysses*" to Luca Crispi's *Joyce's Creative Process*; Dermot Keogh's discussion of divorce in *The Vatican, the Bishops and Irish Politics 1919–1939*; David Fitzpatrick's pithy account in *The Two Irelands 1912–1939* of Church and Free State negotiations, first with Cosgrave in 1922 and 1923 and then with de Valera from 1932 to 1937; and W. B. Yeats's contributions to the 1925 debate on divorce in the Free State Senate.[17]

[16] The proposal to amend the Constitution was rejected following the 1986 referendum (63.5% against to 36.5% in favor) but was accepted following the 1995 referendum (49.72% against to 50.28% in favor).

[17] Leo Bersani, "Against *Ulysses*," *The Culture of Redemption* (Cambridge, MA: Harvard University Press, 1990), 155–78; Dermot Keogh, *The Vatican, The Bishops and Irish Politics 1919–1939* (1986; Cambridge: Cambridge University

To conclude the legal argument, I would like to consider whether the Blooms' English divorce would be recognized in the Irish jurisdiction if Molly or Bloom subsequently decided to return to Dublin married or to remarry. James Roberts, as we have seen, stated in his *Divorce Bills in the Imperial Parliament* (1906) that "despite a Privy Council ruling that domicile is the sole determinant of jurisdiction, there have been many cases [of] persons who were at the time domiciled in Ireland [who] have resorted to the English Court and there have obtained decrees of absolute divorce, as distinguished from that of judicial separation."[18] Having made this observation, which he repeated in 1910 to the Royal Commission on Divorce—and it is an observation which my research has substantiated—Roberts then went on to say, "The question arises as to whether, when a decree has been obtained without fraud or collusion in the English Court, such can or may be recognized in Ireland."[19] This uncertainty remained in the Irish jurisdiction until 1958, when in a dissenting judgment in the case of *Mayo-Perrot v. Mayo-Perrot*, Justice Kingsmill Moore, having reviewed a number of pre-1922 English and Irish divorce decisions and on the basis of these, concluded that "prior to that date the Irish courts would have recognised a divorce decree granted by a foreign court within the jurisdiction of the common domicile of the parties." The cases he reviewed were *Shaw v. Gould* (1868), *Le Mesurier v. Le Mesurier* (1895), *Sinclair v. Sinclair* (1896),[20] and *Bater v. Bater* (1906)[21]—all cases of parties obtaining *decrees absolute* after establishing English residency for the purposes of obtaining a divorce.[22]

Press, 2004), 128–29; Fitzpatrick, *Two Irelands*, 226–34; Yeats, *Senate Speeches*, 89–102, 156–60.

18 Roberts, *Divorce Bills*, 12.

19 Roberts, *Divorce Bills*, 12.

20 *Sinclair v. Sinclair* (1896) 1 IR 603.

21 *Bater v. Bater* (1906) P 209.

22 Shatter, *Family Law*, 153. See also Shatter, *Family Law*, chap. 10: "Recognition of Foreign Decrees of Divorce *a vincula* Article 41.3.3 and Its Interpretation." Subsequent decisions adopted the approach of J. Kingsmill Moore. This was first done by an English Court in *Breen v. Breen* [1964] P 144. The case of *Bank of Ireland v. Caffin* [1971] IR 123 was the first time the question came up as a ratio issue. *Family Law*, ed. Shannon, 172.

But as all good readers of *Ulysses* know, none of the possible courses of action discussed in this book—forgiveness, desertion, separation, divorce—actually takes place, *at least not then.* Bloom's entry into the matrimonial bed wakes rather than arouses Molly. They are reported to have an "increasingly more laconic" conversation replete with evasions and falsity. Bloom is depicted falling asleep while Molly lies awake, musing over what has happened, what she might do, and what the consequences might prove to be.

Glossary

According to Richard Ellmann, *The Consciousness of Joyce* (London: Faber and Faber, 1977), 108, Joyce possessed a copy stamped "J. J." of *Every Man's Own Lawyer: A Handy Book of the Principles of Law and Equity, by A. Barrister; Fifty-fourth Edition, Revised, including New Acts of Parliament and War Emergency and Incidental Legislation of 1918* (London: Crosby, Lockwood, 1919). The book appears to have been Joyce's principal source of legal knowledge. Definitions followed by page number in brackets are from *Every Man's Own Lawyer*. Definitions from the first edition of *Halsbury's Laws of England*, vol. 6 (London: Butterworth, 1909), accessible at https://archive.org/details/lawsofenglandbei06hals, are referenced as *1H6* followed by paragraph number, and definitions from the fourth edition of *Halsbury's Laws of England* (London: Butterworths, 1963) are referenced as *4H*, followed by volume and paragraph number. Definitions from *Dicey, Morris and Collins on the Conflict of Laws*, ed. Sir Lawrence Collins, 14th ed. (1896; London: Sweet and Maxwell, 2006), are referenced as *DMC*, followed by section number. Definitions from the *Oxford English Dictionary* (online version March 2016) are referenced as *OED*. Definitions from *Black's Law Dictionary*, ed. Bryan A. Garner, 10th ed. (1891; St. Paul, MN: Thomson Reuters, 2004), are referenced as Black followed by page number. Other sources are as cited. No citation means the term is explained in *Irish Divorce / Joyce's "Ulysses."*

P. Kuch, *Irish Divorce / Joyce's Ulysses*,
DOI 10.1057/978-1-137-57186-1

Adultery "Voluntary sexual intercourse between a married person and another who is not his or her spouse, regarded as a violation of the marriage vows and hence as a sin or crime; the state or condition of having committed this" (*OED*). Modified to consensual sexual intercourse on the grounds that the term adultery is only applicable to persons of the age of consent.

Affidavit "A statement in writing verified by the oath or solemn affirmation of the person making the statement, made for the purpose of production in evidence in legal proceedings" (2).

Affinity "Relationship in marriage—that is, between the husband or wife, and the wife's, or husband's relations by consanguinity" (2).

Alimony "An allowance made by order of the Court out of the husband's estate for the support of his wife, upon a judicial separation or a dissolution of the marriage being decreed. Alimony may be (i) *Pedente lite*—that is, during the continuation of a pending suit (Lat. *Lis pendens*) or (ii) *Permanent*, to be granted on the conclusion of the suit" (3). "The English courts have the power to allot alimony *pendent lite*, even though a substantial question as to the jurisdiction of the courts has been raised by the other party to the suit and awaits determination; but it is a matter of discretion whether alimony shall be allotted in any particular case. The courts will not restrain a husband from removing his property out of the jurisdiction, for the purpose of defeating a wife's right to alimony, before the order for alimony is made" (*1H*6, §394).

Bigamy "The offence of marrying again in the lifetime of one's lawful husband or wife from whom one has not been divorced" (5). As defined by The Offences against the Persons Act 1867, §1.1.

Breach of promise "The violation of one's word or undertaking especially with a promise to marry. Under English common law, an engagement to marry had the nature of a commercial contract, so if one party broke the engagement without justification, the innocent party was entitled to damages." This has subsequently been abolished by what are known as Heartbalm statutes (Black, 226).

Circumstantial evidence "Circumstances from which a supposed fact may reasonably be inferred" (7).

Collusion "Collusion is a deceitful agreement or contract between two or more persons, for the one to bring an action against the other, to some evil purpose, as to defraud a third person of his right" (*OED*). "However, a request by a wife to a husband to furnish her with such evidence of his adultery as will enable her to present a petition will not be regarded as collusive, unless it amounts to a suggestion that the husband should commit adultery in order that the wife may gain her freedom.... Mere agreement between parties not making an imposition on the Court or a suppression of facts, but merely facilitating proof and smoothing the asperities of litigation, is not collusive or otherwise objectionable, though it is liable to be looked into by the Court." *Laidler v. Laidler* [1920] 36 TLR 510.

Comity of nations a. "The courteous and friendly understanding, by which each nation respects the laws and usages of every other, so far as may be without prejudice to its own rights and interests. b. Apparently misused for: The company of nations mutually practising international comity" (*OED*). "Comity is a term of very elastic content. Sometimes it connotes courtesy or the need for reciprocity; at other times it is used as a synonym for the rules of public international law.... The concept of comity is increasingly used in common law countries not as an explanation for the system of the conflict of laws, but as a tool for applying or re-shaping the rules of the conflict of laws. In particular it is used in a sense which owes much to the rules of public international law, namely respect for the jurisdiction of other States" (*DMC*, 1–008, 1–009). See below Conflict of Laws.

Condonation "Forgiveness and reconciliation, and a blotting out of the offence; and if the petitioner has condoned the adultery or cruelty complained of, the petition will be dismissed, on proof of the condonation. Condonation may be implied from facts and circumstances" (376).

Conflict of Laws "That part of the law of England which deals with cases that have a foreign element.... In the conflict of laws, a foreign element or a foreign country means a non-English element and a country other than England. From the point of view of conflict of laws, Scotland and Northern Ireland are for the most part but not for all purposes as much foreign countries as France or Germany.... The English rules of the conflict of laws differ from those adopted in many continental European countries in one important respect. There are many situations in which, if the English court has jurisdiction, it will apply English domestic law. This is true, for example in most issues in proceedings for divorce and separation.... Conversely, there are many situations in which, if a foreign court has jurisdiction according to English rules of the conflict of laws, its judgement or decree will be recognized in England, regardless of the grounds on which it is based or the choice of law rule which it applied" (*DMC*, 1-001, 1-004). See also *1H6*, §273–79. Note §277: "In petitions for dissolution of marriage and other matrimonial causes, the jurisdiction of the English courts depends upon the domicil or residence of the parties to the suit, according to circumstances" (*1H6*, §277).

Connivance "The complaining party was aware of the adultery or impropriety at the time it was committed, but shut [their] eyes to it, and took no steps to prevent it" (376).

Consortium "The benefits that one person, especially a spouse, is entitled to receive from another, including companionship, cooperation, affection, aid, financial support, and (between spouses) sexual relations" (Black, 374). The action for loss of consortium was abolished by the Administration of Justice Act, 1982 (c. 53) § 2 (*OED*).

Costs (in divorce suits) "As the wife is generally supposed to have no separate income, she is entitled to have her costs taxed from day to day as against her husband, and whether she is petitioner or respondent. When the costs have been taxed, a summons may be taken out, returnable before the Judge Ordinary, who may then order the husband to pay them, and also to pay a further sum into Court, or give security to meet the wife's costs of the hearing. If in a matrimonial suit the wife is unable to go to trial in consequence of the non-payment of her costs by the husband, she should either apply at the Judges' Chambers to have the case stand over, or appear in Court on the day of the hearing and state her inability to proceed. Although a wife is in general a privileged suitor with regard to costs, where she has separate property she is liable, like any other unsuccessful suitor, to be condemned to costs. Upon the principle that the whole property is supposed in law to belong to the husband, he is generally obliged to pay the expenses of the litigation on both sides: except in cases where the wife is found guilty of adultery with a Co-respondent; in which case the Court generally orders the Co-respondent to pay the costs on both sides" (380–81).

Counsel "A body of legal advisers, engaged in the direction or conduct of a cause. (Usually a collective plural, but sometimes treated as a numeral plural; formerly, in 'to desire the benefit of counsel', 'to be allowed counsel', etc., treated as a collective sing.)" (*OED*).

Couverture "The status of a woman during marriage" (9).

Criminal conversation "Adultery. The action for *crim. con.* against an adulterer, which was formerly open to an injured husband, is now abolished, the right to claim damages against a co-respondent in a divorce suit being substituted" (9).

Crown The legal concentration of all the subjects of the realm, whose private rights are injured by delinquents in revenue matters, and they are, in fact, the party who contend with the particular individual.

Decree nisi / Decree absolute In divorce proceedings, when a decree is the result of the suit, a *decree nisi* (Lat. = unless) is first pronounced, to be made absolute if no sufficient cause to the contrary—such as the collusion of the parties—be shown within a proscribed time.

Divorce "By which a marriage tie is dissolved: so that after a decree *nisi* has been made absolute (but not before) either of the parties is at liberty to marry again" (374). See also *Foreign Decrees of Dissolution of Marriage* (*1H6*, §395–99).

Divorce, English Jurisdiction "The English courts have no jurisdiction to pronounce a decree of divorce completely dissolving the marriage-tie—divorce *à vincula matrimonii*—unless the parties are domiciled within the jurisdiction at the time when the proceedings are commenced. And this domicil must be a real and genuine domicil, as defined by English law. It is not sufficient for the parties to consent to the jurisdiction of the English courts, either expressly or impliedly by their conduct. They cannot by such submission give the courts a jurisdiction which they would not otherwise possess. Nothing less than domicil in the fullest sense of the term will suffice. No residence which falls short of domicil will give jurisdiction. If the fact of the domicil at the date of the petition is once established, it is immaterial that the marriage which it is sought to dissolve was contracted elsewhere than in England, or that the parties at the time of the marriage were domiciled abroad, or that the parties are not British subjects, or reside out of the jurisdiction, or that the misconduct alleged took place abroad. The matrimonial domicil differs in no degree from domicil as ordinarily defined. It is the domicil of the husband, and the wife cannot acquire a domicil separate from that of her husband. But (probably) the English courts may decree a divorce in favour of a wife who has been deserted by her husband, or whose husband has so conducted himself towards her that she is justified in living apart from him, provided that at the moment when the desertion or separation took place she was domiciled with her husband in England, and that at the time of the commencement of the suit she is still in England. And (probably) the English courts can decree a divorce in favour of a wife whose domicil at the time of her marriage was in this country, and whose marriage, though valid by the laws of this country, has been declared void by the courts of her husband's domicil. The English courts have no jurisdiction over a co-respondent domiciled abroad, and a petitioner may obtain leave to proceed without citing him; but the proper course is to give him notice of the proceedings so that he may come in and defend himself if he so desires, or apply to be dismissed" (*1H6*, §388).

Divorce *a mensa et thoro* Judicial separation from bed and board once a *decree nisi* has been made absolute.

Divorce *a vinculo matrimonii* Judicial separation from the very bonds of marriage once a *decree nisi* has been made absolute.

Domicile (sometimes spelt domicil) "The place of one's legal home or permanent residence. Upon the question of domicile, even in the United Kingdom,—as to whether one's domiciled in Scotland or in England—may depend the validity of a marriage, or the descent of property" (11). "Domiciled in England means in England as distinguished from Scotland and Ireland as well as from foreign countries, because Scotland and Ireland have their own separate legal tribunals." *Re Mitchell exp. Cunningham* (1884) 13 QBD 418 at 423. Note *4H8*, §421–29, and *1H6*, §280–300. "Every person at birth becomes a member both of a political and a civil society. The former determines his political status or nationality, on which depends his allegiance to a sovereign; the latter determines his civil status. This means that the law which governs the civil society into which he is born, the law of the country of his domicil, is attached to his person and remains so attached, wherever he goes, unless and until he ceases to be a member of that society; and this can only be done by becoming a member of another civil society, or changing his domicil, upon which the law of the new domicil becomes attached to him in the same manner" (*1H6*, §277).

Equity of exoneration "If a married woman charges her property with money for the purpose of paying her husband's debts and the money raised by her is so applied, she is *prima facie* regarded in equity, and as between herself and him and not giving him the money raised on her property, and is entitled to have her property exonerated by him from the charge she has created. The doctrine is purely equitable and . . . is based on an inference to be drawn from the circumstances of each particular case." *Paget v. Paget* [1898] 1 Ch 470 at 474 CA *per cur.*

Equity to a settlement "The right to which a wife had, previously to the *Married Woman's Property Act*, to have settled on her a portion of any property coming to her husband in her right after marriage. Under the Act, the property now comes to her as her separate property" (12).

Feme couvert (couverture) "A married woman" (13).

Feme sole (discovert) "A single woman" (13).

Flagrante delicto "(Lat. = *In the very act of committing the crime*)—Referring to the arrest of a criminal" (14).

Garnishee order "Made by the court when a person (the garnishee) from whom the debt is owing to another person is garnished or warned not to pay the debt, which is thus 'attached' by a creditor of the person to whom the debt is owing" (14).

Holograph "A deed or other writing wholly in the handwriting of the person making and signing it" (16).

In camerâ "(Lat.=*In a chamber*). A case heard without admission of the public, in a judge's private room, is said to be heard *in camerâ*; this course being taken in cases in which publicity would be detrimental to public morals" (17)

In formâ pauperis "(Lat.) As a pauper" (17).

In re "(Lat.) In the matter of—" (18).

Jactitation of marriage "Falsely giving out one's self as married to another" (18).

Jew "In English law has almost always been confined to persons practicing the Jewish religion: the disabilities of Jews have not attached to persons of Jewish race who have become baptized. Thus they are generally described in Acts of Parliament and in legal documents as persons practicing the Jewish religion." Re Michel's Trust [1860] 28 Beav 39; *In re* Cohen [1919] 36 TLR 16.

Judicial separation "Whereby the marriage tie is not dissolved; but the wife is placed in the position of an unmarried woman (except that she cannot marry again, nor can the husband), and her husband cannot interfere with her concerns" (374).

Jurisdiction "The authority which a Court has to decide matters that are litigated before it or take cognizance of matters presented in a formal way for its decision. The limits of this authority are imposed by the statute, charters, or commission under which the Court is constituted, and may be extended or restricted by a similar means" (*4H*10, §715).

King's (or Queen's) Bench "The name given to the common law division of the High Court of Justice, and derived from the name of the former Court of King's (or Queen's) Bench, in which at its first institution the Sovereign sat in person, thus making it the first in dignity, as it was first in authority, of the common law courts. It was presided over by the Lord Chief Justice of England, which title now belongs to the Chief Justice of the King's Bench Division" (19).

King's (or Queen's) Proctor "The legal adviser of the Crown whose duty it is to intervene in divorce suits, after a decree *nisi* has been pronounced, and before the decree is made absolute, if he has reason to suspect collusion between the parties to the suit" (19).

Marriage "The condition of being a husband or wife; the relation between persons married to each other; matrimony" (*OED*). Such a relation may be considered sacramental, symbolic, or contractual. The definition of marriage recited in *The Book of Common Prayer* (Protestant) and the definition of marriage as stated by the Twenty-fourth Session of the Council of Trent (Catholic) are not as relevant in English law post-1857 as the definition established by *Hyde v. Hyde* (1866), which "is understood to involve four conditions: a marriage must be voluntary; the parties must intend it to be for life; it must be monogamous; and it must be between parties of a different sex." Note that "a marriage solemnized in Ireland by a Roman Catholic priest, between two Roman Catholics, according to the ritual of the Roman Catholic Church in use in Ireland, but in the presence of only one witness is by the law of the land valid, although it may not be valid by the law of the Roman Catholic Church, by reason of there not being two witnesses in addition to the priest, as required by the decree of the Council of Trent." *Usher v. Usher* KB [1912] 2 IR 445; 46 ILTR 109. See also *1H6*, §375–87.

Misdemeanor "An indictable offence (or crime) of less magnitude than a felony" (22).

Not proven "A verdict on a criminal charge which is allowed by Scottish but not by English law" (23).

Nullity of marriage "Whereby the marriage of the parties may be declared null and void, by reason of a prior marriage of either of the parties, or insanity, or impotence; or for illegality through force having been used in obtaining the marriage, or by reason of fraud and imposition" (374). Where the Courts (Ecclesiastical and Judicial) regard the marriage as never having taken place and no status of matrimony as ever having been conferred.

Paraphernalia ("Lat. *Paraphernalia* [*bona* understood]: from the Greek παραφερα.")—"The wearing apparel and jewels or other personal ornaments of a married woman" (23). "The Married Woman's Property Act 1882 has not abolished the general law as to gifts or paraphernalia. Consequently, when a husband gives jewellery to his wife, whether the gift constitutes paraphernalia or separate estate is still a question to be determined, according to whether the evidence shows an intention on the part of the husband that his wife shall merely adorn her person with the jewels, or an intention that they shall be hers absolutely" (370) (*4H22*, §1082).

Rape "(As designation of a criminal offence); Having carnal knowledge of a woman by force and against her will" (27).

Recrimination "A countercharge in a divorce suit that the petitioner has been guilty of an offense constituting a ground for divorce" (Black, 1466).

Restitution of conjugal rights "The remedy of either husband or wife, when one of them has without lawful reason separated from the other; in which case the Court can order a return to cohabitation, and if the order be disobeyed, may commit the offender for contempt of Court" (374).

Restraint on anticipation "A provision commonly made in settlements of property, to restrain a married woman from alienating by way of anticipation property or income settled to her separate use, the primary object being to protect the wife from parting with future means of subsistence recklessly or under undue influence from others" (28).

Separation "An arrangement by which a husband and wife live apart from each other while remaining married, either by mutual consent (often but not necessarily in a written document) or by judicial decree" (Black, 1572). However, separation must indeed take place (*Bindley v. Mulloney* [1869] 17 WR 510); and the contract to live separate and apart is one which may be upheld and enforced (*Courtney v. Courtney* [1923] 2 IR 31). "Although parties have agreed in writing prior to marriage that it should be lawful at all times for the husband to live separate and apart from the wife and that the wife should not require or endeavor to compel him to live with her such an agreement is contrary to public policy, and therefore, void in law." *Brodie v. Brodie* [1916–17] All Er Rep 237. "Suits for judicial separation—divorce *à mensa et thoro*—being instituted primarily not for the purpose of dissolving the marriage, but for the protection of the wife or husband, as the case may be, the English courts do not hold that an English domicil is necessary in order to give them jurisdiction, because no change of status of either party is involved in making such a decree. It is sufficient if the parties are resident (that is to say, have their matrimonial residence) within the jurisdiction at the time when the suit is commenced" (*1H*6, §389).

Separation agreement "An agreement between spouses in the process of divorce or legal separation concerning alimony, maintenance, property division, child custody and support, and the like" (Black, 1572). "A decree of judicial separation . . . will have no effect outside the jurisdiction of the court which decrees it, nor, as it would appear, even within the jurisdiction, if both parties afterwards abandon their residence in England" (*1H*6, §390).

Specific performance "The remedy sought by a plaintiff who, instead of damages for a breach of contract, seeks the enforcement of the terms of the contract" (31).

Tort "An injury or wrong suffered by a person at the hands of another, irrespective of any contract between them: but distinguished from a crime as not being a wrong done to the community as well as to the individual, and hence not punishable under the criminal law" (33). "Those civil rights of action which are available for the recovery of unliquidated damages by persons who have sustained injury or loss from acts, statements or omissions of others in breach of duty or contravention of right imposed or conferred by law rather than by agreement are rights of action in tort" (*4H*45, §1201).

Bibliography

Works

Joyce, James. *The Critical Writings of James Joyce*. Edited by Ellsworth Mason and Richard Ellmann. New York: Viking, 1959.

———. *Dubliners*. 1956. Harmondsworth: Penguin, 1967.

———. *Dubliners*. Edited by Hans Walter Gabler with Walter Hettche. New York: Garland Publishing, 1993.

———. *Exiles*. Hammersmith: Paladin, 1991.

———. *Exiles: A Play in Three Acts*. London: Jonathan Cape, 1972.

———. *Finnegans Wake*. 1939. London: Faber, 1971.

———. *Giacomo Joyce, with an Introduction* and *Notes by Richard Ellmann*. London: Faber, 1969.

———. *James Joyce: Poems and Shorter Writings*. Edited by Richard Ellmann, A. Walton Litz, and John Whittier-Ferguson. London: Faber, 1991.

———. *James Joyce's "Ulysses": The Manuscript and First Printings Compared*. Annotated by Clive Driver. New York: Octagon Books, 1975.

———. *Joyce's Notes and Early Drafts for "Ulysses": Selections from the Buffalo Collection*. Edited by Phillip F. Herring. Charlottesville: University Press of Virginia, 1977.

———. *Joyce's "Ulysses" Notesheets in the British Museum*. Edited by Phillip F. Herring. Charlottesville: University Press of Virginia, 1972.

———. *Letters of James Joyce*. Edited by Stuart Gilbert. London: Faber and Faber, 1957.

———. *Letters of James Joyce, II*. Edited by Richard Ellmann. London: Faber and Faber, 1966.

P. Kuch, *Irish Divorce / Joyce's Ulysses*,
DOI 10.1057/978-1-137-57186-1

———. *Letters of James Joyce, III*. Edited by Richard Ellmann. London: Faber and Faber, 1966.

———. *The Little Review "Ulysses"*. Edited by Mark Gaipa, Sean Latham, and Robert Scholes. New Haven, CT: Yale University Press, 2015.

———. *Stephen Hero*. London: Jonathan Cape, 1969.

———. *"Ulysses": A Critical and Synoptic Edition, Prepared by Hans Walter Gabler with Wolfhard Steppe and Claus Melchior*. New York: Garland, 1984.

———. *"Ulysses": The Corrected Text, Student Edition*. Edited by Hans Walter Gabler with Wolfhard Steppe and Claus Melchior. Harmondsworth: Penguin, 1986.

———. *"Ulysses" Notes & "Telemachus"–"Scylla and Charybdis": A Facsimile of Notes for the Book & Manuscript & Typescripts for Episodes 1–9*. Preface by Michael Groden. New York: Garland, 1978.

Critical Works

Ackerley, Chris. "'Tutto è sciolto': An Operatic Crux in the 'Sirens' Episode of James Joyce's 'Ulysses'." *James Joyce Quarterly* 38, no. 1–2 (2000–2001): 197–205.

Adams, Robert M. "Hades." In *James Joyce's "Ulysses": Critical Essays*, edited by Clive Hart and David Hayman, 91–114. Berkeley: University of California Press, 1977.

———. *James Joyce: Common Sense and Beyond*. New York: Random House, 1966.

———. *Surface* and *Symbol: The Consistency of James Joyce's "Ulysses"*. New York: Oxford University Press, 1962.

Ames, Keri Elizabeth. "The Oxymoron of Fidelity in Homer's *Odyssey* and Joyce's *Ulysses*." *Joyce Studies Annual* 14 (2003): 132–74.

Anon. "Defects of Laws Relating to Married Women." *Irish Law Times and Solicitors' Journal* 28 (28 May 1904): 181–84.

———. "Marriage in the Nineteenth Century." *Dublin University Magazine* 59 (May 1862): 542–53.

Aquinas, Thomas. *The Gifts of the Spirit*. Vol. 24 of *Summa Theologiæ*. Edited by Edward D. O'Connor. Cambridge: Cambridge University Press, 2006.

Attell, Kevin. "Of Questionable Character: The Construction of the Subject in *Ulysses*." *Joyce Studies Annual* 13 (2002): 103–28.

Attridge, Derek. *Joyce Effects: On Language, Theory, and History*. Cambridge: Cambridge University Press, 2001.

Backus, Margot. *Scandal Work: James Joyce, the New Journalism, and the Home Rule Newspaper Wars*. Notre Dame, IN: University of Notre Dame Press, 2013.

Bailey, Peter. "Parasexuality and Glamour: The Victorian Barmaid as Cultural Prototype." *Gender and History* 2, no. 2 (1990): 148–72.

Balazs, Thomas. "Recognizing Masochism: Psychoanalysis and the Politics of Sexual Submission in *Ulysses*." *Joyce Studies Annual* 13 (2002): 160–91.

Baldwin, Simeon E. "The Hague Conference of 1904 for the Advancement of Private International Law." Faculty Scholarship Series. Paper 4304. Accessed 6 July 2016. http://digitalcommons.law.yale.edu/fss_papers/4304.

Balzac, Honoré. *Physiologie du marriage*. Paris: Calmann-Levey, n.d.

The Bankers', Insurance Managers', and Agents' Magazine. Vol. 84. London: Waterlow, 1907.

Barbie, Leon. *Guide Pratique du Divorce*. Paris: Librairie Générale de Droit et de Jurisprudence, 1927.

Bataille, Georges. *Eroticism*. Translated by Mary Dalwood. 1957. London: John Calder, 1962.

Bednarska, Dominika. "A Crippled Erotic: Gender and Disability in James Joyce's 'Nausicaa'." *James Joyce Quarterly* 49, no. 1 (2011): 73–89.

Beeton, Isabella. *The Book of Household Management*. London: Ward, Lock, 1861.

———. *Mrs Beeton's Everyday Cookery: With about 2,500 Practical Recipes*. London: Ward, Lock, 1923.

Bénéjam, Valérie. "Joyce after Flaubert: The Cuckold as Imperfect Physician, the Writer as Physiologist." *James Joyce Quarterly* 36, no. 3–4 (2009): 439–53.

Benveniste, Emile. "Active and Middle Voice in the Verb." In *Problems in General Linguistics*, translated by Mary Elizabeth Meek, 145–51. Coral Gables, FL: University of Miami Press, 1971.

Bersani, Leo. "Against *Ulysses*." In *The Culture of Redemption*, 155–78. Cambridge, MA: Harvard University Press, 1990.

Bertolini, C. David. "Bloom's Death in 'Ithaca', or the END of *Ulysses*." *Journal of Modern Literature* 31, no. 2 (2008): 39–52.

Bew, Paul. *Enigma: A New Life of Charles Stewart Parnell*. Dublin: Gill and Macmillan, 2011.

Black's Law Dictionary. Edited by Bryan A. Garner. 10th ed. 1891. St. Paul, MN: Thomson Reuters, 2004.

Blamires, Harry. *The New Bloomsday Book: A Guide through "Ulysses"*. 1966. London: Routledge, 1996.

Bosinelli, Rosa Maria Bollettieri. "The Reader as Detective: Sherlockholmesing Joyce's Texts." In *The Benstock Library as a Mirror of Joyce*, edited by Rosa Maria Bollettieri Bosinelli and Franca Ruggieri, 167–75. Joyce Studies in Italy 7. Roma: Bulzoni Editore, 2002.

Bowen, Zack. *Bloom's Old Sweet Song: Essays on Joyce and Music*. Gainesville: University Press of Florida, 1995.

———. "*Exiles*: The Confessional Mode." *James Joyce Quarterly* 29 (Spring 1992): 581–86.

———. *Musical Allusions in the Work of James Joyce: Early Poetry through "Ulysses"*. Albany: State University of New York, 1974.

———. *"Ulysses" as a Comic Novel*. Syracuse, NY: Syracuse University Press, 1989.

Bowker, Gordon. "Joyce in England." *James Joyce Quarterly* 48, no. 4 (2011): 667–81.

Boyle, Robert. "A Note on Reuben J. Dodd as 'a dirty Jew'." *James Joyce Quarterly* 3, no. 1 (1965): 64–66.

Brooker, Joseph. *Joyce's Critics: Transitions in Reading and Culture*. Madison: University of Wisconsin Press, 2004.

Brown, Richard. *James Joyce and Sexuality*. Cambridge: Cambridge University Press, 1985.

———. "'Perhaps she had not told him all the story': Observations on the Topic of Adultery in Some Modern Literature." In *Joyce, Modernity and Its Mediation*, edited by Christine van Boheemen, 99–111. Amsterdam: Rodopi, 1989.

Brown, Susan. "The Mystery of the *Fuga per Canonem* Solved." *Genetic Joyce Studies* 7 (2007). http://www.geneticjoycestudies.org/GJS7/GJS7brown.html.

Buck, Jesse. "The Role of *Ne Temere* in the Decline of an Irish Custom Regarding the Religious Affiliation of the Children of Mixed Marriages." *Australasian Journal of Irish Studies* 11 (2011): 28–43.

Budgen, Frank. *James Joyce and the Making of "Ulysses" and Other Writings*. 1934. London: Oxford University Press, 1972.

Bulson, Eric. *The Cambridge Introduction to James Joyce*. Cambridge: Cambridge University Press, 2006.

Bunreacht na hÉireann.

Butler, Judith. *Excitable Speech: A Politics of the Performative*. New York: Routledge, 1997.

Callanan, Frank. *The Parnell Split 1890–91*. Cork: Cork University Press, 1992.

The Canadian Encyclopedia. Toronto: McClelland and Stewart, 2000.

Castoriadis, Cornelius. *The Imaginary Institution of Society*. Cambridge, MA: MIT Press, 1987.

Cohn, Dorrit. *Transparent Minds: Narrative Modes for Presenting Consciousness in Fiction*. Princeton, NJ: Princeton University Press, 1978.

Collier, Patrick. *Modernism on Fleet Street*. Aldershot: Ashgate, 2006.

Conan Doyle, Arthur. "A Case of Identity." *The Strand Magazine* 9 (September 1891): 248–59. Republished in *The Adventures of Sherlock Holmes*, 38–50. New York: Harper, 1892.

Connolly, Thomas E. *James Joyce's Books, Portraits, Manuscripts, Notebooks, Typescripts, Page Proofs: Together with Critical Essays about Some of His Works*. Lampeter: Edwin Mellen Press, 1997.

———. *The Personal Library of James Joyce*. Buffalo, NY: University of Buffalo Bookstore, 1957.

Cooper, Louis Blom, ed. *The Law as Literature: An Anthology of Great Literature in and about the Law*. London: Bodley Head, 1961.

Corballis, Richard. "Who Taught Molly to Say 'Yes'?" *James Joyce Quarterly* 48, no. 1 (2010): 156–61.

Corkey, William. *The McCann Mixed Marriage Case: An Address by the Rev. Wm. Corkey, with an Authorised Translation of Ne Temere Decree and Translation of Bull of Excommunication*. Edinburgh: The Knox Club, 1912.

Cornish, William. "Marital Breakdown: Separation and the Coming of Judicial Divorce." In *The Oxford History of the Laws of England: Volume XIII: 1820–1914 Fields of Development*, edited by J. William Cornish, Stuart Anderson, Ray Cocks, Michael Lobban, Patrick Polden, and Keith Smith, 767–801. Oxford: Oxford University Press, 2010.

Cosgrove, Brian. *Joyce's Negations: Irony, Indeterminacy and Nihilism in "Ulysses" and Other Writings*. Dublin: University College Dublin Press, 2007.

Cowgill, Rachel, and Julian Rushton, eds. *Europe, Empire, and Spectacle in Nineteenth-century British Music*. Farnham: Ashgate, 2006.

The Criminal Law Amendment Act, 1885: With Introduction, Notes and Index. Edited by Frederick Mead and Archibald Henry Bodkin. London: Shaw, 1885. https://archive.org/stream/criminallawamen00bodkgoog#page/n30/mode/2up.

Crispi, Luca. *Joyce's Creative Process and the Construction of Characters in "Ulysses": Becoming the Blooms*. Oxford: Oxford University Press, 2015.

Crumb, Michael. "*Sweets of Sin*: Joyce's *Ulysses* and Swinburne's 'Dolores'." *James Joyce Quarterly* 28, no. 1 (1990): 239–45.

Daly, Mary. *Dublin, the Deposed Capital: A Social and Economic History 1860–1914*. Cork: Cork University Press, 1984.

Damasio, Antonio. *Looking for Spinoza: Joy, Sorrow, and the Feeling Brain*. Orlando, FL: Harcourt, 2003.

———. *Self Comes to Mind: Constructing the Conscious Brain*. New York: Vintage, 2010.

Davis, Lance E., and Robert E. Gallman, eds. *Evolving Financial Markets and International Capital Flows: Britain, the Americas, and Australia*. Cambridge: Cambridge University Press, 2001.

Davison, Neil. *James Joyce, "Ulysses", and the Construction of Jewish Identity*. Cambridge: Cambridge University Press, 1996.

de Certeau, Michel. *Culture in the Plural*. Minneapolis: University of Minnesota Press, 1997.

———. *The Practice of Everyday Life*. 1984. Berkeley: University of California Press, 1988.

Deleuze, Gilles. *Masochism: Coldness and Cruelty*. New York: Zone Books, 1991.

Deleuze, Gilles, and Féliz Guattari. *A Thousand Plateaus: Capitalism & Schizophrenia*. Translated and Forward by Brian Massumi. 1983. London: Continuum, 2003.

d'Erme, Elisabetta. "Mr Canvasser Bloom." Paper presented at the 17th Trieste Joyce School, Trieste, 29 June–5 July 2014.

Derrida, Jacques. "The Law of Genre." Translated by Avitall Ronell. In *On Narrative*, edited by W. J. T. Mitchell, 51–77. Chicago: University of Chicago Press, 1981.

Devlin, Kimberly J. "En-Gendered Choice and Agency in *Ulysses*." In *"Ulysses" in Critical Perspective*, edited by Michael Patrick Gillespie and A. Nicholas Fargnoli, 70–87. Gainesville: University Press of Florida, 2006.

Devlin, Kimberly J., and Marilyn Reizbaum, eds. *"Ulysses": En-gendered Perspectives*. Columbia: University of South Carolina Press, 1999.

Dicey, A. V., and J. H. C. Morris. *Dicey and Morris on the Conflict of Laws*. Edited by Lawrence Collins. 13th ed. London: Sweet and Maxwell, 2000.

Dicey, A. V., J. H. C. Morris, and Lawrence Collins. *Dicey, Morris and Collins on the Conflict of Laws*. 14th ed. London: Sweet and Maxwell, 2010.

———. *Dicey, Morris and Collins on the Conflict of Laws*. 15th ed. London: Sweet and Maxwell, 2012.

A Dictionary of Law. Edited by Jonathan Law and Elizabeth A. Martin. Oxford: Oxford University Press, 2014. http://www.oxfordreference.com/view/10.1093/acref/9780199551248.001.0001/acref-9780199551248-e-2425.

The Digest: Annotated British, Commonwealth and European Cases: Husband and Wife, Joint Property and Matrimonial Causes (Part 1–6), Green Band Reissue. Edited by E. C. P. Lascelles, G. F. L. Bridgman, J. T. Miles, and H. W. Clements and revised by Peter Strickland and Deborah Sanders.

Dixon, W. J. *Law and Practice of Divorce and Other Matrimonial Causes*. 4th ed. London: Butterworth, 1908.

Doležel, Lubomír. *Heterocosmica: Fiction and Possible Worlds*. Baltimore: Johns Hopkins University Press, 1998.

Donoghue, Denis. "Is There a Case against *Ulysses*?" In *Joyce in Context*, edited by Vincent J. Cheng and Timothy Martin, 19–39. Cambridge: Cambridge University Press, 1992.

Eide, Marian. *Ethical Joyce*. Cambridge: Cambridge University Press, 2002.

Ellmann, Maud. "The Music of Joyce's Vernacular Voices." *Modernism/Modernity* 16, no. 2 (2009): 383–90.

Ellmann, Richard. *The Consciousness of Joyce*. London: Faber and Faber, 1977.

———. *James Joyce*. 1959. New York: Oxford University Press, 1983.

———. *"Ulysses" on the Liffey*. London: Faber, 1972.

The Empire and the Century: A Series of Essays on Imperial Problems and Possibilities by Various Writers. London: John Murray, 1905.

Every Man's Own Lawyer: A Handy Book of the Principles of Law and Equity, by A. Barrister; Fifty-fourth Edition, Revised, including New Acts of Parliament and War Emergency and Incidental Legislation of 1918. London: Crosby, Lockwood, 1919.

Family Law. Edited by Geoffrey Shannon. 4th ed. Oxford: Oxford University Press, 2011.

Fargnoli, Nicholas A., and Michael Patrick Gillespie, eds. *Critical Companion to James Joyce: A Literary Reference to His Life and Work.* New York: Checkmark, 2006.

Ferris, Kathleen. *James Joyce and the Burden of Disease.* 1995. Lexington: University Press of Kentucky, 2010.

Ferriter, Diarmaid. *Occasions of Sin: Sex and Society in Modern Ireland.* London: Profile Books, 2009.

Fish, Stanley. *Is There a Text in this Class?: The Authority of Interpretive Communities.* Cambridge, MA: Harvard University Press, 1980.

Fitz-Gibbon, Kate. *Homicide, Law Reform, Gender and the Provocation Defense: A Comparative Perspective.* London: Palgrave Macmillan, 2014.

Fitzpatrick, David. "Divorce and Separation in Modern Irish History." *Past & Present* 114, no. 1 (1987): 172–96.

———. *The Two Irelands 1912–1939.* Oxford: Oxford University Press, 1998.

Fordham, Finn. "'Circe' and the Genesis of Multiple Personality." *James Joyce Quarterly* 45, no. 3–4 (2008): 507–20.

Foucault, Michel. *The History of Sexuality.* Translated by Robert Hurley. 1976. London: Penguin, 1990.

Fournier, Leslie T. "Present Railroad Problems in Canada." *The Annals of the American Academy of Political and Social Science* 187, no. 1 (1936): 151–58.

———. *Railway Nationalization in Canada: The Problem of the Canadian National Railways.* 1935. New York: Arno Press, 1981.

Franke, Damon. "Joyce/Foucault: Sexual Confessions (review)." *James Joyce Quarterly* 46, no. 1 (2008): 153–57.

Frazier, Adrian. *George Moore, 1852–1933.* New Haven, CT: Yale University Press, 2000.

Freedman, Ariela. "'Don't eat a beefsteak': Joyce and the Pythagoreans." *Texas Studies in Literature and Language* 51, no. 4 (2009): 447–62.

Friedman, Alan W. *Party Pieces: Oral Storytelling and Social Performance in Joyce and Beckett.* Syracuse, NY: Syracuse University Press, 2007.

Friedman, Isaiah. *Germany, Turkey, and Zionism, 1897–1918.* Oxford: Clarendon Press, 1977.

Frost, Ginger S. *Living in Sin: Cohabiting as Husband and Wife in Nineteenth-Century England.* Manchester: Manchester University Press, 2008.

Frost, Laura Catherine. *The Problem with Pleasure: Modernism and Its Discontents.* New York: Columbia University Press, 2013.

Garvin, John. *James Joyce's Disunited Kingdom and the Irish Dimension*. Dublin: Gill and Macmillan; New York: Barnes and Noble, 1976.

Gibbons, Luke. "Spaces of Time through Times of Space: Joyce, Ireland and Colonial Modernity." *Field Day Review* 1 (2005): 71–85.

Gibson, Andrew. *Joyce's Revenge: History, Politics and Aesthetics in "Ulysses"*. Oxford: Oxford University Press, 2008.

———. "'Nobody Owns': *Ulysses*, Tenancy, and Property Law." *James Joyce Quarterly* 50, no. 4 (2013): 951–62.

———. ed. *Reading Joyce's "Circe"*. Amsterdam: Rodopi, 1994.

Gifford, Don, with Robert J. Seidman. *"Ulysses" Annotated: Notes for James Joyce's "Ulysses"*. 1974. Berkeley: University of California Press, 1988.

Gill, Rebecca. "The Imperial Anxieties of a Nineteenth-Century Bigamy Case." *History Workshop Journal* 57 (2004): 58–78.

Gillespie, Michael Patrick. "A Critique of Ellmann's List of Joyce's Trieste Library." *James Joyce Quarterly* 19, no. 1 (1981): 27–36.

———. *Inverted Volumes Improperly Arranged: James Joyce and his Trieste Library*. Ann Arbor: UMI Research, 1983.

———. ed. *James Joyce's Trieste Library: A Catalogue of Materials at the Harry Ransom Humanities Research Center*. Austin: University of Texas, 1986.

Glasheen, Adaline. "Calypso." In *James Joyce's "Ulysses": Critical Essays*, edited by Clive Hart and David Hayman, 51–70. Berkeley: University of California Press, 1977.

Goloubeva, Irina Rasmussen. "Molly Bloom: A Re-Immersion in the Concrete." *James Joyce Quarterly* 47, no. 3 (2010): 395–415.

Goodrich, Herbert F. "Jurisdiction to Annul a Marriage." *Harvard Law Review* 32, no. 7 (1919): 806–24. http://www.jstor.org/stable/1327742.

Gorn, Elliott J. "The Wicked World: The National *Police Gazette* and Gilded-Age America." *Media Studies Journal* 6, no. 1 (1992): 1–15.

Graham, S. "Treatment of Paediatric Tuberculosis: Revised WHO Guidelines." *Paediatric Respiratory Reviews* 12 (2011): 22–26.

Grandt, Jürgen E. "'Might be what you like, till you hear the words': Joyce in Zurich and the Contrapuntal Language of *Ulysses*." *Joyce Studies Annual* 14 (2003): 74–91.

Grattan, Sheena. "Of Pin Money and Paraphernalia, The Widow's Shilling and a Free Ride to Mass." In *One Hundred and Fifty Years of Irish Law*, edited by Norma Dawson, Desmond Greer, and Peter Ingram, 213–38. Belfast: SLS Legal Publications; Dublin: Round Hall Sweet and Maxwell, 1996.

Groden, Michael. "'Cyclops' in Progress, 1919." *James Joyce Quarterly* 12, nos. 1–2 (1974–1975): 123–68.

———. "Genetic Joyce: Textual Studies and the Reader." In *Palgrave Advances in James Joyce Studies*, edited by Jean-Michel Rabaté, 227–50. London: Palgrave Macmillan, 2004.

The Grove Book of Opera Singers. Edited by Laura Williams Macy. Oxford: Oxford University Press, 2008.

Gula, Marianna. *A Tale of a Pub: Re-Reading the "Cyclops" Episode of James Joyce's "Ulysses" in the Context of Irish Cultural Nationalism*. Debrecen: University of Debrecen Press, 2012.

Gunn, Ian, and Clive Hart. "Rearranging the Furniture at No. 7." *James Joyce Quarterly* 44, no. 4 (2007): 785–92.

H. F. G. "The Domicile of a Wife." *Michigan Law Review* 20, no. 1 (1921): 86–90. http://www.jstor.org/stable/1277099.

Hager, Kelly. "Chipping Away at Coverture: The Matrimonial Causes Act of 1857." BRANCH: Britain, Representation and Nineteenth Century History. Accessed 6 July 2016. http://www.branchcollective.org/?ps_articles=kelly-hager-chipping-away-at-coverture-the-matrimonial-causes-act-of-1857.

Haggart, Kerri. "Bloom's Situated Mind in James Joyce's *Ulysses*: Decoding Character in a Social Storyworld." PhD diss., University of Otago, 2015.

Halsbury's Laws of England. 1st ed. Vol. 6. London: Butterworth, 1909. https://archive.org/details/lawsofenglandbei06hals.

Halsbury's Laws of England. 4th ed. London: Butterworth, 1963.

Hamilton, Claire. *The Presumption of Innocence and Irish Criminal Law: "Whittling the Golden Thread"*. Dublin: Irish Academic Press, 2007.

Hannay, John. "Coincidence and Analytic Reduction in the 'Ithaca' Episode, *Ulysses*." *Journal of Narrative Technique* 13, no. 3 (1983): 141–53.

Hardiman, Adrian. "Law, Crime and Punishment in Bloomsday Dublin." In *Lawyers, the Law and History: Irish Legal History Society Discourses and Other Papers, 2005–2011*, edited by Felix M. Larkin and N. M. Dawson, 54–82. Dublin: Four Courts Press in association with the Irish Legal History Society, 2013.

Hart, Clive. "*Finnegans Wake* in Perspective." In *James Joyce Today: Essays on the Major Works*, edited by Thomas F. Stayley, 135–65. Bloomington: Indiana University Press, 1966.

———. "Gaps and Cracks in *Ulysses*." *James Joyce Quarterly* 30, no. 3 (1993): 427–37.

Hartner, Marcus. "Multiperspectivity." In *The Living Handbook of Narratology*, edited by Peter Hühn et al. Hamburg: Hamburg University Press. Last modified 15 October 2012. http://wikis.sub.uni-hamburg.de/lhn/index.php/Multiperspectivity.

Hatch, H. M. *Popery Unmasked: Showing the Depravity of the Priesthood and the Immorality of the Confessional; Being the Questions Put to Females in Confession Extracted from the Theological Works now Used by Cardinal Wiseman, His Bishops and Priests, as Quoted in "The Confessional Unmasked," together with Extracts from Dowling, Hogan, and Maria Monk; Showing the Crimes Committed in the Black Nunnery and a Description of the Horrid Inquisition Rooms, with Notes.*

Lowell, MA: H. M. Hatch, 1854. https://ia600401.us.archive.org/21/items/poperyunmaskedsh00hatc/poperyunmaskedsh00hatc.pdf.
Hayman, David. *"Ulysses": The Mechanics of Meaning*. New York: Prentice Hall, 1970.
Heffernan, Catherine. "Sexually Transmitted Infections, Sex and the Irish." D. Phil. diss., Oxford University, 2002.
Henke, Suzette. *James Joyce and the Politics of Desire*. London: Routledge, 1990.
Henriques, H. S. Q. "Historical Survey." In *The Law of Aliens and Naturalization including the Text of the Aliens Act, 1905*, 1–61. London: Butterworth, 1906. https://archive.org/stream/lawofaliensnatur00henruoft/lawofaliensnatur00-henruoft_djvu.txt.
Hepburn, Allan. "*Ulysses*, Opera, Loss." *James Joyce Quarterly* 38, no. 1–2 (2000–2001): 63–84.
Herr, Cheryl. *Joyce's Anatomy of Culture*. Urbana: University of Illinois Press, 1986.
Herring, Phillip. *Joyce's Uncertainty Principle*. Princeton, NJ: Princeton University Press, 1987.
Hirsch, E. D. *Validity in Interpretation*. New Haven, CT: Yale University Press, 1967.
Hogan, Patrick. *"Ulysses" and the Poetics of Cognition*. London: Routledge, 2014.
Holland, Merlin. *Irish Peacock and Scarlet Marquess: The Real Trial of Oscar Wilde*. London: HarperCollins, 2003.
Homer. *The Odyssey*. Translated by Robert Fagles. New York: Viking Penguin, 1997.
Hopkins, J. Castell. *The Canadian Annual Review of Public Affairs 1902*. Toronto: The Annual Review Publishing Company, 1903.
———. *The Canadian Annual Review of Public Affairs 1903*. Toronto: The Annual Review Publishing Company, 1904.
———. *The Canadian Annual Review of Public Affairs 1904*. Toronto: The Annual Review Publishing Company, 1905.
Horstman, Allen. *Victorian Divorce*. London: Croom Helm, 1985.
Hynes, Samuel. *The Edwardian Turn of Mind*. Princeton, NJ: Princeton University Press, 1968.
Irish Church Act 1869 (c 42).
The Irish Law Times Digest of Cases Decided by the Superior and Other Courts in Ireland 1867–1893: Reported in "The Irish Law Times and Solicitors' Journal", Vols. I–XXVII. Compiled by William Cotter Stubbs. Dublin: John Falconer, 1895.
Iser, Wolfgang. *The Act of Reading: A Theory of Aesthetic Response*. London: Routledge and Kegan Paul, 1978.
———. *The Implied Reader: Patterns of Communication in Prose Fiction from Bunyan to Beckett*. Baltimore: Johns Hopkins University Press, 1974.

Jay, Martin. "Historical Explanation and the Event: Reflections on the Limits of Contextualization." *New Literary History* 42 (2011): 557–71.

Jenkins, Roy. *Victorian Scandal: A Biography of the Right Honourable Gentleman Sir Charles Dilke*. New York: Chilmark Press, 1965.

Johnson, Michael. "'Just Getting Off': The Inseparability of Ejaculation and Hegemonic Masculinity." *Journal of Men's Studies* 18, no. 3 (2010): 238–48.

Kant, Immanuel. *The Philosophy of Law: An Exposition of the Fundamental Principles of Jurisprudence as the Science of Right*. Translated by W. Hastie. Edinburgh: T. & T. Clarke, 1887.

Kenner, Hugh. "Circe." In *James Joyce's "Ulysses": Critical Essays*, edited by Clive Hart and David Hayman, 341–62. Berkeley: University of California Press, 1977.

———. "Molly's Masterstroke." In *"Ulysses": Fifty Years*, edited by Thomas Stayley, 19–28. Bloomington: Indiana University Press, 1974.

———. *"Ulysses"*. 1980. Baltimore: Johns Hopkins University Press, 1987.

Keogh, Dermot. *The Vatican, The Bishops and Irish Politics 1919–1939*. 1986. Cambridge: Cambridge University Press, 2004.

Kershner, R. Brandon, ed. *Cultural Studies of James Joyce*. Amsterdam: Rodopi, 2003.

———. *The Culture of Joyce's "Ulysses"*. New York: Palgrave Macmillan, 2010.

———. ed. *Joyce and Popular Culture*. Gainesville: University Press of Florida, 1996.

———. *Joyce, Bakhtin, and Popular Literature: Chronicles of Disorder*. Chapel Hill: University of North Carolina Press. 1989.

Kiberd, Declan. *"Ulysses" and Us: The Art of Everyday Living*. London: Faber, 2009.

———. "*Ulysses*, Newspapers and Modernism." In *Irish Classics*, 463–81. London: Granta Books, 2000.

Kirkland, John. *The Bakers' ABC: An Encyclopedic Dictionary for Bakers, Confectioners, and Caterers*. London: Gresham, 1927.

"Dervla Kirwin." *Who Do You Think You Are?* BBC, 18 September 2010.

Knowles, Sebastian D. G. "A Form Endearing: A Performance of Siren Songs; or, 'I was only vamping, man." In *Joyce in the Hibernian Metropolis: Essays*, edited by Morris Beja and David Norris, 213–36. Columbus: Ohio State University Press, 1996.

Knowles, Sebastian, Geert Lernout, and John McCourt, eds. *Joyce in Trieste: An Album of Risky Readings*. Gainesville: University Press of Florida, 2007.

Lamaison, Pierre, and Pierre Bourdieu. "From Rules to Strategies: An Interview with Pierre Bourdieu: Pierre Lamaison and Pierre Bourdieu." *Cultural Anthropology* 1, no. 1 (1986): 110–20.

Latey, William, ed. *The Law and Practice in Divorce and Matrimonial Causes*. 15th ed. London: Longman, 1952.

The Law Reports of the Incorporated Council of Law Reporting for England and Wales from the Commencement of Michaelmas Term, 1865, to the End of Trinity Sittings, 1890. 3 vols. Edited by Arthur Paul Stone. London: The Council, 1892.

The Law Reports: Ten Years' Digest, 1901–1910 of All the Cases Reported in the "Law Reports" and in the "Weekly Notes" from the Commencement of 1901 to the End of 1910 together with References to the More Important Statutes, Rules and Orders and Parliamentary Papers. Compiled by Myron White-Winton. London: The Council, 1911.

The Law Reports: Ten Years' Digest, 1911–1920 of All the Cases Reported in the "Law Reports" and in the "Weekly Notes" and all the Other Contemporaneous Reports together with a List of the Statutes Passed during the Same Period from the Commencement of 1911 to the End of 1920. Compiled by James Robert Vernam Marchant, County Court Judge. London: The Council, 1922.

The Law Reports of the Incorporated Council of Law Reporting for Ireland: "The Irish Law Times" and the Incorporated Council of Law Reporting for Northern Ireland: Digest of Cases Decided by the Superior and Other Courts in Ireland from the Commencement of Hilary Sittings, 1919, to the End of Michaelmas Term, 1928. Edited by R. H. Ryland. Dublin: J. Falconer, 1930.

Lawrence, Karen R. *The Odyssey of Style in "Ulysses".* Princeton, NJ: Princeton University Press, 1981.

———. *Who's Afraid of James Joyce?* Gainesville: University Press of Florida, 2010.

Leckie, Barbara. *Culture and Adultery: The Novel, the Newspaper and the Law 1857–1914.* Philadelphia: University of Pennsylvania Press, 1999.

———. "The Simple Case of Adultery." *James Joyce Quarterly* 40, no. 4 (2003): 729–52.

Lee, J. J. *Ireland 1912–1985: Politics and Society.* Cambridge: Cambridge University Press, 1989.

Legitimacy Declaration Act (Ireland) 1868 (c. xx).

Leonard, Garry. *Advertising and Commodity Culture in Joyce.* Gainesville: University Press of Florida, 1998.

Lernout, Geert. *Help My Unbelief: James Joyce and Religion.* London: Continuum, 2010.

Litz, A. Walton. "Ithaca." In *James Joyce's "Ulysses": Critical Essays,* edited by Clive Hart and David Hayman, 385–405. Berkeley: University of California Press, 1977.

Luddy, Maria. *Prostitution and Irish Society.* Cambridge: Cambridge University Press, 2007.

Lyons, F. S. L. *The Fall of Parnell, 1890–91.* London: Routledge and Kegan Paul, 1960.

Lyons, John Charles. *The Grand Juries of the County of Westmeath. [1727–1853], with an Historical Appendix.* Ledestown: privately printed, 1853.

http://www.askaboutireland.ie/aai-files/assets/ebooks/129_Grand-Juries-of-County-Westmeath/129%20Grand%20Juries%20of%20County%20Westmeath%201727-1853.pdf.

Mackey, Peter Francis. *Chaos Theory and James Joyce's Everyman*. Gainesville: University Press of Florida, 1999.

Maddox, James H. *Joyce's "Ulysses" and the Assault upon Character*. New Brunswick, NJ: Rutgers University Press, 1978.

Maddox, Peter. "The Background of, and Contemporary Reaction to, The Matrimonial Causes Act, 1857." *The Cambrian Law Review* 18 (1987): 62.

Madtes, Richard E. *A Textual and Critical Study of the "Ithaca" Episode of James Joyce's "Ulysses"*. Ann Arbor: UMI Research Press, 1983.

Mahaffey, Vicki. "Joyce and Gender." In *Palgrave Advances in James Joyce Studies*, edited by Jean-Michel Rabaté, 121–43. New York: Palgrave Macmillan, 2004.

———. "'Minxing Marriage and Making Loof': Anti-Oedipal Reading." *James Joyce Quarterly* 30, no. 2 (1993): 219–37.

———. *Reauthorizing Joyce*. Cambridge: Cambridge University Press, 1988.

Malcomson, A. P. W. *The Pursuit of the Heiress: Aristocratic Marriage in Ireland 1740–1840*. 1982. Belfast: Ulster Historical Foundation, 2005.

Manganiello, Dominic. *Joyce's Politics*. London: Routledge and Kegan Paul, 1980.

Marriage Law (Ireland) Amendment Act, 1863 (c. xxvii).

Marriage Law (Ireland) Amendment Act, 1873 (c. xvi).

Marriage of British Subject (Facilities) Act, 1915 (c. xxxx).

Marriage of British Subject (Facilities) Amendment Act, 1916 (c. xxi).

Marriage (Society of Friends) Act, 1872.

Marriages Validity Act, 1899 (c. xxvii).

Martin, Peter. *Censorship in the Two Irelands, 1922–1939*. Dublin: Irish Academic Press, 2006.

Mason, Michael. "Why is Leopold Bloom a Cuckold?" *ELH* 44 (Spring 1977): 171–88.

Matrimonial Causes Act, 1878 (c. xix).

Matrimonial Causes and Marriage Law (Ireland) Amendment Act, 1870.

Matrimonial Causes and Marriage Law (Ireland) Amendment Act, 1871.

McCarthy, Patrick. "*Ulysses*: Book of Many Errors." In *Joycean Unions: Post-Millennial Essays from East to West*, edited by R. Brandon Kershner and Tekla Mecsnóber, 195–208. Amsterdam: Rodopi, 2013.

McClung, Jeff. "The Physical Fitness of Leopold Bloom." *International Journal of Humanities and Social Sciences* 2, no. 2 (2012): 16–22.

McCourt, John, ed. *James Joyce in Context*. Cambridge: Cambridge University Press, 2009.

———. *The Years of Bloom: James Joyce in Trieste, 1904–1920*. Dublin: Lilliput Press, 2000.

McCrea, Barry. "Secrets of Szombathely: The H.E.L.Y.'S Sandwichmen and Irish Citizenship." *James Joyce Quarterly* 41, no. 3 (2004): 397–405.

McGee, Patrick. "Joyce's *Nausea*: Style and Representation in 'Nausicaa'." *James Joyce Quarterly* 24, no. 3 (1987): 305–18.

Mendes da Costa, D., ed. *Studies in Canadian Family Law*. 2 vols. Toronto: Butterworths, 1972.

Merrett, David Tolmie. "The 1893 Bank Crashes and Monetary Aggregates." Research Discussion Paper 9303. Sydney: Reserve Bank of Australia, 1993.

———. "The Australian Bank Crashes of the 1890s Revisited." *Business History Review* 87 (Autumn 2013): 407–29.

———. "Australian Banking Practice and the Crisis of 1893." *Australian Economic History Review* 29, no. 1 (1989): 60–85.

Minutes of Evidence Taken before the Royal Commission on Divorce and Matrimonial Causes: Presented to Parliament by Command of His Majesty. London: His Majesty's Stationery Office, 1912.

Mnyani, C. N., and J. A. McIntyre. "Tuberculosis in Pregnancy." *BJOG: An International Journal of Obstetrics and Gynaecology* 118, no. 2 (2011): 226–31.

Moody, John, ed. *Moody's Manual of Corporation Securities: Fourth Annual Number*. New York: Moody Publishing, 1903.

———. *Moody's Manual of Corporation Securities: Fifth Annual Number*. New York: Moody Publishing, 1904.

Moody, Theodore William, W. E. Vaughan, Francis X. Martin, and Francis John Byrne, eds. *A New History of Ireland*. Oxford: Oxford University Press, 2010.

Moorhouse, E. Hallam. *The Story of Lady Hamilton*. London: T. N. Foulis, 1911.

Mormont, Dorian. "Performance and Analysis of the Oldest Mutual Fund, the Scottish Widows' Fund from 1815 to 2000." *Memoire Presente en vue de l'obtention du Master en Sciences economiques, finalement Management Sciences*. MS Thesis. Solvay Brussels School of Economics and Management, 2011–2012.

Morrison, Mark. *The Public Face of Modernism: Little Magazines, Audiences, and Reception 1905–1920*. Madison: University of Wisconsin Press, 2001.

Mullin, Katherine. *James Joyce, Sexuality and Social Purity*. Cambridge: Cambridge University Press, 2003.

Musser, Amber. "Masochism: A Queer Subjectivity?" *Rhizomes* 11–12 (Fall 2005–Spring 2006). http://www.rhizomes.net/issue11/musser.html.

Nash, John. *James Joyce and the Act of Reception: Reading, Ireland, Modernism*. Cambridge: Cambridge University Press, 2006.

Nicoll, Donald. *Publicity: An Essay on Advertising, by an Adept of 35 Years' Experience*. London: Office of the Parliamentary, Patent and Advertising Agency, 1878.

Nolan, Emer. *James Joyce and Nationalism*. 1995. London: Routledge, 2003.

Noonan, John T. Jr. *Power to Dissolve: Lawyers and Marriages in the Courts of the Roman Curia*. Cambridge, MA: Belknap Press of Harvard University Press, 1972.

Norris, Margot. "Don't Call Him 'Blazes': Hugh E. Boylan's Narrative Caricature." *James Joyce Quarterly* 48, no. 2 (2011): 229–49.

———. "Narratology and *Ulysses*." In *"Ulysses" in Critical Perspective*, edited by Michael Patrick Gillespie and A. Nicholas Fargnoli, 35–50. Gainesville: University Press of Florida, 2006.

———. *Virgin* and *Veteran Readings of "Ulysses"*. New York: Palgrave Macmillan, 2011.

North, S. N. D. *Marriage and Divorce 1867–1906: Part 1 Summary, Laws, Foreign Statistics*. Department of Commerce and Labor Bureau of the Census. Washington, DC: Government Printing Office, 1909.

Nouveau scandale de Londres: l'Affaire Crawford. Paris: Libraire Illustreé, 1886.

Nussbaum, Martha. *Poetic Justice: The Literary Imagination and Public Life*. Boston: Beacon Press, 1995.

O'Brien, John. *Conflict of Laws*. London: Routledge, 1999.

O'Byrne, Simon. *Civil Divorce for Catholics*. Dublin: Frederick Press, 1982.

Ó Gráda, Cormac. *Jewish Ireland in the Age of Joyce: A Socioeconomic History*. Princeton, NJ: Princeton University Press, 2006.

———. "Settling in: Dublin's Jewish Immigrants a Century Ago." *Field Day* 1 (2005): 87–99.

Osborough, W. N. *Law and the Emergence of Modern Dublin: A Litigation Topography for a Capital City*. Dublin: Irish Academic Press, 1996.

O'Shea, Katharine. *Charles Stewart Parnell: His Love Story and Political Life*. New York: Doran, 1914.

Osteen, Mark. *The Economy of "Ulysses": Making Both Ends Meet*. Syracuse, NY: Syracuse University Press, 1995.

The Oxford Companion to Music. Edited by Alison Latham. Oxford: Oxford University Press, 2002.

Paoli, Xavier. *My Royal Clients*. 1911. London: Forgotten Books, 2013. http://www.forgottenbooks.com/readbook_text/My_Royal_Clients_1000499859/241.

Parnell, John Howard. *Charles Stewart Parnell: A Memoir by His Brother John Howard Parnell*. New York: Henry Holt, 1914.

Pettigrew, Jane. *A Social History of Tea*. London: National Trust Enterprises, 2001.

Phelan, James, and Peter J. Rabinowitz. "Character." In *Narrative Theory: Core Concepts and Critical Debates*, edited by David Herman, James Phelan, Peter J. Rabinowitz, Brian Richardson, and Robin Warhol. Columbus: Ohio State University Press, 2012.

Phillips, Roderick. *Putting Asunder: A History of Divorce in Western Society.* Cambridge: Cambridge University Press, 1988.

Pierce, David. *Joyce and Company.* London: Continuum, 2006.

———. *Reading Joyce.* New York: Routledge, 2014.

Plato. *Republic.* Edited and translated by Chris Emlyn-Jones and William Preddy. Loeb Classical Library. Cambridge, MA: Harvard University Press, 2013.

Potts, Willard, ed. *Portraits of the Artist in Exile: Recollections of James Joyce by Europeans.* New York: Harcourt, Brace and Jovanovich, 1986. (Originally published Seattle: University of Washington Press, 1979.)

Power, Arthur. *Conversations with James Joyce.* London: Millington, 1974.

Power, Henriette Lazaridis. "Pantomime Songs and the Limits of Narrative in *Ulysses.*" In *Picking Up Airs: Hearing the Music in Joyce's Text*, edited by Ruth H. Bauerle, 53–66. Urbana: University of Illinois Press, 1993.

Proposal for the Abolition of the Matrimonial Remedy for Restitution of Conjugal Rights. The Law Commission (Law Com. No 23). London: Her Majesty's Stationery Office, 24 July 1969.

Proust, Marcel. *Swann's Way.* Translated by C. K. Scott Moncrieff. 1922. London: Chatto and Windus, 1976.

Rabaté, Jean-Michel, ed. *James Joyce Studies.* Houndmills: Palgrave Macmillan, 2004.

———. *Joyce Upon the Void: The Genesis of Doubt.* New York: St. Martin's Press, 1991.

Radojevic, N., et al. "Multiple Stabbing in Sex Related Homicides." *Journal of Forensic and Legal Medicine* 20 (July 2013): 502–7.

Raleigh, John Henry. *The Chronicle of Leopold and Molly Bloom: "Ulysses" as Narrative.* Berkeley: University of California Press, 1977.

Rawson, Maud Stepney. *Penelope Rich and Her Circle.* London: Hutchinson, 1911. https://archive.org/details/cu31924027985427.

Rayden, William. *Rayden's Law and Practice in Divorce and Family Matters in All Courts.* 13th ed. London: Butterworths, 1979.

———. *Rayden's Law and Practice in Divorce and Family Matters.* Edited by Joseph Jackson. 14th ed. London: Butterworths, 1983.

Regan, Marguerite M. "'Weggebobbles and Fruit': Bloom's Vegetarian Impulses." *Texas Studies in Literature and Language* 51, nos. 4 (2009): 463–75.

Reizbaum, Marilyn. *James Joyce's Judaic Other.* Stanford, CA: Stanford University Press, 1999.

Report of the Royal Commission on Divorce and Matrimonial Causes. London: His Majesty's Stationery Office, 1912.

Reppke, James A. "Journalist Joyce: A Portrait." *James Joyce Quarterly* 45, nos. 3–4 (2007–2008): 459–68.

Richards, Thomas. *The Commodity Culture of Victorian England: Advertising and Spectacle, 1851–1914*. Stanford, CA: Stanford University Press, 1990.

Richardson, Henry Handel. *The Fortunes of Richard Mahony: The Way Home*. Edited by Clive Probyn and Bruce Steele. Melbourne: Australian Scholarly Publishing, 2007.

Ringrose, Hyacinthe. *Marriage and Divorce Laws of the World*. London: Musson-Draper, 1911.

Riquelme, Jean Paul. "Preparatory to anything else: Joyce's Styles as Forms of Memory—The Case of 'Eumaeus'." In *"Ulysses" in Critical Perspective*, edited by Michael Patrick Gillespie and A. Nicholas Fargnoli, 9–34. Gainesville: University Press of Florida, 2006.

———. *Teller and Tale in Joyce's Fiction: Oscillating Perspectives*. Baltimore: Johns Hopkins University Press, 1983.

Roberts, James. *Divorce Bills in the Imperial Parliament*. Dublin: John Falconer, 1906.

Rose, Danis. "The Source of Mr. Bloom's Wealth." *James Joyce Quarterly* 25, no. 1 (1987): 128–32.

Roughley, Alan. *Reading Derrida Reading Joyce*. Gainesville: University Press of Florida, 1999.

Royal Commission on Venereal Disease: Final Report of the Commission. London: His Majesty's Stationery Office, 1916.

Rubenstein, Michael D. "'The Waters of Civic Finance': Moneyed States in Joyce's *Ulysses*." *Novel: A Forum on Fiction* 36, no. 3 (2003): 289–306.

"Rules and Regulations for the Court for Divorce and Matrimonial Causes." In *The Law Journal Reports for the Year 1866: Michaelmas Term 1865 to Michaelmas Term 1866, Forming Part V of Vol. LXIV, New Series, Vol. XXXV*, 1–13, 14–21. London: Edward Bret Ince, 1866.

Ryan, Louise. "'A decent girl well worth helping': Women, Migration and Unwanted Pregnancy." In *Ireland Beyond Boundaries: Mapping Irish Studies in the Twenty-First Century*, edited by Liam Harte and Yvonne Whelan, 135–53. London: Pluto Press, 2007.

Sadowski, Piotr. "Androgyny and (near) Perfect Marriage: A Systems View of the Genders of Leopold and Molly Bloom." *Style* 44, nos. 1–2 (2010): 139–61.

Sato, Y. "Silodosin Improved Spontaneous Ejaculation Induced by Mental Strain." *International Journal of Urology* 21 (August 2014): 841. doi.: 10.1111/iju.12439.

Savage, Gail. "Defining the Boundaries of Marital Sexuality: Bigamy, Incest and Sodomy in the Divorce Court, 1857–1907." Paper presented at the Mid-Atlantic Conference on British Studies Annual Meeting, New Brunswick, NJ, 22 March 2003.

———. "Divorce and the Law in England and France Prior to the First World War." *Journal of Social History* 21, no. 3 (1988): 499–513.

———. "Erotic Stories and Public Decency: Newspaper Reporting of Divorce Proceedings in England." *The Historical Journal* 41, no. 2 (1998): 511–28.
———. "The Operation of the 1857 Divorce Act, 1860–1910: A Research Note." *Journal of Social History* 16, no. 4 (1983): 103–10.
———. "They Would if They Could: Class, Gender, and Popular Representation of English Divorce Litigation, 1858–1908." *Journal of Family History* 36, no. 2 (2011): 173–90.
Schwartzman, Myron. "The V.A.8 Copybook: An Early Draft of the 'Cyclops' Chapter of *Ulysses* with Notes on Its Development." *James Joyce Quarterly* 12, nos. 1–2 (1974–1975): 64–122.
Sclater, Shelley Day. *Divorce: A Psychosocial Study*. Aldershot: Ashgate, 1999.
Senn, Fritz. "Arguing about Law: Cyclopean Language." *James Joyce Quarterly* 37, nos. 3–4 (2000): 425–46.
———. "Dynamics of Corrective Unrest." In *Joyce's Dislocutions: Essays on Reading as Translation*, edited by John Paul Riquelme, 59–72. Baltimore: Johns Hopkins University Press, 1984.
———. *Inductive Scrutinies: Focus on Joyce*. Edited by Christine O'Neill. Dublin: Lilliput Press, 1995.
Seymour, Mark. *Debating Divorce in Italy: Marriage and the Making of Modern Italians*. London: Palgrave Macmillan, 2006.
Shatter, Alan Joseph. *Family Law in the Republic of Ireland*. 2nd ed. Dublin: Wolfhound Press, 1981.
Shloss, Carol. "Molly's Resistance to the Union: Marriage and Colonialism in Dublin, 1904." *Modern Fiction Studies* 35, no. 3 (1989): 529–41.
Simons, Jefferey. "The Soft, the Sweet, and Bloom." *Joyce Studies Annual* 13 (Summer 2002): 86–102.
Smith, Keith. "Offences against the Person." In *The Oxford History of the Laws of England: Volume XIII: 1820–1914 Fields of Development*, edited by J. William Cornish, Stuart Anderson, Ray Cocks, Michael Lobban, Patrick Polden, and Keith Smith, 393–464. Oxford: Oxford University Press, 2010.
Snyder, Carl. *American Railways as Investments: A Detailed and Comparative Analysis of All the Leading Railways, from the Investor's Point of View, with an Introductory Chapter on the Methods of Estimating Railway Values*. New York: Moody, 1907.
Spinoza, Benedictus de. *Ethica Ordine Geometrico Demonstrata*. Translated by R. H. M. Elwes. http://www.gutenberg.org/cache/epub/3800/pg3800.txt.
Stayley, Thomas, ed. *"Ulysses": Fifty Years*. Bloomington: Indiana University Press, 1974.
Stephens, Davy. *The Life and Times of Davy Stephens: Told by Himself*. Dublin: Cahill, 1912.

Stephenson, William. "Eroticism and Lightness in 'Wandering Rocks'." In *Joyce's Wandering Rocks*, edited by Andrew Gibson and Steven Morrison, 121–40. Amsterdam: Rodopi, 2002.

Stone, Lawrence. *The Road to Divorce*. Oxford: Oxford University Press, 1990.

Streit, Wolfgang. *Joyce/Foucault: Sexual Confessions*. Ann Arbor: University of Michigan Press, 2004.

Szczeszak-Brewer, Agata. "Joyce's Vagina Dentata: Irish Nationalism and the Colonial Dilemma of Manhood." *Frontiers* 34, no. 2 (2013): 1–24.

Tanner, Tony. *Adultery in the Novel: Contract and Transgression*. Baltimore: Johns Hopkins University Press, 1979.

Taylor, Charles. *Modern Social Imaginaries*. Durham, NC: Duke University Press, 2004.

Thompson, Frederick Diodati. *In the Track of the Sun: Readings from the Diary of a Globe Trotter*. New York: D. Appleton, 1893. https://archive.org/details/intrackofsunread00thom.

Thornton, Weldon. *Voices and Values in Joyce's "Ulysses"*. Gainesville: University Press of Florida, 2000.

Thwaites, Tony. "Mr. Bloom, Inside and Out: Some Typologies of the 'Initial Style' of *Ulysses*." *James Joyce Quarterly* 47, no. 3 (2010): 363–81.

Tymoczko, Maria. *The Irish "Ulysses"*. 1994. Berkeley: University of California Press, 1997.

Urquhart, Diane. "Ireland and the Divorce and Matrimonial Causes Act of 1857." *Journal of Family History* 38, no. 3 (2013): 301–20.

———. "Irish Divorce and Domestic Violence, 1857–1922." *Women's History Review* 22, no. 5 (2013): 820–37.

Utell, Janine. *James Joyce and the Revolt of Love: Marriage, Adultery, Desire*. London: Palgrave Macmillan, 2010.

Valente, Joseph. "Beyond Truth and Freedom: The New Faith of Joyce and Nietzsche." *James Joyce Quarterly* 25, nos. 1 (1987): 87–103.

———. "The Novel and the Police (Gazette)." *NOVEL: A Forum on Fiction* 29, no. 1 (1995): 8–19.

Venn, John. "John Brinkley." In *Biographical History of Gonville and Caius College 1349–1897*, 107–08. Cambridge: Cambridge University Press, 1898.

Wales, Katie. *The Language of James Joyce*. London: Macmillan, 1992.

Warnock, Keith. "Auditing Bloom, Editing Joyce: Accounting and Accountability in *Ulysses*." *Accounting, Business & Financial History* 18, no. 1 (2008): 81–95.

Wawrzycka, Jolanta W. Review of Janine Utell, *James Joyce and the Revolt of Love: Marriage, Adultery, Desire*. *James Joyce Quarterly* 48, no. 3 (2011): 552–58.

Weiner, Martin J. "Alice Arden to Bill Sikes: Changing Nightmares of Intimate Violence in England, 1558–1869." *Journal of British Studies* 40 (April 2001): 184–212.

———. *Men of Blood: Violence, Manliness and Criminal Justice in Victorian England*. Cambridge: Cambridge University Press, 2006.

Whelan, Yvonne. "Monuments, Power and Contested Space: The Iconography of Sackville Street (O'Connell Street) before Independence (1922)." *Irish Geography* 34, no. 1 (2001): 11–33.

White, Harry Vere. "Divorce." *Irish Church Quarterly* 6, no. 33 (1913): 33.

White, Nicholas. *French Divorce Fiction from the Revolution to the First World War*. London: Legenda, 2013.

Whittaker, E., and B. Kampmann. "Perinatal Tuberculosis: New Challenges in the Diagnosis and Treatment of Tuberculosis in Infants and the Newborn." *Early Human Development* 84, no. 12 (2008): 795–99.

Wicke, Jennifer. "Lingerie and (Literary) History: Joyce's *Ulysses* and Fashionability." *Critical Quarterly* 36, no. 2 (1994): 25–41.

———. "Modernity Must Advertise: Aura, Desire and Decolonization in Joyce." *James Joyce Quarterly* 50, nos. 1–2 (2012–2013): 203–21.

———. "'Who's she when she's at home?' Molly Bloom and the Work of Consumption." *James Joyce Quarterly* 28, no. 4 (1991): 749–63.

Wilde, Oscar. *The Complete Works of Oscar Wilde*. Edited by Josephine M. Guy. Oxford: Oxford University Press, 2007.

———. "The Soul of Man under Socialism." *Fortnightly Review* 49 (1891): 292–319.

Wilson, Richard, and Frank J. Fabozzi. *Corporate Bonds: Structure and Analysis*. London: John Wiley, 1995.

Wittgenstein, Ludwig. *Tractatus Logico-Philosophicus*. London: Kegan Paul, Trench, Trubner; New York: Harcourt, Brace, 1922.

Wright, Danaya C. "Untying the Knot: An Analysis of the English Divorce and Matrimonial Causes Court Records, 1858–1866." *University of Richmond Law Review* 38, no. 4 (2004). http://scholarship.law.ufl.edu/facultypub/205.

Wynne, Brian. "Uncertainty and Environmental Learning: Reconceiving Science and Policy in the Preventive Paradigm." *Global Environmental Change* 2, no. 2 (1992): 111–27.

Yeats, W. B. *The Senate Speeches of W. B. Yeats*. Edited by Donald R. Pearce. London: Faber and Faber, 1971.

Index

P. Kuch, *Irish Divorce / Joyce's Ulysses*,
DOI 10.1057/978-1-137-57186-1

V

W

Y